Builders of a New South

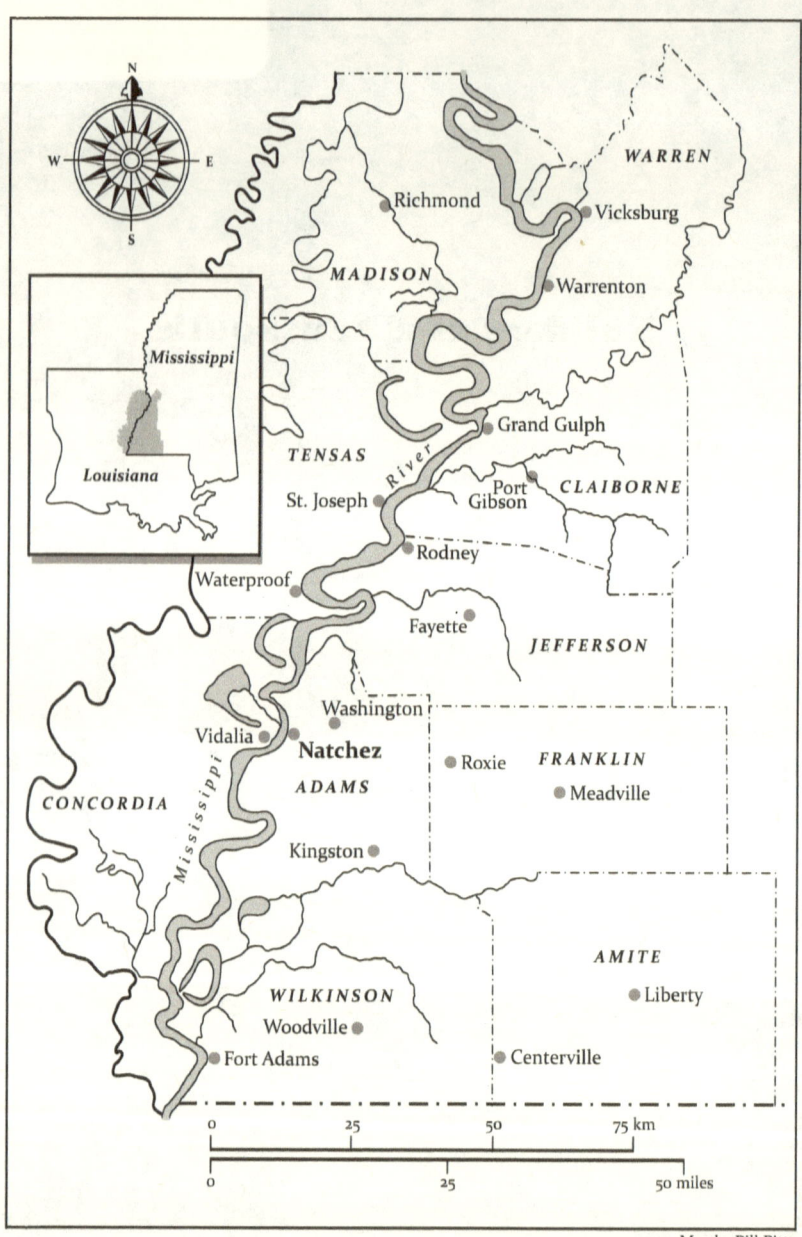

Builders of a New South

Merchants, Capital, and the Remaking of Natchez, 1865–1914

Aaron D. Anderson

University Press of Mississippi / Jackson

www.upress.state.ms.us

The University Press of Mississippi is a member of the Association of American University Presses.

Copyright © 2013 by University Press of Mississippi
All rights reserved

First printing 2013

∞

Library of Congress Cataloging-in-Publication Data

Anderson, Aaron D.
Builders of a New South : merchants, capital, and the remaking of Natchez, 1865–1914 / Aaron D. Anderson.
p. cm.
Includes bibliographical references and index.
ISBN 978-1-61703-667-5 (cloth : alk. paper) —
ISBN 978-1-61703-668-2 (ebook)
1. Natchez (Miss.)—Commerce—History—19th century. 2. Natchez (Miss.)—Commerce—History—20th century. 3. Merchants—Mississippi—Natchez—Case studies. 4. Natchez (Miss.)—Economic conditions. 5. Natchez (Miss.)—Social conditions. 6. Natchez (Miss.)—History. I. Title.
HF3163.N25A53 2013
381'.10976226—dc23   2012020574

British Library Cataloging-in-Publication Data available

Contents

Acknowledgments [*vii*]

INTRODUCTION
A New Merchant System [*3*]

CHAPTER 1
Old Ways and New Realities [*11*]

CHAPTER 2
Merchant Communities [*40*]

CHAPTER 3
Crop Liens, Freedmen, and Planters [*71*]

CHAPTER 4
A New Kind of Planter [*112*]

CHAPTER 5
Merchant Life and Social Capital [*142*]

CHAPTER 6
A Dangerous Business [*180*]

Summary and Conclusion [*214*]

Notes [*221*]

Selected Bibliography [*257*]

Index [*271*]

Acknowledgments

A BOOK IS JOURNEY IN ITS OWN RIGHT, AND IT IS A GREAT pleasure to thank the many people who have helped me in mine over the past eight years. This project was begun at California State University, Northridge, working with Ronald L. F. Davis. I am deeply indebted to Ron for introducing me both to Natchez and to research in southern archives, and it was he who first suggested a version of this topic. Ron is the person most responsible for my start in the field of southern history, and he has been a tireless friend and mentor who helped shape this project in countless ways. I would also like to thank Joyce Broussard, Thomas Devine, Richard Horowitz, and Ralph Vicero at Northridge for their valuable assistance while I was there. This project was greatly expanded and refined at the University of Southern Mississippi, and I would like to offer my most heartfelt gratitude to Louis M. Kyriakoudes for his superb guidance and patient support. Louis is the consummate historian, and his analytical and technical expertise proved invaluable in this research. I also offer my most sincere thanks to William K. Scarborough, Max Grivno, and Pamela Tyler for their invaluable comments and criticism in shaping this work, and also to the staff in the History Department at Southern Mississippi, particularly Shelia Smith. In the years since leaving Southern Mississippi, I have taught at Alcorn State University and would like to thank my colleagues Kenneth H. Williams, Buford Satcher, Dorothy Idleburg, and Alpha Morris for their kindness and support.

I would also like to express my gratitude to the many archivists, librarians, and staff at both research institutions and public records facilities. Many thanks to the staff at the research libraries of the University of Texas at Austin, the University of North Carolina at Chapel Hill, the Baker Library at Harvard, Tulane University in New Orleans, and the

Hill Memorial Library at Louisiana State University, particularly to Mark Martin there. Similar thanks go out to those at the Adams, Franklin, Jefferson, and Wilkinson county courthouses in Mississippi, as well as those in Tensas and Concordia Parishes in Louisiana, especially Becky Zerby in Concordia. A special debt of gratitude is owed to Ron and Mimi Miller at the Natchez Foundation, Anne Webster and Clinton Bagley at the Mississippi Department of Archives, Marianne Raley at the Natchez George W. Armstrong Library, Judy Brady at Temple B'Nai Israel, as well as to Edward Esau and to Brooks Harrington and his family, who were all incredibly supportive and made this research possible. Also, special thanks to fellow historians Cameron Beech and Scott Marler for their valuable help and friendship, as well as to Jennifer Green, John Mayfield, and particularly David Moltke-Hansen, who read the entire manuscript and provided invaluable insight and criticisms that greatly improved this work. Also, I am especially grateful to Craig Gill and the staff at the University Press of Mississippi, who were a pleasure to work with and made this book possible.

This book is devoted to my mother, Kathleen, who was among the first in her family to graduate from college and was the strongest proponent of education in my life. Also to my father, Carl, who taught me the desire to pursue my dreams and the work ethic to see a project through to completion. Although they are no longer with us, I think they both would be pleased. Finally, I owe my greatest debt of gratitude to my wife and best friend, Susan, for her undying patience, understanding, support, and research assistance these past many years. She accompanied me on research trips and spent countless hours recording, processing, and entering chattel mortgage and other data, and her role in this work was indispensable. She gave enthusiastically of her time while engaged in her own busy career, and this book would have not been possible without her.

Builders of a New South

INTRODUCTION

A New Merchant System

THE DAY BROKE SOFTLY IN NATCHEZ ON JANUARY 11, 1898, A pleasant, hazy day in the midst of a mild southern winter. The *Natchez Democrat* predicted the weather would be "Warm, Damp, and Cloudy," and advised that "a good rain will probably be followed by a freeze," indicative of the sudden and unpredictable changes that could descend upon that epicenter of the Cotton Kingdom. Natchez was fairly quiet in January, the off-season for cotton planting, and most of the previous year's cotton crop had already been shipped to market in New Orleans and elsewhere. Business was only "so so on the [Mississippi riverboat] landing," and in fact, the river was "in an uncertain state" due to possible flooding driven by strong winter storms to the north. In many ways, the ebb and flow of the river controlled the seasons of life in Natchez, but the business of cotton was never very far from anyone's mind in the Cotton Kingdom, and reminders were everywhere: "The Leathers [steamboat Captain Leathers and his ship] passed south yesterday afternoon with a good sized load of cotton and seed," and another had "a full load going out to Vicksburg Sunday noon." Soon Natchez would explode in bustling preparations for the coming year's crop, but Harrison Ross was already thinking about his.[1]

Harrison Ross was a black sharecropper. He farmed thirty acres on "Ab Sojourner's" cotton plantation; he had been farming cotton on Sojourner's place for about four years, but had been working on shares in the district for many years. He probably had relatives working on other plantations around Adams County or in town, such as Anderson and Mary Ross on Duck Pond plantation, Amelia or Evaline Ross on Cliffs, and Menora, Jesse, and Elbert Ross in the town of Natchez. Perhaps his family had emerged from slavery somewhere in the area. When Ross got up that day in January, he knew that he would meet with his furnishing merchants,

Wolfe Geisenberger and his son Sam, to sign the crop lien agreement for that year's credit. The firm of Wolfe Geisenberger & Son Company, Dry Goods and Cotton Merchants had been in business since the mid-1860s furnishing the croppers and planters in the area, and they would supply the sixty-one-year-old Harrison and his wife, Veicy, with all the necessities for their survival and to grow a crop of cotton on the Sojourner place with a $60 line of credit. This debt would be secured by a lien on all the cotton they grew on Sojourner's land, maybe ten or fifteen bales, and they would pay Sojourner two bales as rent for their thirty acres and whatever house they would be offered to live in—possibly a shotgun shack or a former slave cabin left over from an earlier age.[2]

Ross had known Wolfe Geisenberger for at least eighteen years. He had first done business with him in 1880, when he, together with Veicy and their four daughters, worked for shares on Louis Pipe's plantation south of Natchez in Kingston. Not much had changed in the intervening years for Ross, as his credit limit on Pipe's was usually the same amount of $50 a year. But he took his business to another Natchez merchant after 1880 or worked with another cropper under that cropper's mercantile account, not returning to Geisenberger & Co. until 1895 to work on terms on Ab Sojourner's plantation. This movement of croppers from one merchant or plantation to another was fairly common among Natchez District sharecroppers and tenants, and Ross may have been part of a larger "squad," or group, of sharecroppers working for Geisenberger or someone else subsumed under the contract name of a lead person in the interim. But between 1895 and 1898 Ross carried over a supply debt from one year to the next: once in 1897, for $34.35, out of $85 borrowed from Geisenberger in 1896 for goods and supplies. Because of his debts, he was limited in the new crop year to a credit of just $40 in goods, a pretty small amount for a married couple to live on for a year in the late 1890s, much less make a crop of cotton. But he apparently made enough that year to pay off his supply bill with Geisenberger and start fresh in 1898.[3]

Ross was in the grips of the economic institution of sharecropping, the premier form of agricultural labor that replaced slavery in the "New South" after the Civil War. He probably did not have much to look forward to except work from dusk to dawn, usually in the hot sun, day after day, just to break even at the end of the year, in a cycle that repeated itself year after year. This system had become fully entrenched since Reconstruction, and while it perpetuated a cycle of debt for men like Ross, it also made wealthy the men who were the new keepers of King Cotton: the postbellum merchant class. How did things transpire in Natchez history to put this system in place? What was the role of these furnishing merchants? And what was the significance of their place in the postwar social and economic life of the Natchez District in particular? To answer these questions, this work explores how the postbellum merchant class used favorable laws and socioeconomic conditions largely to control the petty financing of cotton agriculture and, in the process, rise to the pinnacle of Natchez social, political, and economic power by the turn of the century.[4]

The defeat of the Confederacy and the fall of the institution of slavery brought about a great economic reconfiguration of the cotton-producing South. The transformation of the South's agrarian economy in the wake of emancipation and defeat saw the dominant class of planters lose large portions of their wealth as antebellum credit and marketing relationships that bound coastal cotton factor and interior planter broke down under the stress of postwar economic reconfigurations. The planters were reduced by war-driven destruction and economic inactivity, while losing their greatest economic asset with the freeing of the slaves. The former system of slave-owning planters operating on credit from coastal factors deteriorated as the plantation owners no longer commanded extensive slave labor assets and were unable to secure operating capital just from the value of their lands or on their word as agrarian elites. Simultaneously, the freedmen emerged as a new group of paid agricultural workers under the wage labor and tenancy system, creating an explosive new market for goods and credit. This untried, confused situation produced opportunity for the postwar merchant class to develop economic prowess as prime facilitators of the sharecropping system. Their mercantile activities fulfilled and at least partially remedied the war-induced economic vacuum, and in the process made them the driving social and economic force of the emerging New South.

The postbellum phenomenon of share-tenancy and the new social and economic status of the furnishing merchant occurred throughout the cotton-producing South, but one region in particular offers a striking microcosm to study its dynamic and character: the Natchez District of Mississippi and Louisiana. Long a premier center of Southern cotton production, the Natchez District was home to an entrenched and powerful antebellum class of planters that dominated the region's economy. The war reduced the planter class to a large extent and left great opportunity for a new economic group to challenge and replace its members as the main purveyors of cotton agriculture. The merchants moved quickly into the breech, and a new postwar class of traders comprised of immigrants, Yankees, and loyal Confederates was able to use the economic void and freedmen-driven sharecropping system to gain socioeconomic status surprising in both its scope and rapid development. These merchants proliferated in the postbellum milieu and were highly influential in the economic reconstruction of the region, dominating Natchez economic conditions well into the twentieth century.

My study closely examines an array of records including census, tax, property, and probate records, as well as thousands of chattel mortgage contracts generated by ten premier Natchez mercantile families for the years 1865 to 1914 to establish the time, place, and pace of change over time, developing a social and economic "portrait" of the socioeconomic reconstruction of the Natchez District from the chaos of Union occupation through the local end of the cotton economy in the early twentieth century. I carefully follow the upward trajectory of the rising merchant class as the fresh social and economic leaders of the New South and their political and business contributions to the region. In the process, I both explore their internal interactions as family and mercantile communities and introduce striking new economic and demographic information on the economic relationship of freedmen sharecroppers to these merchants. My purpose is to understand the "new elite" in one influential region of the reconstituted South through close examination of these merchant families and the records of their business activities, to determine the character of their financial success and socioeconomic impact in the first two generations of the postwar era.[5]

The Natchez mercantile community was chosen for several reasons. The Natchez business community was well established long before the war, and its traders had been key players in the local rise of King Cotton. Many of the merchants in this story were in business before the war or were an important part of various local communities of immigrant traders or long-standing Southern planter families. Among the Natchez Jewish mercantile community, for example, several key members were in business in the antebellum period and offered support to an influx of newcomers during and after the war, helping build perhaps the most influential local postwar mercantile faction, one that included as much as one-third of all merchantmen in the area by the turn of the century. Others were Irish,

French, English, or Italian immigrant traders, who in much the same way used local social and economic conditions to construct their own influential communities and greatly contribute to the postwar scene. Some traders were associated with the former planter elite or had close associations with the long-standing Natchez cotton marketplace, which had featured a significant merchant class since the colonial period. Many of these men returned from the Confederate battlefronts to assume a new place and importance in their hometown as postbellum merchants, even if they had not been in business at the war's inception. Still other merchants were Northerners who came with the occupying Union army or shortly thereafter as part of an exploding postwar interest in the cotton business and its potential to make quick fortunes. For would-be merchants from both sides of the Mason-Dixon Line, the possibilities might have seemed endless with the emerging free African American population offering a huge new market for goods and credit. This study assesses the nature of the presence of merchants from the points of view of these new consumers, asking the extent of exploitation in these emerging economic and social relationships.

At the core of this book are ten merchant family groups. They comprised a total of twenty-eight individual traders over the period 1865–1914. While having much in common in the developing Natchez mercantile arena, they displayed a range of circumstances and had diverse fates. Six of the featured families were Jewish immigrants, and each was chosen because of the extent of its members' participation as entrepreneurs and because of specific attributes that help to explain their individual and group success. Some functioned as antebellum merchants in the area, while others were newcomers during the Civil War. The Beekmans and Lemles, for example, came to Natchez early in the 1840s, were significant in the formation of the Natchez Jewish community, and continued to function as prime economic operators who prospered in the postbellum period. The Friedlers, Geisenbergers, Jacobses, and Lowenburgs all arrived in Natchez during the war or shortly thereafter, and demonstrated more of the stereotypical "carpetbagger" character to their story; Isaac Lowenburg actually arrived with the Union army as a provisioner in 1863. Two featured families were postwar traders who began as antebellum merchants and immigrants from other areas: Armand Perrault emigrated from France and arrived in Natchez in the 1840s, followed by the Irish immigrant George T. Payne a decade later. Both the Perraults and Paynes rose from a modest prewar status to prosper greatly in the postwar era. The final two featured family groups, the Carpenters and the combined Abbotts/Flemings, were Natchez natives or internal migrants who arrived in the district during the antebellum decades. Both the Flemings and Abbotts were in business in Natchez as merchants or clerks in 1860 and had close ties to the prewar planter and merchant classes, while the Carpenters were not in the mercantile trade at all, but were local contractors and builders with strong ties to the planter class as well. Several of these men fought in some of the most perilous battles of the Civil War, serving in locally raised Confederate army units, only to return home as new Natchez traders.[6]

The conditions in Natchez and much of the defeated South after the war were highly advantageous for these merchants. They were able to capitalize on economic conditions in the postbellum period to build impressive plantation-furnishing houses and cotton-buying firms that served as the basis for the cotton plantations that made them wealthy as merchants and landlords and planters. They were heavily involved in supplying credit to freed blacks and the surviving planter class alike, and they amassed significant fortunes based on this furnishing business and the attendant land speculation and related agrarian enterprises that supported it. They were able to use existing conditions, and new legal advantages, to succeed in the uncertain marketplace like no other group.

While all were well known as successful merchants within the bustling postwar Natchez mercantile scene, they were also part of vibrant local mercantile communities that often ran along familial or cultural lines—communities for which they provided leadership and from which they benefited socially and economically throughout the entire period of study. As these families rose in social and economic status in the Natchez community, they were or became ardent Southerners who also were important civic and business leaders. The immigrant Isaac Lowenburg arrived with the Union troops in 1863 and rose from nothing to serve two elected terms as the first Jewish mayor of Natchez from 1883 to 1887. He and other merchants also became involved in many fraternal, civic, and business organizations, and they were involved in local railroad construction, hospital building, cotton mill construction and management, and land development. One of Natchez's first residential suburbs, Clifton Heights, was a mercantile project, and many prominent merchants, business leaders, and planters lived there. They were local proponents of a range of technological improvements that swept the country during the Gilded Age, and the

Natchez that these families inhabited in the early 1900s was far different from the one in which they did business fifty years earlier, just before, during, and after the Civil War. Natchez "grew up" and entered the twentieth century during their heyday, and these entrepreneurs were the prime local modernizers of the era. Their businesses constituted a significant economic engine that drove the Natchez postbellum economy, and their presence and activities changed the face of Natchez.

This is also a story about credit and debt. Natchez merchant wealth was in large part derived from the system of debt that the traders facilitated and maintained, and almost all of their business activities involved offering credit at high interest rates. Profiting on the debt of others through real estate transactions like tax foreclosure sales, these merchants were able to secure ownership of many cotton plantations at bargain prices. In doing this, they served those planters desperately in need of supplies on credit to operate their cotton plantations, sharecroppers in need of credit to buy their own supplies and land to farm, and numerous other merchants in need of capital and goods to establish their own businesses. Few of the players in this system of debt emerged intact except for the merchant creditors, and the essential character of their business almost always revolved around the growing, buying, and selling of cotton. Both planters and freedmen croppers found themselves reliant on the new merchant class, and their relationship with the traders was often a financially perilous proposition. The profits derived from the mercantile businesses provided the traders with capital to expand into a host of other entrepreneurial pursuits that built modern Natchez as part of the changing South.

This research builds upon and adds to ideas and themes contained in works of other historians of the postbellum era, offering new depth and synthesis to our understanding of a complex world that created the New South. In his seminal work on the new "retainers" of King Cotton, Harold D. Woodman illuminates the vital role merchants played in the postwar period as the new marketers of the South's cotton crop and the providers of agricultural credit and goods, replacing the antebellum cotton factor system. Building on Woodman's research, Ronald L. F. Davis demonstrates the specific function of the sharecropping system in the Natchez District and its place in the New South as the primary form of labor to replace slavery. Davis's key work provides a sound base for this study's expanded research into the world of Natchez merchants and their cropper customers, the nexus of initial mercantile success. Michael Wayne provides a valuable resource of specific information on the changes affecting the planter class in the Natchez District, particularly the shift that occurred as the planter and merchant classes melded together into a new rising class of businessmen of the New South. The long-contested assertion of "territorial monopoly" forwarded by Roger Ransom and Richard Sutch will be refuted by evidence presented here, but these scholars' contention that "flawed economic institutions" aided the mercantile credit-debt system of the postwar period is key to this analysis. C. Vann Woodward, Don H. Doyle, and David Carlton together provide an excellent framework for understanding the accession of the Southern business and entrepreneurial class but also fall short of fully explaining the small-market regional center conditions that existed in Natchez. Here a model featuring the emerging small regional business center in the postwar South, brought forth by Louis Kyriakoudes, will be found more useful to explain the developing business conditions that existed in postwar Natchez.[7]

These studies help frame a picture of postwar Natchez's sharecropping regime and lay out the manner in which the furnishing and credit system of mercantile agents operated to make and market the South's staple crops in the transition from slavery to freedom. Building on them, this book shows how a specific group of merchants operated and prospered as new postbellum entrepreneurs. It focuses most specifically on the contractual relations of these men with planters and freedmen agricultural workers within the context of their own ethnic communities. The result is a better understanding of the interplay of time, place, culture, law, and economics in the creation of a new world dominated by sharecropping and mercantile credit in the production and marketing of staple crops. This picture emerges from extensive primary research in the Natchez District's records to demonstrate that these merchants made their money by exploiting the troubled circumstances of the once dominant class of slaveholding planters, as well as the distressed condition of freedmen sharecroppers, to prosper in the postwar scene and become the primary builders of a new Natchez. Yet for all their members' power and influence, much of the merchant class eventually fell victim to the same pernicious system they perpetuated. In the end, cotton was still king in this story, and much of this work explores how a new class of merchants emerged as the new retainers of King Cotton in the postbellum Natchez District, and how their fortunes rose and fell with those of the king.

CHAPTER 1

Old Ways and New Realities

REBEL GUNFIRE FROM THE NATCHEZ RIVER LANDING AND THE bluffs above bracketed the sloped sides of the ironclad gunboat USS *Essex*, while its engines strained and threw spray against the strong Mississippi River current as Commodore "Dirty" Bill Porter positioned his ship into firing position midcurrent. Natchez had technically been surrendered to Union forces since mid-May 1862 and had been left unoccupied and largely unmolested. But General Ulysses Grant's push on Vicksburg and the presence of strong Union fleets ascending the Mississippi from New Orleans and descending from Memphis had left Natchez "hemmed in" and its populace in a panic.[1] These tensions exploded on September 2 as Porter sent a shore party to the landing in search of aid for his sick and wounded, and Porter's later report describes his assessment of the actions of his boat and crew that afternoon:

> I had received intimation that the Rebel gunboat *Webb* was at Natchez, to which city she had convoyed supplies transports with supplies from Red River. I followed to that city, but found they had sought protection of the Vicksburg guns.... At Natchez a boat crew was merely sent ashore to procure ice for my sick, when they were wantonly attacked by over two hundred armed citizens, wounding the officer in command and killing one and wounding five seamen. I immediately backed off and opened fire on the lower town and set an number of houses (from whence they were shooting at us) on fire. After the bombarding the place for an hour, the Mayor unconditionally surrendered.[2]

The point of view on the Natchez side was quite different from Commodore Porter's matter-of-fact account, however. Yankee shells holed and set fire to mercantile houses and warehouses at the "under-the-hill" landing, sending merchants, boatmen, black workers, and a host of townspeople running for what cover they could find. The Yankees also targeted the town proper on the bluff above but were limited by the elevation capabilities of their cannons, instead sending shells indiscriminately to burst overhead and randomly hit homes and businesses. The widow of wealthy cotton merchant and planter Frederick Stanton found a ball lodged in the Corinthian portico of her grand mansion, Stanton Hall, while longtime merchant-planter Thomas Henderson found another had pierced the kitchen of his manse, Magnolia Hall.[3] The Natchez citizens held later that the bombardment lasted far longer than Union claims, and the *Natchez Weekly Courier* echoed the rage Natchezians felt about perceived Yankee cowardice when it defiantly announced the next day that

> a collision of our inveterate foe with a small portion of our people, at the Natchez landing, afforded the Essex gunboat an opportunity to open on the city yesterday. The mysterious 9 and 10-inch holes all over the city . . . attest their industry in attempting the lives of women and children, *without any notice* of their bloody intentions. Should this short notice reach the commander of the Essex, he is informed that his shelling of Natchez *murdered one child*; and that the further casualties intended by his malice, were withheld us by an overruling Providence.[4]

Regardless of the difference between Union and Confederate accounts, it is clear that during the melee of that September afternoon in 1862, there were indeed grave casualties suffered in Natchez, both immediately human and overwhelmingly social and economic in nature. The only direct individual casualty on the Natchez side that day was seven-year-old Rosalie Beekman, the daughter of a small but respected German Jewish merchant, Aaron Beekman. As the shelling began, Beekman and his young family fled his modest dry goods, grocery, and plantation supply house under-the-hill and made their way up Silver Street toward the relative safety of the town on the bluff. But as they ran, Rosalie's older sister, Sarah, heard Rosalie fall and called out. Sarah later related that "Papa called out to her to get up, but she answered, 'I can't, I'm killed.' I remember how he picked her up and his dreadful cries as he carried her in his arms, the blood streaming from her wound. She had been struck." Indeed, Rosalie had been hit by a shell fragment and died the next day in the home of fellow merchant John Mayer. As the Beekmans grieved over the loss of their youngest child, they probably could not have fully appreciated that the same socioeconomic forces that brought forth the war and their loss would be the same mechanisms that would make them one of the most important and wealthy mercantile families in Natchez by the turn of the century.[5]

In a larger sense, with every shell that hit Natchez, an irreparable hole was torn in the social and economic fabric of that epicenter of the old Cotton Kingdom. The system of slavery, highly profitable plantation agriculture, and the attendant mercantile trade that had grown with the explosion of cotton production over the preceding half-century was being torn apart to be replaced by a new order. Of immediate concern to the war-diminished local white population was that, as word of the shelling spread through the information network among the massive local slave population, enslaved blacks began leaving their former plantations in increasing numbers, wandering the district's roadways or congregating in surreptitious "contraband" encampments throughout the countryside. Fears of violent slave uprisings gripped the local slave owners, while bands of freed slaves took what they could from plantations and small farms alike to survive. Though most of the Old Natchez District escaped Yankee occupation for a few months longer, the following July General Grant's conquest of Vicksburg ensured that the arrival of Union troops was imminent. Locals either fled to Confederate-held areas or hid their records, valuables, and cotton, awaiting the inevitable as life in Natchez reached an uncomfortable impasse.[6] The wife of Confederate general William T. Martin—easily the most famous Natchez citizen to serve the "lost cause" and a major figure in the postwar business community—wrote of the day it all came to an end:

> On Monday, the 13th day of July, at 1 o'clock, our usually quiet little town was thrown into the greatest state of alarm by the arrival of Yankees and no wonder we were alarmed . . . several regiments came up the hill screaming and whooping like wild Indians. In less than an hour pickets were stationed at our front gate and the yard filled with soldiers.[7]

Freed slaves soon swarmed to Union lines and encampments in Natchez, swelling the local population by thousands, creating a burgeoning refugee problem that overwhelmed occupying Union officials. But in an unexpected way, the emerging free population of former slaves would also soon alter local trade and commerce by providing an exploding new market for food, supplies, and eventually credit that would both change the socioeconomic landscape of the Natchez District and influence large portions of the defeated agricultural South as a whole. Perhaps most important, in doing so they created and drove a new system of labor that forever altered cotton agriculture and produced vast new opportunities for a fresh generation of Southern merchant-entrepreneurs who would reshape Southern society. The local mercantile firms would become the cash and credit nexus that served both freedman and planter alike, and as one prominent scholar of the postbellum period has noted, "emporiums of cheap merchandise rapidly became symbolic of the creation of a new southern economic system from the wreckage of the old. Perhaps no southern institution more nearly embodied so much of the intimate story of the New South."[8] But if major changes were imminent in the Natchez marketplace, what were the origins of the old mercantile order, and what was the nature of the economic system to be altered?

No place in the antebellum South more nearly epitomized the "ascendancy" and domination of the wealthy cotton planter class than the Natchez District, the wealthiest in the Cotton Belt. Historians have long focused on the wealthy landed gentry, or "nabobs," of the area as the prime economic force of the region, with the local mercantile tradesmen and their activities assuming a largely secondary role in the district's history. While no one can deny that planter profits, derived from the cotton staple trade, exceeded the scope of other local businesses, the trade, marketing, and social endeavors of the antebellum Natchez merchant class as a whole were actually quite significant and shaped the development of the area in a distinct way. The history of the Natchez District and the lower Mississippi region is deeply tied to traders, merchants, boatmen, cotton buyers and brokers, erstwhile professionals, and a host of other entrepreneurial sorts who sought their fortunes first on the remote frontier of the American Southwest, and later in the growing regional center of the Cotton Kingdom. The planter class was never a monolithic entity but a consortium of entrepreneurial-minded capitalists: from the very beginning, many of the wealthiest denizens of the district's antebellum planter elite emerged from, made fortunes in, or were intermarried with the local mercantile class.⁹

From the time that French explorer Robert Cavalier de la Salle first came down the Mississippi River and landed at Natchez in 1682, trade and commercial potential were in the forefront of European desires for colonization of the lower Mississippi valley. Seeking an outlet to the Gulf of Mexico to connect French possessions in the upper Mississippi reaches and Great Lakes region, and to thwart British westward expansion by linking these regions, the French enthusiastically sought inroads in the fur and deerskin export trade with the local Indians. Pierre Le Moyne D'Iberville occupied the region in 1698–1699, and as trade and commercial efforts quickened, the first primitive European settlement was established at Natchez with a trading post in 1713. That year the province "had been entirely placed in the hands of a successful merchant, to be developed, if possible, into a money making enterprise," and powerful French merchant-financier Antoine Crozet began introducing settlers and the first African slaves into the region. Fort Rosalie was constructed at Natchez a few years later, in 1716. Its construction is considered the settlement's true establishment.¹⁰

The character of trade, however, maintained a quality of "frontier exchange" between Native Americans and the French, yielding unsatisfactory results for Crozet and his European backers. Due to these poor returns, Crozet relinquished his charter to Scotsman John Law and his Western Company (Mississippi Company). While several land grants were issued and the first Natchez plantations were established on St. Catherine's Creek in 1718–1719, Law also formed an ambitious plan to introduce tobacco and indigo plantation agriculture for staples export from the region, importing some 3,000 African slaves, as many as 300 of whom were installed clearing land and planting for French masters in the Natchez area by the 1720s. The Western Company faltered in 1721, and the region was assumed by the parent Company of the Indies, which continued support of trade in the Natchez District. For a time Natchez thrived as "the King's galleys frequently tied up at the landing to load and unload valuable cargoes, such necessities as arms, nails, and implements of the frontier. Knives, guns, axes and medicines were exchanged for furs, indigo, tobacco, and sassafras. . . . Natchez-under-the-Hill became a busy port with warehouses, wharves and sheds for storage." The settlement grew to 713 people (including 280 slaves) by 1727 and to more than 750 people by 1729, with as many as 6,290 arpents of land in cultivation, growing primarily tobacco.

Despite this early success, local farmers "complained that the reimbursement they received for their crops was not commensurate with the mercantile prices set by the company, which were 70 per cent above prices at Mobile and New Orleans . . . [and] officers at the fort handled the sale of most incoming merchandise and raised as much as 400 per cent above the official levels." Due to the settlement's remoteness, exorbitant prices for incoming goods would prove to hamper Natchez settlers for many decades to come, and one later visitor characterized the district as "the most expensive place in the universe."[11]

The settlement suffered a setback of a more serious nature in 1729 as the nearby Natchez Indians killed or took captive almost the entire French and black slave population of Fort Rosalie and nearby settlements, but by 1732 French colonial soldiers, in league with powerful Choctaw warriors, had exterminated the Natchez. The French Crown reassumed control of the region in that year and, in an attempt to stimulate new settlement, removed all duties on the export of staples and the import of merchandise. Commerce soon grew to new levels in some areas of French Louisiana, but the Natchez District largely reverted back to a frontier state. One source holds that "in 1745 there were eight white males (soldiers), two negro families, and fifteen negro slaves at Natchez. . . . In 1751 there were fifty soldiers in garrison there." French ineptitude and lack of finances nearly doomed the further commercial progress of the Natchez District. It would take a significant change to revive the district's fortunes, and just such a change occurred in 1763.[12]

The shattering defeat suffered by the French in the Seven Years' War and the following Treaty of Paris placed all French possessions east of the Mississippi in British hands, while the Spanish received the portion to the west and the critical port of New Orleans. British officials governing the new province of West Florida initially ignored the district—primarily due its geographic isolation—but by the early 1770s sent troops to repair the fort at Natchez, to be christened Fort Panmure. Soon thereafter they began issuing large land grants in the area. War veterans and Crown favorites received lands ranging from several hundred acres to over 25,000 acres, and many future nabob families appeared in the Natchez area with slaves and began plantation agriculture in earnest. Among them were the Hutchinses, Swayzes, Ogdens, and Ellises. Many of these families settled just south of Natchez, on St. Catherine's or Second Creek, and built a substantial settlement at Kingston in that vicinity. They were soon joined by a torrent of British loyalists fleeing the coming American Revolution, including a group of Connecticut Seven Years' War veterans led by Phineas and Thaddeus Lyman. In 1773 purportedly "four hundred families passed down the Ohio, on their way thither during six weeks of the summer that year."[13]

These early planters engaged in tobacco and indigo production, as well as lumber and livestock. They were also able to build substantial homesteads and apparently demonstrated a strong desire to secure more slaves for their growing plantations. While downriver shipping through New Orleans was problematic because it was in Spanish hands, the British were able to conduct significant commercial activity in the region, shipping staples in return for finished goods. Several mercantile concerns in Natchez quickly emerged. Anthony Hutchins, the largest planter in the area, served as local agent for London commission house John Miller & Co., while British captain John Blommart and influential Philadelphia-connected James Willing now ran thriving mercantile houses at Natchez under-the-hill. "Orders for luxury items, including cases of Madeira, cognac, and port, as well as fine apparel" reached Natchez from Panton, Leslie, and Co. of East Florida, and by 1776 Natchez boasted at least four mercantile establishments. Local plantation agriculture was quickly assuming antebellum form, and the growing export trade in staples brought a significant influx of manufactured goods in return, the beginnings of true mercantile trade in Natchez.[14]

The American Revolution also had exploded that year, and while Natchez was a bastion of loyalists, some community members strongly supported the American cause, especially merchant James Willing. Willing owned "the principal shop in Natchez under-the-hill," and his brother Thomas was senior partner of the major Philadelphia mercantile house Willing & Morris and also a member of the First Continental Congress. James Willing was reasonably well liked and supplied goods to the many gentlemen Tory planters but was dissipated and "squandered his small fortune in drink," and he bitterly closed his doors in 1777. That year he fell into league with friend and wealthy Irish American New Orleans merchant Oliver Pollock and then went to Philadelphia to join the American cause against his former neighbors. Through his connections he gained an officer's commission to lead the only American military expedition against the southwestern frontier to seize or destroy British assets along the river and to solidify a supply chain out of New Orleans from Pollock to American troops in Illinois Territory. He landed with more than 100 volunteers on the gunboat *Rattletrap* and seized Natchez in 1778 before moving on to New Orleans, plundering British supplies and looting the plantations of former friends Anthony Hutchins and William Dunbar, who commented later that "all was fish in their path." Spanish governor Bernardo de Galvez in New Orleans did not appreciate his presence, but allowed Pollock to sell the British plunder. Later that year Willing was captured by British forces.[15]

Spanish willingness to aid the rebel Americans belied their strong desire to occupy the region of British West Florida, and after Spain declared war on Britain in 1779, Galvez seized West Florida and the Natchez District. Although loyalists Anthony Hutchins and merchant John Blommart led a brief Natchez uprising against the Spanish in 1781, Spain's minions were firmly in control by 1783, when the Treaty of Paris fixed the boundary between American and Spanish possessions a short distance below Natchez on the 31st parallel. Natchez was above the line and was a point of contention between the United States and Spain until the Spanish agreed to evacuate to the line in 1795. In the interim, the English-speaking residents of Natchez were required to swear loyalty to Spain, providing a buffer against inevitable American expansion. Otherwise they were largely left to their planting businesses and mercantile concerns. The Spanish maintained the status quo for influential residents but also issued liberal land grants to lure settlers, including future antebellum nabob families—the Minors, Surgets, Lintots, Vidals, Vousdans, and a host of others. It is not an understatement to assert that a fair portion of the Natchez antebellum planter class received their lands during this period.[16]

Under popular district governor Manuel Gayoso de Lemos, who socialized with and married two members of the local planter aristocracy, the Spanish encouraged trade through New Orleans with their possessions in Mexico, the West Indies, and Spain itself. They also subsidized the local tobacco crop, "promising to buy two million pounds of their tobacco yearly at the premium price of ten dollars per one hundred pounds." Area planters produced 1,402,725 pounds in 1789, but production soon fell off with competition from Kentucky growers and the cancellation of Spanish tobacco subsidies. Many planters switched to indigo and, increasingly, cotton. More important, the Spanish opened the Natchez marketplace to credit-offering Caribbean slave traders, and by one estimate there were 2,400 slaves in the district by 1795, while another scholarly analysis has examined over 800 local slave transactions in Spanish records between 1780 and 1796, seemingly making that number a bare minimum.[17]

Direct mercantile trade with traditional British sources and American firms in Philadelphia was hampered, as the Spanish regulated trade and control of river commerce. Still, Natchez under-the-hill bustled with trade, and the river landing thoroughfares were lined with busy shops and warehouses. The strong interrelation between Natchez and New Orleans mercantile houses was cemented during this time, while "with the sudden influx of Spanish-milled dollars . . . the swift rise in trade with Mexico and the Spanish-dominated West Indies brought strange craft to Natchez-under the hill. Sleek ships from Barcelona and Cadiz landed at the wharf and galleons from South America came up the river every few weeks." Yet Natchez's remoteness from established markets on the Gulf Coast and beyond still plagued local planters with very high merchant prices, and this situation boiled over in 1790 when the planters lost their tobacco subsidies. As in the coming antebellum era and beyond, many large merchants were planters, but this did not temper the natural friction between the "Natchez merchant-creditor class and the planter-debtor element." Eleven "opulent" city merchants complained that for the year 1790 they were owed open accounts in the excess of $146,000, while the planters retorted they were victims of outrageous prices and usurious interest rates that exceeded 10 percent or more. Planter John Hutchins wrote that "matters will drift from bad to worse, and the time is not very distant *when the planter must destroy the merchant or the merchant must destroy the planter.*"[18] Infuriated, Hutchins rendered an example of what he was forced to pay:

> I will give you a few items . . . that you may know of the prices of articles in the vicinity in those times of need; one pair of thin three point blankets, $12; one yard of Scotch osnaburgs, seventy five cents; one pound of brown sugar, 50 cents; one pound of coffee, 75 cents; one pound of tea, $12; one barrel of flour, $25.00 or $30.00; freight on a barrel from New Orleans, $5.00 to $7.00; first cost of one barrel of salt at New Orleans, $20.00; molasses from Jamaica, 50 cents per gallon; molasses watered, sugar sanded and salt pebbled to help the weight and measurement.[19]

While friction surely existed, there were never clear-cut divisions between the members of the two classes. Not only was the merchant often a planter, and the planter a merchant, but either could have marital ties to the other. In fact, merchant capital fueled a good portion of the developing local plantation agriculture. Both the planter and merchant elites apparently were prospering sufficiently to begin constructing the first of the large homes in or around Natchez, complete with fine European furnishings and in some cases extensive libraries. Wealthy merchant and book dealer John Henderson, for example, took time from his mercantile pursuits to construct a substantial home, engage in agriculture, and write the only local pre-American period literary work, *Paine Detected, or The Unreasonableness of Paine's Age of Reason* (1797). Similarly, large planter Bernard Lintot ran several successful mercantile establishments in addition to his plantations. However, the dynamics of creditor-debtor relationships are key to the development of Natchez and shaped the local economy for over a century.[20]

By the late 1790s the situation in Natchez had changed drastically in favor of expanded commerce, trade, and agriculture. Convinced they could no longer regulate or contain the burgeoning "western trade" coming downriver from Kentucky and other interior American frontier regions, the Spanish opened the Mississippi River to American flatboats at a 15 percent duty. This decision induced a wave of commodities to flood the Natchez under-the-hill commercial district and jump-started the "flatboat era" of Mississippi River commerce. Then, in 1795, a watershed year, the Spanish signed the Treaty of San Lorenzo, which acknowledged the 31st parallel as the limit of Spain's interests, placing the Natchez District firmly in the United States' hands. American commissioner-surveyor Andrew Ellicott soon arrived with an army escort and pressed for Spanish evacuation of the district. Early Natchez planter and merchant William Dunbar—a noted surveyor-scientist responsible for the modern Natchez street layout—figured prominently in this period for his role with Ellicott in surveying the 31st parallel. But the banner contribution of Dunbar and other local planters that year was the introduction of the cotton gin and a switch to a new concentration on cotton staple production.[21]

Cotton had been grown in the district as early as 1735 but had never become a viable export staple. There was neither a viable marketplace nor a way to remove the seeds from the cotton lint efficiently and cost effectively. All this, however, changed. The expanding industrial revolution in England led to the explosive growth in the textile industry, creating a huge market for cotton. By 1800 the English were importing as much as 56 million pounds of the staple. Planters and merchants in Natchez alike realized this huge emerging market potential, and the local introduction of the cotton gin enabled their participation. Large slaveholding landowners immediately switched to cotton as the premier cash crop. Excellent climactic conditions, superior loess soil (a rich sedimentary accumulation of Great Plains dust and indigenous compost), and prime local bottomlands proved ideal for cotton production, and easy access to transportation on the Mississippi River ensured the crop's economic viability with ready access to market in New Orleans or Liverpool.[22]

Slave-worked cotton plantations became very profitable practically overnight, and wealthy planters began to increase production exponentially. The Natchez cotton crop "exceeded 3,000 bales" in 1797 and may have surpassed 1,200,000 pounds the following year. Nabob William Vousdan became the first planter to ship directly to England, while Stephen Minor produced 2,500 bales, worth $51,200, on nine plantations. William Dunbar wrote Philadelphia-based merchant John Ross that "the foundation of a large fortune may be laid now," and "we continue to cultivate cotton with very great success. It is by far the most profitable crop we have ever undertaken in this country." Representatives from such Liverpool mercantile firms as Green, Wainwright & Co. and Barclay, Salkeld & Co. arrived in Natchez to offer credit and services, and to solicit trade. Meanwhile, local mercantile firms quickly moved into the cotton-handling and plantation supply business. Commerce exploded. Soon incorporated as an American town, Natchez quickly expanded the range of conveniences supplied by cotton factors and local merchants. Slaves poured into the town's hinterland, as the cotton planters took advantage of the relatively cheap slave and land prices supported by good prices for cotton in the domestic and international markets. By 1798 Natchez had become the capital of the new territory of Mississippi, and a new era of business had begun.[23]

The business of the Natchez District increasingly was planting, but in the town of Natchez itself, mercantile trade was the focus of activity. With the crops coming in, fall was the best time of year to make money selling merchandise to planters flush with cotton to trade for goods. In October 1801 the *Intelligencer* announced that another sort of busied enterprise was well under way at one of the local mercantile houses, in anticipation of the year's imminent harvest:

On Monday the 19th instant, will be sold at the vendue office, a large quantity of

Dry Goods

Consisting principally of the following articles, viz.
Rose blankets, 3 point ditto, 2 1–2 point ditto, 2 point ditto.
Blue and red bordered duffield ditto.
Blue cloth, blue and olive fearnought.
Belt French britannias, nankeens, umbrellas, fine cotton shirting, cotton cambrick, fine handkerchiefs, mosquito netting, and &c.
The sales will be continued from day to day. Cotton, in in square bales, delivered at this place on or before the 25th instant, will be taken in payment at 24 dollars per 100 wt.

John Henderson, V.M.
Natchez, Oct. 12, 1801[24]

The goods offered that week by Henderson & Co. were just a small sampling of the items available in Natchez that October for payment in cotton, cash, or credit. In one advertisement, merchant Job Routh—whose family would become very wealthy planters by midcentury—touted that he had a "large quantity of the best Monongahela liquors, viz. Whisky, Peach Brandy, and Cherry Bounce; all which he will dispose of low for cash. . . . The above liquors were made by R. Noble, who is known to make equal to any in that country." Stephen Douglas announced that he had "For Sale, Thirty Barrels of Flour," while New Orleans commission merchant John Lynd promoted the ability to service planters in the local hinterlands with his "Commission, Grocery, and Liquor Line; all orders from the country will be executed with care and dispatch," a very early example of the developing coastal cotton factor trade. Every issue of the *Intelligencer* seemingly contained more mercantile advertisements than the last, and within a few short years literally page after page of the local paper would be packed with offerings of everything from "fashionable European goods" to "Hardware, Stationary, Chocolate, Mackerel, and Salmon" or "Ladies Spangled Kid or Moroco Shoes."[25]

As the district burst in a frenzy of cotton production and attendant mercantile activity, a new generation of successful merchants or merchant-planters entered the scene and laid the groundwork for the local mercantile configurations that endured through the Civil War. Cotton was selling at 44 cents a pound in 1801 and was already the nexus of local wealth, and most mercantile efforts were directly related to the cotton trade or its beneficiaries. And as the previous advertisement of Henderson & Co. indicates, cotton was also a medium of exchange, as good as cash and maybe better, because handling cotton presented opportunities to profit further by offering a depreciated local cash value and then selling at the greater true market price in New Orleans. Often the merchant acted as a local agent and charged commission, shipping, and handling charges for essentially the same service. Or the merchant "would hail passing riverboats (flatboats) laden with the products of the Northern country—flour, cornmeal, bacon, and the like," and then buy both the cargo and boat. He then "advertised his new purchase and advised local planters to bring their cotton to the river to exchange for the supplies they need.... When his stock was exhausted, he loaded the cotton on the flatboat and took it downstream to New Orleans to be sold."[26]

It is unclear how many local Natchez merchants used this ingenious approach, but judging by the numbers of advertisements that offered "Hoes and axes, to be sold low for cash or cotton," and "Brandy, Demarra Rum and Coffee, which they will exchange for cotton on very good terms," the merchants were more than happy to trade their wares for cotton to be sold downriver. There are abundant examples as well of offers "Wanted to Purchase, 100 Bales of Cotton; For which cash will be given.... Apply at the store of M. Snyder," or "The Subscribers will give cash for 100 Bales of Cotton.... Claiborne & Wooldridge." The nature of the goods or commodities often sold for cotton indicates that local plantations were far from self-sufficient in meeting their food requirements and that a dearth of hard currency or specie necessitated a commodity exchange for goods. These elements endured in the plantation economy through the cotton era.[27]

The experience of one of the largest and most successful merchants of early antebellum Natchez demonstrates the mercantile strategy described above, the fluidity of the merchant-planter interrelationship, and also the importance of local merchants in Natchez society and economics. Samuel Postlethwaite came from a wealthy family in Carlisle, Pennsylvania, that had solid ties to the Philadelphia mercantile class. After achieving success himself as a merchant in Kentucky, he came down the Mississippi in 1800 on a flatboat loaded with commodities and landed at Natchez, where he sold his "small cargo of flour, bacon, and wood, including the raft on which he traveled," for $75 to Abijah Hunt, a very successful merchant-planter. He was shocked to find that the next boat in his traveling group sold their cargo for $7,000, although on partial credit. Apparently impressed by the business opportunities, he stayed in the district as a merchant and was soon advertising his wares: "CHEAP GOODS. S. Postlethwaite and Co. Have on hand, a great variety of excellent goods, which will sell on the most moderate terms for CASH or COTTON. *They have lately received three bales of* BLUE GUINEAS, *to be disposed of on very easy terms.*"[28]

Young Samuel was a most ambitious man, and within the space of a few years had married the daughter of wealthy but ailing nabob William Dunbar, taken over Dunbar's many business concerns, invested in his own plantations, and inherited yet more land and slaves as executor of Dunbar's estate after Dunbar's death in 1810. Postlethwaite made the transition from newcomer to member of the landed aristocracy quickly. He soon was such an important local businessman that he helped charter the Bank of Mississippi in 1809 and later served as its second president. Postlethwaite's nephew from Carlisle, twenty-one-year-old Dr. Stephen Duncan, arrived in Natchez in 1808 and soon followed the same path to riches, marrying a daughter of the powerful Ellis family in 1811. He received his first cotton lands and slaves as dowry, and became perhaps the largest and wealthiest cotton planter in the entire South by midcentury, having succeeded his uncle Samuel as the third president of the Bank of Mississippi in 1825.[29]

Men of all ranks, including the professional classes of doctors, lawyers, bankers, and newspapermen—even preachers—flooded the Natchez District upon word of the quick and easy fortunes to be made on what were still the reaches of the southwestern frontier. The landed gentry, comprised of old-line land-grant families such as the Minors, Surgets, Vousdans, and Bingamans, may have derived their wealth from plantation empires in the country, but others found their opportunities in town. The wealthiest men in the district during the period included merchants Samuel Postlethwaite, Abijah Hunt, and James Wilkins, also physicians John Carmichael and Fredrick Seip, and lawyers Charles Green and Lyman Harding. Regardless of a man's initial profession, however, the lure of cotton loomed large and drew just about every successful businessman into cotton planting as the *main chance* eventually.[30] One young Yankee teacher and minister later described the phenomenon of "cotton mania":

> A plantation well stocked with hands, is the *ne plus ultra* of every man's ambition who resides at the south. Young men who come to this country, "to make money," soon catch the mania, and nothing less than a broad plantation, waving with the snowy white cotton bolls, can fill their mental vision, as they anticipate by a few years in their dreams of the future, the result of their plans and labor. Hence the great number of planters and few professional men of long or ancient standing in heir several professions.[31]

Not all professionals or merchants gave up their occupations for planting. Though some did, others managed to do both. Wealthy merchants in particular were unlikely to abandon their mercantile activities. James Wilkins, for example, owned 4,678 acres and 277 slaves by 1815, but still made the majority of his income from his Natchez commission business. Also, there was plenty of lucrative work available for doctors and lawyers. Yellow fever, among a host of other subtropical maladies, regularly scoured the area in the late summer and occasionally reached epidemic proportions; a severe occurrence in 1823 reduced the local population by 312 souls. Lawyers were always in demand as well, and by one account over 144 lawsuits were filed between 1803 and 1805 alone (a ratio of more than one lawsuit for every fourteen white Natchez citizens), while two years later local lawyers-planters Lyman Harding and William B. Shields defended treasonous ex–vice president Aaron Burr when he was apprehended nearby. Merchants in particular needed their services in the continuing planter-merchant credit and debt dilemma as perhaps 70 percent of the local cotton-related trade was conducted on credit. Debt-related newspaper advertisements were common, and one issued by mercantile partners Ferguson and Woolley indicated that "the subscribers give notice that their books of account, will on the first of December next, be placed in the hands of their attorney at law, for recovery of their debts, when suits will be immediately commenced against all persons without discrimination, who stand indebted to them."[32]

By the second decade of the antebellum era, over 8,000 slaves worked in the cotton fields of Adams County, the population of Natchez approached 2,000, cotton sales moved toward $1 million annually, and local dry goods firms, groceries, and commission merchant houses numbered well over thirty. The Mississippi flatboat era had transformed Natchez into an important regional commercial shipping center, supply depot, and the most important American city on the southwestern American frontier. The flatboat men who had brought a myriad of products and commodities south on the Mississippi from the interior, and often returned north by land on the adjacent Natchez Trace, had transformed the under-the-hill landing into a crowded area of stores and warehouses—but also prostitution, drinking, and gambling establishments, making it one of the most notorious locales on the western frontier. Also notorious was the appearance of slave traders. They operated in town until local ordinances forced them outside the city limits in the 1830s, when they created a slave market on the edge of town known as Natchez "forks-in-the-road," which emerged as one of the most important slave marketplaces in the country. Infamous slave merchants such as Franklin & Armfield made fortunes there feeding the local hunger for slaves, but even petty local merchants engaged in this trade, and it was common to have an advertisement like "M. Robitaille, Offers For Sale at His Store, A Likely Negro Man, Aged about twenty-two years, for cash or short credit." This appeared right below a solicitation for "Dry and Fancy Goods" in the for-sale section of the newspaper.[33]

In contrast, the town above the hill became an opulent and aristocratic community, whose economic, social, and political influence affected the entire Mississippi valley and (old) Southwest region. In this social climate, the tradition of the grand old Natchez families and nabobs quickly solidified and became entrenched. A rising new contingent of middle-class merchants came to dominate local city and county politics until the Civil War, while the local planting, mercantile, and professional aristocracy gravitated toward state office and largely dominated politics in the capital until the Jacksonian era. The steamboat age arrived in 1811 when the *New*

Orleans first docked at Natchez, and by the time Mississippi became a state in 1817, regular service to New Orleans, Memphis, and Louisville was available. The next year merchant Samuel Postlethwaite, together with his nephew Stephen Duncan and a host of other merchants and local businessmen, formed the Natchez Steamboat Company to profit from the new form of conveyance. Always intimately tied to the rise and fall of cotton prices, Natchez fortunes also benefited from such investments significantly during the first quarter-century of the steamboat era.[34]

In these first decades, too, several other social and economic changes began to shape the development and character of the Natchez merchant class into the postbellum period. As local import commerce and the staple export trade became national and even global in nature, a dual mercantile system developed that was comprised of the coastal commission merchant, or cotton factor, in addition to the local merchant. In the Natchez District, most coastal factors servicing the area resided in New Orleans, but some were also based out of New York, or occasionally Liverpool. This convoluted system displayed many overlapping functions that both factors and the local merchant fulfilled, though often the differences lie in the scale of credit offered or cotton handled in conjunction with direct access to markets. Cotton factors were generally commissioned agents of the planters who dealt with European and Northern cotton buyers or textile manufacturers and serviced the market for the cotton that planters grew, supplying credit, cash, foodstuffs, and finished goods in return.[35]

Some of these coastal factors had local representatives in Natchez, usually more modest merchant houses, but increasingly most worked directly with individual planters, often removing the local merchant from the equation. The factors also provided bookkeeping and banking functions, had access to much larger pools of capital, and visited the region intermittently during the crop year, while handling the planters' provision and marketing needs by correspondence—a level and scale of service few local merchants could provide. The middle-size merchants in town also supplied household goods to planters and in addition provided farm supplies to outlying small farmers in the region, as well as a variety of store goods to townspeople and local customers, who did not offer the scale of business necessary to make it economically feasible for coastal factors to pursue. While a broad pattern and trend, this was by no means a hard-and-fast rule, and Natchez maintained several local commission houses that rivaled New Orleans firms until the Civil War. But in general, as the antebellum period progressed, the local merchants usually offered goods on credit and purchased cotton on a smaller scale than coastal cotton factors or northeastern supply firms, whom they often served as local middlemen.[36]

As these trends developed through the antebellum period, Natchez society was becoming more class-driven and stratified. Many early settlers who enjoyed large land grants were from privileged backgrounds, or quickly climbed the social ladder to the aristocracy through the explosion of cotton agriculture and its attendant trade. Decades of intermarriage between nabob families created a society apart that was becoming increasingly more difficult to penetrate by marriage. Even during the wide-open period of the early nineteenth century, when men like Samuel Postlethwaite and Dr. Steven Duncan quickly married into the planter class, a good percentage of those newcomers were from privileged backgrounds themselves. Money and privilege usually married money and privilege, while increasingly "the prerequisites for entry into the gentry class by the late antebellum period were 'connections' as well as wealth." Connections and "social capital" proved invaluable to antebellum planter-merchants. For the burgeoning merchant capitalist class of the postwar period, these ties played even greater roles in success.[37]

The nabobs and quick-acting newcomers occupied large swaths of available farmland in the district by the mid-1830s—one reason why a large contingent of small subsistence farmers never emerged there. As soil depletion became a factor in that decade, the planters quickly expanded their holdings as part of a "speculative mania" into adjacent counties, onto the Mississippi delta, and across the river in Louisiana. Joining them was a sizable contingent of smaller planters. In turn, too, there were middle- or lower-class tradesmen, mechanics, clerks, teachers, clergy, small shopkeepers, peddlers, and the like. Then, starting in the 1830s large immigrations of Irish, Germans, English, and other groups bolstered these classes. By 1850 almost one white resident in three was foreign-born—one-third of these were Irish. Natchez also was home to over 200 free blacks, many of whom worked in the trades. Opportunity still abounded in the district, and it was still possible for young men on the make to join the landed gentry. The odds of doing so, however, declined with each decade for several reasons.[38]

The panic of 1837 hit Natchez hard and sent the district into an economic downturn that endured into the 1840s. Both planters and merchants alike were highly dependent on outside Northern credit, and when cotton prices fell below 10 cents a pound in the early 1840s, profits in the marketplace contracted. Because the number of local mercantile houses had increased to unsustainable levels, competition became fierce. The newer merchants were unlike some of their freewheeling merchant-planter predecessors. They borrowed from their Yankee peers: saving, thrift, hard work, time management, temperance, and public reputation and involvement were core values. These merchants were intimately tied to credit offered by wholesalers and manufacturers in the Northeast, Midwest, and New Orleans, and the introduction of the Northern credit rating service R. G. Dun & Co. during this era placed merchantmen seeking credit under scrutiny like never before. Many of this generation of businessmen rose from modest means and learned their trades from the bottom up as clerks or traveling peddlers, and they began to specialize along the lines of smaller retail shopkeepers, grocers, or larger wholesale merchants. They read business literature and often made purchasing trips to the Northeast or Midwest wholesale centers, increasing their ties to Northern merchant capitalism. Business-minded immigrants who emerged from European shop-keeping traditions began arriving in Natchez in larger numbers, particularly German Jews like Aaron Beekman, who would figure prominently in Natchez postwar business development.[39]

This is not to say that large cotton commission houses or multifaceted "plantation supply" firms run by nabob merchant-planters were no longer part of the Natchez marketplace, or that fortunes were no longer made in that arena. Irish immigrant Fredrick Stanton, for example, got his start in New York as a clerk in the 1820s and by the 1830s was a very wealthy regional commission merchant in partnership with H. B. Hamer and Henry S. Buckner, one of the largest New Orleans cotton factors after the war. But the partners suffered heavily after the panic of 1837, and Stanton lost everything and was apparently $700,000 in debt, but was able make a second mercantile fortune during the boom of the 1850s and died as a nabob in 1859 with perhaps the grandest mansion in Natchez, 15,000 acres in cotton, and 444 slaves. Bostonian lawyer Alvarez Fisk arrived in the district around the same time as Stanton and by the 1840s was "the most influential merchant-financier in Natchez," operating hugely successful commission houses in town and in New Orleans. He was wealthy enough to provide the land and capital to construct the Natchez Institute in 1846, one of the most successful public schools of the antebellum

South. Philadelphian Charles Dahlgren, former banker for the Second Bank of the United States and future Confederate general, owned one of the district's largest plantation supply houses—large firms that did not specialize and carried myriad products from groceries to dry goods or farm implements and served planters with one-stop shopping—and made a fortune through his mercantile pursuits and over 6,000 acres of land obtained by marriage to a member of the powerful Routh family.[40]

Thus by the 1850s and the last great cotton boom before the war, a stratified "dual economy" had emerged in Natchez that encompassed elite planters, merchants, and professionals, on the one hand, and a emerging cadre of bourgeois middle-class merchants and other midlevel professionals who serviced both the aristocracy and the lower classes, on the other. The domination of the upper tier had actually begun to retard growth in Natchez, as large portions of cotton wealth never found their way into the local economy, but rather often went for goods and services through factors in other regions. Cotton wealth rarely found its way into infrastructure and manufacturing investment, and while Natchez had long been the manufacturing leader in Mississippi, by the 1850s it was being eclipsed by other cities with larger middle-class segments and more opportunities for migrants of that class. For example, this "top heavy" condition was evident in the "capital invested in manufactures" figures for 1860, which listed Natchez at $161,000, while Vicksburg, a short distance upriver, was listed at $643,550. Vicksburg had outstripped Natchez with a viable railway connection to the North via the New Orleans & Nashville Railroad, which also boosted its shipping revenues by handling cotton from the growing Mississippi delta region. Natchez was still isolated without a rail line, although leading merchants and planters had made an abortive attempt at constructing a railway to connect with Canton before it collapsed under the weight of the depression after 1837. Railway construction and new manufacturing endeavors would be of major interest to the Natchez merchant class in the postwar period.[41]

Nevertheless, Natchez on the eve of the Civil War was a vibrant commercial and import-export center with all of the modern conveniences and a well-developed municipal government that provided services on par with cities much greater in size. In 1860, 6,612 free people lived in the town of Natchez, amid a slave population of 14,292 in the surrounding county, while the port shipped around 50,000 bales of cotton worth well over $2 million, and local mercantile sales approached $2 million.

The census of 1860 reveals seventeen individuals who lived in town with property worth more than $300,000. Five were local merchants. Many wealthier slaveholders lived on plantations in Adams County and the surrounding counties and parishes that composed the Natchez District. Indeed, Adams County was home to as many wealthy men as anywhere in the South and had perhaps the greatest concentration of millionaires of any place in the nation outside of New York City. In addition, middle-class merchants made large gains during the 1850s, and there were over twenty local merchants with the solidly bourgeois net worth of between $20,000 and $50,000 of personal property, and nine who owned ten or more slaves. The 1858 Natchez city directory listed over 100 retail firms of various specialties, including clothing dealers, confectioners, druggists, grocers, and jewelers, as well as purveyors of dry goods, plantation supplies, variety goods, western produce, and wines and liquors. It must be mentioned, of course, that large parts of the nonslave population were middle-class tradesmen and tradeswomen, small shopkeepers, peddlers, middling-scale farmers—most of whom owned slaves—and the common folk made up of boatmen and skilled or unskilled workers.[42]

The start of the Civil War changed the situation in Natchez drastically. A conservative, Whig stronghold before the war, the city had delivered the largest contingent of pro-Union votes in the 1860 Mississippi secession referendum. Many planters and merchants, with Northern business and family connections, had pro-Union sympathies; some were absentee owners who spent large amounts of their time in the North. The cotton crop of 1860 was the last sold before the Union blockade disrupted the economic system in Natchez. Coastal cotton factors could not sell or ship cotton to the North or England or receive new goods in return, and this forced many merchants and planters to the brink in the first year of the war. Although many had great assets, these men were often cash poor, and the credit-supply factor system had been disrupted. Also, many were creditors themselves and were now unable to collect on debts owed them by others.[43]

The concentration of fighting around the fortress town of Vicksburg upriver from Natchez, as well as the pro-Union sentiment of some of its largest planters and merchants, saved Natchez from extensive war damage. These conditions explain the large contingent of antebellum mansions and structures that survived the war but also provoked the ire of Confederate guerrillas operating out of the Louisiana swamps who terrorized loyalists and killed their workforce. This is not to say that Natchez did not suffer during Union occupation, or that Natchez was a Union stronghold. The majority of its white residents supported the Confederacy, and once the war began even those who opposed secession joined the cause. In the ensuing occupation cotton was confiscated or burned along with some plantations; economic and social structures were upended; fortunes were destroyed; and the district's thousands of slaves were freed. Planters, coastal factors, and local merchants were weakened or put out of business and had their goods seized, and the traditional supply and credit system offered by factors and merchants was disrupted almost beyond repair. As a result, few Natchez planters and merchants were able to conduct much *real* business during the war, and many were severely weakened from the outset. Dying planter Benjamin Wailes summed up the sentiments of many when he wrote, "In the unhappy state of our Country I may have already lived too long." Nonetheless, this confused social milieu and economic void provided an array of opportunities for those with a sharp eye for sizing up the situation and exploiting the uncertainties of the moment.[44]

※ ※ ※

As General Grant's occupation forces filed into Natchez in July 1863, bringing up the rear of the columns was the train of wagons and carts that comprised the contingent of Yankee sutlers, the merchant-peddlers who supplied goods to the Union troops for a price. Among them, and among the dust and the clatter, was Isaac Lowenburg. The twenty-seven-year-old German Jewish immigrant had only been in America for five years but apparently had enough wisdom to appreciate opportunity when he saw it and sufficient command of the language, American customs, and business savvy to take advantage of it. Lowenburg moved quickly to make himself part of the Natchez scene and the small, local Jewish community. With the help of his Northern friends and supply and credit contacts, before the year's end he was in the grocery, dry goods, and cotton-factoring business in a marketplace practically devoid of available goods. He sold to the shaken townspeople, Union soldiers, what few planters remained, and, increasingly, freed blacks with a bill or two of hard Union currency in hand gained from occupation work details or a black soldier's pay. Within a year Lowenburg had a lease to run the abandoned cotton plantation Loch

Levin and Union permits to ship cotton and receive goods. Within two he had a local rebel bride. Within ten he had one of the largest mercantile houses in town. Within twenty he was a leading businessman, wealthy merchant-planter, and the first Jewish mayor of Natchez.[45]

Lowenburg had company in his endeavors. In its last issues before the Union occupation, the *Natchez Daily Courier* had published only a small handful of advertisements offering meager goods for sale, including "For Sale, A Fine Lot of Milch Cows . . . J. Mayer & Son" and "Choice Brown Sugar, For Sale by the hogshead, Barrel or less . . . Fleming & Baldwin." After only two months of occupation, however, the *Courier* reemerged in September 1863, and every new issue included a growing number of solicitations from Northern firms seeking local business, as many wholesalers moved quickly to get a market share. "F. H. Clark & CO. . . . Memphis, Tenn.," invited "attention to our present Stock of new and choice Goods, which is full and complete in all its branches." In another instance, the ad read: "SUTLERS, ATTENTION! NEW GOODS, JUST RECEIVED AT THE WELL KNOWN SUTLERS EMPORIUM OF HOPPE, WOLFF & CO., MEMPHIS, TENN. . . . FANCY GOODS, NOTIONS, etc." Another was from "ST. LOUIS TO THE SOUTHERN TRADE, E. G. TUTTLE & CO., WHOLESALE DEALERS IN HATS, CAPS, AND STRAW GOODS . . . AND VARIETY OF NOTIONS." Not to be outdone, soon Yankee men on the make flooded the newspaper with other offers like "D. B. SMITH, SUTLER 28th Ill. Inf'y Vols., HAS OPENED AT THE POSTLEWAITE STORE ON MAIN STREET, A LARGE STOCK OF SUTLERS, MILITARY, AND OTHER GOODS," or "BY C. W. FORD, FOR SALE, A LARGE AND FINE STOCK OF DRY GOODS." This rapidly growing new marketplace contained few recognizable mercantile firms from before the war, but by July 1864, after only a year of Union occupation, the pages of the *Courier* were so loaded with new dry goods, grocery, and commission firms that it started to resemble its former prewar character.[46]

Some antebellum Natchez merchants had found ways to eke out a living and survive before the occupation forces came, and soon prospered thereafter. For example, Bavarian emigrant John Conrad Schwartz had been a prosperous and solidly bourgeois purveyor of confections and liquor during the 1840s and 1850s, worth $37,000 in real and personal property in 1860, including fifteen slaves. After Natchez was shelled in September 1862, he apparently found himself bereft of goods to sell and resorted to procuring tobacco and coffee perilously close to Union lines—and perhaps smuggling these goods—for wartime profits. His daybook from December 1862 to March 1863 lists trips to Jackson, Mississippi, to purchase "a sack of coffee gross weight—229 lbs." for $823.62, and a second for over 1,000 pounds of tobacco, pipes, related goods, and shipping at $3,383.20. Of this total, nervous draymen alone charged "freight to Brookhaven 38.00" and "freight from Brookhaven to Natchez 54.70," while the total shipping charge came to $156.70. He recorded fifty-four coffee sales in Natchez from December 19, 1862, to January 12, 1863, including the entries "Dec 23 Mr. E. Dixon 5 lbs. 4.50 . . . 22.50," or "R. W. Phillipps 7 1/8 lbs . . . 32.00," for a total profit on the coffee of $56.12. These prices exceeded prevailing Mississippi Confederate government wartime standards for allowed prices of $1.50 a pound. Concerning the tobacco sales recorded between February 13 and April 3, 1863, he recorded total receipts of $4,267.20, or a profit of $208.39. His efforts yielded a total profit of $264.52, which he promptly reinvested that spring in the remaining hardware stock of Armand Perrault & Co. for $5,000 Confederate currency, a business that carried him through the remainder of the war and later made him wealthy.[47]

The trajectory of Schwartz's new hardware business over the following year is indicative of the emerging marketplace taking shape. Schwartz's "Cashbook 1863–1881" provides an example of the huge difference in business from 1863 to 1864. As he noted, he:

> Bought out the stock of A. Perrault March 31st. From this stock sales were made for confederate currency as follows:
>
> | 1863 | March 31st | 78.15 |
> |------|------------|-------|
> | | April | 561.15 |
> | | May | 672.45 |
> | | June | 222.90 |
> | | July | 110.00 |
> | | August | 25.00 |
> | | | $2,379.50 |
>
> After which sales were made only in United States currency and were for the remaining half of

1863	August	18.80
	September	70.50
	October	460.00
	November	129.00
	December	132.00
		$811.1548

Schwartz clearly struggled after May 1863, when occupation was imminent, and from August through the end of the year as occupation was under way. In actuality, however, he probably did much better than it appears, as he gained back almost half of his $5,000 investment in the first few months with the $2,379.50 in sales. After the switch to U.S. currency, he may have done almost as well because of the much greater value of that medium, all the while engendering future business as perhaps the only local hardware firm up and running during that difficult transitional period. In the figures for 1864, it is clear he had turned the corner, and his business gamble was paying off:

864	January	264.45
	February	314.35
	March 31st	522.75
	April	950.65
	May	1640.30
	June	1286.95
	July	1140.70
	August	872.80
	September	628.00
	October	716.00
	November	492.00
	December	584.05
		$8,913.0049

These much-improved sales figures only reveal a portion of the accelerating changes that would shape the postwar scene. With the new and renewed access to Northern and New Orleans markets and wholesalers, new goods were again available and moved quickly, as these businesses pursued Southern outlets with vigor. Schwartz, for example, seems to have had stronger connections to New Orleans, whereas many of the Yankee newcomers had theirs in the North. In the period between April 12 and May 5, 1864, alone, Schwartz placed orders for at least $2,035.21 in dry goods, hardware, and clothing from "Stark, Stuffer & Co., Blake & Tower Co., and Folger & Co.," all of New Orleans. By the first week of July he placed an additional $2,563.09 in orders with those firms and others for a little of everything: cutlery, tools, glassware, pots and pans, pocketknives, personal shavers and combs, cotton packing, cotton gin parts, paints and oils, and an expansive list of other items. And almost certainly he received credit terms on those orders ranging from ninety days to six months net depending on the wholesaler. The new goods were not just sitting on the shelves either. In May he sold merchandise both needed and whimsical to a telling range of customers: merchants, planters, and Union soldiers and authorities—but also, in surprising numbers, freed blacks and African American soldiers. Below is a small sample of who bought what by date purchased:

1864	May 3	Rich'd coll'd Coffee Pot (Richard colored)	1.00
	May 4	Beekman 200 Fish Hooks (Aaron merchant)	5.00
	May 9	Freedman's Hospital 3 Locks (U.S. authorities)	6.00
	May 11	Ann coll'd Broom	.50
	May 12	Lisa coll'd Looking glass	.75
	May 14	Wm Stanton Ice Cream Freezer (planter)	5.00
	May 19	Mrs. Stockman Hair Brush (merchants wife)	2.50
	May 20	Soldier coll'd Fishing Tackle	5.00
	May 20	Julia coll'd Flat irons 12 (hair)	.50
	May 25	Gun Boat Officer 2 doz. Vest Rings	2.00
	May 26	Mary coll'd Mouse Trap and Spectacles	3.00
	May 31	Soldier coll'd Tin Ware	.75[50]

Those purchases represent a very small portion of Schwartz's sales that May, which at $1,640.30 was his best month in 1864. By the end of that year his total receipts of $8,913 represented a tripling of business, conducted in all hard Union currency. His orders for goods increased exponentially the following year, and his suppliers included the Northern firms of "Plant & Bros. . . . St. Louis Mo., Waters & Fox . . . Louisville Ky., William McCulley & Co. . . . Pittsburgh, [and] Heron, Rodger & Paddock . . . Cincinnati O.," more than doubling his gross receipts, to $20,508. Meanwhile, in addition to the burgeoning marketplace of newcomer Yankee merchants, a few familiar Natchez prewar mercantile firms besides J. C. Schwartz & Co. reemerged or started advertising once again, including Meyer, Deutsch, & Co.; Fleming & Baldwin; and Pollock & Mason. While many of the carpetbagger firms would prove transitory and would disappear during the first few years of Reconstruction, other new firms would emerge during this time that would become stalwarts of the Natchez postbellum marketplace. Rickey, Shelton & Co.—backed by capital provided by Union general Herron of New Orleans—was advertising heavily by the spring of 1865 as "The leading House In Natchez," but by 1867 it was bankrupt and gone. At the same time, however, new firms Rumble and Wensel, Henry Frank, and H. M. Gastrell & Co. became leading houses and businessmen of the dawning age.[51]

A few planters even made tentative steps toward resuming business. While many had suffered greatly at Union hands, particularly Frank Surget, who had his suburban villa Clifton dynamited and burned, or Gabriel B. Shields, who was driven from his home Montebello and incarcerated with his son, a handful of others made small progress, particularly if they had known Union sympathies. Having literally been a prisoner in his suburban villa Concord in late 1863 when he penned, "I don't go into town unless on business. . . . I have two guards (Union) here at present," nabob Henry C. Minor wrote: "I am happy to say I shipped this evening, by steamer 'New Orleans' four hundred bushels of cotton seed. It was put up in barrels, as barrels are cheaper than sacks. I have four hundred bushels ready at John's lower place (his uncle). I will ship on Friday if the gunboat is in the neighborhood."[52]

It must be remembered, however, that any work or commerce Minor managed to conduct during occupation was certainly reliant upon remaining ex-slaves and black laborers now working for wages under the watchful eyes of Union troops, the Treasury Department, and, soon, the Freedmen's Bureau. His success—and that of other planters—however, was not assured. As a class, the planters were prostrate after years of little or no income and the loss of slaves and the immense capital they represented. The labor situation was far from resolved as well. Its eventual resolution would create great opportunity for the postbellum merchant class.

❈ ❈ ❈

With the defeat of the Confederacy in the spring of 1865, the marketplace in the Natchez District was already deeply involved in a frenzy of mercantile activity. The area was flooded with Yankee and Southern merchants seeking to capitalize on the burgeoning opportunities presented by the rising new social and economic order. With stocks of fresh goods arriving daily, they were more than eager to supply goods and credit to the war-weary Natchez townspeople and planters but also to Union troops, occupation officials, and carpetbaggers of all stripes who attempted to provide order and structure to the largest emerging market of all—freed blacks. While recent hatreds and upheavals of the war certainly did not evaporate overnight, people who came from both sides of the Mason-Dixon Line seemed determined to channel their energies and bury their fears by moving forward into the possibilities of an uncertain new age, demonstrating a strong desire to get back to the business of conducting business. One glib purveyor of goods may have inadvertently summed up the desire to move ahead with his proclamation that "Richmond has Fallen, SO HAVE GROCERIES!" while another reiterated this urge to seek new commercial opportunities in the wreckage of an old, defeated system: "*Wanted*. A CAPITALIST to engage in the TRADE business. Permits and Authorities correct, and ready for shipment. Address A,B,C, Natchez Post Office."[53] As some men eyed the possibilities and profits to be realized from the resumption of full-scale cotton production, many others realized the potential of the emerging new marketplace.

And this was as it should have been. The Natchez District from its colonial inception had been instituted and built upon the desire for trade and profits, and indeed European mercantilism preceded and fed the rise of cotton agriculture. The vaunted planter class had never been far removed from mercantile pursuits, and many planters had emerged from trade or made much of their fortunes in the commercial arena. Southern agrarian capitalism had always worked hand in hand with merchant capitalism, inexorably intertwined in a credit and supply nexus. With the destruction of slavery, the old antebellum system of agriculture and trade was shaken to its foundations, and while many basic market forces remained, new realities were emerging that changed the Southern economic landscape forever. Cotton remained king for two generations to come, but the old elites had been damaged and weakened, and the agricultural labor force was now open to and dependent upon the marketplace for goods and credit, making the former supply and credit mechanisms increasingly unable to meet the demands of the new postwar economy. Into the breach emerged a new bourgeois generation of merchant-businessmen-entrepreneurs who more closely represented the sweeping Gilded Age changes in the nature of commerce that swept the nation, and who became, more than any other group, the true builders of a New South.

CHAPTER 2

Merchant Communities

NINETEEN-YEAR-OLD JOSEPH N. CARPENTER HAD BEEN AT WAR for over two years, serving in the Breckinridge Guards cavalry unit, comprised of Natchez volunteers and attached to Confederate general John C. Breckinridge. He had fought in some of the most hotly contested battles and campaigns of the war: at Missionary Ridge, Nashville, and the Atlanta Campaign, where he had his horse shot out from under him but emerged intact. His last action was the desperate rebel attempt to stop General Sherman's advancing Union army at Bentonville, North Carolina, in March 1865, the final major Confederate military action of the war. But the powerful Union elements quickly brushed aside the outnumbered Southerners, and a little over a month later, on April 26, the war ended for Carpenter, as General Joseph E. Johnson surrendered his army and Carpenter's unit to Sherman. Paroled and released from service, Carpenter was owed $1,400 for the cost of his horse and back pay by the failed Confederate government, but he "took the dollar and a quarter that was paid out in Mexican silver, accepting this in satisfaction of all claims," and began the long trip back to Natchez "by train, raft, wagon, steamboat and on foot." The trip was "filled with hardships" but also "attended by . . . many ludicrous situations and novel adventures." Like many young Southern soldiers uprooted and disrupted by the war, Carpenter returned home imbued with a strong entrepreneurial desire to find business opportunity among the wreckage of the old order. Within a year he was in business with his father, Nathaniel, as N. L. Carpenter & Sons, which quickly became one of Natchez's most successful cotton-handling, -ginning, and -supply firms. From these beginnings, Carpenter would build the most successful business empire in the region by the turn of the century.[1]

Carpenter was joined by a host of young Natchezians returning from the war that year, men who would quickly form a substantial portion of an emerging postwar business and mercantile class. If the Natchez community had held significant pro-Union sympathies before the conflict, once hostilities commenced local men had swarmed to the rebel banner, including many of the young clerks and middle-class merchants who would constitute the postbellum mercantile bourgeois. Participation in the Confederate war effort would become a proud badge of honor and a common cohesive element in the postwar mercantile community. Former Kentuckian Lieutenant Samuel Dryden Stockman and Irish immigrant Thomas Hart served in the Natchez Southrons at Shiloh, Chickamauga, and New Hope Church. Italian immigrant Sergeant Paul Botto, Irishman John Marron, and Connecticut-transplant William Abbott toiled at Malvern Hill, Manassas, and Gettysburg with the Natchez Fencibles. Natchez brothers Edward and Samuel Perrault were at Fredericksburg, Gettysburg, and Spotsylvania Courthouse with the Natchez Light Guards. And four feet eight inch, "too short to shoot" German Jewish immigrant Simon Mayer rose to major as Confederate general Jacob H. Sharpe's aide-de-camp in the Atlanta campaign. Like Carpenter, these men all made their way back to Natchez ready to assume or reassume their places in the booming mercantile marketplace.[2]

These former Confederate soldiers constituted part of an emerging vanguard of merchant-entrepreneurs who would change the face of Natchez and the New South in the coming years. Some were Southern survivors from the antebellum marketplace as well as Confederate veterans. Joining them were Yankee newcomers or European immigrants. Others, like the Carpenters, though staunchly Confederate, were new to commerce. One of the salient features of all those who prospered in the postwar marketplace was that they enjoyed local ties or family relationships to one or more emerging groups in the larger community. These provided attachments, support, and cohesiveness in an uncertain postbellum marketplace. Some of the communities were well defined and formed along cultural or religious lines, as in the case of vibrant local communities comprised of immigrant Jewish, Irish, or Italian merchants, while other informal groupings among longtime Americans relied more upon antebellum familial relationships or loose ties engendered by common regional heritage or business connections. In each case, these communities were critical factors in a merchant's success. German Jews usually formed partnerships with German Jews, while natal Southerners went into business with natal Southerners. This pattern also carried over into the arena of intermarriage between families, further reinforcing these communities' claims. Yet while at the beginning of the postbellum period the lines of separation between communities were fairly solid, as the period progressed, entrepreneurialism crossed ethnic lines, particularly in the second generation of mercantile families, when sons of immigrant merchants teamed with sons of native families in new entrepreneurial combinations representative of the new business age. As will be demonstrated later, as a result, second-degree associations of networking and "social capital" created new and larger opportunities in business, finance, and politics that often superseded old cultural, familial, and group rivalries by the turn of the century.[3]

The Natchez merchant class had achieved a surprising amount of diversity by 1860, perhaps an indication that the wealthy planter-merchant class was actually in decline on the eve of the Civil War and that small and middle-class merchants were gaining market share before the postwar period. An examination of the available figures for 1860 reveals some startling demographic trends that would continue into the postwar era. The 1860 census for Natchez Township, for example, indicates that out of 139 individuals who listed their occupation as some form of mercantile pursuit, 54 were American citizens, while fully 85 were foreign-born, translating into a proportion of 39 percent native and 61 percent foreign. This surprising figure is partially a function of the prewar predilection among natives to list cotton agriculture as their primary occupational endeavor if involved in a planter-merchant configuration, or changes within family firms. For example, Cyrus Marsh, a prosperous merchant for several decades was listed as a "farmer," while his son, Cyrus Jr., ran the firm in town as his father retired to his agricultural pursuits. Similarly, Thomas Henderson, a member of the long-standing nabob merchant-planter Henderson family, is also listed as a farmer, while the Natchez city directory lists Thomas Henderson & Co. as doing business on Main Street as a cotton commission firm. Also, the labels of merchant and farmer were fluid within the realm of native versus foreigner and transformed often due to family changes. For example, Hulda and Thomas Stanton were American-born beneficiaries of the mercantile fortune of Irishman Frederick Stanton (wife and son) and listed their occupation as "farmers" after Fredrick died in 1859. Yet their mercantile interests were continued by Frederick's

Irish brother Thomas as part of the burgeoning Stanton, Buckner, & Newman Co.[4]

The foreign-born numbers still are striking. The influx of merchant-minded immigrants from Europe who emerged from European mercantile traditions was dramatic and important; furthermore, it would continue into the postbellum period. Having long been part of the Natchez social fabric as a smaller but industrious segment of the emerging merchant middle class, in the postwar era immigrant merchants would gain significantly in importance. In the 1850s alone at least seventy-eight Irish and English, thirty-three German, seven French, and three Italian immigrants came to Natchez, and many entered the marketplace as petty merchants, grocers, and peddlers. The Irish, English, German Jews, and Italians, in particular, increased embryonic merchant communities of their antecedents that existed from the 1840s or earlier. The 1858 Natchez city directory indicates that in terms of size and ability or means to advertise, the larger and wealthier firms were generally native owned and run, while the newcomers were making inroads, especially in the grocery and dry goods business (see Table 1).[5]

The figures in Table 1 reflect that in 1860, while superior in numbers, the immigrant merchant communities had often centered on small shopkeeping pursuits and were purveyors of clothing, confections, liquors, and groceries, which could include various specialties such as "Fruit Merchants." In other cases some acted as traveling peddlers of notions and small goods—Jews were well known for this. The immigrant traders also

Table 1. Origin of Natchez Merchants, 1860					
Origin					Total (%)
U.S.-born	Mississippi	South (other)	Northeast	Midwest	
	14 (26%)	8 (15%)	26 (48%)	6 (11%)	54 (39%)
Foreign-born	Germany	Ire.–G. Brit.	Italy	Other	
	28 (33%)	27 (32%)	18 (21%)	12 (14%)	85 (61%)
Source: U.S. Census (1860), MS Population Schedules, Adams County, Mississippi*					
*The table contains only the top three immigrant groups as listed by name, the "other" twelve foreign-born merchants are from: France, 7; Spain, 2, Russia, Cuba, and Canada, 1 each. The term "merchant" was undefined and could mean dry goods, cotton, or clothing merchant, or perhaps any number of variations. The major mercantile types listed in the 1860 Census include by number: "Merchant," 90; "Fruit Merchant" (Grocer), 25; "Druggist," 4; and miscellaneous listings ("confectioner, liquor, lumber, coal, fancy store, and jewelry"), 16. Tailors, milliners, and other trades were not included.					

were known for a willingness to sell to and trade with slaves, or the "black trade." Few rose to the importance or wealth like that of the Irish Stanton family in the cotton commission business, but increasingly they began to make inroads into the multifaceted "plantation supply" arena that could include groceries and dry goods. Aaron Beekman is an example of this trend, and in the postwar period, these immigrant traders became major players in this business. The 1870 census reflects this trend but also demonstrates the shift in the merchant community composition due to wartime changes (see Table 2).[6]

Although no figures exist for the period immediately following the war, an examination of the 1870 census in Table 2 reveals that demographic changes in the marketplace under way during Reconstruction would shape the character of the Natchez merchant class. The predominance of the immigrant community in sheer numbers was tempered somewhat. By a slim margin, the most numerous group was now comprised of native citizens. While still a very diverse marketplace, the totals in 1870 reveal that Natchez Township was now comprised of at least 159 individuals who listed mercantile pursuits as their occupation, with 55 percent native-born Americans and 45 percent from foreign lands. Many of the emerging new merchants were eager young men who were clerks in 1860, served in the war, and came home determined to be successful. Others like Joseph N. Carpenter and his former contractor father, Nathaniel, recently entered the mercantile business from the trades, increasing the percentage of

Table 2. Origin of Natchez Merchants, 1870					
Origin					Total (%)
U.S.-born	Mississippi	South (other)	Northeast	Midwest	
	35 (40%)	15 (17%)	23 (26%)	12 (14%)	87 (55%)
Foreign-born	Germany	Ire.–G. Brit.	Italy	Other	
	31 (43%)	19 (26%)	9 (13%)	13 (18%)	72 (45%)
Source: U.S. Census (1870), MS Population Schedules, Adams County, Mississippi*					
*The table contains only the top three immigrant groups as listed by name, the "other" 12 foreign born merchants are from: Russia-Poland, 8; France-Alsace, 4; and Switzerland, 1. The nomenclature of how various merchants were listed was much improved in the 1870 census and more clearly represented the nature of the Natchez marketplace and its merchant components. For example, in 1870 the census listed firms in the following categories and totals: "Merchant," 52; "Grocer," 49; "Dry Goods," 24; "Storekeeper," 15; "Druggist," 7; "Proprietor," 2; "Cotton Factor," 1; and miscellaneous listings ("confectioner, liquor, lumber, coal, fancy store, and jewelry"), 4. Only S. Dryden Stockman & Co. is listed as a "cotton factor," when in reality a large majority of merchants, grocers, and dry goods firms handled and shipped cotton as a portion of their business.					

locally born merchants, while Northern newcomers inflated native-born numbers. The German Jews began to dominate the foreign contingent, supplemented with growing numbers of German-speaking Jewish newcomers from Alsace-Lorraine (France). Later, increasing numbers of Jews from the eastern European areas of Russia (Poland) arrived, while the Italian and Irish English merchant communities remained static or decreased in number slightly. Calculating the percentage totals of American-born, however, can be deceptive. Second-generation sons of foreigners started entering the market as native-born individuals, but they also maintained ethnicities.[7]

Also, many of the antebellum Natchez merchantmen and their families, who had migrated to the area from other regions of the United States and grown wealthy with the explosion of cotton agriculture, were natives with their means reduced at war's end. The grandees of inherited merchant capital were in many instances third or even fourth generation by 1870, and few, if any, enjoyed the former status of their nabob forbearers. A. J. Postlethwaite, the descendant of the wealthy early merchant Samuel Postlethwaite, started the postbellum period by selling out to a German Jewish newcomer from the North, Henry Frank. John W. Henderson, son of the first-tier merchant-planter Thomas Henderson, commenced business with a former clerk and war veteran, William Abbott, without marked benefit of his father's previous firm. In fact, most of the "opulent" merchants of the previous age were dead, financially shattered, or scattered to parts elsewhere by 1865, and most of the grand and wealthy mercantile houses of the antebellum era had been destroyed by the war or seen their owners grow too old, rigid, or mired in the past to make an impact on the new marketplace. Tellingly, of the four merchant-planters worth $300,000 in 1860, none was in business during Reconstruction. Probably the greatest mercantile survivor was Mississippi native James Carradine, who boasted $111,000 in real and personal property in 1860 and still had $35,000 in property left in 1870. The middle-class element would demonstrate the greatest gains during the early postwar period, and the rising young entrepreneurial class was swiftly and almost entirely replacing the former grand element.[8]

※ ※ ※

In 1867 the emerging business of Samuel Dryden Stockman was in many ways emblematic of what it took for the native-born portion of the emerging postwar Natchez mercantile class to get ahead in business. Touting that his firm would "make liberal advances in CASH and SUPPLIES on cotton assignments to our New Orleans House,"[9] the thirty-six-year-old Stockman enjoyed all the necessary elements to succeed in a changing Natchez marketplace: he emerged from a modest local middle-class merchant family that had strong ties to other local mercantile families; his father had been a president of the Natchez Board of Aldermen (city council) in the 1840s; he was a highly regarded Confederate officer and war veteran; he had learned his trade first as a clerk in his father's small mercantile auction and cotton commission firm and later received his start in business working for the wealthy merchant-planter Stanton family at Stanton & Stockman, Plantation Supplies and Family Grocery Store. Perhaps most important of all, he had been associated with Henry S. Buckner and Samuel B. Newman during his time at Stanton & Stockman Co. before the war. One of the strongest Natchez-associated New Orleans cotton-factoring firms both before and immediately following the war, Buckner & Newman Co. proved an invaluable association to a rising young merchant. Buckner and Newman soon formed two major new factoring firms as Buckner & Co. and S. B. Newman & Co. Newman apparently thought highly enough of the credentials, connections, and demeanor of Stockman to appoint him as the company's local representative in Natchez:[10]

| S. B. Newman, | S. D. Stockman, | S. B. Newman, JR |
| New Orleans | Natchez | New Orleans |

COTTON FACTORS
AND COMMISION [sic] MERCHANTS
S. B. Newman & Co.,
No. 171 Gravier St., New Orleans, La.
S. D. Stockman & Co.,
*At the old stand of Thos. Henderson & Co., foot
of Main Street, Natchez, Mississippi*[11]

Armed with as much as $700,000 in combined Northern capital to invest loaning to planters and merchants alike—while handling vast amounts of cotton in return—the connection with Buckner and Newman also practically assured Stockman's success, as this glowing report from the local representative of the R. G. Dun & Co. credit rating firm would indicate:[12]

S. D. Stockman + Co.

10232 July 16/66 Impossible to estimate amt. of capl. The house is a branch of "Buckner + Newman" in N.O. Their cr. is unlimited. All the members of this are bus. men + pers reliab. Their bus. is immense. Of course, 250 NY will not cover thr capl. We put this amt. as the lowest limit.[13]

Inasmuch as Stockman demonstrated the wherewithal to inspire the confidence of his new backers, he also had the characteristics that we will witness time and again as the absolute prerequisites for membership in the emerging bourgeois entrepreneurial elite: family, community, and business connections; access to capital and supply sources; knowledge of the business and shrewd ability to gauge risk; an opportunistic openness to the new emerging marketplace conditions; and the simple ability to be in the right place at the right time. In the developing business community in Natchez, these attributes were almost always combined with a strong sense of belonging to the portion of the cultural (ethnic or religious) business community with which one identified. Such identification, however, did not unduly limit a young man with pluck, a burning desire to advance, and courage to try new ventures and branch into new entrepreneurial pursuits. Stockman demonstrated as much in another business pursuit, outside of his mercantile and cotton commission firm: "ARE YOU INSURED? If not, why not? The cost is trifling; the duty is manifest; the result may be escape from ruin . . . POLICIES ISSUED WITHOUT DELAY . . . S. D. STOCKMAN, AGENT."[14]

Stockman also sold Aetna insurance for a time. Thus he not only insured the cotton that he and others stored and shipped against fire, but he profited in the process as well. As his commission business grew, however, he saw that franchise later go to John A. Dicks, a future business partner of Joseph N. Carpenter in the cotton business. To understand Stockman's success, one also needs to take into account the web of familial connections on which he drew. His uncle, merchant John Fleming, had migrated to Natchez in 1835 from Virginia, had married Stockman's father's sister Mary, and was soon the senior partner in perhaps the premier prewar Natchez middle-class plantation supply and commission firm, Fleming & Baldwin Co. By the 1850s John Fleming and New York–native Hiram Baldwin were lending significant amounts of money to local planters and handling their cotton, with S. D. Stockman's older brother James N. acting as "trustee" for Fleming & Baldwin on several agricultural loans. R. G. Dun gave them superior personal and business ratings:[15]

Fleming + Baldwin Cott. Groc. + c.

10023 Dec 12/56 Sales last yr $ 100NY. Per prop (each) abt $5m. RE (each) say $6m. char, habts, cap and prospects first rate. Cap in bus prob over $50NY. Altogether unencumbered @ both men age abt 35 yrs. and Bus improving.[16]

In April 1861, with war imminent, John and Mary Fleming sold S. D. Stockman his first storefront on Main Street for $5,000 cash—the same building in which he started out after the war as S. D. Stockman & Co. until he took over the former Thomas Henderson & Co. facilities mentioned earlier. Fleming and Baldwin also boasted connections with Buckner and Newman, and in April 1866 Stockman and Fleming & Baldwin both served as trustees for Buckner & Newman on a huge loan to the nabob planter James Metcalfe to operate his plantations Woodland, Montrose, York, and Bourbon—over 5,000 acres mortgaged for a total of $48,305.40 due over two years at 8 percent interest—and in the process received rights to ship all of Metcalfe's cotton for a commission. Fleming & Baldwin emerged from the war as probably the top Natchez plantation supply and commission firm, a distinction it would hold until the 1870s. Fleming's son James S. Fleming, ironically, later married planter James Metcalfe's niece Anna, and James S. Fleming will figure prominently later in this study. S. D. Stockman became successful enough to move his operation to New Orleans early in the 1870s, handling many large planter and mercantile accounts in conjunction with Samuel B. Newman Jr. as Samuel Sr. aged. Stockman and his younger brother John were instrumental in providing capital to the growing mercantile and cotton-handling concerns of Joseph N. and Nathaniel L. Carpenter, and the familial bonds and interconnected nature of these two native white mercantile families were significant. The

1880 census reveals that the S. D. Stockman household was host to businessman Joseph N. Carpenter's sister Helen and her attorney husband, William F. Mellon, when the Mellons moved to New Orleans to set up his law firm in that large market.[17]

About a block away from Stockman's new commission house, a business of a different sort arose that would rival any in the district within a few years. Joseph N. Carpenter and his father, Nathaniel L., opened their new firm as N. L. Carpenter & Sons. The Carpenters enjoyed many of the same local strengths that Stockman did: a long association with the community, a good middle-class standing, a respected family name, honored service in the Confederacy, and a modicum of capital to invest. But the trajectory that brought this family to prominence was considerably different than that of the Stockmans. Nathaniel L. Carpenter emerged from a Vermont family that had fought in the Revolutionary War. He married a woman from New York and arrived in Natchez in the 1830s. Carpenter entered the building trades and appeared in records as early as 1837, when he contracted to build a home for leading Natchez journalist L. A. Basaucon on Main Street in a "good and workmanlike manner" for $2,000. While a middling tradesman, he had dealings with some members of the Natchez elite during the 1840s and 1850s, including leading planter Stephen Duncan and renowned steamboat captain Thomas Leathers of the *Natchez* versus *Robert E. Lee* steamboat race fame. Carpenter owned a handful of slaves and took in an apprentice in the building trade, demonstrating a no-nonsense Yankee view of responsibility and working habits by offering his sixteen-year-old apprentice Lineas Risley "meat, drink, washing and lodging and any and all necessities in sickness and in health, clothing excepted," but also sternly warning him not to "haunt or frequent hotels, taverns, saloons, or other places of amusement or dissipation."[18]

But Carpenter apparently did not want a career in the trades for his sons, Joseph and Allen, and perhaps sensing opportunity in the reduction of the antebellum order and the exploding possibilities in the new marketplace, put up a gin stand sometime in 1864 to profit from the renewed cotton market by ginning and handling cotton. In the fall of 1865 advertisements appeared for "COTTON GINNED AND BALED . . . on REASONABLE TERMS and without delay. FRESH CORN MEAL constantly on hand. N. L. CARPENTER."[19] When his sons returned from the war, the newspaper soon announced:

N. L. CARPENTER & SONS,
CORNER OF WALL AND JEFFERSON STREETS, NATCHEZ, MISS.

Having just completed extensive improvements in the establishment, we are now prepared to

Gin Cotton

    Grind Corn

        Farnish Laths

            Dress Lumber

Our new gins produce a very large yield of the finest cotton.

A continuation of the patronage heretofore so liberally bestowed is respectfully solicited.[20]

As their advertisement indicates, the Carpenters demonstrated a mechanical and technical bent as part of their entrepreneurial endeavors—ginning cotton, grinding corn, pattern sawing—a logical progression for a trades family, and they would become leading proponents of the local manufacturing and technological improvements in the postwar period. But as with most Natchez merchants, their base was in the cotton business, and soon after their firm appeared, they began advancing financing and plantation supplies at 8 to 10 percent interest to plantation owners, including nabob William S. Cannon on his Bluff plantation and Edward Dixon on Majorca. Joseph N. Carpenter soon rose to the pinnacle of the local cotton business as president of the Natchez Cotton and Merchants Exchange and handled some of the largest planter supply and credit accounts in the district. Apparently the Carpenters did not rely on backing directly from a New Orleans factoring house, however, instead carefully building their business using their own modest capital and that from their local associates, including James Stockman, acting as trustee for the premier local bank Britton & Koontz. Joseph N. Carpenter also soon forged varied new businesses with fellow Natchezian John A. Dicks and planting-mercantile concerns across the river in Concordia Parish with Pennsylvanian newcomer George G. Klapp. In keeping with the tendency to conduct business within their own group, many planters preferred to do business with native firms composed of local men they knew, making N. L. Carpenter & Co. and S. D. Stockman beneficiaries of their history and connections. This notion seemed to benefit the Carpenters almost immediately, and R. G. Dun gave them sparkling credit ratings from the beginning, which got even better over time:[21]

N. L. Carpenter + Son Grist Mill + Cotton Gin

10232 July 16/66 Capl 5NY w 10NY outside, owes 0o*f*, pay promptly.

10232 Dec 10/67 Cap. 15NY$ gd. for contracts, during past yr have added at least 8NY$ wor. of improvements.

10232 July 1/70 Same, making money rapidly.[22]

The family of Connecticut-born William Abbott took a more circuitous route. They would combine a connection with the Fleming family to eventually produce the only major female player in the Natchez plantation supply and cotton business: his wife, Ann. A clerk for Fleming & Baldwin before the war, Abbott had been disabled during his service with the Natchez Fencibles. Upon his return from the war, he married Ann E. Wells, the daughter of a prominent local master painter, and teamed up with Lieutenant John W. Henderson of the Breckinridge Guards, a member of the antebellum merchant-planter Henderson family. Henderson was also an agent for and had backing from the New Orleans factoring firm Henderson & Peale Co., advertised as successor to his father's Thomas Henderson & Co.[23] The local R. G. Dun representative noted: "'H' is an hon man, has a large estate but yet to establish a bus. reputation. His father deceased [had] unbounded credit." Abbott & Henderson brought in Joseph Stone, son of a local attorney, and bought out a Northern grocery firm J. B. Gilbert Co. The same R. G. Dun agent reported, "Dec 10/67 (style now Abbott, Henderson, & Stone) cap 5NY to $7500 Liabs. sm gd chars. H+A particularly." Abbott went on his own in the grocery business as William Abbott & Co. by the mid-1870s, as Henderson left to go in the clothing business and Stone formed his own grocery firm. R. G. Dun rated Abbott as a cautious businessman, never one to overextend himself. He was a rarity in the local mercantile trade, moreover, because he did not extend credit: "Mar. 2/78 He is one of our best citizens + does bus in a strictly cash basis, never have been sued since being in bus, cap in bus abt 4NY 42 yrs old man."[24]

Actually, the R. G. Dun agent had it partially wrong. Abbott had been acting as a trustee for plantation credit advances for many years, monitoring the repayment of other people's or investor money for a percentage, and therefore had a hand and significant experience in the plantation supply and credit business beyond a cash basis. At the same time, he was training his young clerk James S. Fleming—the son of John Fleming of Fleming & Baldwin Co., where Abbott had been a clerk before the war—in plantation cotton crop financing. Abbott's wife, Ann Elizabeth, apparently was learning a thing or two about the business as well, because after Abbott died unexpectedly, James Fleming and Ann E. Abbott joined together to expand the William Abbott & Co. grocery firm into the plantation supply and credit offering business in a large way. Ann E. Abbott assumed control of the firm and named Fleming as her store manager, while she handled the gathering of new planter and cropper business for the firm, as well as watching over their growing plantation assets in the countryside. Fleming later started his own firm, after Ann E. Abbott died, and became one of the major local supply merchants in his own right. Thus, during the years 1890–1910, the Abbott/Fleming combine had local plantation accounts that rivaled other firms in the district and gained control of significant cotton lands, becoming landlord-merchants in the process.[25]

Clearly, within the native merchant community there existed a level of local family interconnections that not only gave many merchants their start as clerks and junior partners for other firms but also provided staying power, capital infusion, and a level of general support and shared identity that many outsiders did not enjoy. Like groups tended to join with like groups within the merchant community, and ties garnered in the antebellum period among the rising middle class were particularly strong and useful, while most of the wealthy nabob firms of the older age faded from the scene. Camaraderie among the new class of young Confederate veterans was particularly strong, and these men often elected to start their new business careers together, joined by their local family members or rekindled antebellum business relationships that they had shared as clerks and junior partners. Several other major firms not detailed in this section—for example, Rumble & Wensel Co., E. B. Baker & Sons, and Pollock & Mason—exhibited these same sorts of root configurations. Northern outsiders seemed to be viewed with more suspicion—as carpetbaggers. Unless taken in by one of these local familial groups, as was George G. Klapp by the Carpenter family, they often had a much more difficult time getting established or achieving persistence in the postwar marketplace.[26]

In fact, by 1867 the legal section of the newspaper was littered with evidence of new Northern firms being sued by creditors or in receivership. Particularly notable was the spectacular failure of two huge firms, Rickey, Shelton & Co. and Murphy & Gairnes. In a testament to the ability of the R. G. Dun agents to ferret out a bad risk among the merchant community, only a few months before the Ricky Shelton & Co. financial meltdown commenced, the Dun agent noted of the firm: "Dishonest & Unsafe . . . consid'd embarr'd not consid'd honest, or reliable, not well estab'd, not gd." Meanwhile, the members of the locally born or associated mercantile community generally enjoyed a significant share of the planter-class business, at least initially.[27] A cotton statement advertised by S. D. Stockman & Co. in July 1869 is instructive of who was shipping large amounts of cotton associated with Stockman's factorage firm and within the local native merchant community:

Cotton Statement

Total receipts to 1st July, 1869, 14,999 bales
Total shipments to 1st July, 14,851 bales,
leaving on hand 148 bales.
Cotton in store, July 1, 1869:
 E. B. Baker & Son have 23 bales
 S. D. Stockman & Co. have 75 bales
 B. Wade 19 "
 Pollock & Mason 24 "
 N. L. Carpenter & Son 7 "
  Total, 148
  S. D. STOCKMAN & Co.,
   Cotton Factors[28]

All these firms had strong local familial and business connections—combined with solid Confederate credentials and reputations for loyalty and service—but they were by no means the only mercantile players and movers of cotton in the Natchez marketplace.

Not long after General Grant's troops occupied Natchez in the summer of 1863, three young Union sutlers walked into the store of Natchez

German Jewish merchant John Mayer in search of a local supply source. Mayer had been among a vanguard of European Jews who had fled rising anti-Semitism and had found their way to Natchez in the 1840s. There they had formed an embryonic Jewish merchant community of modest shopkeepers and dry goods purveyors that included Aaron Beekman, Marx Lemle, and David Moses. Mayer's family had firm Confederate loyalties, and his son Simon was at that moment a few hundred miles to the north as part of the Army of Tennessee, where he soon would fight at Missionary Ridge and Chickamauga. Yet Mayer was apparently kind to the Yankee newcomers regardless, particularly after learning that two were German Jews as well. He took them in as fellow Jews by asking them if they would like to attend local Hebrew services and inviting them to socialize at his home. Soon sutlers Isaac Lowenburg, Henry Frank, and former peddler Julius Weis were regular visitors to the Mayer home and were becoming integrated into the growing Natchez Jewish community. They were becoming integrated in other ways as well, because Mayer had three blossoming daughters who would marry these three young men within the next few years. Mayer almost certainly could not have known that day in 1863 when he met the Union sutlers that he would become a nexus of familial associations that would bind the vibrant postwar Natchez Jewish mercantile community. Within a decade his three future sons-in-law, Lowenburg, Frank, and Weis, would respectively own the largest Natchez plantation supply and commission house, its most expansive dry goods firm, and perhaps the most successful cotton factorage in the entire American South.[29]

As among the native local merchants, familial associations were of major importance in the postwar Jewish community. Intensifying the bonds was the propensity of Jews to marry within their religion. The base of the Jewish mercantile community formed by the Mayers, Beekmans, Lemles, and others, who had been in business in Natchez for years, helped provide cohesive support and group identity and attachment to several Jewish newcomers who would arrive in the district during the war or shortly thereafter. As in the native community, the combination of cultural, social, and business ties was a strong indicator of future success, and many Jews would become stalwarts of the rising postbellum merchant and entrepreneurial class. Like other Natchez merchants, they sought opportunity in the economic vacuum created by the destruction of slavery and the emergence of the new market of freedmen. The introduction of tenant farming as the premier local labor configuration, in Reconstruction and after, was the basis of this success. In fact, the Jewish merchant community became the prime purveyors of plantation supplies and mercantile credit to the emerging black croppers, and this activity provided sufficient wealth for the Jews to become major landlord cotton planters and entrepreneurs in other arenas by the turn of the century. The Natchez city directory reveals that in 1858 there were at least twelve firms owned by Jews, mostly dry goods and clothing purveyors, but by 1866 that number had grown to eighteen firms, many of which now ventured into areas previously dominated by native firms with planter-class connections—for instance, plantation supply and cotton factoring. The members of the local planter class initially seemed to prefer to do business with native firms, but this changed over time as Jewish firms gained respect and reputation. Jewish firms soon rivaled competitors like Fleming & Baldwin, S. D. Stockman, or Rumble & Wensel, and by the end of the century had surpassed many of those competitors. Indeed, the count of local Jewish firms rose to over forty, roughly half of the premier local mercantile firms.[30]

Jews had been in the district since the colonial period, and there are records of a planter, Benjamin Monsanto, and a peddler, Henry Jacobs, residing locally in the 1790s, and a druggist, William Lehmann, who arrived in 1819, among several others. But many German Jewish peddlers plied the rural areas of the Natchez District during the 1820s and 1830s, and their presence contributed to the growing mythos and phenomenon of the "Jewish Mississippi peddler." Some early Jewish immigrants to Mississippi relied on peddling a myriad of small goods and notions—everything from paper fans to thimbles—in rural areas where people traveled only occasionally to town for supplies. This often meant bartering items like needles and thread for eggs, corn, or even pigs, which could be taken back to town and sold for a profit. These peddlers also gained valuable experience trading with slaves for produce and locally caught fish or game. This would serve them well in dealing with freed blacks in the postwar marketplace. These peddlers traveled the back roads of Mississippi in hopes of raising enough capital to open a proper store or business in town.[31]

This experience was almost a rite of passage for the hopeful young Jewish merchant: he learned to speak English and abide by American ways—and, more important, Southern ways—and made valuable business connections and created a solid customer base. The typical early Jewish immigrant interested in the mercantile trade was a nearly penniless young man in his teens who had made his way across the Atlantic with little money on a grueling sixty-to-ninety-day boat trip. He landed in New York or New Orleans and then made his way to a Mississippi town, where he hoped to find a fellow Jew from back home already in business—someone whom he could rely on for help and advice if not always employment. This chain or cycle is very important in early Mississippi, and the Jewish community in Natchez probably started out with a few peddlers who sent word back home to relatives or friends. Word eventually got around about prospects in the South, and more merchant-minded Jews soon followed. Extended Jewish families often developed in the same locations. One such Jewish migrant commented on this pattern: "No Jew was ever the first person to go anywhere. There was always a cousin or uncle ahead of him."[32]

Among these early Jewish immigrants was Bavarian Julius Weis. Weis likely arrived in New Orleans sometime in the early 1840s and apparently continued on to Jefferson County, Mississippi (a short distance north of Natchez), where his sister Sara lived with his brother-in-law Daniel Scharff, who was working as a peddler. Weis soon plied the country back roads as a peddler himself, armed with his pack full of notions and trinkets, and he later reminisced that

> for a few days I happened to strike a very poor piece of country, about Brandywine Spring, Copiah Country, Miss. This country was settled mostly by poor white farmers, with very few negroes. My sales were very small, and I got very much discouraged. As the country was entirely strange to me, one day I had to do without my dinner, as I did not happen to get to a house at dinnertime (noon). Shortly after noon, I came upon a negro who was on his way to Port Gibson with a load of cotton, and who had stopped beside the road to feed his oxen and eat his dinner. I went to him and asked him to give me a piece of his cornbread and a piece of meat, which he did, and I ate it with a great deal of relish, giving him a cotton handkerchief in payment. The next day I started out in a different direction, and met with much better success.[33]

Weis traveled the dusty back roads of Mississippi in hopes of raising enough capital to open a proper store or business in town, which he soon did. When he appeared upon the Natchez scene in 1859, the R. G. Dun agent noted of him: "Sept. 22, 59 A Peddler—carries all his ppy in his pack

+ pocket. Age abt. 40. but little is known here as to his character or claims to confidence." Weis soon joined the largest Natchez Jewish dry goods firm, Meyer, Deutsch & Weis, as a partner, and in 1864 he married John Mayer's daughter Caroline—which gave him local family ties to John Mayer & Son, I. Lowenburg & Co., and Henry Frank Dry Goods. Soon after the war he and Meyer, Deutsch & Weis moved their operation to New Orleans as major cotton factors. Weis became a stalwart and nexus of the Jewish mercantile community in postwar Natchez, and, like S. D. Stockman, he primarily made his mark in the local marketplace as a New Orleans cotton factor. He was a major financial backer of several top Jewish firms and handled their cotton, had unlimited access to New York capital, owned or leased many local plantations, and had close family ties to at least five prominent Jewish mercantile families. His clout eventually superseded community lines, and several native planters and mercantile firms received capital and did business with him by the mid-1870s, by which time he may have become the largest cotton merchant in the American South.[34]

Peddlers aside, the Mayers may have owned the only Jewish firm in Natchez when they opened a store under-the-hill in 1841, but soon after they were followed by Aaron Beekman and Marx Lemle, two men who would develop major mercantile and plantation supply firms in the postbellum marketplace. In 1843 Aaron Beekman, probably the most successful of the antebellum Jewish merchants in the postwar marketplace, arrived in Natchez. Born in Bavaria, Beekman likely arrived in America in the late 1830s or early 1840s, and eventually went into the dry goods business under-the-hill as well. He later moved to the "Cotton Square" on Franklin Street above the hill after a fire in 1858.[35] Beekman was apparently affluent enough to own four slaves and maintain a clerk by 1860, and the local R. G. Dun agent commented about Beekman during that period:

10023 Sept 14/58 This last spring he bot a house + lot here on Cr + did bus two weeks since he was burnt out + lost a good part of his stock wh was a small one—he is rebuilding a fireproof store. I have also learned since the fire that he owns 250 acres of land w prob 6ny$ is also possible that he may have cash. These sm German Mrchts make + have money when no one suspects it—learned that his land is paid for + it is presumed that he has raised money to build on faith of this—So other mortgages or other encumbrances appear on record.[36]

Beekman weathered the Civil War intact and in fact added to his real estate holdings with devalued Confederate cash and emerged in the postwar marketplace ready to resume business and grow. The R. G. Dun agent wrote of him: "Janie 8/66 Has a small RE wor 5NY$ & consd wor. 10NY$. Don't owe much, gd habs + char. as money mak'g man." If Beekman had a fast start in Reconstruction, he also had eleven children, whose marriages eventually connected or linked him to many other prominent Jewish mercantile firms in the postwar era, including Henry Frank Dry Goods, A. & M. Moses, and Meyer, Weis & Co. Beekman would remain in business from 1843 until his death in 1901, probably longer than any other Natchez merchant on record, and his influence on Natchez was profound. He became one of the largest cotton-buying and -supplying merchants in the area as well as a prominent cotton planter with considerable land holdings throughout the district.[37]

Marx Lemle also arrived from Bavaria with his wife, Sarah, in 1843 and opened a dry goods store under-the-hill on Silver Street. Lemle had one daughter and no male heirs, but he had an expansive local family comprised of at least four brothers or sisters and a number of nephews, nieces, and cousins, who connected him to a considerable amount of business in the district. Before the war, the local R. G. Dun agent placed Lemle & Co. as a middling dry goods house: "July 27/59 Taxes last yr on 4NY of stk. No R.E. or other visible means, except his stock in trade + little household furniture. A German Jew of good habits, trade mostly with Negroes + c." But the local land deeds indicate that Lemle had actually purchased his store under-the-hill for $1,800 cash in 1858, and he added to real estate holdings considerably during and shortly after the war, while doing a bustling trade with local blacks. When rated by R. G. Dun a few years later, his situation had improved in the new marketplace considerably: "July 16, 69. Capl 10NY. RE is 20 @ 30 NY$ Stands well; cr. gd." Lemle also had considerable family ties to the mercantile community, both in Natchez and across the river in Louisiana. Relatives Daniel, Isadore, Gustav, and Herman Lemle were considerable merchants, planters, or lawyers in their own right in Vidalia, Concordia Parish, during the 1870s and 1880s, often receiving their goods through Marx Lemle in Natchez. The Lemles had major mercantile connections as well to the ex-sutler firm I. Lowenburg & Co. through Daniel—who at one time teamed up as partners with Lowenburg's cousin Samuel Block—and niece Sophia, who married Lowenburg's brother, Samuel, who ran that firm's Vidalia office. In a twist of fate, Samuel Lowenburg served in the Confederacy in the Adams Light Infantry while at the same time his brother Isaac was a Union sutler in Grant's army. This also raises the question of whether Samuel Lowenburg had Natchez connections before the war that drew Isaac there in 1863.[38]

When Isaac Lowenburg and Henry Frank walked into John Mayer's store looking for supplies for the Union troops in 1863, it changed the course of Natchez history. The paternal Mayer gave the young newcomers an entrée into Natchez Jewish society, and his association deepened dramatically when Ophelia Mayer—Mayer's high-spirited twenty-year-old daughter and ardent Southerner—and her friends ran afoul of the Union occupation authorities concerning some inflammatory anti-Union letters. Timely intervention by Lowenburg and Frank with their Northern friends and associates got the young women released from custody and probably saved whatever meager merchandise resided in Mayer's store from confiscation by Union troops. Family legend has it that Isaac and Henry supplied hard-to-get Union army passes to three of Mayer's young, unmarried daughters, and they allegedly used these passes to cross Union checkpoints and smuggle supplies under their hoop skirts to Confederate family members. But regardless, it is clear that these local Jews embraced Isaac Lowenburg and Henry Frank whole-heartedly. When Lowenburg wed Ophelia Mayer in 1865 and Henry Frank wed her sister Melanie in 1868, they joined Julius Weis as Mayer sons-in-law and made it clear that they were committed to staying and prospering in the Natchez Jewish community. Both I. Lowenburg & Co. and Henry Frank Dry Goods were doing a brisk business at war's end, and within a couple years Frank appeared in the R. G. Dun ledgers with the notation "Apl 6/67 He is now dg the largest Dry Good bus in this place and seems to be permanently established," while Lowenburg was listed as "March 15/1868 Capl in business $3500. Reputation of being honest. Have engaged since war in planting [cotton]." Lowenburg was also the Natchez agent for his brother-in-law Julius Weis of Meyer, Weis & Co., and the two ran several plantations on both sides of the Mississippi River. Over the years both Lowenburg and Frank became local business stalwarts involved in the Natchez Cotton and Merchants Exchange, the Natchez Cotton Mills, and local railroad concerns and politics.[39] Soon it became commonplace to see their advertisements splashed across the local newspaper pages:

I. Lowenburg   John Hill

I. Lowenburg & Co.,
Corner Main and Pearl Streets,
-DEALERS IN-
PLANTATION SUPPLIES AND FAMILY GROCERIES OF ALL KINDS,
WHOLESALE LIQUOR DEALERS,
CASH ADVANCES MADE ON CONSIGNMENTS OF COTTON.
Highest Market Price Paid for all the Products of the Country.
We are prepared to sell goods, either at wholesale or retail, as cheap as any other house in the city.
GIVE US A CALL.[40]

Not long after Lowenburg and Frank arrived in Natchez, another Jewish family destined for mercantile prominence appeared on the scene—the Geisenbergers. Born in Alsace-Lorraine in 1819, Wolfe Geisenberger had immigrated in the 1840s with his family to the town of Port Gibson, Mississippi, another Jewish enclave fifty miles north of Natchez that had a distinct Alsatian flavor and background. Through his wife, Fannie, they were related by marriage to the Ullmans, another major postwar Natchez Jewish mercantile family that came to town in 1865. Samuel Ullman, a Confederate veteran of the Sixteenth Mississippi Infantry Regiment, married yet another Mayer family daughter, Emma, and ran Ullman & Laub Plantation Supplies with David Laub, while Marcus M. Ullman ran one of Natchez's largest clothing stores, M. M. Ullman & Co., well into the twentieth century. Wolfe Geisenberger partnered with another Alsatian and Confederate veteran who was also related to the Ullmans and formed Geisenberger & Benjamin, a dry goods and plantation supply firm. R. G. Dun later rated Geisenberger in 1870 as "Lately started. Age 45 to 50. Marr'd char hab + capacity gd. Capl in bus 10NY," and he continued to the turn of the century with his son Ben as Wolfe Geisenberger & Son, a major plantation supply firm. The Geisenbergers were related to or intermarried with practically every Jewish mercantile family mentioned so far in this section, and Wolfe's sons carried on into the twentieth century in no less than three separate mercantile firms.[41]

Other business-minded Jewish families came in the years after the war, notably the hugely successful Friedler and Jacobs families. Isaac (Ignatz) Friedler, a Northern immigrant like Lowenburg and Frank, came to the Natchez area in 1866 or 1867. Born in Bohemia, Friedler most likely arrived in New York from Bremen in December 1854, and indications are he worked as a merchant in Ohio for several years before the war. Unlike the other merchants discussed, he chose to settle in Vidalia, across the Mississippi River from Natchez, and he began as a merchant there, working with the Austrian brothers Jacob and Nathan Lorie, who had backing from Aaron Beekman in Natchez. But he was in business on his own by 1870 with backing from Meyer, Weis & Co., and the Natchez R. G. Dun agent noted: "February 3/70 Stk on hand w. 5 @ 8 NY dg a fr bus. steady + sober," and within three years his rating with R. G. Dun had skyrocketed to "Owns his own store house + dwelling. Est wor. 35NY . . . sells for cotton is close + saving money." His success supplying the croppers and planters on the very large and productive plantations in Concordia Parish rivaled that of anyone in the district, and he translated those profits into serious cotton-planting interests, both on his own and with New Orleans factor Julius Weis. Vidalia's close proximity to Natchez also ensured that Friedler would emerge as a prominent member of the Natchez business community, and, like other prominent mercantile Jews, he and his family cemented these connections by intermarriage; he married into the Lehmann family while his son, Joseph, married the daughter of Henry Frank. He remained in business in Vidalia until 1896, before moving to the upscale neighborhood of Clifton Heights in Natchez, where he lived in semiretirement and worked for Henry Frank Dry Goods. His son, Joseph, however, carried on his business interests in Natchez and formed a successful dry goods firm with Sam Geisenberger—Wolfe's son—styled as Geisenberger & Friedler Co.[42]

About the same time Friedler appeared, another immigrant arrived, who, with his brother and their sons, would over the coming decades challenge the hegemony of the German Jews within the Natchez Jewish mercantile community. An eastern European Jew, Simon Jacobs had emigrated from Russia (Poland) to Canada sometime in the 1850s and married an English immigrant in Toronto, but by 1860 they lived in St. Louis, where Jacobs worked as a shoemaker. They arrived in Natchez in 1867, and Jacobs went into the dry goods business a short time thereafter with his younger brother Adolf working as his clerk. They first appeared in the R. G. Dun ratings in July 1870, when the local agent noted: "In bus 1 yr. Age 35. marr'd char + hab gd. capacity fair. In bus 5NY. No RE or other outside means. No judgments or other liens." Simon and Adolf formed a plantation supply and commission firm a year later as a partnership styled S. & A. Jacobs, and their fortunes quickly accelerated as they became one of the busiest Natchez firms supplying African American croppers. This showed in their R. G. Dun ratings: "Jan/72 Capl 75 NY Quiet, unassuming, attentive + building up a good business, making a good reputation. No mortgages, judgments or suits. . . . S. Jacobs pd 5NY for residence a few days ago." The Jacobses differed from the majority of the Natchez Jewish mercantile community in that they were eastern European, and apparently there was a fair amount of condescension among the German Jews toward their eastern brothers; Isaac Lowenburg dissuaded his daughter from wedding Simon's son Hyman for this reason. Nonetheless, the Jacobses were intermarried with the mercantile Roos, Scharff, and Frank families and were leading businessmen for decades. They owned three separate mercantile firms and served on the Natchez Cotton and Merchants Exchange and the board of aldermen, and Adolf and his son Albert became wealthy enough to open a local bank in 1906, largely with their own capital.[43]

Thus the immigrant Jewish merchants joined their local counterparts in the Natchez postwar mercantile community, all seeking opportunity in a bustling new marketplace committed to extracting profits from the wreckage of the old regime. The Jewish merchant community was a combination of immigrant shopkeepers from an earlier age, their proud young Confederate sons, and newcomers often with Northern experience. As in the case of the local merchant or planter elites, identity with a cultural and social community was as much an element of success as business acumen or access to capital and credit. Robert Somers wrote of the South in 1871 that "much of the storekeeping business is conducted by sharp, active young men of the Jewish aspect . . . sent down by firms in New York and other large towns to sell goods at a profit of 100 to 200 per cent." This characterization was at least partially true in Natchez: it was a place where "among the new generation of shopkeepers were many Jewish families who brought a new energy and vitality to the town." But surprisingly little tension arose among the competing groups as the city continued to be a relatively liberal haven, where the language of business and wealth spoke louder than religious or cultural derivations.[44] The mercantile and entrepreneurial milieu in Natchez was multifaceted, and David Rattray perhaps best described its character in 1881: "English, Irish, Scotch, Italians, a few French and Germans [who were Jewish], of origin and nativity, make up the population. Between the latter and the Christians, the social line is less distinct than in any part of the Union, and Jews and Gentiles freely intermingle in every enterprise of commerce, charity or public advancement."[45] As we will see in the coming chapters, Rattray could not have been more right in his assessment about the character and associations of Gentiles and Jews among the entrepreneurial and business-minded men who changed the face of Natchez by the turn of the twentieth century. But what of the English, Irish, French, and Italians he also mentioned?

On May 7, 1835, the port of New Orleans was lined with graceful ocean-going merchantmen and stout river steamboats extending up and down the Mississippi riverfront shoreline, while the attendant wharves and docks bustled with the hurried activity of loading and unloading goods, staples, and particularly the last year's crop of white baled cotton. Late spring was a busy time of year in New Orleans, and somewhere along the waterfront, the *St. Paul*—a ship out of Le Havre, France—sidled in dockside and disgorged a new wave of eager European immigrants into the American South. Among them likely was the young French mercantile clerk Armand Perrault. Perhaps related to several Perraults who had recently arrived from France and settled in New Orleans, Armand seems to have had his sights set on continuing on inland to Louisville, Kentucky. At that growing interior mercantile hub he married a local woman and had two children before relocating down the Mississippi River to Natchez, a major recipient of the Louisville trade. By 1845 he was in business in Natchez as A. Perrault & Co., a general store on the north end of town. Over the next forty years he would develop a web of family and business associations that would touch an amazing array in the varied Natchez merchant community. He would sell his first store to his longtime clerk and Irish immigrant George T. Payne in 1859. The non-Jewish German immigrant John C. Schwartz (the hardware dealer detailed in the first chapter) would purchase his second in 1863. Perrault used those funds to gather plantation lands and Natchez city property with devalued Confederate currency, and also to establish his own plantation supply house in 1865 with his two Confederate veteran sons. The same two sons also later opened other firms in addition to their mutual family business. One took a Mississippi-born son of Scottish immigrants as a partner, and another teamed with a locally born son of Irish immigrants. His other five sons ended up as merchants as well, one of whom opened a firm with his father's former clerk and an English immigrant, while two married sisters from an Italian immigrant merchant family. By 1900 the family was involved in no less than five mercantile firms, was related to several different mercantile groups through marriage or close business association, and commanded substantial plantation lands as merchant landlord-planters.[46]

The experience of the Perrault family brings to light the third tier of the diverse Natchez mercantile community, immigrant groups smaller or less engaged in mercantile activities than the local indigenous and immigrant Jewish communities, but still a vital part of the entrepreneurial Natchez milieu. Like the other mercantile communities, these varied groups relied upon their family and friendship associations and ties for cohesiveness and support in the emerging New South, and many had a significant hand in the reshaping of Natchez. They also sought wealth and prominence through the changed Natchez market conditions. Interestingly, however, they displayed a greater propensity to disregard national origin in marriage, particularly the Irish, French, and Italians, who all shared the common Catholic religion. This may have very well been the case with the Perrault brothers. As with the Jews, a handful of small shopkeepers from the antebellum period provided a base for future members of their groups to build upon in the postwar period. But whereas the Jewish community continued to receive many new immigrants in the postwar period, the Irish, Italian, English, and French communities were largely complete by the end of the war and would receive only a modicum of newcomers thereafter to supplement their numbers. In some cases their numbers would actually decline by the turn of the twentieth century. But those who remained demonstrated Natchez mercantile persistence and produced many local entrepreneurial leaders who helped reshape Natchez.[47]

Among these leaders was George T. Payne, one of the Irish who flocked to Natchez during the 1840s and 1850s in the wake of the potato famine. By 1850 he lived in the Armand Perrault household and worked as clerk at A. Perrault & Co. Later he brought his two sisters to Natchez from Ireland. They lived with him until his death in the 1890s. The Irish were the most numerous immigrants in Natchez, and they dominated the local physical labor and building trades. But a good many had also entered the mercantile field like Payne, who was in the same business in Ireland. After almost a decade of working for Perrault, he apparently had built up enough capital or an interest in Perrault's store to begin on his own, to which Perrault agreed and sold out the shop to Payne.[48] The R. G. Dun representative noted the change under Perrault's rating:

10232 Oct 20, 59 Has sold out his Gro. + Variet to G. T. Payne . . . was form'ly clerk for A. Perrault . . . very little known among bus. men + cannot be said what bus char, his locality is where most of the negro trade is done, + that constituted the bulk of his business, of both of Perrault & Payne, he is sober + seems Indus. Abt 25 or 28 yrs. old.[49]

Payne was listed in the 1860 census with $15,000 in assets, which he put to use during the war and bought a substantial mercantile complex on Franklin Street in three separate transactions for over $11,000 in Confederate currency. This would serve as his mercantile base in the postwar period. He apparently also engaged in smuggling or other illegal trade to further his postbellum position, because the local R. G. Dun agent noted soon after the war that Payne "engages in illicit traffic" and "pays promptly, but is regarded as tricky." In fact, the mercurial Payne was probably one of the few Natchez merchants to surpass a bad reputation early on to prosper mightily in the coming years. On one occasion he was arrested and accused of breaking into rival Jewish Marx Lemle's store in 1868 to "take some cloth," which probably made him none too popular with the Jewish business community. But he was a part of a tight-knit Irish mercantile faction that included successful postwar supply and cotton merchants Thomas Pollack and Confederate veterans Patrick Burns, John Marron, and John Hart. Payne and Pollock in particular would also vie with Jewish community leaders in the 1870s and 1880s for influence in city and county government. Backed by and shipping large amounts of cotton through the wealthy New Orleans commission house Nalle & Cammack, and drawing on his prewar experience in the "black trade," Payne saw his business with black croppers explode during Reconstruction. Soon he was respectable enough—or at least his money and influence were—to occupy a position on the board of the Natchez Cotton Mills, the Natchez Cotton and Merchants Exchange, and the board of alderman. All the while he was accumulating significant plantation lands. The R. G. Dun agent noted the change by the 1870s, finding that he was "getting rich . . . [and] we doubt if there is a more solvent man in Natchez."[50] Meanwhile, Payne and his Confederate Irish clerk Thomas Hart, later a successful merchant and planter in his own right, touted their services thus:

GEORGE T. PAYNE
DEALER IN
DRY GOODS, GROCERIES, &

WESTERN PRODUCE.
A COMPLETE STOCK
LADIES' AND GENTS BOOTS AND SHOES,
AND GENTS' CLOTHING.
MY MOTTO IS
QUICK SALES AND SMALL PROFITS.[51]

If the web of Natchez immigrant mercantile associations tied the French Perraults to the Irish mercantile community through Armand's former clerk George T. Payne, the myriad associations after the war continued through the many Perrault sons. Although all the Perraults were technically part owners of the bustling Perrault & Co. plantation supply firm, they also branched out in other directions as well. After Samuel Perrault returned from his Confederate service with the Natchez Light Guards, for example, he teamed up as partners with the son of Scottish immigrant John McPherson and bought out another Scottish merchant, John Foggo, to form McPherson & Perrault, a clothing and fancy goods firm. R. G. Dun rated them as "young men of energy + prudence, reliable," in the early 1870s, but after they were in business a few years they sold out to Samuel's brother Thomas. T. E. Perrault clothing would remain a fixture on Main Street for decades, and R. G. Dun rated his firm highly, noting approvingly that his "Capital in bus ass'd at $8,000, should be 10,000 No RE ass'd Est. worth $10,000 clear char, habits and capacity good, prospects good." The Dun agent had it wrong in one particular: Thomas owned no outside real property because he had a share of the extensive Perrault plantation supply business and their cotton plantations.[52]

Ironically, the location of Perrault's fancy goods store on Main Street brings out yet another Perrault connection to other members of the Natchez immigrant merchant community: next door at 91 Main Street resided for years the same hardware firm, J. C. Schwartz Hardware, sold by his father in 1863 to the Bavarian immigrant John Conrad Schwartz. Schwartz exploded onto the scene after buying Perrault's store, and in early 1866 the R. G. Dun agent gushed that Schwartz "Is considered one of the safest

+ most reliab bus men in Natchez . . . is shrewd, quick in perceptions, of excell't judgment . . . in short he possesses every element of success." Indeed, the Dun agent claimed that Schwartz was worth $50,000, and he quickly grew wealthy through the firm and also served on the Natchez Cotton and Merchants Exchange. Among other things, he also invested in land with Christian Schwartz (likely his brother), who became a successful planter and occasionally partnered with Jewish merchant Isaac Lowenburg on plantations in Concordia Parish.[53] A prolific advertiser with money to spend, J. C. Schwartz firm's notices were a fixture in every local media source:

J. C. SCHWARTZ
NEW IRON BUILDING,
NO. 91 MAIN STREET,
IMPORTER AND DEALER IN
FOREIGN AND AMERICAN
HARDWARE,
PLANTATION & BUILDERS HARDWARE,
COOK STOVES,
AND AGRICULTURAL IMPLEMENTS, SHOT GUNS,
AMMUNITION, &C.
NATCHEZ, - - - MISS.[54]

After selling his fancy goods store to his brother Thomas, Samuel Perrault formed a new partnership with Frank O'Brien and formed O'Brien & Co., probably the largest and most successful purveyors of bricks and masonry in Natchez. From an immigrant Irish family, O'Brien was also a Confederate veteran, and he and Perrault dealt substantial amounts of city property in Natchez, while Perrault also owned a share and stake in Perrault & Co. The relationship between these immigrant families was further cemented when Perrault married O'Brien's sister Mary during the 1870s. Meanwhile, the web of immigrant mercantile associations branching from the Perraults continued through the intermarriage of fancy goods and clothing dealer Edward and his younger brother Armand Jr., who both married into the Italian immigrant Signaigo family. Significant numbers of Italians had immigrated to Natchez in the 1840s and 1850s and had come to dominate the middle-class local "fruit merchant" and "confectioners" trade, which often included groceries, tobacco, cigars, and liquor in addition to fruit and confections. A. J. Signaigo was a successful confectioner in 1860 who reported $11,000 in personal wealth, and after he died following the war his two daughters, Mary and Adeline, married Edward and Armand Perrault, respectively, while their mother, Carrie Signaigo, continued to operate the family fruit shop and grocery on Main Street. R. G. Dun noted that Edward "bot out his mother in law M + C Signaigo" to form "E. J. Perrault," a "confectioner, cigars + notions" establishment across Main Street from Thomas's clothing firm, where he operated a store until 1880, when he sold out and went to work in one of the other family establishments as a clerk. Carrie Signaigo seems to have opened another confectionary firm a few doors down from Edward's store on Main Street a short time later, meaning there were a least three Perrault-related businesses within one city block on Main Street, and two that were in direct competition with each other. The Perraults also had close associations through business with Frank Arrighi—the son of Italian fruit merchants, fellow Confederate veteran, and longtime city treasurer—as well as successful Italian supply merchants and plantation owners Prospero De Marco, Joseph Reale, and Louis Botto.[55]

One final Perrault son extended the family's web of association in the immigrant community in yet another direction, to the handful of Englishmen operating in the Natchez mercantile realm. Younger than the other four Perrault sons, Vincent Perrault got his start as a clerk in the main family business Perrault & Co., and while there he worked with a young English Irish immigrant, Fred Maher. Maher had emigrated from England in 1860 to New Orleans with his mother and brother, and the three arrived in Natchez shortly thereafter. Maher received a good education at the Natchez Catholic cathedral and started as a clerk at Perrault & Co. at fourteen years of age, while his brother Robert became a Natchez school principal. Maher was soon handling the Perraults' expansive plantation supply lending operations in northern Adams and Jefferson Counties as their agent. He oversaw several large agricultural supply loans and the consequent plantation acquisitions there by the Perraults for debt foreclosure. Included were Emerald Mound, White Hall, and Blue Ridge. After Armand Perrault Sr. died, Vincent Perrault and Fred Maher conducted much of the day-to-day operations of Perrault & Co. before striking out on their own and forming Perrault & Maher groceries and dry goods, which became one of the leading Natchez plantation supply firms and endured into the twentieth century. Meanwhile, Maher also was appointed by the mayor and board of alderman to replace merchant John Fleming as city treasurer.[56]

Maher shared a place in the immigrant merchant arena with another very successful Englishman, Henry M. Gastrell. Gastrell appeared in 1865 as a former Union army lieutenant who had been discharged for a severe wound to the head. As a former Union soldier, he was a relative rarity in that he apparently had no local ties yet was one of only a few newcomers outside the Jewish mercantile community who succeeded and endured past the first years of Reconstruction. Gastrell does not appear in prewar records, but we know that he and his wife came from Bristol, England, and he was only twenty-two years old when he appeared in the marketplace with this notice in 1865:[57] "NEW STORE! H. M. GASTRELL & Co., *Dealers in all kinds of* HARDWARE and CUTLERY, STOVES, TINWARE, LAMPS, LANTERNS, and PLANTATION IMPLEMENTS . . . Main Street opposite CITY HOTEL, NATCHEZ, MISS."[58] Hardware was a good business in Natchez, and money could be made quickly and, often, largely in cash. While Gastrell was the major competitor of J. C. Schwartz's hardware firm, there seemed to be enough business to go around for the two, and Gastrell's stock in the mercantile community rose quickly. Only three years after his appearance he served on the local railway committee to bring rail service to Natchez; other committeemen included some of the most influential merchants in Natchez. A few years later the R. G. Dun agent noted, "States he has clear $231,000 in assets (including 70NY in RE 2 small farms ½ interest in 30,000 ac land, 12 NY residence)," and if Gastrell was exaggerating his worth, it was not by much as he soon owned a large share in a local railway with Jewish merchant Samuel Block and a Mississippi river steamboat packet named after his wife—the *Lucy E. Gastrell*.[59]

# # #

The Natchez mercantile community was thus emerging from its prewar and wartime configurations, driven by a combination of old and new to meet the challenges of a changed marketplace and to confront the needs of an altered society. Clearly, in tracing the familial and close mercantile associations that branched from the members of just three families—the Stockmans, Mayers, and Perraults—a social and economic picture emerges to reveal the intricate interconnections between families and people that drove the complex composition of the emerging postwar Natchez merchant community. This web of connections also reveals the place of each of the ten families featured in this work, and their ties to one another. Middling immigrant shopkeepers who could barely speak English in the antiquated slave-driven world were now working at the same dream of advancement as members of formerly elite families on near or complete parity; the nabobs were waning quickly. Ties to the past were indeed important, not because of inherited wealth among agricultural and mercantile grandees, but instead because of connections forged among families and their associates. Often, service in the war seems to have united men in their new business configurations, as they appear to have worn their shared experience as a badge of honor. Meanwhile, select and active newcomers *could* find an enduring place among the Natchez mercantile community with the right connections or, perhaps, a fair amount of luck and determination. Yankee became Southerner as southron became Northern-styled merchantman, while the immigrant from an earlier age found new opportunity and belonging and a greater respect. The natives who had dominated Natchez for so long and the newcomers alike were now all remaking themselves into a new kind of Southerner, a Southern businessman of a new age. On one occasion, at the urging of and for the "welfare of the merchants who have so generously aided its publication," a local newspaperman was eager to publicize the new Natchez with a broadside meant to allay fears that the New South was still full of hostile rebels:

> The editor is an Ohioan, who, after a residence of almost two years here, conceived of the idea of telling the "up-country" people something of this portion of the Sunny South and thought to attract attention by the title "Points to the Yankees." It did attract attention, but at the wrong end of the line. A number of most prominent citizens at once objected saying: "We like your idea, but your title, never! The epithet 'Yankee' was applied in a time of war, with all hatred, and was intended as mortal insult to our invading enemies. But that time has long since passed, and, sir, WE ARE ALL YANKEES NOW."[60]

CHAPTER 3

Crop Liens, Freedmen, and Planters

IN THE SUMMER OF 1863, AS GENERAL GRANT'S TROOPS OCCUPIED Natchez and Northern traders of all stripes began to swarm the district, a human movement of a different sort was under way that would soon transform the local marketplace like no other force. Some twenty miles to the east of Natchez in Adams County lay the cotton plantation of William and Jonathan Rucker, the 975-acre Rucker home place. Part of an expansive planter family that held hundreds of slaves on plantations in Adams, Chickasaw, Pontotoc, and Yazoo Counties of Mississippi, the Ruckers had at least ninety-four enslaved blacks on Rucker plantation ranging from three to eighty-six years old. Among them were brothers George, James, and Nathaniel Wright. Once word was out that Natchez was securely in Union hands, slaves from the surrounding countryside began making their way there, as the local planters' tenuous hold on their slaves broke down. That August the three Wright brothers left with three other Rucker field hands for Natchez and joined the Fifty-Eighth Colored Infantry of the occupying Union army. But conditions at Camp McPherson in Natchez were horrific, as disease raged among the recruits, and over 30 percent died, while many more deserted, including the Rucker field hands and two of the Wright brothers. The twenty-four-year-old Nathaniel Wright alone remained. He spent his first two years and eight months as a free man serving as a private in the Union army. His brothers, James and George, might have spent the next eighteen months in "contraband" camps around the area, avoiding rebel guerrillas, but they returned to the Union army in June 1865 and were officially discharged with Nathan in May 1866. Thus embarked the Wright family into a brave new world of freedom that certainly must have seemed full of promise, only to find that the reality was far less than anticipated.[1]

While it is unclear what the three brothers did the next few years, by the early 1870s George and Nathaniel were both married and raising their families back on Rucker plantation, working for their former owners as sharecroppers. The census lists their worth at $500 and $1,500 in personal property, respectively, probably mostly livestock and a wagon or two. Starting in 1873 both began a business relationship with Natchez merchant George T. Payne, giving him a lien on their yearly cotton crop in return for supplies to make a crop and support their families for the year. On April 11 that spring, Nathaniel "received from G. T. Payne of the City of Natchez in money and for the purchase of supplies, farming utensils, working stock and other things necessary for the cultivation of a plantation" and a $75 credit line for the year 1873, both secured by "the crop of cotton to be raised by me during the present year, and also, the following property to wit; one Black mule, [and] one milk cow." Wright also agreed to pay a 2.5 percent commission upon any advances in addition to 10 percent interest on the total of goods already marked up as much as 50 percent, while agreeing to "ship G. T. Payne all cotton" produced for handling and sale. Nathaniel's brother George agreed to the same terms with Payne & Co., except he borrowed $150 to make his crop and survive for the year. Thus began a cycle of yearly debt for both men as they depended on Payne for their advances and supplies, paying over 12 percent interest on top of a heavy markup for the privilege, and remitting a good deal more for Payne to handle and ship their cotton. Both Wright brothers apparently were productive farmers and good for their accounts, because they never recorded an amount owed from one year to the next; both used Payne's mercantile firm for several years, borrowing amounts ranging from $50 to $200 per year, before apparently moving on to a competitor for their supplies. Meanwhile, plantation supply merchant J. W. Roos bought Rucker plantation from Peter Rucker in 1887 for $4,276 and began renting land to the croppers like the Wrights. In 1902, almost forty years after he set out upon his new life as a free man, Nathaniel Wright was still on the same plantation where he had been enslaved, renting land from merchant J. W. Roos and plowing cotton on Rucker. He and his eighteen-year-old son, Nathan, were now getting their supplies from Natchez merchants Adolf Jacobs & Son, with a $200 lien on their crops and the same highly unfavorable terms of debt Wright first experienced with George T. Payne back in 1873. Nathaniel died a few years later, and his son Nathan gave up farming in 1910 and moved his young family to Memphis, Tennessee, to start anew. Many years later the freedom ex-slave Nathaniel worked so diligently to achieve became embodied by the work of his grandson Richard Wright, who gained acclaim as the finest black writer of his generation, and who talked about the Wright family's difficult life in Mississippi in his autobiography, *Black Boy* (1945).[2]

The Civil War, in destroying slavery, also destroyed the slave-based economy and labor system of the Natchez District, creating both turmoil and opportunity. While a few antebellum merchants like Fleming & Baldwin, A. Perrault & Co., and A. Beekman & Co. survived the war intact and formed the postbellum nucleus of the mercantile community, new members arrived in the district, altering the character and the economic activities of that community in fundamental ways. Many came with the Federal troops or soon thereafter. Isaac Lowenburg, Wolfe Geisenberger, and Isaac Friedler are examples discussed above, together with others, like Joseph N. Carpenter and William Abbott, who returned home from the Confederate military shortly after the fighting ceased to take up positions in the local mercantile scene. Regardless of these men's previous positions, their postwar role in Natchez reflected a capacity for exploiting the economic conditions emerging with the reduction of the slave labor system and the bankruptcy of most of the wealthy planters who perpetuated it. By the end of the war, the tradesmen were poised to embark on careers in Natchez as successful merchant-entrepreneurs; by the end of the decade they had established themselves as key players in the new labor system of sharecropping; and by the 1880s they had become the major economic power brokers in the district in ways that few residents would have deemed possible on the eve of the Civil War. A team of social anthropologists that studied the caste and class character of Natchez later described the town as a place where "the wholesale merchants . . . who once rivaled the banks as credit agencies for the planters . . . were socially of the middle class . . . but a few had risen into the upper class."[3]

The postwar situation favored all local merchants, as a vast new market for goods and credit emerged with the freed slaves. The Natchez District was awash with black refugees in 1865, and the Freedmen's Bureau became the premier employment agency for the former slaves, backed up by the authority of the occupying Union army. Federal authorities attempted to put the freedmen back to work in agriculture by negotiating employment and wage agreements with planters, but this left the freedmen and women with little stake in the success of the crop or their labor. Clearly a new labor system was needed to replace slavery in the Natchez District. Indebted planters and blacks alike needed credit and goods to carry on cotton planting and to get the region back on its economic feet after the destruction of war. Cotton was still a very profitable crop, particularly at high postwar prices. New agricultural laws issued in Mississippi and throughout the South during Reconstruction addressed this concern and ensured that merchants would occupy a central position in the postbellum period by virtue of "prior liens," whereby merchants had first rights to cotton grown over any liens held by planters for rent and freedmen for wages. Out of this new crop lien system emerged a new system of labor in the Cotton Kingdom: tenant farming and sharecropping. These forms of labor would dominate the Natchez District by the mid-1870s and became the primary means by which black croppers were able to access goods, credit, and even land. Tenancy and sharecropping also became the defining economic institution of the agricultural cotton-producing New South well into the twentieth century. While share-tenant farming allowed landless and cash-poor African Americans access to goods and land to farm, the high interest rates merchants charged for goods on credit ensured that sharecroppers were seldom able to meet their financial obligations and come away with any profit for themselves. In fact, at the end of the growing season these croppers often found themselves deeply in debt—debt that the merchants could carry over into the new crop year. This mechanism perpetuated a cycle of debt that often left freed blacks in an economic position perhaps worse, in terms of their material standard of living, than the one they had known in slavery.[4]

In Reconstruction, Natchez District blacks enjoyed a relatively brief period of real freedom under the protection of occupation forces. They held many elected offices on the local, state, and even national levels as part of the Republican Party; they voted regularly to further their condition; and some became prominent landowners. Hiram Revels, the first African American to serve in the U.S. Senate (1870–1871), owned Sandy Creek plantation; lawyer Louis J. Winston served as Adams county clerk for twenty years and owned Mount Welcome; while the Speaker of the state assembly, John R. Lynch, and his brother William owned part if not all of six plantations, including Providence, Homochitto, Hedges, Grove, Saragossa, and Ingleside. Surprising numbers of African American farmers were able to purchase lesser tracts of lands or smaller plantations. Still, most freed blacks were poor croppers, and racial discrimination compounded the cycle of debt they had to endure. After occupation ended and Union troops left Natchez in 1877, the position of African Americans in Mississippi and the Natchez District deteriorated under the attack of those whites who opposed voting and economic rights for African Americans, culminating during the 1890s in the legal disfranchisement of all black males. Many hapless African American share-tenants now found themselves not only locked in a cycle of debt but also reduced to second-class citizenship and often the targets of racial hatred.[5]

This system reduced the former slave-owning elite as well. Many planters began the period of Reconstruction deeply in debt after years of limited cotton income, while the natural disasters of floods and insect infestation along with the resumed tax collection by federal and local authorities added to their plight. Many of these hard-up planters turned either to local merchants for credit and cash to make their crops or to people who would lease the lands and work them on their own accounts. In a process few predicted at the time, many of these once prominent and wealthy landowners ended up losing their lands to their merchant creditors through debt foreclosure or overdue tax sale. In a distinct way, these merchants rivaled, and in some cases replaced, the vaunted planter class as the new economic force in the Natchez District during the postbellum period. By the early 1880s many of the featured merchant families owned several cotton plantations of their own at the expense of this group. Consequently, they were in a far superior position to engage in the often uncertain cotton plantation business, thanks both to their access to Northern credit and goods and to the cash that their bustling cotton plantation supply business generated.[6]

Consequently, numerous merchants prospered and became wealthy men. Cotton was still the king, and most of their income in the Natchez District came from the sale of plantation supplies and cotton. Despite a significant economic downturn in the mid-1870s, cotton remained the only real cash crop, and this meant that there was always plenty of business for those merchants furnishing plantations and croppers or buying and selling their cotton. These merchants became prominent local businessmen, owning large homes in town and plantations throughout the Natchez District, and in many instances assuming political office and positions of influence in local organizations and business ventures—all built upon supplying credit and goods, handling cotton, and perpetuating the local labor system. The share-tenancy system irrevocably changed the character of the labor and supply system in the district, and became firmly entrenched as the foundation of the area's economy and society. The merchants recorded hundreds of crop lien agreements with black croppers every year in the Natchez District, and all of these liens were contracted with an impoverished people one generation out of slavery who were forced to rely on this system to procure even the simple necessities of life. In 1902 the world was quickly changing, and even rural Natchez now hummed with telephones, electricity, and rail service, yet to find Nathaniel Wright after twenty-nine years approaching Adolf Jacobs & Son for essentially the same credit arrangement he first found with George T. Payne in 1873, with no net gain in assets or circumstance, is sadly indicative of the prevalence of the new system and its ties to the merchants. The sharecropper's situation was much the same, perhaps worse, and the firmly entrenched system dominated all aspects of African American life in most plantation districts. Tenant farmers like Wright started the twentieth century in an almost medieval form of debt peonage, far removed from the promise of freedom that characterized black hopes in 1865. And nothing represented the cropper's plight more than the yearly mortgage agreement in which he bargained away his blood and sweat for a few dollars to support his family and farm for another year:[7]

Mortgage—Lien On Crops

I have received this day from *I. Lowenburg & Co.* in money, and for the purchase of Supplies, Farming Utensils, Working Stock, and other things necessary for the cultivation of a Plantation, the sum of *One Hundred* dollars, for the use and cultivation a Plantation situated in the County of *Adams* and the State of Mississippi to be cultivated by me during the present year, and the said *I. Lowenburg & Co.* has agreed to advance me during the present year in money, and for the purchase of Supplies, Farming Utensils, Working Stock, and other things necessary for the purpose of carrying on said Plantation, the further sum of ---- dollars, for the payment of which sums of money and supplies so advanced, and to be advanced by the said *I. Lowenburg & Co.* has a lien by the law of the State of Mississippi, approved February 18, 1867, upon certain property named in the said law; and as further security to said *I. Lowenburg & Co.* for the payment of the said money so advanced and to be advanced as aforesaid, and also for the payment of *Ten* per cent commissions for advancing said money, and for interest on such advances, at the rate of *One* per cent per *Month* till paid, I hereby bargain, sell, mortgage, and pledge to said *I. Lowenburg & Co.* the crop of cotton to be raised by me during the present year, and also the following property to wit:

Sam'l Brandon's Plantation

And I bind and pledge myself to ship *to I. Lowenburg & Co.* in *Natchez* as soon as gathered, and in condition to be sent to market, the whole of the crop of Cotton that I may raise during the present year, to be sold by them and the proceeds to be applied by them in payment and satisfaction of the sums due and to become due to the aforesaid.

Given under my Hand and Seal, this 26 day of *March* A.D. 1869

Henry X *Lincoln* [*Seal*] (His Mark)
Lucinda X *Lincoln* [*Seal*] (Her Mark)[8]

The above mortgage lien on the cotton crop of Henry and Lucinda Lincoln, working on Samuel Brandon's Seltzertown plantation in 1869, is one of the oldest in existence for I. Lowenburg & Co. Indeed, it is a very early example of an emerging lien contract form that would become institutionalized throughout the Natchez District by the mid-1870s. Lowenburg had been in business since 1863 as one of the first of the emerging "new" plantation supply houses, and the firm's trade grew along with the new system of labor and credit that was coming to dominate not only the Natchez District but also large parts of the postwar South. From the very beginning, Lowenburg's business had depended on, and was largely built by, servicing the burgeoning new market of freed black cotton croppers and the planters for whom they worked throughout the district. The Lincolns likely emerged from slavery from somewhere locally and may have even been former slaves of Samuel Brandon's, and they probably took the surname of their emancipator, President Lincoln, as their own. In March 1869 the Lincolns sought a $100 credit line to farm their assigned ten acres on Seltzertown, although the exact nature of their agreement with Brandon is unknown. But this early lien agreement is representative of a solidifying system of labor and debt and demonstrates that by 1869 the crop lien system and share-tenancy were taking firm root in the Natchez District. Within a few years this system would become the standard for the area, with large leather-bound "chattel mortgage" ledgers at the county and (across the river in Louisiana) the parish courthouses. By the mid-1870s the cropping and lien system would dominate African American life and local agriculture, and it would continue to do so until the early twentieth century. But if this system came to dominate the local environs and cotton production, how did it arise, and how did it function?[9]

With the occupation of Natchez by Union troops in midsummer of 1863, runaway and emancipated slaves from the Louisiana and Mississippi countryside flocked to Natchez following the fall of Vicksburg to Union forces on July 4, 1863. Official Union policy in the occupied areas of the Mississippi River valley tried to contend with this problem by putting all women and children and elderly males to work on abandoned plantations or plantations run by Union loyalists. Able-bodied men like Nathaniel Wright and his brothers from Rucker plantation were invited to serve in the Union army, but the conditions they encountered were terrible, and many deserted. For those put to work on the plantations, a contract labor system paid fixed but barely subsistence wages. The Union army became the chief employment agency in the Natchez District, and Union officers instructed the freedman in their labor contracts and oversaw the negotiation and signing process. Although refugees were encouraged to remain on their home plantations, if such places were controlled by the army and safe from Confederate raiders, few plantations any distance from Natchez were safe in 1863, including Rucker, twenty miles east of town. Most blacks wanted to make a break for freedom in any case. The impulse resulted in masses of freedmen filling up poorly run refugee camps in and around Natchez. This situation prevailed for most of the third and fourth years of the war, but numerous plantations were up and running by 1864 under the protection of the Union army and operated by Northerners, the army itself, or even loyal planters on their own places.[10]

Refugee freedmen were paid a subsistence wage on the government-run plantations during the war, and the Freedmen's Bureau, a government agency established to assist and protect those who were formerly enslaved as they made the transition to freedom, supported this set wage policy in the face of substantial opposition from former slaveholders in the area. Some thought was given to redistributing confiscated and abandoned lands—the idea of "forty acres and a mule"—to those who were formerly enslaved immediately after the war to give them a stake in the system through ownership. But this idea had little support from the administration of Andrew Johnson and all but disappeared during the reign of Presidential Reconstruction, which lasted into 1867. In the immediate aftermath of the war and during the first months of Presidential Reconstruction, local whites tried to control labor by a system of so-called black codes, which prohibited black vagrancy and unemployment, forcing the freedmen to work under barely subsistence, fixed-wage contracts without any real stake in the success of the crop. The Freedmen's Bureau refused to enforce the black codes but did support the idea of wage labor at first. The numerous difficulties that arose with a fixed-wage system, however—such as how to dock blacks for poor work, absconding landlords who fled before paying wages, issues of discipline, and the refusal of freedmen to work for their former owners or any former slaveholders—forced the bureau to look to share-tenant farming and sharecropping as a solution. And this was a scheme generally supported by blacks because of the independence it allowed them from white supervision of their labor.[11]

Under this system the agricultural worker, in theory, rented a portion of land for a fixed dollar amount (such as $300) or a fixed amount of cotton (such as one bale) or a fixed share amount in cotton (such as one-third of the crop), and thereby shared in the risk of making the crop as well as the reward of a good crop. In this setup, the worker became a kind of tenant farmer, with the cash rent or share rent paid when the crop was made at the end of the year. Only those workers who could provide tools and work animals would participate in this fixed rent arrangement because landlords would not contract on a fixed rent unless the tenant could supply all other resources for making the crop. For those who had no assets to bring to the arrangements, such as tools or work animals, the usual scenario for former slaves, the worker entered into an agreement with the landowner, or his agent, and was advanced the necessary means to make a cotton crop on a portion of land with the understanding that a percentage of the future crop, or a "share," would be due the landlord as rent with the supply bill to be covered out of the worker's share of the crop. Under share-tenancy, the worker paid a specified share of the crop or a fixed amount of cotton as rent. Under sharecropping, workers received a share of the crop as a sort of wage, out of which they supplied themselves. In both cases the share arrangement gave freedmen and freedwomen, in theory, the freedom to exercise their labor and directly reap the profits without owning the land they worked, or investing, in the case of sharecroppers, any capital; the only collateral provided was their labor and the prospect of a future crop.[12]

Disastrous floods that hit the Natchez District in 1867–1868, principally due to failed levees destroyed during the war, and an armyworm infestation combined to ruin the crops, thereby severely taxing the resources of those planters who had tried to make a crop on their own by paying wages. Desperate planters and landowners were thus more accepting of the new share-tenancy system because they did not have to pay set wages regardless of the crop yield. Also, the share system enabled them to operate on credit for provisions until the crop came in. This lowered their need for operating capital and lessened financial exposure to a bad crop, because it spread out the risk between them and the freedmen. Most important, the new system allowed them to shift the supply bill to the freedmen tenants and sharecroppers. In most cases this was acceptable to those who were formerly enslaved because it permitted them to seek supplies from someone other than the former slaveholders who still controlled the land. In fact, many freedmen and freedwomen refused to contract with the antebellum planters if it meant working under their supervision and being fed from the plantation store. This social reality combined with two other aspects of the postbellum economy: the loss of equity in land that was practically worthless without an enslaved labor force to work it, and the severely weakened position of the antebellum factor as a source of credit due to losses experienced by these agents during the war. As a result, a huge new market for goods and staples and credit to make a crop emerged, and it was a market not easily serviced by the former means of credit and supply, because it was made up of thousands of individual freedmen farmers in need of supplies on which to live and to make a crop as sharecroppers or share-tenants. In this context, the crop rather than land and slaves became the collateral for credit.[13]

Mississippi and Louisiana met this new reality by enacting agricultural crop lien laws in 1867 designed to guarantee that workers and suppliers of provisions to make a crop held first claim to the crop over any claim by landowners for rent. "An Act for the Encouragement of Agriculture" essentially gave anyone who provided goods, supplies, cash, or credit for the production of a cotton crop a lien on that crop when harvested. This enabled the sharecroppers to place a laborer's lien on the crop to guarantee payment for raising the crop. This law demanded that landlords pay workers their share of the crop prior to any other expenses being paid by the landowner. Perhaps most important, it also allowed merchants to have the first claim on the worker's share of the crop for supplies advances as well as first claim on any crop due the landlord by renters supplied by merchants. This development encouraged surviving antebellum planters to lease or rent out land for cash or a share of the crop directly to tenants. The tenants were usually black croppers, but often the actual lessors were the supply merchants who provisioned the sharecroppers on the place and took a share of the cotton as rent. The linchpin in the new agricultural system was the merchant, who always held first claim to the crop because of the new laws protecting merchant interests. And here lies the crux of the new opportunity for postbellum merchants: a new system in which merchants provisioned agricultural workers as advances on the crop, and at highly inflated prices to cover their risks of crop failure by holding a crop lien on the future crop to ensure payment. Often these merchants bypassed the landlords altogether by leasing lands or by buying lands at bargain prices from debt-ridden landowners—lands they operated on their own accounts. In these cases they made money as both landlords collecting rents and as suppliers of goods obtained on credit, often from Northern wholesalers. This process of supplying the new market of black agricultural workers as sharecroppers and share-tenants, supported by law and the new social reality of the times, enabled some postbellum merchants to achieve substantial success—a success that they parlayed into an array of activities from land speculation to manufacturing, transportation, and banking.[14]

Preeminent among these new mercantile men in the Natchez District were the groups of merchants discussed in the preceding chapter, all of whom enjoyed several advantages for various reasons. Antebellum Natchez merchants like Fleming & Baldwin and A. Perrault Co. had close local ties, good reputations, and crucial supply networks and large credit resources through New Orleans cotton factors and wholesalers like Buckner & Newman Co. Returning Confederate veterans like Joseph N. Carpenter and William Abbott brought home a burning desire to move on from their war experiences and also commanded strong local ties and financial resources, sterling reputations, and the growing cachet of their service in the "lost cause," a key component of local respect in the coming age. Northern newcomers, like the former sutlers who made up I. Lowenburg & Co. or discharged Union lieutenant H. M. Gastrell, enjoyed close relationships with the occupying Union troops as well as access to Northern credit and goods through their contacts with suppliers in New Orleans, like the firm of Meyer, Weis, & Co., or with firms in the North such as Bettman, Bloom & Co. of Cincinnati. These advantages found them setting up wholesale supply houses early on in downtown Natchez and Vidalia. I. Lowenburg & Co. opened as a wholesale supply house and cotton brokerage at the downtown Cotton Square in Natchez on 97 Franklin Street in 1863, across the street from Aaron Beekman & Co. dry goods, grocers, and cotton buyers already residing there at 108–110 Franklin Street. William Abbott opened with planter John W. Henderson as Abbott & Henderson Co. plantation supplies, and they went in at 18 Commerce Street, right next door to Marx Lemle's dry goods and cotton-buying firm, down the street from H. M. Gastrell Co. hardware. N. L. Carpenter & Son ginned and brokered cotton on Wall Street, while across the river, Isaac Friedler followed with his own plantation supply and cotton-buying business on Carter Avenue in downtown Vidalia with Nathan Lorie. These firms were in the starting gate for serving a wide range of customers, including townspeople, outlying planters, small white farmers, and freedman sharecroppers.[15]

What these merchants did as businessmen stemmed principally from their new role as suppliers of credit to the producers of the cotton crop, whether they were sharecroppers and tenants or landlords trying to make a crop using freedmen as wage hands or share-tenants. Although most of their business at first involved supplies, the nature of the new situation soon found the merchants supplementing and even replacing the cotton-buying activities of the coastal cotton factor. Merchants who held claim to a crop through a crop lien found themselves protecting their interests by actually collecting the cotton upon harvest. This was especially the case if the merchant leased the land or owned it outright. Even in the case of landowners who worked the crop on their own accounts, merchant suppliers got paid with delivery of the crop. In a short time the merchant began to operate as the handler of the crop itself in the final stage of shipment to the coast, profiting thereby as the middleman between the grower and the market. In fact, several local merchants made major inroads in this direction before the war had even concluded. Union authorities granted Isaac Lowenburg and his sutler partner Henry Hill a lease and cotton-shipping permits for the abandoned cotton plantation Loch Leven in Wilkinson County in 1864, less than a year after they arrived with the Union army. Their legal trade in cotton differed from the activities of those who smuggled cotton out of the Confederacy and thereby plagued occupation authorities for most of the war. Still, the lines were not easily drawn during the war years because substantial trading in cotton occurred in the district, sometimes with the enemy. The local R. G. Dun agent felt sure that the Irishman George T. Payne was involved in wartime smuggling, as he commented on several occasions that Payne "does illicit traffic" and "engages in illicit traffic . . . [and is] regarded tricky." General Grant became so exasperated with the illegal cotton trade of some Jewish operatives in the Mississippi valley that he banned all Jewish traders for a time from the region, although that did not seem to influence Lowenburg, Beekman, Friedler, or Lemle to any great degree in Natchez. President Lincoln quickly rescinded this edict on banning Jews from the region as traders while nevertheless noting, "Every foul bird comes abroad, and every dirty reptile rises up."[16]

There is no evidence that any of the Jewish merchants who rose to prominence in the Natchez District were involved in such illicit trade, but the opportunity for such activities was always there. In fact, Lowenburg's brother, Samuel, served as a soldier in one of the Confederate militia units organized in Natchez during he war. This suggests that he may have lived in the Natchez District before the war or else had joined the unit elsewhere. Samuel Lowenburg's presence in a Confederate unit from Natchez clearly indicates that Isaac Lowenburg had some knowledge of the area prior to his arrival as a sutler with his partners Hill and Frank. Indeed, given the controversy over the role of Jewish merchants in the area, it is likely but not certain that Lowenburg was drawn to Natchez because of the opportunity for such speculation in cotton, both legal and illegal. In any case, Lowenburg shipped cotton legally from the district during the war, as did several other merchants with whom Lowenburg was closely associated in the Jewish merchant community, including Aaron Beekman, Marx Lemle, and Wolfe Geisenberger. But there were many local merchants outside the Jewish community shipping cotton during that time, including Fleming & Baldwin, Pollock & Mason, and Cyrus Marsh, often acting as agents for New Orleans cotton-factoring firms like Buckner & Newman Co. or Ober Atwater & Co.[17]

Clearly, these merchants operated as cotton buyers even before they began operating as suppliers of freedmen sharecroppers. Still, their role in supplies solidified their hold on cotton crops—not as buyers but as receivers of crops collected in rent and for supplies advanced in making the crops. This supply business and the legal use of the crop liens constituted the basis of their mercantile enterprise in the postwar years. Chattel mortgage records and land deeds showing crop lien agreements or contracts still survive and are extant in various forms throughout the four counties and two parishes that make up the Natchez District. For example, separate chattel mortgage ledgers for Adams County exist for the years 1875–1903, although some contracts exist in the land deeds as early as 1867. Jefferson County offers the longest span of surviving contracts of any Mississippi county in the Natchez District; they cover the years 1876–1910. They are the last available contracts in this form because chattel mortgage ledgers increasingly fell out of favor after the turn of the century, as local banks began to replace the merchant class as the primary petty agricultural lenders of the district. A few contracts survive for the period 1871–1904 in the land deed ledgers in Wilkinson County, while Franklin County has chattel mortgage ledgers dating from 1871 to 1903, and, once again, more in the land deeds there. There are no separate ledgers, but chattel mortgage records for the Louisiana parishes of Concordia and Tensas exist for the years 1865–1910 in the land deed and general mortgage records, thus providing significant material for examining the plantation supply business and interaction of Natchez merchants with black croppers.[18]

Although merchants issued crop liens prior to the recording of such claims in official record books, earlier incidents were not uniformly reported. Fleming & Baldwin and Miller & Marsh issued primitive agreements, starting in 1867, and George T. Payne did so in 1868. The I. Lowenburg & Co. lien agreement displayed at the beginning of this chapter is the oldest example found that was preprinted and was made especially for crop liens, while Marx Lemle soon followed with his first chattel mortgage on the Palatine plantation in April 1870. Between that date and 1875 similar contracts show up in the land deed records as "Chattel Mortgages." Before 1870 contracts between planters or merchants with freedmen sharecroppers were recorded in instruments of rent agreements, leases, fixed-wage labor agreements, and other forms of written contracts. Louisiana never used chattel mortgages per se as the legal instrument, instead issuing "General Mortgages," which were referred to as "Affidavits" or "Merchants Liens," within the realm of land deeds. One of the earliest records of any lien being issued for an annual supply bill to one of the merchants featured in this work from a planter occurred between I. Lowenburg & Co. and Charlotte Surget in Concordia Parish in 1867, followed by one from William S. Cannon to N. L. Carpenter & Son in 1868 in Natchez. Most of the early crop lien activity found in the records occurred in places other than Adams County. Wilkinson County recorded "Chattel Deeds" in separate ledgers as early as 1871, but these were destroyed by flood sometime in the 1880s. The index for these ledgers survives, however, and it is possible to at least discern if any of the featured merchants issued any chattel mortgages in that region. Also, records in the Mississippi counties of Franklin, Jefferson, and Wilkinson stretch back to 1871, although the contract of choice seemed to have been a "trust deed." This instrument became the favored legal device in all areas by the end of the period studied, when large amounts of valuable land served as collateral. These agreements differed significantly from county to county, and parish to parish, but they all essentially did the same thing: provide the merchants with a lien on chattels, cotton, and land to ensure payment on supply and cash debt.[19]

The general procedure for securing chattel mortgages and crop liens was as follows: the creditor (a cropper or planter) would approach the merchant for credit (usually goods, but sometimes cash), or else the merchant would approach the potential debtor, usually after the first of the year or sometime during the spring before cotton planting. The two parties would agree on a set amount of credit for the coming season. This amount could vary from as little as $30 to as high as several hundred or even thousands of dollars, depending on resources and size of the cropper's or planter's operation. Often several people, or a family unit of croppers, a "squad," would be listed on the mortgage, as these groups would combine their resources and labor to manage a larger and more successful crop. The cropper or planter would then give the merchant a mortgage on the season's crop, due and payable at the end of the harvest, and this line of credit was secured with personal property, usually horses, mules, and wagons, often the only items of value that the cropper owned. The planters generally put up their land as collateral as part of a trust deed in the event that the crop failed or they failed to pay, but on many occasions they also put up chattels as security, and a mortgage lien might have fifty or more head of livestock, plows, wagons, and even a cotton gin set up as security. Thus there were no hard-and-fast rules to this process, and the security could literally be anything of value that the debtor was willing to encumber and the merchant was willing to accept as collateral. The county or parish office of records legally recorded these mortgages and deeds for a fee, usually paid by the lendee, and they formed the legal basis of the lien system that gave merchants the legal right to foreclose on the collateral if the crop failed or if the debtor failed to repay the note.[20]

For this study, all existing contracts (crop liens and trust deeds) issued by members of the featured ten merchant families were gathered in the six counties and parishes of the Natchez District: Adams, Franklin, Jefferson, and Wilkinson Counties of Mississippi, and Concordia and Tensas Parishes in Louisiana. Examination of these crop lien and trust deed records generated some impressive numbers. During the forty-three-year period starting January 1, 1867, and ending in December 31, 1910, the combined totals from the region indicate that members of these ten merchant families recorded at least 13,233 individual chattel mortgage agreements and trust deeds, an average of 307.74 contracts per year in the district. The aggregate total of these mortgages and deeds was $2,669,289.09 in credit extended, or an average of $62,076.49 per year, and $201.71 per individual crop lien or trust deed contract. While these totals might not seem that large by contemporary standards, in today's terms the monetary conversion, accounting for inflation, would render an aggregate mortgage total of $61,663,726.35, or a yearly average of $1,434,028.87, with a per contract average of $4,643.34. These totals and averages represent credit extended on these contracts and actual yearly supply bills when available, not the actual amounts due at the close of each contract, which often far exceeded the credit amount given on the contract (see Tables 3–5).[21]

The figures display as much as can be determined of each mercantile family's total credit business conducted in the district for the period studied and how the income was divided between chattel mortgages and trust deeds. Some merchants offered large amounts of credit in both mortgage configurations—chattel mortgages and trust deeds. The Beekmans and the Jacobses did so. Others, like the Friedlers and the Carpenters, primarily specialized in one type of mortgage or the other, because they dealt mainly with either croppers or planters. However, no other merchant family came close to the huge figures generated by the many members of the Jacobs family. The figures also portray just how large these individual family totals were in today's terms: the Jacobs family wrote about $15.5 million of business, the Friedlers $8.8 million, the Beekmans $7.7 million, and so on. In fact, even the least prosperous featured family, the Lemles, wrote $2.1 million in contracts, indicative of the relative scale of business and affluence

Crop Liens, Freedmen, and Planters

Table 3. Credit Totals and Averages by Merchant, 1867–1910

Merchant	# Crop Liens	Total $ Crop Liens	Ave.	# Trust Deeds	Total $ Trust Deeds	Ave.	Combined Total	Ave.
Abbott	911	$139,715.41	$153.36	41	$33,130.04	$808.05	$172,845.45	$181.56
Beekman	1566	$283,035.52	$180.74	160	$51,300.24	$320.63	$334,335.76	$193.71
Carpenter	155	$125,240.82	$808.01	27	$65,855.71	$2,439.10	$191,096.53	$1,049.98
Friedler	2608	$384,720.14	$147.52	0	0	0	$384,720.14	$147.52
Geisenberger	1291	$192,653.77	$149.23	13	$3,423.33	$263.33	$196,077.10	$150.37
Jacobs	2980	$560,369.93	$188.04	102	$108,476.29	$1,063.49	$668,846.22	$217.02
Lemle	933	$91,937.61	$98.54	2	$750.00	$375.00	$92,687.61	$99.13
Lowenburg	528	$176,686.26	$334.63	72	$114,208.59	$1,586.23	$290,894.85	$484.82
Payne	944	$122,641.00	$129.92	7	$2,103.94	$300.56	$124,744.94	$131.17
Perrault	865	$170,467.23	$197.07	28	$42,573.26	$1,520.47	$213,040.49	$238.57
Totals	12,781	$2,247,467.69	$175.84	452	$421,821.40	$933.23	$2,669,289.09	$201.71

Source: All existing chattel mortgage and trust deeds records for the ten featured merchant families in the six county/parish Natchez District, 1867-1910.*

*The figures contained here probably represent far less than one-quarter of the total business conducted in the district among all merchants and croppers or planters for the period studied. The currency conversions were calculated at 1885 dollar values (midpoint of the data series) in 2008 values as placed and converted by the changes in the Consumer Price Index (CPI), one of several ways arriving at currency conversions. See "Measuring Worth," Consumer Price Index currency calculator of measuring relative worth in dollars, http://www.measuringworth.com/uscompare/.

that these families attained for their time. The trajectory of these credit contracts is interesting as well, because the majority of this business actually occurred in a relatively short period of time (see Table 4).[22]

Table 4 demonstrates the ebb and flow of the credit business at a quick glance. For example, the graph clearly shows the meteoric rise of credit offered as the crop lien–trust deed system became well entrenched in the mid-1870s, and that this aspect of these merchants' business was at its height during the 1880s and spiked again in the 1890s, but trailed off precipitously after the turn of the century with falling cotton prices, increasing competition from local banks, and the introduction of the cotton boll weevil, which decimated the local cotton business. Also, downturns in the graph correspond with well-known economic downturns in the mid-1870s and early 1890s, and it is clear that the merchant credit system and local cotton production were at their height during the 1880s and 1890s. Thus the apex of the merchants' credit-offering business occurred during a twenty-five-year period starting in the early 1870s, and ending around the turn of the century.[23]

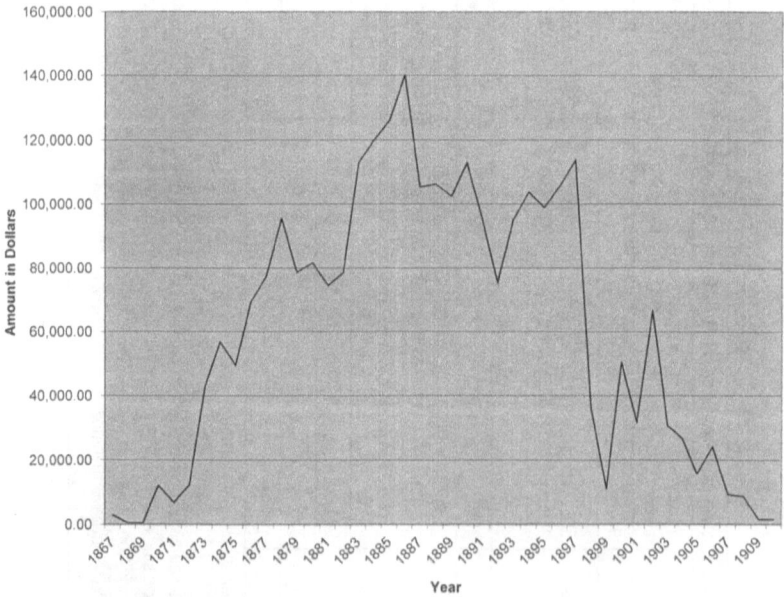

Table 4. Total Credit Extended by Year, 1867–1910
(Total of the Ten Merchants—$2669,289.09)

These contracts were usually made during the first part of the year before planting, and the year's credit for supply and store purchases was usually given in set amounts like $50 or $100 for a small cropper with the future cotton crop, livestock, or personal items as collateral (chattel mortgages), to as much as $5,000 or $10,000 given to a planter on a good-size plantation with cotton lands put up as security (trust deeds). But large amounts were also lent to planters on chattel agreements as well, with sometimes tens of mules, horses, cattle, or farm implements offered as security. In either case, the crop of cotton was almost always encumbered, and it had to be sold and shipped with the lending merchant. And often the contract, whether a chattel mortgage or trust deed, would record a specific amount initially purchased, like a $59.36 store bill at the beginning of the season, and then offer an additional "credit line" from which the cropper or planter could draw from for the remainder of the crop season. The merchant might stipulate that only a certain sum could be drawn in supplies every month, to protect himself from the cropper or planter overspending his credit line—something that often happened anyway. Close examination of these records reveals important information on the flow and stages of the mercantile credit-offering business, and how this system actually functioned in the Natchez District. The vast majority of these merchants' crop lien and trust deed activity is concentrated between the years 1875 and 1900, indicating that the mercantile hold on local petty agricultural financing was at its peak during that quarter-century period. Before that time the system was still developing and not well entrenched. Afterward an explosion of local banks began to fulfill the lending function, and there was a general decline in the cotton markets due to low prices. Consequently, many members of the merchant class moved on to different businesses—particularly after the cotton boll weevil smashed local cotton production after 1907. The peak year for liens was 1878, with 841. The twenty-year period 1875–1895 as a whole saw 10,475 contracts issued. The combined periods of 1867–1874 and 1896–1910, on the other hand, saw only 2,758 total chattel mortgages and trust deeds (see Table 5).[24]

Table 5 details the actual number of contracts issued every year and is indicative of the volume of this business, not the amount in dollars this business generated. Examination of both Table 2 and Table 3 indicates that peak volume in contracts did not necessarily correlate with peak dollar amounts, and the amounts in dollars depicted in Table 2 seems to be a better indicator of the general state of the economy, a valid assumption

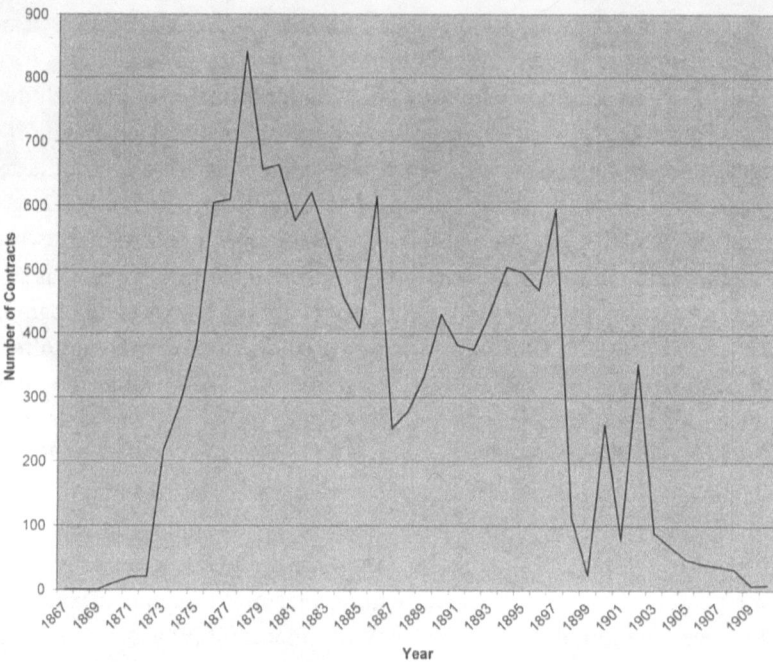

Table 5. Total Contracts Extended by Year, 1867–1910
(Total of the Ten Merchants—13,233 Contracts)

perhaps because the dollar totals do better correlate with known economic downturns, like the periods 1873–1878 and 1890–1896. While more contracts were given in peak years of cotton production or in anticipation of good production, this is at least partially representative of the willingness of the merchants to lend in relation to the fluctuating prices of cotton; a huge downturn in contracts occurs during the period of very low cotton prices around 1900. Also, the number of contracts issued is not necessarily indicative of a merchant's business strength: Carpenter issued far fewer contracts than Geisenberger, but their totals were nearly same because Carpenter's contracts were generally much larger and more concentrated on planters. One $5,000 supply contract with a good-size planter in one year could equal tens of small contracts with sharecroppers. The amount of contracts per year is also indicative of the logistical and time requirements on large contract writers like Friedler or the Jacobs family during the peak period, who wrote hundreds per year during the peak and must have been taxed to their limits to write, monitor, and collect on their vast numbers of yearly contracts.[25]

Other interesting patterns and characteristics emerge as well from the data, such as the geographic distribution of the contracts. Many of these merchants demonstrated a remarkable ability to do business over a surprisingly wide swath of the Natchez District, while a few others appeared to concentrate in one area. All the mercantile families detailed in this study were based and had their main facilities in Natchez, except for Isaac Friedler, who did business exclusively across the river in Vidalia. As such, while all ten merchants were clustered in the same general locale, many penetrated deeply and often into the geographic "territorial" markets of outlying small rural merchants—even those of larger competitors in relatively distant towns. Marx Lemle & Co., for example, was one of the smallest lien recorders of the period, with 933 liens issued from 1870 to Lemle's death in 1883. With the help of his brother Isadore, however, the firm ran a satellite store in Vidalia and had a pretty evenly split business, with 460 contracts in Adams County surrounding Natchez and 480 agreements across the river in Concordia Parish, with a single lone account from the outlying area in Franklin County. Thus all of Lemle's business was concentrated in a twenty-five-mile radius from his store in Natchez. Similarly, Isaac Friedler appears never to have ventured outside of Concordia Parish to offer crop liens, although he conducted land investments also some twenty-five miles north in neighboring Tensas Parish. He recorded more crop liens in Concordia than any other merchant studied and the second highest total out of all traders, negotiating 2,608 liens, or 131.5 average contracts per year over a twenty-four-year period from 1870 to 1893. This number is at least partially representative of the kind of contract used in Louisiana, a variant on the singular crop lien contract used in Mississippi. Louisiana-based merchants issued a "merchant's lien" that would often include "open accounts" for literally hundreds of freedman sharecroppers on just one contract, a procedure that reflected the large landholdings and extensive cotton planting that occurred in the rich soils of Concordia, perhaps the premier cotton area in the entire Natchez District. Friedler possibly had as much business as he could handle without having to venture into neighboring counties or parishes. Interestingly, Lemle contracted only two trust deeds and Friedler none. Both merchants did most of their business with small croppers on crop liens (see Table 3).[26]

Several other merchants made at least some inroads into outlying areas, achieving market penetration and garnering a significant amount of their business in a fifty-mile radius from Natchez. Wolfe Geisenberger & Co. is the fourth largest merchant in terms of the number of liens found for this study, with 1,304 total contracts issued in the district from 1874 to 1903; the majority (1,291) were written locally in Adams County. Yet Geisenberger also made some effort to pull in business from afar, issuing 76 liens in Jefferson County, 49 in Franklin, and 7 in Wilkinson. In all, he wrote 10 percent of his business in areas at least thirty miles distant from his store in Natchez. Geisenberger also concentrated on the cropper business, issuing only 13 trust deeds in the period. George T. Payne & Co. and William Abbott Groceries Co.—comprised of widow Ann E. Abbott and her manager, James S. Fleming—developed similar totals and geographic reach. Payne wrote 951 contracts, of which 722 were in Adams County, but he also managed to garner 141 accounts in Franklin County, 85 in Jefferson County, and 3 in Concordia Parish. It appears, then, that Payne pulled in almost 25 percent of his business from afar. He also maintained a plantation store over thirty miles distant, on his Payne Place in Franklin County. Abbott and Fleming demonstrated even greater ability to gather accounts from the hinterlands, writing 73 liens in Jefferson County, 75 in Franklin County, 5 in Wilkinson County, and 2 in Concordia Parish. These numbers were nevertheless dwarfed by the 797 liens in Adams County. Payne & Co. concentrated mainly on the small cropper business, issuing only 7 trust deeds over the period for a relatively small average of $131.17 per contract, while Abbott and Fleming pursued more planter business and wrote 41 trust deeds, generating a higher average contract of $181.56. Armand Perrault & Co. also demonstrated similar behavior, maintaining 83 percent of its accounts in Adams County, while generating just 27 in Franklin County and 126 in Jefferson County, where it owned several plantations over the period. Like Abbott and Fleming, however, Armand Perrault & Co. wrote considerably more planter business, at 20 percent of the company's total generated income, and it did so at a much higher average contract at $238.57 per lien (see Table 3).[27]

The Lowenburgs', Beekmans', Carpenters', and Jacobses' approach to business was different as they made strong inroads into a number of areas a good distance from Natchez, their businesses were quite widespread, and they pursued more planter business as cotton factors. For example, I. Lowenburg & Co. recorded 600 lien contracts in the period 1866–1906, with 345 occurring locally in Adams County, but they also appear frequently at great distance, with 82 contracts in Jefferson County, 20 in Franklin County, and 2 in Wilkinson County, while writing another 151 in Concordia Parish, garnering an astonishing 42 percent of the firm's business from outside Adams County. In fact, some of the earliest examples of I. Lowenburg & Co.'s participation in the new lien system came from thirty miles distant from Natchez in Jefferson County, where the company recorded several liens in 1871 and 1872, while also recording liens as early as 1874 in Franklin (thirty miles distant) and Wilkinson Counties (forty miles distant). Lowenburg leased Loch Ness plantation in Wilkinson County and Fletcher plantation in Concordia Parish in 1864, before the war's conclusion, and he was clearly willing to range out in search of business right from the beginning of the study period, before the crop lien system existed. His early experiences with these plantations may have made him more prone to accept geographical separation, and this could be related to his plantation-buying and cotton-growing activities a little later in the period. He later owned plantations in all of the Natchez District areas listed except Tensas Parish. Perhaps most important, I. Lowenburg & Co. was more of a *cotton factorage* that dealt in large contracts with planters, writing seventy-two trust deeds, for a per contract average of $484.82, much higher than the merchants previously discussed (see Table 3).[28]

Aaron Beekman & Co. demonstrated the greatest geographical reach, as it is the only Natchez merchant house to appear in every county and parish in the district, and in greater numbers. Of the 1,726 contracts the company recorded for the period 1871–1906, an astounding 715 contracts (41 percent) were written at least thirty miles distant from the company's store in Natchez, although it also maintained a plantation store on its plantation in Franklin County and wrote many there. Beekman had a midrange business of planters and croppers that generated an average contract of $193.71, yet did only a small business just across the river in Vidalia, while others like the Lowenburgs, Friedlers, and Carpenters looked to that cotton-producing hub for large lending totals to planters. Beekman recorded just two contracts in Concordia Parish, yet one contract in 1893 for $400 in plantation supply debt ended up snowballing into plantation ownership, with Beekman getting the Lone Pine plantation in a debt settlement in 1896. But Beekman, like Lowenburg, invested in plantation ownership at some distance from his home base, and he eventually owned Kibbeville in Franklin County, Penny Place in Jefferson County, and Bitterwood in

Wilkinson County. Meanwhile, the Carpenters were the only true cotton factors in this story, making only 182 contracts total, with 62 percent in Adams County and 38 percent in Jefferson County, Concordia Parish, and Tensas Parish. The Carpenters dealt mostly with planters, and their average contract was the largest, at $1,049.98. The Jacobs family, probably the largest merchants in the region, generated an impressive $668,846.22 in total business with 3,082 contracts in every area except Concordia Parish, with 25 percent of their accounts residing at least thirty miles distant from Natchez and an average contract of $217.02. The Jacobses also ended up owning several plantations in Adams, Franklin, and Jefferson Counties (see Table 3).[29]

Clearly, the Natchez merchant class was able to penetrate markets up to fifty miles from their home stores to gather substantial portions of their business, which naturally leads to the issue of competition among the merchantmen for the local or not-so-local supply business. Some historians contend that merchants typically carved out and held "monopoly" control over a given geographic area, enabling them to dictate supply prices and credit terms within that region. In the course of this research in all areas of the Natchez District, there seems to be abundant evidence to the contrary, and in fact the merchants were widely distributed within their available market, often writing lien contracts on cotton lands and plantations far from their stores, or on those owned or leased by other merchants. Louis Kyriakoudes has provided a better model for the conditions in the regional cotton supply and shipping center of Natchez, where merchants instead exhibited geographic "clustering" in the developing urban areas in combination with a penchant for distribution—the ability to penetrate the far-off markets of the "county stores" that supposedly enjoyed these territorial monopolies. Every one of the counties and parishes mentioned previously had its own cadre of local merchants in the form of country stores, yet larger Natchez merchants operating from a distance appear to have consistently siphoned off 25–30 percent of local business. This seems to be largely a function of the ability of larger "urban" Natchez merchants to offer greater credit resources, lower credit prices, larger product selection, or superior cotton shipping and sales capabilities.[30]

In another form of competition for business among merchants who controlled or owned their own plantations in the district, one might assume that the merchant-landlord would want to control all the supply debt on his own plantation and channel that business through his own store, thereby collecting double shares as landlord-furnishing merchant, but this was not always the case. For example, in Concordia Parish, we know through land records that I. Lowenburg & Co. held a lease on Cheripa plantation from 1871 to 1877, and that during Lowenburg's control of that plantation competing Vidalia merchant Friedler & Co. maintained at least ten accounts with the sharecroppers there amounting to almost $2,000. This indicates that Lowenburg and Friedler competed for contracts with sharecroppers on Lowenburg's own plantation, because during the same period I. Lowenburg & Co. maintained eight accounts there for $1,600. In another case, between 1877 and 1884 Friedler wrote at least twenty-five supply contracts on the "Lowenburg's" plantation in Concordia (probably the Fletcher plantation), although Friedler and Lowenburg were closely associated as part of the same Jewish mercantile community, had ties by marriage, and may have had some kind of agreement.[31]

There were many examples of merchants doing business on another's plantation in other areas, as well as examples of several merchants operating on the same plantation at the same time. For example, in the 1870s and early 1880s Marx Lemle owned Wade's Woodyard, a large 2,280-acre plantation in Adams County that Lemle received for a defaulted supply bill debt from planter Clarence J. Wade in 1875. During his ownership, Lemle maintained at least twelve supply accounts with his sharecropping tenants on the plantation, worth $1,045 in supplies and cash advanced. But during the same period Wolfe Geisenberger & Co. issued six supply contracts worth $375 to Lemle's tenants, George T. Payne & Co. wrote two supply contracts worth $190, and Armand Perrault & Co. negotiated another for $75, all conducted with Lemle's sharecropping tenants while he himself had several supply contracts on his own plantation. In probably the largest example, between 1877 and 1902 Marx Lemle Co., S. & A. Jacobs, Adolf Jacobs & Co., A. F. Jacobs & Bros., I. Lowenburg & Co., Wolfe Geisenberger & Son, George Payne & Co., and William Abbott Co. combined to write no less than thirty-seven contracts worth several thousands of dollars on the Carpenter family's Point Place plantation, all while the N. L. Carpenter & Son factorage firm wrote contracts there as well. There are many examples of this, suggesting a fairly wide-open market for the local sharecropper and plantation supply business, where there was significant competition but also enough business to go around. Of course, what appears to have been rampant competition might have been just the opposite—that is, merchants willing to supply some credit-risky freedmen in cases where other merchants were not, based on their past experiences.[32]

There are also examples of these merchants furnishing supplies to the sharecroppers and share-tenants on their own plantations without allowing outside mercantile competition. For example, Aaron Beekman & Co. operated Beekman's plantation in Adams County between 1883 and 1897, and during that time the firm maintained no less than twenty-nine supply accounts for the tenants worth $7,835.07 at 8 percent interest. During that fifteen-year span a competing merchant wrote only one contract on Beekman's plantation: one crop lien by Wolfe Geisenberger & Son for $30 in February 1886. In another case Friedler & Co. leased Waverly plantation in Concordia Parish during the period 1874–1876 and actively furnished its sharecroppers and share-tenants. During the year 1874 Friedler recorded at least twenty-seven merchant liens with African American households on Waverly, extending supplies by August 12 of $1,436.53. This was not the full supply bill because two or three more months remained in the growing season during which the tenants needed additional supplies. Assuming at least a 30 percent markup on the price of the goods sold to share-tenants on credit—which is a conservative estimate in the view of most historians—Friedler might have turned a $430.95 profit on the goods alone. And it might have been more if he also collected interest on the supplies advanced, typically 8 percent. Additionally, Friedler undoubtedly collected rents from these workers as share-tenants on the place.[33]

In Friedler's case, although it is unclear how much income he derived from his accounts on Waverly plantation in 1874, some educated estimates can be made. He usually charged around three bales rent per family or squad (bales ran about 450 pounds), meaning he probably collected roughly eighty bales of cotton for those twenty-seven contracts (3 bales x 27), a conservative estimate based on the records. With cotton selling in New Orleans at around $.18 a pound, his income from the cotton collected in rents came to around $6,480 ($.18 x 450 pounds per bale x 80 bales). In addition, Friedler typically bought and shipped most or all the cotton that his tenants owned after paying their rents—perhaps a total of an additional eighty bales, assuming that the tenants produced five to seven bales on the twenty-acre plots that were commonly rented at that time. Typically, merchants paid a cent or two below New Orleans prices, which rendered a profit for services in buying eighty bales of around $360 ($.01 x 450 pounds = $4.50 x 80 bales = $360). Merchants also charged a commission of 2.5 percent for shipping, baling, and compressing the cotton, which produced an additional $162 ($6,480 x 2.5 percent). This means Friedler could have grossed around $7,000 for his part in this crop ($360 markdown on the New Orleans price + $162 commission + $6,480 in cotton rents). After subtracting 20 percent for overhead costs, he probably netted $5,600 ($7,000 x 20 percent = $1,400, which is subtracted from $7,000 to equal $5,600). His New Orleans cotton factor charged a 2.5 percent commission for selling the cotton, possibly reducing the $5,600 by around $162, meaning that he might have cleared around $5,438 in profit before paying insurance and shipping costs, which possibly reduced his net by several hundred dollars more. In most cases commissions paid to the coastal factor were usually split with the interior merchant, and insurance and shipping costs were typically deducted from the price paid for the cotton in the local market. Out of these proceeds of around $5,000 to $6,000, Friedler paid an additional $1,000 in rent for his lease, leaving him with a net income of at least $4,000. In addition, there are the profits he made for supplies and advances to his tenants to make the crop at a 30–50 percent markup percent plus 8 percent interest, payable in cotton. It is likely that Friedler acquired at least another forty bales of cotton in payment for supplies advanced, adding another $2,000 or more in net profits. He worked on lease three similar plantations in Concordia Parish in 1874, generating an income after expenses of $12,000 to $20,000, not counting the supply business he carried on in that year on other plantations that he did not lease.[34]

Clearly, profits could mount quickly. Occasionally, the amounts of cotton charged croppers for fixed-rent contracts were included on the chattel mortgage agreements. Thus we at least have examples of what cotton merchants were receiving as rents in cotton on their plantations: Marx Lemle Co.—18 bales in rent (1876–1883); Wolf Geisenberger & Son—92 bales and an additional 52,550 pounds (1880–1898); I. Lowenburg & Co.—180 bales and 5,000 pounds (1876–1886); Aaron Beekman & Co.—168 bales and 182,045 pounds (1876–1898); and Friedler Co.—172 bales and 5,000 pounds cotton (1873–1885). These figures barely scratch the surface of the yearly amounts of cotton that actually passed through the hands of these merchants, however, because the vast majority of the croppers in the Natchez District worked on shares, not fixed rent; neither do these totals include cotton bought and sold or received from landowners supplied by the merchants. For example, the Carpenter family usually dealt with large landowners as cotton factors, and they often demanded, on the pain of financial penalty, huge set amounts of cotton to be shipped by planters to whom they then advanced money: in March 1887 planter B. B. Parham agreed to ship no less than 1,200 bales of cotton at 2.5 percent commission on his Shamrock plantation in return for an $15,000 advance at 8 percent interest (due by January 1888), and agreed to pay Carpenter, Dicks & Co. $1 for every bale short of 1,200. Parham apparently made the shipment and repaid the advance because no legal trouble erupted, and Parham received an even larger advance the following year. Thus business with larger planters and landowners could easily generate hundreds of bales of cotton to ship, creating opportunity to profit from just handling the cotton.[35]

In one example, during the period September 1880 to March 1881, the New Orleans factor and commission house of Nalle, Cammack, & Co. received 317 bales from A. Beekman & Co., 627 from G. T. Payne & Co., 238 from Marx Lemle Co., 459 from A. Perrault & Co., and 139 from S. & A. Jacobs. Using Beekman and Payne as examples, and assuming that they handled their bales as middlemen rather than owning them outright, by applying the same equation used above, Beekman would have netted $1,500 for just handling the 317 bales. Here is how it might have worked: he made around $1,426.50 in marking down the price he paid on the 317 bales bought (317 bales x 450 pounds = 142,650 pounds x $.01 = $1,426.50); he probably collected an additional $641.95 in commission for handling and shipping (142,650 pounds x $.18 = $25,677 x 2.5 percent = $641.95), for a total of $2,068.45 gross profit. Shipping and insurance costs of $.005 per pound of cotton as well as the 2.5 percent commission paid to the coastal factor or handling agent were undoubtedly deducted from the price he paid for the cotton rather than being added on as costs to him. Other expenses for overhead and labor probably equaled less than 20 percent of the gross, or around $413, suggesting that he earned around $1,600 for handling the 317 bales. In the same way, Payne could have made around $3,000 for his 627 bales. If the two merchants owned the cotton outright, the net profit would have been much larger. And these figures and calculations represent only a small portion of the business handled by the merchants under investigation. Indeed, the coastal factorage firm of Julius Weis & Co. was the New Orleans factor most closely related to the Jewish merchants of Natchez and the largest handler of cotton from the Natchez District, receiving as much as $1 million in yearly shipments.[36] A key component of the merchant's supply business involved provisioning sharecroppers, tenants, and planters with the livestock, plantation tools, wagons, carts, and equipment to make a crop. Mules, oxen, and horses were needed to cultivate and harvest the crops, not to mention cows and other livestock kept on these farms and plantations as food sources. Judging by the chattels listed in the crop lien contracts, thousands of animals and farm implements were provided by these merchants every year. Beekman and Friedler handled so many animals that they purchased land and constructed sizable stockyard facilities. Mules and horses, for example, were the "tractors" of that day, and they were not cheap. The typical forty-acre spread needed at least one mule to work the land and perhaps a milk cow feed the family. Friedler Co. typically rented mules for $30 each in 1876 and for a 425-pound bale the next; I. Lowenburg & Co. was selling mules in 1880 for $60; and in 1879 Lemle Co. was selling a horse for one bale of cotton or a wagon for $50. When Friedler bought Forrest plantation in 1884, the deal included forty-two mules, six wagons, six cotton-planting machines, seven harrows, six plows, one mowing machine, countless small hand tools, harnesses, and 800 sacks of cotton seed. Clearly, the supply business generated a significant demand for livestock and tools, which the supply merchants advanced as part of the crop lien contract, charging high markups and healthy interest rates.[37]

After the war, doing business always carried elevated risks, especially for merchants advancing supplies on credit. A certain percentage of business always consisted of bad debts that had to be collected. When this happened the merchant could file in the local district court for a judgment and attachment of the collateral that the debtor put up as security or simply take the matter up with the local justice of the peace. Usually the sheriff, as an agent of the court, seized the personal property or cotton of the debtor, until the debtor rendered payment, which seldom happened. In this case, the merchant took the seized cotton or chattels, like livestock or implements, as settlement of the debt. In one example, Friedler Co. recorded 398 merchant liens on the plantations in Concordia Parish in 1878 for a total of $39,428.36 in credit extended (Friedler's peak year), and from this crop lien activity it was necessary to sue six individuals for payment on unpaid supply bills totaling $1,257.71, or around 5 percent bad debt. In each case, the judge found in Friedler's favor for the full amount plus 8 percent interest until paid and court costs, giving him judgments totaling around $1,500.[38]

This suggests that liens were an effective legal means for ensuring payment, but it is equally clear that few such actions were taken. Most likely, bad debts were considerably higher and simply were not pursued off the plantation principally because sharecroppers and tenants were captive customers of sorts. If the crop failed, the debt could be carried over, but there was little sense in paying court costs to collect debts from people who had no assets. Rather, when the courts were resorted to it was usually in a case of a landowner or a tenant with assets to be attached. The high markup on the goods advanced meant that Friedler's real debt was always about a third lower in actual costs to him, or around $850 in this specific case. The merchants did not always win their debt cases, and their accounting methods did not always go unchallenged. In 1886 Friedler sued planter John Hart in the Ninth District Court in Vidalia for an annual plantation supply bill in the amount of $398.51, plus 8 percent interest and court costs. Hart challenged Friedler's accounts: "The defendant has since learned that the said account contains excessive numerous charges, amount in the aggregate as the defendant is informed and believes, to more than three hundred dollars." He complained that Friedler's charges were "excessive" and "illegal," and that Friedler had agreed to "furnish the defendant with goods and supplies at reasonable market prices." Apparently he owed something, but the bill was too high by around $300, and the judge thought that Hart's complaints had enough merit to set the matter over for trial. Unfortunately, the ledger does not contain the verdict.[39]

It is hard to gauge the reliability and honesty of the merchants, particularly in a system that contained so much opportunity for dishonesty. The merchants of this study were family men and women of large stature in the local community, and in many cases local business and political leaders. This does not mean, however, that these merchants were anything less than hardboiled in their collection of debts or in their business dealings. The plantation supply and cotton-handling business built fortunes for these merchant families, largely by offering highly marked-up goods on credit terms, to those who could not get these services elsewhere, for a pernicious premium. By 1875 the Natchez merchant class had cornered the local market of supplying petty agricultural credit to the burgeoning class of African American share-tenant farmers and rivaled the large New Orleans cotton factors as prime handlers of local cotton and suppliers of the planter class as well. The lien system made the merchant class and gave them strong legal protection against planter and cropper alike, and both classes of debtors increasingly found themselves in the grasp of merchantmen offering credit. The Natchez traders ranged far into the countryside and dominated those environs, armed with the same financial advantages, rivaling local traders and largely controlling the plantation supply and cotton-handling business within a fifty-mile radius. Only the rise of the local banks, low cotton prices, and the boll weevil would break their grip after the turn of the century. But who were the croppers and planters from whom the merchantmen gathered their business in the Natchez District?

※ ※ ※

The new growing season would soon be under way in Natchez on February 4, 1886, as Daniel and Louisa Jackson made their way into the store of Wolfe Geisenberger & Son Dry Goods and Plantation Supplies at 118 N. Commerce Street. The Jacksons had been working on shares and farming about 30 acres on the Stanton family's 2,200-acre Brandon Hall plantation in northern Adams County since at least 1877. They may have emerged from slavery somewhere in the area—perhaps from the Stantons on Brandon Hall—although the census lists Daniel's birthplace as North Carolina and Louisa's as Tennessee. On that day in February they sought out Geisenberger's firm to open a new credit account for the year 1886 to purchase the necessary food to survive and supplies to farm on Brandon Hall, and they received a $100 credit line at 8 percent interest backed by a lien on their cotton crop to draw upon until they could harvest in the fall. The hope was their share of cotton that fall would make enough profit from the sale through Geisenberger & Son (at an additional 2.5 percent commission) to pay off their credit account and leave a little extra to live on until the following spring, when they would receive a new credit line for the following year. The Jacksons were well acquainted with the crop lien system: they had been good customers of George T. Payne & Co. on Brandon Hall since 1877, borrowing about the same average of $100 per year and apparently paying their balances to continue the credit relationship with Payne. But for whatever reason, perhaps better credit terms, they were making a switch to Geisenberger's firm. They stayed with Geisenberger & Son until at least 1897, occasionally working as a squad with Ab Stanton, but by 1900 the now seventy-year-old Daniel was a widower and living with his son Murphy, who was also a cropper. Daniel must have died a few years later, and all that remains of his and his wife's presence in the district over those many years is a handful of still-existing lien records for a little over $1,000.⁴⁰

On February 20, about two weeks after the Jacksons visited Geisenberger & Son in Natchez, their planter landlords on Brandon Hall—Aaron Stanton and Elizabeth Brandon Stanton—made a trip of their own to Natchez, but they went to call on I. Lowenburg & Co. Plantation Supply and Cotton Merchants. Wed in October 1865, the Stantons represented a union of two of the largest and most powerful antebellum Natchez planter families: Aaron Stanton was the son of David Stanton, brother of Fredrick Stanton and a wealthy cotton merchant and planter from Ireland; and Elizabeth E. Brandon was the granddaughter of the first native-born governor in Mississippi and large planter Gerard Brandon. Between the Stantons and Aaron's cousin Robert, they had control of over 8,000 acres on Brandon Hall, Windy Hill, Egypt, Cedar Grove, and Sandy Creek plantations, but like many members of the planter class, their interests had suffered since the war, and they were desperately in need of financing of their own to conduct planting operations in 1886. In fact, all of their plantations except Brandon Hall had been in tax foreclosure to the state of Mississippi as recently as 1883, although they managed to emerge intact. On that twentieth of February, Elizabeth and Aaron negotiated a lien agreement with I. Lowenburg & Co., where they mortgaged their entire cotton crop and agreed to ship it all with Lowenburg for a 2.5 percent commission, and put up twenty-eight mules as security to receive an initial advance of $2,739.13 in cash and supplies, as well as a credit line of $3,000 (all at 8 percent interest) to carry them through until the crop was harvested and sold. The Stantons were also very familiar with the merchant lien system: between January 1, 1874, and November 3, 1898, Aaron and Elizabeth concluded no less than thirty-five crop liens and trust deeds with Natchez merchant firms Aaron Beekman & Son, N. L. Carpenter & Son, J. N. Carpenter & Co., and I. Lowenburg & Co, for a total credit received of $62,435.35, or $1,388,991.18 in current dollar value. And while they apparently never defaulted on any of these loans or lost their plantations to supply debt foreclosure, they also apparently never got sufficiently ahead in their finances to do without merchant financing; within a few decades the family would be out of the planting business altogether.⁴¹

Clearly, the merchant lien system of crop financing greatly influenced both cropper and landlord alike and often placed great stress on both as it funneled outside capital into the district in the form of Northern goods, financing, or proceeds from cotton sales in New Orleans, New York, or Liverpool. The outside capital was essential to local agricultural pursuits as part of a dependent South largely devoid of its own cash resources. But the cost of the credit was high. While many planters had become reliant on the merchant class for financing, others were able to steer clear of the merchant-class debt through access to local bank financing or funds procured through New Orleans or New York. The powerful Surget family owned more local cotton lands than anyone in the district but received their financing from New York and dealt mainly with New Orleans factors or Northern wholesalers for their supplies. But the thousands of local croppers had no such options and almost uniformly dealt with local plantation supply merchants for all of their needs, both agricultural and personal, and large numbers fell into a life of perpetual indebtedness to these merchants. While it would be too much to say that these individual merchants were responsible fully for the plight of those who were formerly enslaved, it is nevertheless accurate to say that they were an essential part of the problem and profited from the helplessness of the African American croppers whom they provisioned and worked. Indeed, supplying the freed slaves constituted a main element of their success as merchants, and the relationship between the croppers and the traders was perhaps the most defining relationship of several of these merchants' careers and perhaps also the most personal.[42]

Earlier in this chapter the character and volume of the financial numbers generated by this relationship were presented, but these numbers do little to demonstrate that each one of the chattel mortgages filed as contracts also tells a human story about the continual struggle that the debtors endured. The merchants' activities greatly contributed to the postbellum character of the African American community. These merchants replaced the support system of slavery with a new market-oriented and perhaps less paternalistic economic arrangement. The traders helped the newly freed blacks secure credit, supplies, goods, medical care, and even land to farm, often serving as bankers for the freedmen and helping them conduct many other forms of business, including paying taxes or arranging funerals. And after the war no other group was willing or able to help the freedmen's transition to freedom besides the federal authorities, and the agricultural laws of 1867 firmly cemented the merchants' pivotal role in black life. Conversely, the merchants clearly profited from the new system, and they supported conditions in the African American community that often left blacks little better off than they were in slavery. These merchants took the sharecroppers into debt and kept them there, perpetuating their hardship and even enforcing a new economic class system, creating conditions that defined the new labor institution in the New South: the share-tenancy system.[43]

A principal element of this new relationship was the simple willingness of the merchants to pursue the African American market and the strong preference of freed blacks to do business with whomever offered them the best terms—or harbored the least amount of racism. They knew that there was great competition among the merchant class, and it certainly did not hurt that these merchants comprised a group with whom they could do business, bypassing the former slaveholding elite. All the merchant families detailed in this study were first-generation European immigrants except the Abbotts, Carpenters, and Flemings, and there is a good reason for the others' selection. In the antebellum period, newcomers like Aaron Beekman, Armand Perrault, and George T. Payne gathered most of their business in the "black trade," doing business with slaves who were allowed to come into town by their masters and trade in truck goods, game, fish, and the cash they occasionally earned. The foreigners clearly had less compunction about trading with blacks and fewer ties to the planter class, and it was an easy transition for them in the postbellum period to move headlong into the exploding black marketplace. Also, the burgeoning Jewish merchant community was comprised of formerly persecuted European Jews who tended to look upon business as business, regardless of the color of the customers.[44] Even early in the postbellum period the Yankees noticed this willingness, as one Northern observer, Frederick Law Olmsted, wrote in 1865: "A swarm of Jews, within the last ten years, has settled in nearly every Southern town, many of them of no character, opening cheap clothing and trinket shops; ruining, or driving out of business, many of the old retailers, and engaging in an unlawful trade with simple Negroes, which is found very profitable."[45]

The above description could only in part describe the upstanding Friedlers, Geisenbergers, Lemles, and Lowenburgs of this study but also could be applied to the non-Jews from the other merchant communities as well. The trade with the freedmen certainly did not endear these merchants to the defeated local populace, at least at first, but it also became the very foundation of these merchants' postwar success: the willingness to conduct business with blacks and pursue the emerging economic market comprised of the newly freed slaves. These merchants were economic opportunists, and they were "more interested in customers than in customs of racial discrimination, more committed to making sales than making trouble, more worried about inventory than about integration." There is a definite truth in the view that these merchants were motivated by money and not racism, but they were well aware of the racial ramifications of the sharecropping system and their part in it. One historian has noted that many of these merchants were uncomfortable with the continuing Southern racism they encountered, particularly after the occupation ended and a new racist wave swept the South in the form of Redemption and Jim Crow. There is scant evidence, nevertheless, that the merchant class ever did anything to make the system more equitable. Indeed, they dug into the system that favored them with both hands.[46]

Natchez blacks knew that they held the key to local labor, and in a sense this empowered them, at least for a time—that is, so long as the Freedmen's Bureau and the U.S. Army operated in the region. The former slave-owning plantation owners had to scramble to get labor to bring their crops in, and blacks, being more astute than the planter class and many other Southerners gave them credit for being, went where they were given the best financial terms and living conditions. They proved quite shrewd in their dealings for a "preindustrial people" just out of slavery. While the planter class attempted to limit the options available to the freedmen and freedwomen with the "black codes," those who were formerly enslaved simply "voted with their feet" and moved from plantation to plantation, going where they not only got the best financial arrangements but also the widest range of personal freedom, as much as possible away from supervision by whites. The sharecropping system was attractive to them partly because it gave them a modicum of freedom of choice. This desire for independence remained important throughout the era, manifested as it was in the freedom to move about and conduct business with whom they pleased. As a result, the freedmen often appear in the records one year only to disappear the next, while others appear one year and do not reappear again for several years. During the Jim Crow era, this pattern in the records indicates not only the commitment of freedmen to moving their business from one merchant to another but also their attempt to retain one of the only freedoms they possessed in the impoverished state to which sharecropping had reduced them.[47]

All freed blacks were not sharecroppers. During the period of occupation and Reconstruction, freedmen enjoyed many of the same rights as anyone else and played a large role in local politics, and some made significant inroads into mainstream society. In the dark years of Jim Crow, some African American families prospered, even flourished, particularly those families descended from free blacks of the antebellum period or those advantaged ones who had received land from their former masters. African Americans owned many plantations in the Natchez District, and there are abundant instances where local merchants dealt with these plantation owners or other prominent local blacks. For example, August and Sarah Mazique purchased China Grove plantation from Wilmer Shields in 1869 and later bought Oakland. Several Natchez merchants had supply contracts with this family or the sharecroppers on their plantations. Brothers William and John Lynch, both born into slavery in the Natchez District, emerged as influential politicians and landowners during Reconstruction, and they eventually owned at least part of five plantations; all of the merchants in this study did business with the sharecroppers on these plantations, with the exception of the Friedler Co. in Vidalia. I. Lowenburg & Co. supplied Hiram Revels, the first African American from Mississippi to sit in the U.S. Senate, on his Mount Welcome plantation. Beekman & Son also did business on Revels plantation. In fact, most of the merchants in this study had dealings with a small group of African American plantation owners in the Sandy Creek area northeast of Natchez. Even Abraham Geisenberger, Wolfe's son and the first prominent lawyer to emerge out of the Jewish merchant community, had many prominent blacks as clients in land transactions, including Louis J. Winston, a lawyer, planter, and Adams county clerk for many years. Many of these landowning African Americans employed cadres of their own black sharecroppers, under conditions that were quite similar to those experienced under white planters.[48]

The simple fact, however, was that the overwhelming majority of contracts entered into by the ten merchant families studied were with African Americans on terms that seldom lifted them out of debt. Out of 13,233 chattel mortgages and trust deeds examined for this study, well over 10,000 were chattel mortgages with black croppers. Almost all of these croppers had entered freedom with only the clothes on their backs, and they clearly contracted from a position of severe disadvantage. Careful study of these thousands of contracts finds few instances where blacks profited or advanced much over the course of their lives as a result of the provisions under which they worked, regardless of how hard they worked. They entered into these contracts pledging their labor and the labor of their families, as well as the security of their few possessions, in return for the right to make a crop. What they largely found was an economic trap in which their debt balance was often carried over with the merchant from one year to the next, with the only escape that of trying to work for a different merchant on a different place, but usually with no gain for themselves.[49]

Debt could ruin the sharecropper in the space of a few years, or leave a cropper in an endless cycle of debt for years on end. Take the case of married sharecroppers Nelson and Cressey Page, who did business with A. Beekman & Co. over a three-year period from 1875 to 1877. The Pages started out in 1875 by giving Beekman a chattel mortgage for $70 in supplies on Dunbar plantation, and they listed as their only chattel a single mule, which actually put them better off than many croppers who could muster no security—other than the cotton crop—and had to rent their mules. Apparently, they did not care for the conditions on Dunbar, or found a better deal elsewhere, because the next year, they appear on Mount Ida. They must have made a crop on Dunbar because they did not carry over a balance with them to Mount Ida with Beekman & Co. This time they teamed up with another couple, Basil and Betty Williams, to form their own small squad, perhaps in an attempt to farm more land and bring in a bigger crop. Beekman fronted them $240 in supplies for the year, and the four tenants put up a mule and a horse as collateral. The year did not go well for them, however, and the next year found them carrying $246.73 in debt held over from the previous year. Williams does not appear in the new contract, and Beekman advanced only $40 in supplies, thereby increasing the Pages' debt to close to $300, although they still managed to contribute two mules toward making the crop. In other words, for three years of hard work under the Mississippi sun, Page and his family were worse off than when they started. Apparently, their cotton made each of the previous years was barely enough to cover their rents, with little left over for supplies. This family disappeared from Beekman's records and did not show up in any other chattel or census records for Adams County until 1910, when Cressey reappeared as a widowed tenant farmer living with a twenty-three-year-old daughter.[50]

In another case, sharecropper Henry Rice had a twelve-year run with Beekman & Co. Rice first recorded a chattel mortgage with Beekman in

1876 on Seltzertown, receiving $175 in supplies and putting up as collateral one mule, two cows, and a horse. The next year he carried over a $97.19 balance, or debt, at 8 percent interest, and he took another $50 in advances. In 1878 he owed $83.95, and took another $50. The following year he moved to Lewis plantation and started fresh with a $75 advance, indicating he had managed to pay off the previous $207.19 debt plus interest. This time Rice offered as collateral one horse, one mule, and one buggy. He ended that year again in debt for $37.98, and took another $60 advance from Beekman for supplies. In 1881 Rice worked under a squad contract with three other sharecroppers, assuming his share of a $125 advance. The following year he was back on his own and $95 in debt, taking another $80 in supplies. In 1883 he worked with two other sharecroppers on Lewis, carrying over $29.98 and taking $100 for the year. He owed $101.15 and accepted a $100 advance the next year. In 1885 his debt amounted to $135.53 plus $100 in supplies advanced. The same pattern held true for the next two years, with Rice nearly $300 in debt at the end of the contract year for 1887. In 1888, however, something quite remarkable happened. Beekman advanced Rice $400, suggesting that he had managed to pay off his previous year's debt. Nor did Beekman require Rice to list his animals as security for the advance. The records do not reveal what happened, but the possibilities are many. Perhaps Rice's crop in 1887 was large enough and cotton prices high enough for him to settle his debt. Perhaps he had some kind of windfall. Neither of these explanations seems likely, however, simply because cotton prices did not show any marked improvement nor did cotton lands yield more than what was average year-in and year-out. Something else must have happened that broke the pattern. The next year Rice also disappeared from the records, and it is possible that the seventy-seven-year-old widower moved on or finally died, having worked countless years in the cotton fields of Mississippi with little to show for it in the end.[51]

Whatever the case was with Page and Rice, or the thousands of others like them and their families, their stories make one thing clear. The only hope for the typical sharecropper required breaking the debt cycle with the local merchant suppliers. This generally could only happen through some windfall, the gain of landownership, and fiscal restraint in combination with self-sufficiency in food production. Perhaps this is what happened in the cases of the more fortunate blacks who did manage to become landowners in the Natchez District. All that is certain is that Rice must have been a diligent and hard-working person to survive all those years of debt until he somehow broke the cycle. What the thousands of mortgage records show, however, is that most croppers struggled in diverse ways to survive in a difficult and unforgiving system.[52]

There nonetheless also are cases of black cropper success—those who were able to use the credit system to their advantage and to succeed in farming—among the land deeds and chattel mortgage records involving the Natchez merchants. In 1872, for example, the Natchez firm of Fleming & Baldwin Co. leased the 450-acre Grafton plantation north of Natchez for $500 to the McGrew family, a group of two brothers and their sons who had apparently emerged from slavery somewhere across the river in Louisiana. The McGrews worked as a squad with a couple of other cropper families and ran Grafton with success and made a good crop in 1872. The following January Fleming & Baldwin were having financial trouble of their own and offered to sell Grafton to the McGrews. The fifty-seven-year-old patriarch of the clan, Simon McGrew, took Fleming & Baldwin up on its offer and in probably a cash combination among the entire family bought Grafton from the Natchez merchants for $3,000 cash. Thus began a long-running and apparently successful family cotton-farming business on Grafton run by the McGrews that stretched into the twentieth century. The McGrews did business with Natchez plantation supply merchant and feisty Irishman George T. Payne until his death in 1892, taking modest advances in supplies on crop liens for sixteen years and on trust deeds for two, but always paying their balances. They also ran for many years their own plantation store on Grafton, supplying their own share-tenants on the place. After Payne died, they switched their business to A. F. Jacobs & Bros. and Adolf Jacobs & Co., recording small advances until 1893, when they apparently quit taking advances altogether and began operating on cash, requiring their many cropper tenants to get their own mercantile accounts. Thus the McGrews shifted their focus to that of planters, making their living on the rents collected on Grafton from the croppers there. In 1900 the now eighty-five-year-old Simon McGrew still presided over Grafton, with as many as ten cropper tenants, having made use of the mercantile crop lien system to his advantage for a quarter-century through careful management, a fair amount of luck, and strong family support.[53]

The postbellum merchants of Natchez, in sum, emerged in a postbellum milieu that favored their particular talents as mercantile entrepreneurs, and they demonstrated an incredible ability to work well with all players in the postwar world of Natchez: established merchant communities, Union soldiers, the vanquished planter elite, and especially the formerly enslaved people in the district. Equally important, they brought important contacts with sources of supply and credit from outside Natchez in ways that allowed them to help in the resuscitation of the cotton economy. They also helped establish a new system of labor in which blacks worked the land as tenants and sharecroppers, while functioning as the linchpin of the economy. Offering credit through crop liens to sharecroppers and planters was an essential part of the merchant's place in the economy, particularly in the early postbellum years. They pulled business in from many different plantations, even regions, an indication that they actively marketed their services throughout the Natchez District. The merchantmen competed vigorously and often vied for contracts on plantations owned and operated by one another. Cotton was still king, and they made the lion's share of their money from growing, buying, selling, processing, and shipping cotton. They acted as local cotton factors, controlling the crops of their debtors, and making a profit from each aspect of its sale. They had a nucleus of freedman and planter customers who stayed with them for years, while others came and went. This indicates either fairness in business and a good reputation, or, more likely, an unerring ability to get sharecroppers and planters in debt and to keep them in debt.

These merchants were more opportunistic than they were racist, but because most aspects of their involvement with African Americans were defined by the standards of profit and loss, they did not function as engines of social justice for the African Americans around them. The freed people well understood that working with men who looked at them from the perspective of the bottom line allowed them some modicum of freedom beyond what they had working for the local white planter class. And there really was no other option for the freedmen and many stressed planters to get the credit they needed to survive and continue farming. In the end, the debtor-creditor nexus reduced a large majority of African Americans to an impoverished caste of agricultural workers, except for a few exceptions where they endured the system through perseverance or luck to achieve success or at least more than survival. None of these merchants seemed to see this as a significant issue of equity and justice; if they did, none did anything about it, and perhaps a well-worn ditty popular with black croppers of the day about their relationship with the furnishing merchants says it all:

> *An ought's an ought*
> *And a figger's a figger*
> *All for the white man*
> *And none for the nigger.*[54]

CHAPTER 4

A New Kind of Planter

IT WAS A SPRING DAY IN JEFFERSON COUNTY ON APRIL 17, 1876, the time of year that filled planters and croppers alike with the anticipation of a successful coming crop year. It was also a stressful time of year, as overly wet weather could flood the fields and make it impossible to tend the young cotton, or a hard late frost or excessive dry weather could stunt its development or kill it altogether. Yet at the many cotton plantations in the countryside surrounding the county seat of Fayette, work was in full motion finishing the season's cotton planting. On the front steps of the Jefferson County courthouse, however, there was activity of a different sort as the local magistrate conducted a sheriff's sale for the collection of defaulted property debts. Debt sales were a common occurrence in cotton country, particularly in 1876 with the nation in a deep depression. Among the men who took the fore that day to auction off lands for unpaid mercantile bills was John R. Bledsoe, a trusted associate and bookkeeper for I. Lowenburg & Co. who often acted as trustee for land trust deeds to secure supply debt to the firm. Bledsoe was empowered to auction to the highest cash bidder a 975-acre portion of the large cotton plantation Galilee, called the McCoy Place, to repay a defaulted trust deed from 1874 in the amount of $3,884 due I. Lowenburg & Co. James and Richard McCoy, the indebted planters who owned Galilee, and Isaac Lowenburg himself were probably among the crowd that day. As Bledsoe called out for bids on the McCoy Place, Lowenburg managed to secure high bid with a $3,500 cash offer, and when Bledsoe struck the property off, Lowenburg secured title to the plantation by paying the amount owed to his own firm—in other words, paying himself back and securing the McCoy Place in the process.[1]

The McCoys likely had seen the outcome of that April's sheriff's sale coming for quite some time. Their troubles with Lowenburg had begun almost three years earlier, when Lowenburg had purchased a tax deed on their 2,800-acre Galilee plantation for a high cash bid of $676.97 at a sheriff's sale in May 1873. Tax deeds were redeemable in Mississippi if the landowners could pay the tax bill within two years (six months in Louisiana), and the landowners could remain on the land until the time period expired. The McCoys apparently approached Lowenburg and worked out an arrangement, because they contracted with I. Lowenburg & Co. to supply their cotton-farming operations on Galilee in 1874 while he held their tax deed. They gave two chattel mortgages to Lowenburg early in that year for supplies in the amounts of $150 and $250, secured by their farming implements, livestock, mules, and all cotton produced. But the McCoys still wanted to pay their back taxes and redeem Galilee, so in August Lowenburg refinanced the entire debt—the $1,874 back taxes, which included the $676.97 Lowenburg paid for the tax deed plus interest, and any additional amount they owed him for supplies or cash advances—as a trust deed in the amount of $3,884 secured by the title on the McCoy Place. Thus in August 1874 Lowenburg received a deed to 975 acres to guarantee promissory notes totaling $3,884 due in payments over three years at 10 percent interest. As part of this same flurry of transactions, the McCoys also mortgaged another 636 acres in Adams County, called the Covington Tract, with Lowenburg for an additional $2,900 trust deed, featuring the same terms of payments over three years at 10 percent interest. The McCoys defaulted on the Covington Tract loan the very next year and lost it to Lowenburg at a sheriff's sale on May 1, 1875, for $1,500. Then they defaulted the following year on the McCoy Place, when John R. Bledsoe seized the property and sold it back to Lowenburg in April 1876 for the same debt of about $3,500. The McCoys remained in the area for years on other plantations, and they would record a similar scenario of debt with Aaron Beekman & Son some twenty years later.[2]

This episode of land ownership and debt between the McCoys and I. Lowenburg & Co. was common in the economic relationships between Natchez merchants and area planters and small landowners. Among the merchant families included in this study, similar situations were played out countless times during the postwar period and well into the twentieth century. But this particular case is emblematic of the complex nature of the land dealings that members of the merchant class conducted as a part of their entrepreneurial and mercantile endeavors, and it contains three elements of debt crucial to merchant land dealings: plantation supply liens on crops, lands mortgaged by trust deed, and tax debt. For Lowenburg's part, he clearly was looking to gain control of the lands of indebted planters for a mere fraction of the lands' worth, but he also had other motivations that address his larger entrepreneurial endeavors. While he sought to control the sale of cotton produced on the plantations in question and to supply the McCoys and their tenant croppers with goods at a markup and premium, he may not have been primarily interested in owning and operating the plantations. He seems to have had intimate knowledge of the future route of the soon-to-be-constructed Natchez, Jackson, & Columbus Railroad, as he was on the board of directors, and probably wanted the McCoy Place as right-of-way for the railroad: barely a year later he deeded land across the place for the railroad's construction. Keeping strategic right-of-way parcels that bordered the line for the railroad, he then sold the McCoy Place for a modest profit a year later to another would-be planter, whom he kept in debt for years through a mortgage on the sale, a recurring supply contract, and the requirement that he handle and ship all the cotton produced for a percentage of the sales. Meanwhile, he acquired additional parcels along the future rail line and constructed his own whistle-stop town, Lowenburg Station, in Jefferson County. There he built a new store to service the surrounding plantations as a new outlet for goods and a means of shipping local cotton. In the three-year interim while his plan came to fruition, he collected cotton produced on these plantations, which may have yielded more than his initial investment in just one year's cotton crop, not to mention all the rents and income on supplies advanced that Lowenburg collected from the McCoys and the sharecroppers who worked the place. He might even have known about the McCoys' tax and debt problems and targeted them for a potential debt sale because of the coming railroad.[3]

Clearly, the Natchez postbellum merchants were indeed a "new kind of planter" who on countless occasions owned, operated, or leased plantations in their own right. But they also were always searching for other means of entrepreneurial endeavor that would complement their plantation holdings and existing businesses or open possibilities for profits in new areas. These businessmen used their mercantile position in the local cotton trade—plantation supplying and cotton buying—to gain a foothold and, later, a major stake in the cotton plantation business in the Natchez District. This became one of the most profitable aspects of their enterprise, and they amassed impressive plantation holdings, some of which they held for years and operated as landowner-merchants, and others that they sold quickly if the price was right and they could make a substantial immediate profit without the trouble of operating the plantations themselves. While the commodification of land was common in parts of the Old South, in the Natchez District the idea of ownership of vast cotton empires seized many men of the antebellum era. However, the statement that "a plantation well stocked with hands, is the *ne plus ultra* of every man's ambition" no longer necessarily held true. Cotton plantations were an instrument of profit, and while the cotton produced was a major source of those profits, collecting rents, supplying croppers, and speculating in lands were often equally lucrative. The merchants also made large sums by extensive residential and commercial land speculation and land-development interests in Natchez, Vidalia, and other Natchez District communities. These merchants moved quickly and deeply into all local land markets, missing few sources of profit related to land acquisition and plantation operations. They were involved in just about everything directly or indirectly related to agrarian enterprise in the district.[4]

A host of favorable conditions existed in the Natchez District during Reconstruction and, indeed, into the twentieth century. These conditions enabled merchants initially to gain a foothold and then to command the local land business scene. In the war's wake, not only was land cheap, but many planters were severely weakened or nearly bankrupt. Furthermore, the new emerging market of freed blacks and the advent of the crop lien system supplying these blacks provided an ample source of income capital to invest in real estate—capital generated largely by selling goods received on credit from the North. Finally, foreclosures on defaulted mortgage and trust-deed debt generated by the plantation supply business ensured a steady built-in source of cotton lands, often acquired at well below market value.[5]

Perhaps most important, the merchants were highly organized and integrated in their varied activities across sectors, from the construction of the Natchez cotton mills and local railways to civic projects such as hospitals and other facilities and local government. As the period progressed, members of competing factions and communities could increasingly be found teaming as partners or working together to achieve similar business interests. But throughout the period, within like groups or communities there was often a strong element of mutual support, particularly in the realm of raising capital for land purchases. In the Jewish merchant community, for example, if a member of their business circle needed funds for a land transaction, he could often go to his peers at the synagogue or the Jewish Ezra Lodge #134 for a short-term loan to complete the purchase. The same also occurred among other groups who had familial, social, and business bonds. Even if a merchant could not raise the necessary capital for a given venture, he often referred the opportunity to another member of his circle. And here lies the nexus of their entrepreneurial and mercantile success: advantageous local economic conditions, a business that generated access to cheap land, and a strong support system underlying their enterprise. Deft engagement in these conditions is what separated these merchants from others in the Natchez District.[6]

Members of the ten mercantile families examined herein recorded well over 1,000 land conveyances, acquisitions, mortgages, and leases from 1865 to 1910 in the Natchez District. These land acquisitions display a remarkable range of varying circumstances: some are straight purchases of land in town or agricultural lands in the country; some are quitclaim deeds and transfers where a debtor simply signed over all interest in a given property to satisfy debt on mortgages, crop liens, or deeds of trust; others were purchases of land in tax or debt foreclosure obtained at a tax, trustee, or sheriff's sale—a major source of undervalued land. While the nature of plantation ownership was fluid and often changed from year to year as the merchants continually acquired, bought, and sold agricultural lands, a cursory count of the lands involved in these transactions reveals that these merchants owned at one time or another during the period 1865–1910 at least thirty major cotton plantations of over 500 acres. The merchants leased many more large properties. Joseph N. Carpenter may have owned the largest single place when he held title to the 3,500-acre Clermont just north of Natchez for several years in the 1870s, while the Lowenburg family probably owned the greatest amount of all types of land, having title to 27,000 acres in all at one time or another. The merchant families also owned well over 100 lesser plantations, smaller parcels and unattached or unnamed tracts of agricultural lands in the district, and these types of lands were acquired and sold with a yearly regularity, often to black croppers striving for property ownership.[7]

The merchant families in Natchez and Vidalia in addition built or owned almost 200 parcels, lots, and structures there and in other district towns. At one time in the 1880s Lowenburg and judge Thomas Reber alone owned 100 separate building lots in their Woodlawn subdivision, while Henry Frank and Lowenburg held many more in their Clifton Heights development. These businessmen were involved in financing or building homes in both projects. The merchant families also operated or acquired at least six steam-driven cotton-ginning facilities or gristmills, two cotton oil manufactories, many more urban or country stores, cotton-shipping depot-warehouses and steamboat landings, and stockyards to handle their constant business in mules, horses, and livestock. Joseph N. Carpenter, John A. Dicks, and George Klapp owned two cotton oil manufacturing firms, a gristmill, and two steam-powered cotton gins during the 1880s and 1890s, in addition to at least four stores and attendant facilities. Natchez merchants also bought vast tracts of unimproved or uncleared forest and swampland to secure right-of-way for railroad construction or for future clearing and planting of cotton. All combined, these merchants controlled at one time or another well over 50,000 acres of land in the Natchez District. But all the merchants in question followed and shared a common "cycle" of entry and involvement in the land business that took advantage of the same local conditions and legal mechanisms to gain control and ownership of land—particularly cotton plantations.[8]

※ ※ ※

ATTENTION CAPITALISTS

We have for sale and lease over 60,000 acres
of both hill and bottom Cotton Lands,
comprising some of the most fertile and best improved Plantations in the South. Also a number
of Residences in and near the city of Natchez,
Miss. Parties wishing to invest, will consult their
interest by applying personally or by letter to
WM. DIX & CO.,
Real Estate Agents, Natchez, Miss.[9]

Before General Robert E. Lee's signature on the surrender at Appomattox Courthouse was dry, the Natchez District marketplace for plantation sales and leases had already exploded. Many members of the planter class, desperate after years of no crop sales and income, reeling from the staggering loss of capital suffered when their slaves were freed, or simply unwilling to embrace the new free labor configuration under watchful Union eyes, made a sweeping exodus to market their cotton lands for lease or sale. Stephen Duncan Jr., the proud and racist son of the largest cotton planter in the South, complained about the "Machiavellian diplomacy" required in dealing with his newly freed black field hands: "Payday was unbearable. I have just paid off the negroes & a more unpleasant, disgusting business I have never attended to." Another planter of a similar ilk cast about for "some Northern man to manage the niggers." The local newspapers were literally inundated with notices placing plantations for sale or lease, while a new breed of would-be Northern planters trolled the countryside in search of land to make quick fortunes on resumed cotton production. At 30 to 40 cents a pound, historically high cotton prices drove the frenzy, and Northerner George G. Klapp secured a lease agreement from nabob Alfred V. Davis on Pittsfield in Concordia Parish. Some years later he would be partners with Natchez merchant Joseph N. Carpenter as J. N. Carpenter & Co., and they would run Pittsfield and operate a plantation store there.[10]

But most Yankee planters were not as fortunate as Klapp, and within two years an armyworm infestation and heavy flooding had ruined two crop years in a row and wiped out most of the Northern speculators, who left en masse back north. That, coupled with the resumed collection of now-high Reconstruction-era property taxes, had created a much different marketplace. The remaining planters-landlords were becoming increasingly desperate as fewer eager new lessees appeared, and, consequently, lease prices plummeted. One cotton factor commented: "Everything is going to the devil here in a hard gallop," as short crops, unpaid tax bills, mortgages owed to creditors from even before the war commenced, or yearly supply bills owed merchants under "vendor's liens" now burdened planters. Soon notices of a different sort appeared in the newspapers. "Sheriff's Sale ... Monday, the 1st day of April, 1867, within the hours prescribed by law," one read, continuing: will "sell to the highest bidder, FOR CASH, at the door of the Courthouse of said county, the following described property (under vendors lien) to wit: all that tract or parcel of land ... containing seven hundred (700) acres, more or less ... B. F. B. Hunter, Sheriff of Adams County."[11] Other notices appeared with plantations for sale seeking outright cash, handled for a percentage of the sale by local merchants like Fleming & Baldwin as agents: "*Plantation for Sale. ...* I OFFER MY PLACE for sale, situated in Franklin County, near Hamburg, consisting of 980 acres.... Possession can be given immediately. Apply to FLEMING & BALDWIN, Natchez, or to F. READ, on the premises."[12]

Perhaps no one was in a better position to step into the breach than the merchants, particularly Fleming & Baldwin. After emerging from the war as Natchez's top supply house, Fleming & Baldwin moved into the land business with a vengeance in hopes of quick and perhaps enduring profits. With capital accumulating from the company's burgeoning plantation supply firm, and financial backing from Buckner & Newman Co. of New Orleans, New York financier David D. Withers, and the local Britton & Koontz Bank, Fleming & Baldwin bet heavily on planting and ran a large group of plantations, which the company leased or owned over a 100-mile radius. The R. G. Dun agent noted in 1866 that Fleming & Baldwin had "Capt in bus 125 to 150 NY, wor. more than double that amount," and the company leased 1,557-acre Loch Leven and 2,002-acre Lochdale forty miles south of Natchez in Wilkinson County, and owned 450-acre Grafton and 550-acre Mount Welcome in Adams County. But the firm was hit hard in 1866 and 1867 with poor crops, and the Dun agent warned that the company "had lost a great deal in the past two years," before it had a spectacular year in 1868 and may have made as much as $70,000 that year on one Wilkinson County plantation alone. In 1869 Fleming & Baldwin gained control of the massive 3,294-acre Locust Hill—thirty miles northwest in Tensas Parish—from an antebellum debt settlement with the nabob Routh family for $17,850 and another $15,000 in cash. It also leased Homestead, Somerset, and Via Mede plantations in Tensas in the early 1870s, adding several thousand more acres to production. But the firm would become perilously overextended soon after, and following Hiram Baldwin's death in 1873, the company went out of business; its demise will be detailed in chapter 6.[13]

But other Natchez merchants were also buying and shipping cotton during the early Reconstruction years and leasing lands on their own account, especially after 1867 when new crop lien laws allowed them to parlay their mercantile ventures into land acquisitions. High cotton prices but scant credit found surviving landowners and Northerners alike leasing lands and planting cotton by borrowing supply advances from local merchants, and several years of poor cotton crops put landowners and renters—already overextended in credit for provisions, seed, tools, animals, and wages—even farther behind. The merchants' plantation supply and cotton-shipping business grew exponentially. The dearth of goods, the lack of credit, and the burgeoning new market of black sharecroppers all fueled the demand. By the 1870s the merchants were poised to begin acquiring land leveraged as security for supply advances or gained in default of loans secured by mortgages, and during the next twenty years an explosion of merchant land ownership occurred.[14]

Essentially, there were four basic mechanisms by which merchants gained control of cotton lands and cotton plantations: debt foreclosure on mortgages or deeds of trust, purchases of cotton lands in tax foreclosure at a sheriff's sale, straight purchases with cash or on credit, or simply securing leases for cotton lands. Foreclosure on debt occurred in one of two ways, representative of the aggressive nature of these entrepreneurs in their business dealings. Chattel mortgages were one avenue, where typically a small planter or farmer would get into supply debt with the merchant for a given year and make a poor crop, or sometimes no crop at all, carry the deficit over into the next year, and experience another bad crop, and the obligation would accumulate into an unmanageable debt that the merchant was no longer willing to carry. The merchant would call in the debt when it got bad enough, and whatever chattels that were mortgaged as collateral in the crop lien agreement would be seized by the sheriff and put up for sale to pay the debt, or held until the debtor was able to pay the obligation with interest, which usually did not happen.[15]

Some small planters and farmers simply signed over their land to satisfy these debts through quitclaim deeds, and the merchants would collect small parcels of land in this fashion, ten acres here, forty acres there, and on occasion a significant plantation. The merchants often encouraged the debtors to get in over their heads by carrying over debt from year to year, maintaining that they were acting in the best interests of their customers by holding over deficits in the hopes of a better year and everyone getting paid. But carried-over debt was a bad sign for all the parties involved, and once the deficit equaled the value of the chattels put up as collateral, the merchant had little reason to continue in this risky situation and would often foreclose. While this legal mechanism was used primarily for smaller transactions, mainly the sharecroppers or small farmers who owned little or no land, merchants did on occasion obtain a significant tract through this method.[16]

While chattel mortgage debt could occasionally be parleyed into land ownership, the most common method and legal device favored by the merchants was the use of land-backed mortgages or "trust deeds." The primary difference between land-backed mortgages and trust deeds lies in the scale of lands involved, and the use of a "trustee" to hold title until the contract was satisfied and paid. Essentially, merchants would contract with the same sort of individuals as in chattel mortgages—generally smaller plantation owners, cash-poor but once prominent planters who had fallen on hard times, and occasionally black landowners, most of whom did not have sufficient lands to warrant this device. The owner would deed cotton lands to a trustee, handpicked by the merchant, who held title in trust to provide collateral for the yearly plantation supply bill or cash loan. The indebted landowner could redeem the deed and title to his land when the cotton crop came in, and he paid the bill. The expense of running a plantation and bringing in a cotton crop required significant capital over the course of the year, and many of these owners, often with little operating capital of their own and frequently in debt already, were willing to "bet it all" on the prospect of a good crop year that could wipe out their debts and leave them with a cash windfall with which they could operate in the coming years.[17]

Things did not always go according to plan, however. Plantation owners typically incurred supply bills and cash loans amounting to thousands of dollars, and one or two bad cotton crop years in succession would be enough to break them financially, as the bills and attendant interest, usually 8 to 10 percent for any unpaid balance on top of goods already marked up as much as 50 percent, piled up to the point of no return. The trustee would then seize the plantation and arrange with the local sheriff for a trustee's sale of the plantation to pay the merchant's outstanding supply bill or loan. At the trustee's sale, usually conducted on the county courthouse steps, the land would be sold to the highest bidder, often the same merchant to whom the bill was owed, meaning that the merchant bought the land at a very low price to pay himself back. Usually, the lien holder was the only one bidding for the property because the assets in question were encumbered with debts that had to be paid off no matter how cheaply the land was obtained in the bidding. This is exactly the scenario played out between the McCoy family in Jefferson County and I. Lowenburg & Co. Thus merchants could take goods received on credit, mark them up as much as 50 percent, sell them to planters, seize their valuable cotton lands when they could not pay, and then buy these lands at low prices to pay themselves back. Often no cash came directly out of the merchant's pocket, except for what was due wholesalers. This mechanism worked time and again as cash-strapped farmers fell into the familiar cycle of debt and lost their plantations to merchants.[18]

During the first years of Reconstruction, however, most Natchez merchants approached the plantation business with more caution than did Fleming & Baldwin. It took time to leverage enough planters to obtain lands through debt. Leasing plantations was the preferred method, and many were available because planters were initially reluctant to part with cotton lands, and leasing provided the opportunity to make a cash windfall on a good crop without the capital outlay for purchase. This scenario would change over time, however, as planters were increasingly cash strapped and merchants gained leverage through supply contract debt. I. Lowenburg & Co. had barely opened its doors in 1864 when partners Lowenburg and Henry Hill leased the abandoned Fletcher plantation in Concordia Parish and Deerpark and Loch Leven in Wilkinson County—the same Loch Leven leased later by Fleming & Baldwin—whose owner, S. Chase, was listed in Union wartime records as "absent" but "loyal." Yankees Lowenburg and Hill had excellent connections with occupation authorities as Union sutlers and were also able to gain valuable permits to ship cotton to New Orleans, a keen advantage while operating their own plantations and handling their own cotton. Lowenburg and Hill continued to lease Fletcher, and in 1868 the R. G. Dun agent noted that they "have engaged since the war in planting . . . [and] made money in planting this year." In 1870 they also gained a five-year lease on Cheripa and Concordia plantations in Concordia Parish from Charlotte Surget for $2,000 per year, and the following spring also teamed with Christian Schwarz to lease the 3,000-acre Morville plantation from Eustace Surget for another five-year term at $3,000 per year. By 1871 the two were running three plantations and an interest in a fourth in the same area of Concordia. Henry Hill lived on one of the plantations and ran a plantation store there, while Lowenburg ran the main store in Natchez, until Hill died of yellow fever in late 1871. Lowenburg then operated Cheripa and Concordia for several years with new a planting partner, George W. Jones. At the same time, he maintained his interest in Morville and later gained title to Fletcher in 1885 through supply debt foreclosure.[19]

But I. Lowenburg & Co. and Fleming & Baldwin were certainly not the only firms involved in leasing. Marx Lemle's plantation supply house worked the plantations Palatine Hill and Lanquedoc on lease terms in the early 1870s, while carrying on many supply contracts with his tenant croppers there. Across the river, Isaac Friedler gained his entrance into the plantation business when he leased Waverly from J. S. Harris in Concordia for $600 in 1875 and $700 in 1876, when he gained a three-year extension at $1,000 per year. Leasing could be profitable, and in 1876, for example, Friedler had sixteen supply accounts with croppers on the place generating $1,408.11 in supply sales, while he collected at least thirty-six 450-pound bales of cotton in rent—worth $1,944 at $.12 a pound—a good return on his $700 investment. Friedler leased for years in Concordia, and a decade later he was still leasing on the large Scotland and St. Genevieve plantations for $2,500 a year. During the same time, J. N. Carpenter & Co. leased Good Hope and the 2,000-acre Pittsfield in the same area. It was not uncommon for a merchant to sublease portions of these lands to others, or to lease out lands they actually owned. Lowenburg and Hill subleased a portion of Cheripa to Concordia merchants Wallace & Scoffield for $800 a year in 1871, and Lowenburg later subleased Fletcher to Michael Phelen for several years during the 1880s. Merchants also leased riverboat landings and store facilities in other communities: Isaac Friedler leased the L'Argent river landing and store-warehouse complex at St. Joseph in Tensas Parish for five years in the 1880s for $3,000. The list goes on, including dozens of such transactions. These merchants consistently made money on leased plantations and often looked at this arrangement as a temporary situation, vigilant for the opportunity to buy.[20]

A few merchants did own plantation lands early on or later purchased plantations to operate on their own account. Aaron Beekman apparently owned 250 acres of cotton lands as early as 1858, because the local R. G. Dun agent commented that year that "I have also learned . . . he owns 250 acres of land w prob 6ny$ . . . [and] that his land is paid for," although existing land deeds show no record of this. Armand Perrault owned plantation lands that he purchased and sold during the war in devalued Confederate currency, and he later sold part of this property at a profit while values were high right after the war. When he bought 682 acres on St. Catherine's Creek north of Natchez in November 1862 for $6,000 in Confederate cash, he turned around two months later and sold the same plantation for $7,000, and then took the proceeds of that sale and nine days later bought another 450-acre tract south of Natchez for $6,000 in Confederate notes. In November 1865, when the land market was at its peak, he sold that 450-acre tract for $3,600 cash and a $1,000 note at 10 percent interest in U.S. currency, about a $1,500 profit when the value differential between Confederate and U.S. money is accounted for. But in December 1866 Charles Rowley deeded back the original 682 acres sold him by Perrault in 1863 for $7,000 Confederate currency with a new consideration of a $5,000 cash payment in U.S. currency. Speculation had its risks, as Perrault essentially received these lands back at a loss, although it is possible that the $5,000 represents some settlement between the two. Perrault rented smaller parcels of that plantation to croppers for several years afterward, before selling the land in 1875 for $3,000 mortgaged at 10 percent interest over three years maturity.[21]

In the 1870s and 1880s, however, the tempo and scale of land transactions involving the merchants exploded as they now had become more entrenched in the district's plantation supply business, and had more funds to employ and held more plantation owners in debt. I. Lowenburg & Co. gained ownership of the 1,400-acre Clifton in Jefferson County in December 1869 when Lowenburg received title from the major New Orleans cotton-factoring firm Meyer, Weis & Co. Julius Weis was Lowenburg's brother-in-law, and Lowenburg served as his local agent, and he was acting in that capacity on Clifton. He held a series of mortgages and trust deeds on Weis's behalf from planters Orange and Ann Miles, including one contract dated in March 1871 for $3,615.77 and another mortgage that year for a $2,000 credit line. Several months earlier, in May 1870, Joseph N. Carpenter made a straight purchase of the 650-acre Point Place south of Natchez for $4,000, paid with $2,000 cash up front and two yearly payments of $1,000 at 8 percent interest. The Carpenters would operate Point Place well into the twentieth century with Joseph's brother Allen living on and running the plantation, while the croppers there were supplied by J. N. Carpenter & Co., which also handled all the cotton grown. In another large example, Emma and Rufus Ford of Franklin County, about thirty miles east of Natchez, sold Aaron Beekman & Son the 1,500-acre Kibbeville plantation in October 1882 for $9,000, payable with $1,000 in cash and $8,000 in notes at 8 percent interest over four years. Beekman rented smaller parcels and supplied the croppers on Kibbeville, while he maintained his relationship with Rufus Ford and advanced supplies and cash to operate Ford's Tate plantation through several trust deeds during the 1880s.[22]

One of the largest examples of a mercantile land purchase occurred in 1884 and serves as an example of the close relationship between local merchants and select New Orleans cotton factors, while demonstrating the complex nature of how local merchants used the legal system to their advantage. That year cotton factor Julius Weis, a major backer of the Jewish business community in the cotton business, sold Isaac Friedler and his business partner, LeGrand Page, the 2,549-acre Forest plantation in Concordia Parish with all its livestock and farming implements—including at least forty-two mules and numerous other livestock—for $42,500 on terms of $10,000 cash paid, with the rest to be paid in ten installments at 8 percent interest. Friedler and Page planned to operate a supply store for sharecroppers at Forest along with the plantation itself, and they obtained a line of credit from Weis for plantation supply goods, promising to ship all cotton from Forest through Weis's cotton factorage firm in New Orleans. For reasons unclear, but possibly related to Page's untimely death, a lien for $371.05 in unpaid taxes was placed on the property in 1885, which Weis paid off at a sheriff's sale in January 1886, receiving in turn a tax deed from Friedler. Weis must have then allowed Friedler to redeem title to the property by assuming the tax payment as a loan from Friedler, because between the tax payment in January 1886 and March 1887 Friedler held title to Forest once again under the original terms. But in March 1887 Weis foreclosed on Forest for $9,191 plus the 8 percent interest, the unpaid note for that year by Friedler. He then sold Forest back to Friedler for $25,000, including $14,560 in cash, with the remainder payable in ten notes at 8 percent interest for the remaining balance.[23]

But there was more to this arrangement than is obvious from the legal records. First, Friedler and Weis were long-standing business partners, with the former acting as the latter's agent in land operations and the supply business in Concordia Parish. Friedler obtained supplies on credit from Weis, managed plantation properties owned or leased by Weis or Friedler, and channeled cotton to New Orleans for Weis to handle. This supply business between the two had been going on for years. Viewed in this context, the transaction on the Forest place was a practical way of clearing title to the property after Page's death and was probably the best way to avoid succession problems and related entanglements by letting the property revert back to Weis. And it is likely that the original cash payment to Weis by the partners Friedler and Page came principally from Page, who was now dead. So Friedler allowed Forest to go into tax foreclosure, with Weis paying off the tax lien as a kind of loan to Friedler, which increased his debt to Weis. A year later Friedler defaulted on his mortgage payments to Weis, who then gained legal title to the property, and was thus free to sell it to Friedler, so that the supply and cotton-handling arrangement could begin again. Such legal manipulations enabled merchants to partner in land ownership and the supply business, as well as what resembled the antebellum factorage business, to the mutual advantage of all involved. To get an idea of how much money Forest could produce, a plantation of 2,549 acres in the rich soils of Concordia Parish could be expected to produce over 3,000 bales of cotton at a conservative estimate of 1.5 bales per acre, with half going to croppers and half to Isaac Friedler. The 1,500 450-pound bales of cotton, even at a low $.10 a pound, would yield about $67,500 for Friedler—not including profits he made from supplying the croppers at a 50 percent markup. And Weis would collect a 2.5 percent commission totaling $16,875 for just selling the cotton in New Orleans, plus the interest and profits made from the plantation sale and the supplies he furnished. Thus Weis operated as landowner, mortgage holder, source of supply goods, and cotton factor as well, all in cooperation with his old friend Friedler, who was also technically a landowner.[24]

While leases and purchases were a significant part of merchant land acquisitions, the vast majority arose from debt. In many cases merchants simply purchased lands sold at sheriff's sales for unpaid taxes, much like the tax purchase involved in the saga of debt between Isaac Lowenburg and the McCoy family in Jefferson County. Large landowners in all areas of the district were stressed by high taxes from a number of sources. In low-lying Concordia Parish, for example, taxes were especially high as planters were subject to Louisiana state taxes, local Concordia Parish taxes, and levee taxes for upkeep of the abundant local levees. Failure to pay taxes in the two decades following the Civil War was common, and one source indicates that at least 150 district planters lost some or all of their lands to tax sale by 1875. Natchez merchants were often on the lookout for undervalued property through this means, and hundreds of these conveyances appear in district land deed books during Reconstruction, and after, into the twentieth century. A large majority represented small farms of less than 100 acres operated by families who got behind after a bad crop year, but frequently larger plantations or tracts of land appeared at tax sale and caught the attention of merchants looking for a bargain. The merchants often sold the title to lands obtained in tax sale for a quick profit, particularly lands in tax foreclosure that were partially or completely unimproved. This also occurred when owners were likely to redeem their delinquent tax deeds by making payment of overdue taxes and could also pay the holder of the deed for his expenses and interest on that sum as a penalty.[25]

Concordia Parish by far offers the most examples of significant lands sold at tax sales. In November 1872 Isaac Lowenburg bought 1,737 acres adjacent to the Red River in Concordia Parish for $650 cash at a sheriff's sale in Vidalia, and followed that purchase with another of 1,362 acres at the same venue in June the following year—all remnants of the huge estate left by antebellum planter Levin R. Marshall and lost by his cash-strapped heirs—for a paltry $.30 an acre. Three years later, in 1875, Lowenburg found another excellent opportunity in Vidalia when he bought the 2,570-acre Tekoa plantation in Concordia at another sale for $1,250 cash to pay back taxes. Lowenburg operated Tekoa for four years, renting and supplying croppers as well as leasing a portion to George W. Jones for cotton, before he sold the place to his brother-in-law Julius Weis for $5,000 cash in 1880. Lowenburg was highly adept at identifying and procuring lands in tax sale, and Concordia Parish was one of his favorite operating grounds. On another occasion, while involved in a new venture, to construct the Natchez, Red River & Texas Railroad with leading merchants Henry Frank, Isaac Friedler, and S. E. Rumble, Lowenburg sought a vast tract of unimproved land for railroad right-of-way and acquired 6,434 acres in a single tax sale for $277 in Vidalia on May 22, 1882. Lowenburg was secretary on the railroad's board of directors, and he was compensated with 14,000 shares in company stock for his efforts.[26]

But tax sales occurred throughout the district, and in addition to buying the McCoy Place for taxes in 1873, Lowenburg received a state tax deed on the large Stampley Place (800 acres) in April 1877 in a favorable ruling from the state auditor of public accounts for $220.07. Much like the McCoys, members of the Stampley family were in debt to I. Lowenburg & Co. on several occasions for supply debt as well. In one of the largest cases to occur close to Natchez, in Adams County, and well past the flurry of postwar tax sales, State Auditor W. W. Stone sold a tax deed to the 978-acre Rowandale to S. & A. Jacobs Co. for $1,280 cash in November 1889. As in the case of many other large landowners in tax debt trouble, James H. Rowan negotiated a settlement with S. & A. Jacobs by financing the tax debt and combining it with a supply contract with S. & A. Jacobs for his Rowandale plantation and 718-acre Bayridge plantation in a trust deed for $3,300 two months later. Since tax deeds were redeemable, the merchant's focus often was not to gain outright ownership, but rather to force the owner into accepting an accommodation to continue planting. This same sort of scenario was played out many times by Natchez merchants, who purchased tax deeds to supplement their claims on lands already encumbered by supply debt, possibly even targeting financially weak individuals and forcing them into interest-bearing supply contracts, because the merchant held significant leverage with tax title to their lands.[27]

By far the most common way for the merchants to gain cotton lands was through foreclosure on large mortgage or trust deed debt generated by supply accounts and agricultural loans. Examples of this device in action are common throughout the period and account for at least half of the plantation lands to which merchants acquired title. Often played out over a series of years and marked by escalating accumulated debt for supply accounts and loans, the primary goal of the merchant was not necessarily to gain ownership, but rather to control the cotton and perpetuate interest-bearing accounts based on marked-up goods. In the case of the 640-acre Bitterwood plantation in Wilkinson County, one of the first plantations acquired by Aaron Beekman, the merchant received a trust deed as collateral for supplies in 1871 from owners William and Sina Hastings. The plantation was located thirty miles south of Beekman's store in Natchez, at least a hard day's wagon ride. This supply relationship between the Hastingses and Beekman continued throughout the 1870s and into the early 1880s, with at least four deeds of trust recorded during this period for varying amounts owed each year, until it became a substantial debt. An 1878 deed indicates that William Hastings was in debt for $463.05 from the previous year at 10 percent interest, and he borrowed a further $150 in supplies for that year. This cycle of debt continued until 1882, when the debt became unmanageable, and the trustee William Hewitt seized the property for sale, and the Hastingses were forced to sign over Bitterwood with a deed of conveyance for a $1,100 supply debt. After years of teetering on the economic brink, the Hastingses finally toppled, and Beekman now had 640 acres of prime Wilkinson County cotton land—after collecting thousands of dollars over this period in supply bills and interest—all gathered at some distance from Natchez with little cash expended for the purchase.[28]

In another example of trust deed debt that created a very large plantation acquisition, Orange and Ann Miles executed several trust deeds and mortgages with Isaac Lowenburg and factor Julius Weis during the period 1871–1873, for a total of $10,615.77. These were to operate their 812-acre

Blue Ridge and 1,200-acre Clifton plantations in Jefferson County. Like many other large planters at that time they apparently were cash poor, and they got behind on several occasions but were able to pay off their notes and keep their land. In fact, they became friendly with Lowenburg and his family, and he may have assisted them in securing their own cotton depot on the Natchez, Jackson & Columbus Railroad. The Mileses recorded no further debt with Lowenburg, but in July 1885 they secured a trust deed with Perrault & Co. for $2,091.73, with Blue Ridge and Clifton as well as the 316-acre White Hall and the 900-acre Emerald Mound as collateral. The debt came due in January 1886 with 10 percent interest, but they could not repay the note, and later that year Orange Miles died, leaving the debt with his wife, Ann. Perrault & Co. foreclosed on the trust deed sometime that year, because on February 21, 1887, Perrault's trustee, Fred Maher, offered the properties for sale at a sheriff's sale in Fayette. As often happened, the Perraults secured the high bid with a $1,800 cash offer to pay back the debt owed them. Thus, for an investment of $2,091.73 initially loaned in supplies or cash, and an additional $1,800 cash payment, the Perraults secured four plantations with 3,228 total acres for a total of $3,819.73. Ann Miles apparently let the land go rather than attempt to work out an arrangement to repay the debt because she never appeared in further records with the Perraults, who were already leasing a 95-acre portion of White Hall to a cropper only one week later. The new owners sold small portions of this land and leased the remainder to croppers or small farmers, particularly at Emerald Mound, where they recorded at least twenty-seven supply accounts between 1887 and 1902 with nine separate lessees. In 1903 Vincent Perrault, of Perrault & Maher Co., bought out his four other brothers to control these plantations by borrowing $33,000 at 7 percent interest from the First Natchez Bank, operating them before selling Clifton in 1907 for $7,000 cash—perhaps in debt himself.[29]

There are many examples of supply debt driving land acquisitions. Isaac Friedler bought the D'Armond plantation at a sheriff's sale in Vidalia on April 9, 1877, for a cash bid of $533 for a debt seizure. Later that year he leased it to William Majors for one bale of cotton per 10 acres and a supply contract. In December 1875 Marx Lemle received the 2,280-acre Wade's Woodyard in Adams County from Clarence J. Wade for a $1,000 cash payment and forgiveness of at least $750 in supply debt. Lemle rented to croppers and issued a number of supply contracts on Wade's Woodyard until his death in 1883. Black politician John R. Lynch—who served several terms in the U.S. House of Representatives representing Mississippi during the 1870s and 1880s—lost his 220-acre interest in Providence plus another 192 acres to Adolf Jacobs & Son for a $1,005 cash payment and "assumption of debt" in December 1904, after taking out two trust deeds with the company for $4,120 in the mid-1890s. Ann E. Abbott bought 42 acres of Deerpark at a sheriff's sale May 1891 for $195 cash. The sale was occasioned by a $578.87 judgment against William Davis. She later received 75 acres of Spokane plantation and 175 acres of Clifford plantation from planter Calvin S. Bennett in February 1892 to resolve a bad trust deed debt of $1,052.84 from a supply advance given in 1888. This type of transaction was the dominant means by which the Natchez merchants gained cotton lands from the 1870s right up to the turn of the century.[30]

By the 1890s and into the first decade of the twentieth century the nature of the cotton business was changing, however, as more local banks came into existence, and they and other national or even international lending institutions began to compete for supply debt, reducing the mercantile hold on the agricultural lending business. The First Natchez Bank, the People's Bank, the Bank of Vidalia, and the Safe Deposit Trust Co. were all incorporated locally—and all with members of mercantile families in key positions—between 1889 and 1903, while both domestic and foreign capital flooded the marketplace, including that of the American Mortgage Bank of Scotland and De Nederlandsche Amerikaanishe Land Maatschappy (The Dutch-American Land Co.). Also sons now controlled the mercantile houses that their fathers had built and were highly influenced by new Gilded Age business configurations, particularly the publicly or privately held corporation. Consolidation of plantation lands under the aegis of a land company became the new wave of plantation ownership as land companies sprang up throughout the district. Merchant families still held some plantation lands on their own account in the first years of the twentieth century, but this new trend would come to dominate local large plantation agriculture. As a result, more and more of merchant-class lands and capital found their way into land companies formed by a new generation who were more modern businessmen than nineteenth-century merchants.[31]

For example, in 1899 Simon Lowenburg and Emanuel Samuels of I. Lowenburg & Co. lent $20,000 at 8 percent interest to Wecama Planting Company LTD in Concordia for the operation of Wecama, Pittsfield, and Windermere plantations. With at least 5,600 acres in production, they must have thought it a good business, because in 1906 they formed their own public corporation, Dunbarton Planting Company LTD. Capitalized at 1,500 shares valued at $100 each, Lowenburg and Samuels owned 140 shares, valued at $14,000, invested to operate Dunbarton and Lowenburg's long-held Fletcher in Concordia. Joseph J. Friedler; his father, Isaac; and Sam Geisenberger, armed with their accumulated capital and plantation lands, incorporated Concordia Planting Company LTD in January 1903, capitalized with $100,000 divided into $100 shares. Joseph and Isaac Friedler sold their 1,236-acre Tacony in Concordia to the corporation that same year for $25,000—$18,000 cash plus notes for $7,000—pulling their money out of Tacony while still maintaining control of the land by their position on the board of directors and their part ownership by their shares in the company. Even the seemingly unrelated-sounding Natchez Investment & Insurance Agency, formed in part by second-generation traders A. C. Jacobs, Simon Lowenburg, and Sam Geisenberger in 1906, actually was created to "handle and dispose of real estate and rent property."[32]

But did these changes in land ownership configurations and the way plantations were held and profited from really alter the core business that began the long merchant-class participation in cotton lands many years earlier during the Reconstruction era? Perhaps the best answer can be found in the goals for operating a mercantile business included in the charter papers Lowenburg and Samuels filed when they incorporated I. Lowenburg & Co. in 1913:

> The purpose for which it is created: is to do a general mercantile business, to buy and sell at wholesale or retail all manner of goods, wares, and merchandise and buy and sell cotton; may borrow money and secure payment of the same by mortgages or otherwise, and may lend money and take security therefore in like manner; may receive money on deposit; may acquire, buy and hold real estate in the man-years [sic; manner] before the civil war authorized by law; may sell, rent, or lease real estate, and may buy all manner of personal property and sell the same and do all things necessary to conducting of a general mercantile business.[33]

Thus the involvement of the postwar mercantile class in cotton lands was almost always related to or an outgrowth of their core business interests in the plantation supply business, or in the buying and selling of cotton.

Plantation ownership was not the primary goal in itself, as in the antebellum era. Rather than a way of life and a residence, plantations had become transactional vehicles for mercantile profit. The merchants sought to control the land to facilitate their business in offering supply accounts to croppers, the collection of rents, the handling and sale of cotton for a profit, and, when advantageous, the speculation in these lands for financial gain.

※ ※ ※

There were other ways to speculate and collect rents as well, perhaps right next door to a merchant's thriving store: "For Rent. A desirable residence situated On Silver street Under-the-hill, containing four rooms, hall, kitchen, &c. . . . Apply to A. Beekman, 108 Franklin St."[34] Aaron Beekman bought Magnolia House listed for rent above, in March 1862, for $1,500 cash in Confederate currency, probably a good value for a sizable house in which his growing young family could live. On the east side of Silver Street, it was one of his initial land purchases in Natchez and was next door to his first storefront under-the-hill, until he later moved his mercantile operation to the Natchez Cotton Square. In fact, he and his family may have been fleeing this house when his daughter Rosalie was killed during the Union shelling of 1863. But as time progressed the Beekmans purchased other properties in Natchez—some in which to live or work, but many others to rent, lease, or sell for a profit. This activity is representative of the second major aspect of postwar mercantile land involvement: the ownership and speculation in urban property. Magnolia House was assessed by the county in 1875 as being worth $2,250, about a threefold increase in value from just twelve years earlier, with the value of Confederate currency accounted for, and the Beekmans rented out this home for forty years, collecting a substantial profit. Over time, too, Beekman accumulated property steadily; on the 1875 assessment Beekman was taxed for three properties in the city worth $9,650. Several years later, in the 1883 assessment, it had grown to six properties worth $11,750, and by the 1886 assessment he had increased that number to ten properties worth about $16,000.[35]

As important as the buying, selling, and leasing of cotton plantations was to the business of the postwar Natchez merchant class, it formed only one of the two vital components of their land acquisition and ownership activities. The merchants became deeply involved in all forms of urban property acquisition and speculation in several Natchez District municipalities during the postbellum period, and this activity was at times as important to their growing financial concerns as their agriculture-related business. Sometimes this activity was tied to their core mercantile concerns, such as the acquisition and construction of their stores, warehouses, and livestock-holding or cotton-ginning facilities, as well as commercial lending to other merchants for their stores. In other cases it was related to a different form of entrepreneurial endeavor: the buying, selling, and construction of residential and commercial facilities, which represents the first local examples of the modern land-development business. Natchez lots and parcels of municipal land were bought cheaply and resold for a profit, or incorporated into expanding commercial complexes, and tracts offered for unpaid tax and debt sales often were purchased below market value. Acquisition of Natchez property was highly speculative in the short run, but brought good profits fairly easily in the long run, although some sales turned quick profits. The merchants of this study dealt in a host of residential properties and purchased or built fine homes and mansions for themselves and their families, while always vigilant for opportunities to profit from homes and residential lands both large and small. They also made commercial land transactions for profit or to help facilitate municipal improvements. Their activities during the last half of the nineteenth century changed the face of Natchez, and many examples of their work endure today.[36]

Aside from Fleming & Baldwin, who were well established and owned substantial homes and store facilities during the 1850s, most other postwar merchants followed basically the same business cycle on their way to success in the local urban land business, although the circumstances and time frame varied. In this progression, usually a merchant would first purchase land in town for cash or a mortgage, often his first store building or residence, and then progressively add land purchases as his postwar mercantile businesses grew. Several of the postwar merchants bought their first properties before or during the war. The Carpenter family, for example, bought and sold occasional properties in the course of their contracting business in the antebellum years before opening their first commercial cotton-ginning and cotton-factoring business in 1864 on land they had purchased in the late 1840s. Armand Perrault bought his first storefront and lots on Franklin Street in 1856 for $2,000 cash and a $3,000 mortgage due over three years at 8 percent interest. He then rented the building to his former clerk, George T. Payne, for a few years after he purchased the business in 1858, before Payne bought his own facilities on Pine Street with $8,000 in Confederate cash in March 1863. After the war, Perrault & Co. opened a plantation supply store in the firm's original building and operated there for decades. German storekeepers Aaron Beekman and Marx Lemle became American landowners for the first time within a month of each other in 1858, buying portions of antebellum merchant Peter Little's estate on Silver Street in the under-the-hill area for storefronts. Both of these men had been in business there for well over a decade as renters before they amassed enough capital to purchase commercial buildings of their own. Like George T. Payne, Beekman and Lemle also managed to buy property in 1862 and 1863 with Confederate cash—smart purchases in devalued currency that appreciated significantly after the war in the much more valuable U.S. currency.[37]

During the first decade after the war, a few merchants made ventures into land speculation, while many others purchased their store facilities and homes. Lemle bought new store facilities on Commerce Street for $6,000 in 1866, while Beekman bought a storefront and two lots in Vidalia on Concordia Avenue for $450 the same year. Beekman turned around and rented the store to fellow Jewish merchant Jacob Lorie for $400 a year, nearly recouping his investment in the first year, and he rented out this property for years. Union sutler Isaac Lowenburg followed soon with help from his new family, receiving his first store building in January 1866 from his father-in-law, John Mayer, for a $2,500 mortgage with no down payment, probably representative of Mayer helping his son-in-law's family "get a start" in postwar Natchez. The Lowenburgs lived for several years in a house owned by the Mayers as well, presumably on favorable terms, before buying a sizable home in July 1873. In one of the first postwar examples of mercantile home building and "mansion" ownership, George T. Payne was doing well enough to construct his own substantial home: the land deed boasted of "his new mansion recently finished" on Main Street in 1873, while it was really more a fine townhome.[38]

Meanwhile, in related commercial lending, in 1869 I. Lowenburg & Co. issued credit lines for merchandise advances totaling $5,000 at 8 percent interest plus 2 percent for cash advances to Michael Mack and James W. Coleman, for them to open their own stores in Vidalia. Lowenburg secured payment with mortgages on their land in Vidalia, a common practice among district merchants that occasionally yielded land and store facilities through debt foreclosure if these businesses failed. Isaac Friedler bought his first store in Vidalia from the same James Coleman in January 1871, then sold it for $1,200 cash to pay the mortgage Coleman owed Lowenburg. Other late-coming members of the merchant community who did not open businesses until after the war, like the Jacobs brothers and Wolfe Geisenberger, took a little longer to secure their own homes or store facilities. Although they did not make any urban land purchases until the mid-1870s, we know from other records that they were in business operating out of rented buildings. Regardless, the capital they gathered was soon also used in a flurry of land acquisition and speculation.[39]

Many of the same factors that led to an explosion of mercantile plantation ownership in the 1870s and 1880s fed the buying and selling of urban lands. Flush with a decade of profits derived from trading with both planters and croppers in the plantation supply and cotton-handling business, and able to access lines of credit from their merchandise wholesale suppliers and in turn mortgage their stocks and stores, or by approaching their closely allied cotton-factoring firms, like Meyer, Weis & Co. and S. B. Buckner & Co., many members of the Natchez merchant class now had significant capital to invest in real estate. Often, as in the case of their agricultural land dealings, opportunity came in the form of undervalued property, cash-strapped landowners, or the occasional sheriff's sale for taxes or debt. Considerable land in town was owned by the same planter class experiencing trouble retaining their agricultural lands but also by other entrepreneurial individuals who had got caught up in the boom-and-bust cycle of the 1860s and 1870s—people who had either failed to make a profit in the new marketplace or had bought land high in the 1860s and suffered in the severe economic downturn of the mid-1870s. As such, mercantile businessmen bought and sold properties with frequency but also held properties as investments if they had promise as rentals or as speculations with an eye toward future sales in a better marketplace, which is exactly what happened in the 1880s. These same conditions also made it an ideal time for mercantile firms to expand their operations and mercantile facilities, invest in new entrepreneurial endeavors, or purchase fine homes.[40]

Some merchants were simply looking for profits in a speculative form. Marx Lemle, for example, had purchased a lot on Broadway Street on the bluff right before the war, for $450 cash, and turned around and sold it in February 1870 for $1,200. After he had purchased a new store on Franklin

Street, Lemle also took his first store building and Silver Street property under-the- hill, purchased in 1858 for $1,800, and sold it to fellow Jewish merchants Joseph and Matilda Frank for $4,500 in April 1875. As part of the same transaction, Wolfe Geisenberger bought the Franks' old store property on Commerce Street, which he sold later in 1884 for a $1,000 profit. Across the river in Vidalia, in 1874 Isaac Lowenburg bought a one-third interest in four lots on Front Street at a sheriff's sale for $600 cash and then purchased the remaining interest a few months later for $638, before selling the lots for $1,600 cash fourteen months later. A year later he bought two lots on Concordia Avenue for $1,500 cash and sold them six months later for $2,000, being paid $500 in cash and two notes of $750 at 8 percent interest. Vidalia merchant Isaac Friedler proved to be very good at this type of speculation as well and bought two lots on Vernon Street separately in 1872 and 1873 for $125 and $200, respectively; he combined the two, and then turned around and sold them later for $2,000. On another occasion, in 1882 he paid Dr. Robert Carter and his wife, Pauline, $150 cash for two lots on Concordia Avenue, which he later sold for an $800 mortgage at 8 percent interest. The Carters were frequent debtors to Friedler through annual plantation supply bills on their River and Lake Place cotton plantations, and these transactions might have been in partial satisfaction of their debt. R. G. Dun noted in 1874 that Friedler "Owns his own store house + dwelling . . . wor. 5NY," and he remained heavily involved in Vidalia land speculation. Concordia records indicate that he recorded almost twenty-five purchase-sale transactions by the turn of the century.[41]

There were a host of transactions for other purposes as well, particularly business-oriented expansion and development that drove the local economy. In 1881 Isaac Lowenburg bought a one-acre facility that included a steam-driven cotton gin in Vidalia. He paid $1,600 at a sheriff's sale. The gin was to process the cotton gained from his cotton-handling accounts in Concordia Parish. Aaron Beekman purchased a sizable livery stable facility and building on Franklin Street for $1,350 and then leased it in 1883, on an initial five-year agreement, to the livery firm Alexander Eltringham & Co., which occupied the property for at least a decade. In 1882 the merchants-businessmen Joseph N. Carpenter and John A. Dicks of Carpenter, Dicks & Co.—a cottonseed oil manufacturing firm—combined with Joseph's father, Nathaniel, to purchase, for $2,500, several large lots near their firm and the newly constructed Natchez Cotton Mills. The men then sold the lots to their new firm, the Adams Manufacturing Co., for $4,000. In these cases the lands never really changed hands but simply went to a new use, in the process generating a paper profit of $1,500. The Carpenters, John A. Dicks, and other partners, including Northerner George G. Klapp, bought several more lots in this same vicinity during the 1880s to add to their growing mercantile and manufacturing complex, which now included N. L. Carpenter & Son (cotton gin–grist mill and cotton factorage); J. N. Carpenter & Co. (cotton factorage and plantation supply); Carpenter, Dicks & Co. (the Lee Oil Works); and Adams Manufacturing Co. (ice, soap, cotton-batting, and cottonseed oil factories). By this time, too, Joseph N. Carpenter was becoming wealthy enough from these various business concerns to buy the grand home Dunleith for $22,000. It was perhaps the finest antebellum mansion with expansive grounds in Natchez.[42]

About this same time, judge Thomas Reber and Isaac Lowenburg made a purchase that would change the face of Natchez and would begin a local process that marked the approaching modern era. On June 2, 1882, they bought a multiacre tract, just north of downtown, from Citizens Bank of Louisiana, paying $1,110. A few days later the *Natchez Democrat* noted:

> Within the past days a syndicate of Natchez capitalists have effected the purchase of the "Woodlawn" place, on the northern suburbs of the city, which are to be laid out in lots, to be sold at reasonable prices. . . . It will be laid out in about one hundred lots, with broad streets and avenues, and those lots not disposed of will be built upon by the syndicate. . . . The gentlemen who have made the purchase will at once begin the laying out of the lots, designating the streets, beautifying the tract, fencing it in &c. Their object, as far as we can learn, is to furnish cheap building lots for persons of small means, thus enabling the poorer classes of our people to secure homes. As soon as matters in connection with this enterprise shall have been put in practical shape it will be fully announced in our paper.[43]

Completely a first of its kind, and clearly oriented toward the growing class of both white and African American wage earners working for local enterprises like the Natchez Cotton Mills, or perhaps even one of the Carpenter family's manufacturing concerns, this project promised to create quite a local stir. The tension may have been palpable during the weeks following the notice as word made its local rounds, but as promised, on July 4, 1882—Independence Day—an advertisement was splashed across the pages of the *Natchez Democrat*:

Better Than Gold!
A HOME

Within Six Blocks of the Business Centre of Natchez.
SURROUNDED BY THE MOST ELEGANT PRIVATE RESIDENCES
On and Near Fashionable Thoroughfares

Having recently acquired by purchase the property known as Woodlawn, we are offering for sale the cheapest, the most desirable and finest unimproved lots in Natchez, at a price below their actual value. This is

The Opportunity of a Life-Time.

Remember this offering is limited and those wishing a cheap home must apply soon. A plat of the property may be seen at the store of I. Lowenburg & Co., 79 Franklin street, where pur-chasers can get full information.

LOWENBURG & REBER.[44]

As advertised, through Lowenburg's Natchez store, Lowenburg and Reber began selling lots and houses in the Woodlawn subdivision, primarily to lower-income black and white families. They worked in conjunction with the newly instituted Adams County Building and Loan Association, headed by leading Natchez African American community leader and Adams County circuit clerk Louis J. Winston. It appears, however, that a few more affluent members of the local community also bought lots in Woodlawn themselves as speculations. Among them was planter Kate E. Sojourner. Reber sold out part of his share in the development to Lowenburg in early 1883 for $2,000, intent on constructing a municipal railway. From 1883 to 1887 Lowenburg sold lots and finished houses within the subdivision at considerable profit. In just two examples of sales, between January 12 and February 9, 1883, Lowenburg made six sales on Garden Street ranging in price from $300 to $2,600. In December 1886 he sold a multilot tract in Woodlawn to the Adams County Building and Loan Association for $6,154.36.[45]

The Woodlawn subdivision was emblematic of the quickening pace of development in Natchez that endured through the early twentieth century. The *Natchez Democrat* commented that "there is considerable house-building going on in Natchez, we understand that the demand far exceeds the supply, and the moment the foundation for a new house is laid, applications from renters begin to pour in to the builders. . . . [Landowners] say that there would be many more buildings going up were it not for the scarcity and high prices of building materials." Regardless of building material prices, a boom ensued. Lowenburg had not even finished with Woodlawn before he bought part of the old Clifton plantation, located on the bluffs overlooking the Mississippi River and burned by Union forces in 1863. He got it from fellow merchants Ullman & Laub for $300 cash, and subdivided it into residential lots for the upscale Clifton Heights subdivision. As Natchez's second suburb, it became an enclave of many fine nineteenth-century Victorian homes that are still standing today, and the sales it generated provided income for the Lowenburg family into the twentieth century. Joseph N. Carpenter followed in 1890, when he and his father purchased several acres on Canal Street for $700 and subdivided them into the Carpenter Addition, comprised of forty building lots on the south edge of Natchez. Other local businessmen took notice and joined the rush to develop city lands, with the Arlington Addition, Maple Terrace Addition, and Reed & Brandon subdivisions between 1897 and 1907. The same year that Carpenter began work on his subdivision, he also formed the Natchez Hotel Co. with John A. Dicks to construct a modern five-story steel-frame hotel downtown. Two years later Carpenter also provided a store building and facilities to the newly incorporated Mallery Grocery Co. The first incorporated mercantile firm in Natchez, it quickly became one of the city's largest. Carpenter built the company into a leading grocery firm and served as its chairman until the 1920s.[46]

The mercantile business class provided land or had a hand in countless building ventures during this period. These included municipal projects like the construction of a new hospital; the county jail; a city railway and bluff-side incline; electric street trolley service; city water, sewer, and electric service; ice-producing facilities; and improved harbor and river dock facilities. The merchants also provided land for churches, orphanages, and schools. Isaac Lowenburg deeded land for a small symbolic sum to construct the Windy Hill Baptist Church; Samuel and Vincent Perrault did the same for the Devereux Orphanage Asylum. In perhaps the largest instance of civic benefaction in the city's history, in 1909 the Carpenter family donated multiple lots and $80,000 to construct two large new schools in Natchez. These businessmen were responsible for much of the town's new construction and for most of its outstanding postbellum commercial and residential buildings. Many of these buildings still grace the Natchez downtown area, including the Levy building on Main Street, the Frank building on Franklin Street, the Carpenter schools numbers one and two on Union and Washington Streets, and the Jacobs building and Natchez Institute on Commerce Street.[47]

※ ※ ※

The Mississippi historian David Sansing has noted, "Unlike their prewar predecessors, the new Natchez merchants did not sink their capital in land." This statement is only true in that Natchez postbellum merchants did not sink their capital *in the same way* as their antebellum predecessors. The new postwar market conditions formed by the emergence of free labor, the existence of a troubled land-owning class, commensurate reduced agricultural land values, and new, more modern views of capital and its uses dictated a different approach and mentality about involvement in land ownership. The notion that the cotton plantation was the pinnacle of land ownership in the Natchez District no longer held true. Cotton lands were now largely a means to achieve gain, not only through the control and sale of cotton but also through the sale of goods and supplies on credit at high interest rates to an often near-captive customer base with few other options. While plantation ownership sometimes resulted in lesser but quick profits through the speculation of buying low and selling high, the ownership and retention of vast acres of land in cotton had lost much of its symbolic significance and meaning, as plantations now often functioned as confederations between the landed and the laboring in uneasy fellowships of shared risk but often competing interests. In this way planter dominance gave way to merchant dominance only to see the rise of corporate capitalism in the end, as larger Gilded Age and twentieth-century business configurations came to Natchez. The main chance was not in producing the cotton; it was in controlling and profiting from all of its myriad production and market functions. Another Southern scholar has described the situation thus: "The road to the New South plantation ran through the marketplace."[48]

And it was clearly a natural progression for the merchant class to dominate the urban setting. No other group had such a stake in or desire to build, hold, improve, and control the city environs, the home of the marketplace and those who ran it. In Natchez, the postwar shift included the transfer of urban land from planter class to new bourgeois merchant; the grand mansions formerly held by cotton kings now housed captains of local business and shrewd purveyors of goods and credit. But the process was also a transformation of a marketplace dominated by a planter elite to one inhabited by New South merchants who became landlords by virtue of their mercantile profits. The difference lay in a commitment to mercantile activities first, and merchantmen were surrounded by opportunities that abounded in town for those with a modicum of capital to profit from the development and perpetuation of the world that they created for themselves. The building of a new Natchez was the building of *their* Natchez, and for a time from the 1880s to the first years of the twentieth century their hopes for the future and fervor for the present seemed unbounded. A special advertisement meant to tout the city to potential new residents from the North perhaps best expresses the local merchant classes' enthusiasm for Natchez during the period: "Natchez is on a boom, and has been for several years—not a fictitious boom . . . but a steady natural improvement, caused by the outside world discovering that on the bluffs overlooking the great Mississippi, stands a beautiful city just far enough south for a pleasant home, just high enough to insure health, and surrounded by a fertile country which insures a good living."[49]

CHAPTER 5

Merchant Life and Social Capital

ON THURSDAY, JANUARY 20, 1881, THE OFFICES OF THE DEPUTY clerk of the Ninth District Court in Vidalia, Louisiana, were packed with the Natchez elite. Appearing before prominent attorney and district clerk Phillip Hough that day were a cross section of the leading members of the Natchez District legal, business, and planter classes, assembled as directors to incorporate the new Natchez, Red River, & Texas Railroad Co. (N.R.R. & T.R.R.). They included Concordia District Attorney Hiram Steele; judge, developer, and entrepreneur Thomas Reber; former Confederate general and president of the Natchez, Jackson, & Columbus Railroad William T. Martin; prominent area merchants Isaac Friedler, Samuel Block, Henry Frank, and Isaac Lowenburg; leading Natchez banker George W. Koontz; local lumber mill owner Rufus R. Learned; prominent planters James Surget, H. B. Gaither, and Francis Shields; and local steamship captain L. H. Clapp. All of these men had a keen vested business interest in the project, and their purpose was to lay a railway line that would connect the regional supply center of Natchez-Vidalia with the interior Louisiana parishes and, eventually, with the city of Alexandria and then on to the Sabine River in Texas. This line could produce a significant local economic boost and enable the easy shipment of cotton from the isolated but rich cotton plantations of the interior and facilitate the flow of goods and merchandise in return. Soon these investors' efforts blossomed into a flurry of local activity. Over the following months they acquired the franchise and equipment of a smaller existing line in Concordia Parish, while merchants Isaac Lowenburg and Samuel Block purchased thousands of acres of unimproved lands as right-of-way at tax sales. Initially capitalized at not more than $1.5 million in $100 denominations of shares and bond issues, by late September the N.R.R. & T.R.R. board of directors had increased the amount to a $2.25 million limit and added a host of new major shareholders of at least 100 shares each (a $10,000 investment), including *Natchez Democrat* newspaper owners James Lambert and Louis Botto, leading merchant S. E. Rumble, Natchez mayor Henry C. Griffin, and even New Orleans cotton factor Julius Weis.[1]

Natchez merchants were involved in a host of local and regional railway endeavors in the postwar decades, and as early as 1869 a local railroad committee formed of merchants, bankers, and other business leaders had promoted an "experimental line" connecting the state capital of Jackson with Natchez. By the early 1880s it was completed as the Natchez, Jackson, & Columbus Railroad—giving Natchez its first major rail line, and connecting the area to the American interior and East Coast. It also provided an opportunity for mercantile expansion to I. Lowenburg & Co., which, as detailed in the preceding chapter, constructed a new regional mercantile outlet on the line in Jefferson County. But in a larger sense, merchant interest in connecting Natchez to other towns and regions was imperative for continued business success, and the incorporation of the N.R.R. & T.R.R. in 1881 was emblematic of a developing Gilded Age phenomenon among the emerging Southern business class in Natchez. Railroads often have been portrayed as the first tier of nineteenth-century business modernization. Alfred Chandler Jr. has noted that "rail and telegraph companies were themselves the first modern business enterprises to appear in the United States." Indeed, Natchez had begun the postwar period with no viable rail connections, and while still a vital small-size regional center predicated on its location on the Mississippi River, local business leaders recognized early on that ready access to modern manufacturing, marketing, transportation, and distribution systems was key for the town's economic survival in the new business age. But the involvement of local businessmen in railroads was much more than that; it was the adoption of new ideas, structures, uses of capital, and ways of doing business that tied Natchez to the rest of the nation and united the various factions of the local business community in a rising new social and economic order.[2]

Natchez had clearly been dominated—and its economic growth limited by—an antebellum confederation of planters or planters-merchants in league with coastal factors. This group controlled local commerce, available capital, and, most important, that capital's source, the sale of cotton. The middle-class shopkeepers and businessmen in town largely functioned on the periphery of cotton agriculture, its finance, and its marketing. As such, they were often relegated to a secondary economic role, and significant capital rarely accumulated in the hands of the emerging local middle class. Rather than remain in the local economy, cash flowed through New Orleans and other financial or trade centers. The fundamental shift to a free market economy and the loosening of the landowning elite's grip on agricultural lands provided the opening for merchants not only to prosper but to claim center stage in the immediate postwar years, and the money they made more often stayed in Natchez and was used for local business and municipal development. Nevertheless, the initial business configurations that emerged in Reconstruction were often still structured in the older forms of family-held businesses or frequently short-lived mercantile partnerships. While these types of businesses endured among the Natchez merchants into the twentieth century, the embrace of more modern business forms—hierarchal business structures, the use of managers, even primitive regional attempts at vertical and horizontal integration—marked the fundamental shift in the nature of the local business class, particularly among the emerging new generation of merchant and planter sons who were well educated at leading universities. By the 1890s local businessmen presided over an explosion of newly incorporated business and municipal interests that were often tied to the technological improvements of the day, including local railroad, cotton mill, and manufacturing concerns. Starting a decade earlier, new companies formed to provide for investment and banking, land development, lumber processing, the sale of new agricultural machinery and fertilizer, as well as a host of improvements including electric power, telephones, water and sewer systems, and other modern conveniences and services. While Natchez never reached the level of development seen in leading Southern cities such as Atlanta, the transformation of Natchez by the local mercantile and business class was nonetheless far-reaching. Throughout the postwar era, local business leaders endeavored mightily to emulate the improvements occurring elsewhere, bringing them to Natchez. In this regard, there was a distinct "break" with the old regime, a break supporting the argument of many historians for the "discontinuity" of the New South.[3]

At once the basis and fruit of the transformation in Natchez business culture was another element: the rise of "social capital" among merchants and the entrepreneurial community. This capital expressed itself through various organizations, habits of association, and rising political roles. Family and cultural or religious communities proved crucial to success in mercantile and business endeavors, especially early in the postwar era. But it was only one pillar of the local construct of "families, friends, and firms" that drove and lubricated the Natchez political economy. Networking and the importance of social groups were nothing new in the South or elsewhere for that matter—the planter class had long maintained its local dominance through intermarriage and exclusive group associations. But with the rise of the postwar entrepreneurial bourgeoisie, new forms of networking, group associations, and activities multiplied as trade associations, social clubs, charitable endeavors, and municipal volunteer groups sprang into existence. Particularly important were organizations meant to honor the Confederate past and "lost cause," formed by war veterans and their supporters to bring like-minded individuals together to honor the Southern past. These groups and organizations gave the entrepreneurs of the New South venues to interact and socialize on a personal and business level, to form bonds outside their family or ethnic circle, and to build patronage and financial relationships that spawned new business endeavors and configurations. The groups also helped form the emerging social order as newly successful mercantile and business elites sought out other members of like social standing and circumstance for both social and business interaction. Interestingly, this also included new combinations of "old money" and "new money." The still wealthy remnants of the old monied planter class—and not all planter money and influence were destroyed in the postbellum reconfigurations—increasingly associated with the "parvenus" of the rising entrepreneurial class in the social, business, and political arenas. This was particularly true among the younger postwar generation. The sons of former planter gentry were likely to attend the same universities as the sons of merchants, or to serve as clerks at the local mercantile house or bank alongside an entrepreneur's sons. Many planters' sons established themselves in Natchez as doctors, lawyers, bankers, and businessmen of the new age, in some cases reestablishing the fortunes of their planter families, which had declined in the postwar milieu. This interaction was particularly prevalent in the political arena when monied interests coincided, and goals for civic and economic improvement united Old and New South scions. Thus traditional lines of social and economic separation blurred, as "merchants" and "planters" increasingly became "businessmen" of the New South.[4]

But underneath the sweeping changes lay the mercantile families themselves, and the way they lived in the new age. A strange dichotomy in lifestyle developed. The families were at once dominated by conservative Victorian social mores, thoroughly indoctrinated in "Southern" allegiance and tradition, locked into well-established habits and rhythms of conducting business, and still intimately tied to the land through their active participation in the local cotton business. Yet they also acted as local leading-edge proponents of change in a small but progressive regional center that longed for big city comforts, services, and sophistication. The mercantile families detailed in this study attained a level of affluence in lifestyle that probably would have been unimaginable to them previously, and they attained this affluence in a relatively brief amount of time. Yet the routines of business dominated their time and family relationships, while a mixture of the old and new characterized their activities. For the first postwar generation—partly as a result of their semirural status and close ties to the plantation supply business—traders faced long hours at their stores six or seven days a week in a constant motion of ordering, receiving, stocking, and selling their goods while keeping books and credit files. Yet they also had to find time on their infrequent days off to check on the progress of the year's crop, which was mortgaged to them. Because of this workload, most merchants had partners to share the burden and had young live-in clerks who were learning the trade. They also usually encouraged at least one son to follow in their trade to assume the family business. But things were changing. By the late 1880s the now middle-aged Natchez merchants could place a telephone call to conduct some form of business from a store recently lit by gaslights and, soon after, electricity. Yet they almost certainly still maintained the same large, leather-bound "credit-debit" ledgers, used for decades, and marked their goods in the same cryptic "cash price–credit price" letter codes in use since the antebellum era. All the while, they were sending out business correspondence typed on their new typewriters. Meanwhile, they supplied their homes and families with the latest wares, fashions, and conveniences, and sent their children to the finest schools and took them on regular trips to the North and even Europe, or on annual purchasing trips to New Orleans, Louisville, or Cincinnati. For the sons who followed into the mercantile trade toward the twentieth century, this began to change as they increasingly embraced corporate structures that featured store managers to handle their business while they pursued other entrepreneurial concerns, politics, or additional professions. The world these second-generation Natchez merchantmen inhabited in 1900 little resembled the chaotic Natchez milieu that their fathers found and shaped immediately after the war. Yet for all the technological changes and improvements the new age had brought forth, their lives and businesses in the small town of Natchez were still intimately tied to the whims of King Cotton.[5]

※ ※ ※

It was a crisp winter's morning in Natchez on Tuesday, January 1, 1901, and New Year's Eve celebrations from the night before had wound down as many local residents prepared to go visit friends and family as part of the traditional New Year's Day festivities marking the first day of a new and exciting century. At the fine Victorian home on 300 Pearl Street—the household of successful wholesale and cotton merchant Adolf Jacobs—the day's celebrations and visiting friends were likely a part of the plans, what the local newspaper termed "those of our fashionable people who contemplate making New Year calls." While the Jacobses were Jewish and also observed Rosh Hashanah, the Jewish New Year celebrated in September, they were an integral part of the larger Natchez community and observed all traditional American holidays or their Southern variants. Only days earlier Adolf's eighteen-year-old daughter, Vivian, had hosted a large holiday party, and "a number of young folks spent a delightful evening with Miss Vivian Jacobs at her home." But there was also business to attend to, and if Jacobs's prior habits were any indication, that business was likely attended to forthwith, holiday or not. Sometime that day, the fifty-six-year-old Jacobs and his twenty-four-year-old son and future partner in Adolf Jacobs & Son, Albert C. Jacobs, made their way out, past next-door neighbor and leading dry goods merchant Henry Frank's equally imposing home, and continued on down to their store or their lawyer's office. There they met prominent local attorney and politician Abe H. Geisenberger and Adolf's nephew, Aaron F. Jacobs, of A. F. Jacobs & Bros. Geisenberger, the son of plantation supply merchant Wolfe Geisenberger, was a brother of the owners of three separate local mercantile houses—Geisenberger & Son, Geisenberger Brothers, and Geisenberger & Friedler. He met with the Jacobses that day to attend to several of their agricultural customers and draw up the year's first plantation supply contracts backed by trust deeds, with Geisenberger serving as trustee.[6]

Being New Year's Day, their customers apparently came as a group that day. Neighbors in the same plantation lands south of Natchez, they may have made the trip into town to socialize and visit friends themselves, and also to take care of pressing business needs without a wasted trip. Meeting on a holiday was likely an accommodation to suit the schedule and desires of good customers, but such meetings were never conducted on a religious holiday like Christmas, which, as mainstream Americans, most Natchez Jews celebrated as well. In fact, in over 13,000 chattel mortgage contracts examined in this study, only 14 were concluded on New Year's Day, of which eight were drawn by Adolf Jacobs, who was clearly willing to make allowances to suit his customers. Before the three Jacobses' work was through they had met, negotiated, and signed contracts with four different sets of customers: prominent African American planters Harriet Ligon and her sons, Robert Lee and Isaiah, who obtained a total of $8,568.42 in direct financing and an additional credit line of $2,400 to operate the 1,786 acres that comprised their Duncan Homochitto, Woodland, and Deerpark plantations for 1901; their neighbor and smaller planter Scott Washington, who owned 285 acres of Woodland and received an $800 credit line for the year; and Joseph Hargrave, who owned the 524-acre Ellis Cliffs and secured a $1,358.24 advance. Just for good measure, while they were in the office, the Jacobses also met with George Walker and his wife, African American farmers from north of town who owned 180 acres of "Cotton Fields and Cottage Home" and received a $500 credit line for their cotton planting operation in 1901.[7]

That the Jacobses were willing to conduct their business on a holiday and start the new century on a business footing is indicative of the lifestyle of the hard-charging merchants of Natchez. Mark Twain had referred to the rising New South business class as comprised of "brisk men, energetic of movement and speech: the dollar is their God, and how to get it was their religion." Adolf Jacobs was a soft-spoken family man who taught religious school. But he certainly fit Twain's description in other ways: during the period 1874–1910 he bought, sold, and ran countless plantations and farms and probably recorded more supply contracts than any other merchant in the district. And in 1906 he joined with his son Albert to incorporate a privately owned local bank, the Adolf Jacobs & Son Banking Co. His energy must have been well known, and he demonstrated a penchant for business expediency, consistently recording many of his supply contracts in December and January, earlier than most other merchants; he usually had his yearly lending nearly completed before the cotton was planted in March. This habit is demonstrative of his business style, and his accommodationist character, which allowed cash-hungry farmers to draw their yearly funds a little earlier than most to prepare for their crop year. It was also risky because spring flooding or adverse weather could ruin the year's crop. But make no mistake, he was all business, and if he was willing to lend a little early, he almost never lent late, particularly if his customers spent foolishly and ran out of funds or credit before the crops were brought in and sold. He was one of the first local merchants to write "equally divided" (advances) into his lien contracts to limit monthly credit draws for this reason. He also on occasion required a borrower to agree that "he will not accept nor take any advances in no shape or form from the landlord" if he was worried about a planter-landlord seeking to garner a competing lien on the crop in question by offering additional supplies or advances to his cropper customers.[8]

Most merchants had a distinct style of running their businesses, but all lived an often harrying and complex lifestyle that their trade necessitated. It also dominated their relationships and family life. And while their era brought sweeping changes in technology and new improvements—which the merchant class heartily embraced and indeed invested in—in other ways the basic lifestyle of the furnishing and cotton merchant remained much the same. Merchants faced long hours, meticulous bookkeeping, business trips, riding the fields to check on the progress of mortgaged crops, and a never-ending cycle of store-keeping tasks—all while watching over and training their employees and dealing with customers. Most important, traders had to know when to extend credit and when to hold firm. These myriad responsibilities usually made it necessary to have the support of a shrewd, businesslike partner and a small cadre of devoted younger clerks to a run a successful firm. The business was not for the slothful or faint of heart, but close business practices, in combination with energy, steadiness, shrewdness, understanding, evenhandedness, and a willingness to react quickly to changing circumstances, offered the successful merchants and their families an affluent bourgeois lifestyle full of comforts and privilege. The family was the first pillar of Natchez mercantile life; many business partnerships were formed with sons, brothers-in-law, uncles, or cousins, and the ebb and flows of family life both supported these endeavors and were the prime beneficiaries of their success. Marriage matches often arose from an association with a partner's sister or cousin, and just as often a new business partner came to a mercantile firm after marrying a merchant's sister. These "strong ties" of immediate family relationships form the first tier of building mercantile success and facilitated bonds to larger outside social and economic networks and organizations, the "weak ties" that helped develop a new Gilded Age social and economic order.[9]

Business and family ties existing hand in hand was nothing new, and in fact such combinations of strong and weak ties were already robust in the colonial period and continued into the twentieth century. It was a hallmark of tight-knit immigrant communities but occurred with frequency in the American mercantile community as well. German Jew Aaron Beekman married the sister of his business partner David Moses in the 1840s, while Virginian John Fleming of Fleming & Baldwin married into the local mercantile Stockman family during that same time. Leading postwar hardware purveyor and German John C. Schwartz saw his sister married to his employer, Frederick Crone, in the 1850s, and Schwartz married a cousin of Crone's about the same time. Perhaps no single family had connections to more Natchez mercantile firms than that of the German Jew John Mayer, whose fourteen children entered marriages during the war and shortly thereafter that united the Lowenburg, Frank, Weis, Beekman, Friedler, Roos, Ullman, Jacobs, and Samuels families in an extended confederation that by the turn of the century accounted for roughly one-quarter of all Natchez firms. After the war Nathaniel L. Carpenter partnered with his sons Joseph N. and Allen Delos to form perhaps the most successful Natchez mercantile-manufacturing family, which intermarried with the merchant-lawyer Mellon family. The many Perrault sons not only partnered with their father, Armand, to form Perrault & Co. but also intermarried and ran businesses with the Irish O'Brien and Italian Signaigo families. Even the previously mentioned Jacobs family was intermarried with the Jewish Roos, Scharff, and Frank families. In fact, out of the merchants included in this study, only Irishman George T. Payne developed no family-business associations and never married, but his two unmarried sisters, Lettitia and Marie, lived with him and formed their own small family, albeit quite different from the Natchez mercantile norm.[10]

If the family was important for the formation of partnerships and business associations, it was also usually a part of everyday mercantile life. Most merchants in the small town of Natchez followed a similar daily routine. Almost all lived within a short distance of their stores and often came home for meals with their family during the business day. Isaac Lowenburg's daughter Clara wrote a detailed memoir of the postwar period, and her writing offers a rare glimpse into Natchez mercantile life and routine. By the early 1870s her father had built one of the top wholesale grocery, plantation-furnishing, and cotton-buying mercantile houses in Natchez after starting from nothing as a Union army sutler in 1863. He and his family were becoming increasingly affluent, yet Lowenburg rose at dawn six days a week and made his way to the Natchez "markethouse" to purchase fresh meat and produce for the home and his grocery business. "He always went to market in the morning as many men [merchants] did and sent the full basket home, while he drank his coffee at the good coffee stand, then opened his store, read his mail and came home in time for our big eight o'clock breakfast." The city of Natchez had long maintained the markethouse with stalls for rent to local farmers who brought "meats of all kinds, meal, flour, fish, wild game, poultry, cheese, butter, eggs, suet, lard, tallow, wax, fruits, and vegetables of all kinds." Lowenburg's large breakfast could include "either fried lake fish or brains or liver and grits and some sort of hot bread and eggs. . . . And in the summer hot boiled river shrimp and freshly picked figs, dew berries, cream cheese and coffee." Meals were a very important part of the daily routine, and Lowenburg would probably also return for "dinner" at 2 p.m., the largest meal of the day, which could include "meats and fowl . . . with the gravy and inevitable rice." Merchantmen often worked late, and the evening "supper" might not be a family meal, as the men were often still at their stores until well after dark. But as part of their lifestyle, mercantile families placed a premium on the quality of their meals, and "even in the most precarious of financial moments there was no economy in the kitchen . . . [and] one could never go without good food."[11]

The daily routine at the store, however, began with the merchant and clerks opening the doors well before breakfast, and might not end until twelve or more hours later. Saturday was the biggest day of the week, as croppers and planters came to town from the countryside to draw their weekly supplies, meet and greet, and generally make a day of it. Many merchants had clerks who lived in rooms above or behind the store itself—often cousins or relatives of the family—but it could also be a young black man from a trusted family—and their day started as early as the merchant's did, perhaps earlier. Other traders had sons who shared the daily routine with their merchant fathers and followed them to work. Their pay could range from a modest monthly salary of $25 to perhaps as much as $2 a day, and they worked closely with the merchants on a daily basis. They learned the trade in often friendly and paternal relationships at perhaps "the finest place in the world to acquire a knowledge of business."[12] The responsibilities and duties of a clerk in a Southern store were many, and the hours were long. "Storekeepers expected their clerks to wait on customers, stock shelves, conduct regular inventories, and occasionally assist with the bookkeeping. . . . Clerks worked at least twelve hours a day . . . [and] during rush periods, when the remnants of the previous year's stock had to be sold and the new unpacked, clerks often worked eighteen-hour days." These duties might even include traveling to a competitor's store in a nearby town to purchase a particular item for a valued customer.[13]

In a typical plantation supply house, the items stocked could range from barrels of salt pork and flour to harnesses, trace-chains, plows, or "extra parts belonging to the Eagle Gin Stands," all to be loaded when sold onto wagons hitched out front. The pace of activity was cyclical, and the level of business conducted was directly tied to the status of the cotton crops. In July 1882—the slowest time of the year, before the crops came in and when few farmers had much money—the local newspaper noted, "Though trade is excruciatingly dull at this time, all of our merchants anticipate a big business in the fall." Only two months later, with the crops coming in, the paper trumpeted: "Cotton was rolling into town pretty lively yesterday . . . a big trade is expected today. . . . Judging from the extensive stocks of goods our merchants are receiving, we should think that they are calculating upon a very much larger business the coming season than they have done before for many years. Verily, the boom continues."[14]

For the merchant or his partner, besides supervising the activities mentioned, the day was heavy with bookkeeping, price marking, and negotiating with customers. If a merchant like Lowenburg went through his mail first thing in his business day, he likely found a plethora of business correspondence, advertisements, and bills. Over a couple days in June 1876, Natchez hardware purveyors Schwartz & Stewart paid invoices to "Fred J. Meyers—Covington Wire Works, Covington, Ky. . . . $26.63—Assorted Louvers/Screens," and "Sam'l Cupples & Co.—Manufactures of Woodenware, Cordage, Paper Bags &c.—Established 1851, St. Louis . . . 4 cases Axe Handles—$42.25." Invoices usually included charges for "Package + Drayage" (shipping) and usually were on terms of sixty to ninety days net credit, but often included discounts for immediate payment. Schwartz usually paid his due accounts forthwith by "draft in the Bank of America N.Y." for Northern suppliers or on drafts issued by Canal Bank of New

Orleans for his Southern suppliers in the Crescent City, all drawn on the local Britton & Koontz Bank in Natchez for payment. The same stack of mail could also include solicitations for orders and business by faraway wholesalers. The "Office of Coleman & Bro., No 82 Main St., Louisville, Ky.," wrote to Schwartz: "Dear Sir, We solicit your order for 200 kegs 'Belmont' nails at 2.75 card, factory, 60 days or 2% off for cash—we can fill promptly and at lowest rates of freight + trust to hear from you." The firm "Jones Brothers, Dealers in Cutlery, Hardware, Stoves, Tinware, and Agricultural Implements . . . No. 200 and 202 Main St., Little Rock, Ark." sent word soliciting Schwartz to "Handle our Gins, Feeders & Condensers this season. . . . We will make you prices and terms. . . . Our Dis'ct' (discount) is liberal, our machines excelled by no one and equaled by few if any." By the 1880s mailed advertisements, order cards, and wholesale solicitations could literally overrun a merchant's daily mails. Considerable time was spent filling out orders for merchandise—which required a clairvoyant ability to read the future and order and stock the right goods in the right amounts—or writing letters of complaint about goods that were shipped late, arrived damaged, or were missing parts.[15]

Another huge responsibility was keeping the leather-bound business ledgers and maintaining the pricing system. Regardless of technological improvements, one enduring facet of merchant life was the time-tested system of simple accounting, and Southern merchants needed to know how to keep books for their furnishing businesses. Like most Southern storekeepers, Natchez merchants kept their own versions of "daybooks, journals, ledgers, invoice books, cotton-gin reports, cotton sales books, guano accounts and long strings of cash orders," and it did not matter "whether they used single or double-entry systems, or whether they itemized their sales in their journals and transferred the prices to their ledgers, or observed other rules so long as they could make sense of each year's business." As much as 90 percent of Natchez mercantile business was conducted on credit, making the bookkeeping extremely important. Schwartz & Stewart's account ledger for 1878–1882, for example, listed credit account numbers of both local mercantile and planter accounts in an alphabetized section in the front, including the commercial accounts "William Abbott 149, Aaron Beekman 455, 151, Britton & Koontz 29, N. L. Carpenter & Son 31, 203, Isaac Friedler 429, 127, S. & A. Jacobs 462, 457, Isaac Lowenburg, George T. Payne 371, 158, [and] A. L. Perrault 17, 74, 229." But the firm had large planter accounts as well, like "Daniel F. Ashford

28, 162, James Surget 367, 52, [and] Mrs. Katherine Surget Minor 10, 53." Account numbers would be used in the "Daily Journal," which held daily sales in both cash and credit by account, and below is a small sample of the entries from the same firm on Friday, September 28, 1877:

Acct #			Credit Pur.	Amt.
707	Carpenter, Dicks & Co. Shaw		Do	
	1 Tubular Lantern		1.50	1.50
148	Judge Reber By Cash (payment on acct.)		15.00	15.00
702	Joe K. Stone Self		Do	
	1 Corn Shelling Machine		58.00	58.00
?	K. S. Minor Order		Do	
	2 lbs Shot		.25	
	1 Powder		.50	
	1 Box Caps		.40	1.15
712	Cotton Mills Co.			
	3 Kegs of 8p (nails)	3.15	9.45	
	3 10 (p)	2.90	8.70	
	4 6 (p)	(2.90)	11.60	29.75
713	W. Geisenberger Self		Do	
	1 Keg Duponts #14g Powder		7.00	7.00[16]

The various ledgers and bookkeeping methods were supplemented by an ingenious price-marking system, or "cost mark," which used a letter code to place both "cash" and "credit" prices on merchandise that was immediately recognizable to the merchants and their clerks, but left their customers—who often could not read or write anyway—mystified and unaware of what the real prices were. Soon after the war, John C. Schwartz adopted following code:

H	E	L	P	U	S	G	O	D	F
1	2	3	4	5	6	7	8	9	0

Either Schwartz was deeply religious, had a sense of the dramatic, or had a keen appreciation of irony with the symbolism of his "HELP US GOD F" coding choice—particularly on the heels of the stunning Confederate defeat. He certainly did not seem to need the help of divine intervention as he was one of the most successful merchants in Natchez in the postwar period, but maybe it gave him luck. The way the code functioned, however, was simple. If the minimum cash price of his two-inch Calhoun Plow was $8.50, then he would apply one mark on the plow that read OUF, corresponding with numbers assigned to the letters in the above code. If his credit price was $12.75 (a 50 percent markup), then the code applied to the plow in turn was HEGU. Some merchants might also mark the actual cost of the merchandise to them, in this case we know it was $7.34, or on the plow, GPL. His heirs in business were still using a similar cryptic code for pricing merchandise in the early 1920s.[17]

While a merchant's duties in the store were considerable, he also spent large amounts of time out of the store pursuing his plantation interests, attending property auctions and tax sales, checking on crop progress, and traveling on purchasing or business trips, during which time he left trusted clerks or his partners to run the store—one reason for having family or friends in these positions. Isaac Lowenburg made time to spend with his family by combining these functions with personal time and taking his children along. Lowenburg only took Sundays off and "stayed in bed late," but made a weekly family ritual of checking on crops and visiting his plantation interests that day. His daughter recalled that "every Sunday morning papa had our high carriage 'hitched' up with two fine big dray mules and we went for a long drive in the country. Sim [his son] always sat up high on the driver's seat with the coachman and all the rest of us were stored inside, there was enough room for six or eight." Lowenburg was apparently quite familiar with the croppers on his plantations and saw them often, and his daughter claimed that she witnessed his paternalism with them firsthand: "The Negroes on the plantations honored him and trusted him to take care of them. . . . One of the Negroes in charge of a squad of workers said one year, 'Massa, we was sure better off when we was slaves and had nothing to lose, but on your plantation we know we will be well took care of.'" Clara Lowenburg was clearly biased and romantic about the cropper's views of her father, but several merchant families were known for their paternalism; the Carpenters, Lowenburgs, and Abbotts were often lauded for their "benevolence" and "goodness" and were frequently portrayed, in print at least, as well liked and respected both within the business community and among their less fortunate clients.[18]

One facet of merchant life that all engaged in and likely anticipated was extended business travel. Natchez merchants often traveled to regional cities and even New York on annual purchasing trips or other business-related functions. Early in the era business travel was arduous and was usually carried out only once or twice a year, because "there was no railroad travel and boats and wagon trips took a long time." Most travelers took several daylong steamboat trips to New Orleans, St. Louis, or Louisville, where they could also catch connecting rail lines to other interior cities. But by the early 1880s, with the completion of the Natchez, Jackson, & Columbus Railroad, Natchez now had service to the growing rail hub of Jackson, Mississippi, which made connections to a host of destinations possible. It became a commonplace daily feature in the local newspaper to have small announcements of prominent merchants' and businessmen's comings and goings: "Capt. J. B. O'Brien (coal yard proprietor) expects to get off this evening on a business trip," or "Judge Hiram R. Steele, president of the Natchez, Red River & Texas railroad returned . . . yesterday from a trip to New York." There were even examples of how quick travel had become, as "Mr. Henry Frank, the big dry goods merchant, got home from New York on the train yesterday afternoon. . . . Mr. Frank consumed just sixty-seven hours in making the trip from New York to Natchez, which is pretty good time." Clara Lowenburg, Frank's niece, loved "to get some of the wonderful candy that Uncle Harry (Henry) brought from New York, where he went to buy goods for his wholesale dry goods store." In fact, Clara's father, Isaac Lowenburg, occasionally took his family along on purchasing trips, particularly to visit his brother-in-law, commission merchant, goods wholesaler, and financial benefactor, Julius Weis. Clara described that, on one occasion, "Papa took me and grandma on his annual business trip to New Orleans where he went to make arrangements for handling the cotton plantation products with his commission merchants, Meyer, Weis and Company," and she was impressed to find "Uncle Jule [Julius Weis] had built a . . . magnificent palace, furnished anew with much elegance, real bathrooms and toilets in the bathroom instead of at the end of the back galleries."[19]

As the above description indicates, merchant families and their associates often lived in fine style, and their families were direct beneficiaries of their business life. Indeed, their business life intimately shaped their family life and was directly related to the social and economic position Southern merchants occupied as the rising new Southern middle class. While not extraordinarily wealthy, or perhaps as affluent as New Orleans cotton factor Julius Weis, many Natchez merchant families were solidly bourgeois and enjoyed many elements of an urban Victorian lifestyle, in combination with conditions unique to a small town in the South. By the later stages of Reconstruction, most successful Natchez merchant families had settled into a lifestyle that would endure into the twentieth century, and this lifestyle began in the home itself—homes representative of their rising status. The Lowenburgs, for example, bought a substantial home in 1873, and Clara Lowenburg described it as occupying "half a city block with an old fashioned plantation style house, a wide sixty foot long front gallery, [and a] wide hall with two rooms on each side." In fact, the Lowenburgs enjoyed a home that rivaled that of anyone in town, and Clara proudly boasted that "our parlor was very grand and had stiff Brussels lace curtains hanging from gilt cornices at the four windows . . . [and] the front hall had beautiful varnished marble paneled paper and lovely square shaped chairs and was like a room, with big book case and hat rack and a wall game table."[20]

In contrast, yet also in keeping with the "small-town" or "semirural" configuration in Natchez, the house grounds included a "pasture lot for the cows and horses and Papa kept there his two magnificent mules, Rose and Jane, that he worked in the dray at the store . . . [and] there was a wood and tool house too, and a poultry yard." Until most Natchez urban land had been filled in with houses and buildings of other types by the turn of the century, it was fairly common for homes to have attached lots to keep livestock, chickens, and outbuildings, including outhouses until indoor plumbing became common in the 1890s. Lowenburg's neighborhood was filled with other members of the Natchez merchant and business class, including banker George Koontz, merchant Peter Walsh, and planter Christian Schwartz. The Lowenburg home was probably representative of the upper middle class in terms of size and furnishings, but by no means palatial or a "mansion." A few merchants lived in far grander style: bachelor George T. Payne had a substantial townhouse on Main Street, John Fleming's family lived in the large Towers on Myrtle Street, and Joseph N. Carpenter's family lived in the fine antebellum mansion Dunleith on Homochitto Street.[21]

Several merchant families maintained live-in servants to assist in keeping house, cooking, and raising children. Many of these servants were black—in some cases ex-slaves who had been with a family for years. The merchant family's outlook toward their servants is representative of both their racism and perceived paternalism. Clara Lowenburg's family spent her first years in the home of her grandparents, John and Jeanette Mayer, and she recalled that "over the kitchen lived Aunt Ann, she had been a slave and had nursed all of grandma's children and refused to be free after the war." After Clara's father Isaac purchased their first home, they hired some of the Mayers' servants and took them along. Clara noted that "Grandma must have had some misgivings, as she gave mama our old loved black fat Aunt Jinny who was her cook, even Bill Shaw came and they lived in one of the rooms in the servant's house. . . . Aunt Jinny had been the nurse who went to Europe with us." The Lowenburgs employed other live-in servants as well, and Clara recalled that "Jane Brown was our nurse and the house maid and we loved her too . . . [and] Cornelius Dixon drove the surry [sic] and did all sorts of yard jobs. . . . There was a three room cottage in the yard, where they all lived."[22]

In addition to the Lowenburgs, Joseph N. Carpenter, Marx Lemle, Wolfe Geisenberger, and Ann E. Abbott all employed at least one African American live-in house servant, nanny, or cook by 1880, and others hired "day" servants who lived elsewhere. As in the antebellum era and earlier, whites and blacks frequently lived together under the same roof, and their families were often intimately tied together. House servants were not always black, however, as Irishman George T. Payne employed a white female servant from Bavaria for years. By the turn of the century, it became less common to have African American live-in servants as the racial divisions codified by Jim Crow precipitated a trend toward hiring day servants who lived elsewhere. Close family bonds between blacks and whites began to break down under racist pressure. Tellingly, the wealthy Julius Weis employed four African American live-in servants at his home in New Orleans in 1880, but by 1900 he only had one and instead employed two white immigrant girls from Europe. Nonetheless, Henry Frank still had two black servants living in his home in Natchez in 1900; Sim Lowenburg (Isaac's son) had an African American servant in his household in 1910, and two resided with his family in New Orleans in 1920.[23]

Most Natchez merchant marriages were "companionate" unions, in which "husbands and wives . . . [were] linked by mutual attraction and should provide affectionate support for each other while rearing a family." The trader's wife was responsible for maintaining the home, family, and children. If the husband was clearly head of the household, the home was largely the wife's domain and responsibility. In a large household with servants, these bourgeois Victorian women spent a good portion of their day supervising the various housekeeping activities such as cooking the large daily meals, cleaning an expansive house, washing, caring for the children, sewing, and a host of responsibilities.[24] Clara Lowenburg described a portion of her mother's daily routine: "Next to the dining room was a large store room called the pantry where groceries were kept. 'Giving out' the meals was a daily rite, as no one trusted the negro servants to take what they needed. Housewives carried bunches of keys. A key basket was one's first gift given a housekeeper. The cook came in with measuring pans and a basket for the day's provisions."[25]

While the Lowenburgs may not have trusted their black servants with the food, they trusted them to raise their children. "Jane dressed us and combed our heads very carefully with a fine toothed comb and plaited my hair so tight I could scarcely close my eyes," and their African American nannies physically punished the children on occasion, as "I, trying to curl my hair myself, only succeeded in wetting my fresh dress . . . and got a spanking from Aunt Jennie in the bargain." Or even nursed them, as "Jane often suckled Sallie (Clara's sister), if mama was out and the baby was hungry." The close relationship and bonds between these children and their servants formed the paradox of Southern living in a racist social climate. But it also allowed the merchant wife to attend to the myriad household responsibilities, which included frequent houseguests and rounds of socializing on Friday and Saturday nights or Sunday afternoons. Initially, prevailing social mores required most housewives and girls not to be seen "too often" out shopping or on the streets without a male escort, and they were very much tied to their home lives, socializing among themselves in the privacy of the home. But this was changing with the growth of women's social and religious clubs. Merchant Ann E. Abbott bucked this convention, for example, when her husband, William, died in 1882, and she hired his lead clerk, James S. Fleming, as her store manager and out of economic expediency ran their wholesale grocery firm for two decades until her death in 1903. And throughout the period, merchant property and family assets were often put in wives' names to avoid taxation or the possibility of loss in a lawsuit or debt settlement.[26]

A successful merchant's children enjoyed significant advantages in lifestyle. Their homes frequently had pianos and other musical instruments, and children often took music or singing lessons. Clara Lowenburg had a music teacher and was required to practice piano for an hour daily, while her mother's younger sister, Theresa Mayer, stayed in New Orleans with Julius Weis's family so she could "study all winter with a great opera singer." Their homes were often filled with books, games, and toys, and the Lowenburg household had a collection of classic literature and historical novels, including many in German and English by authors such as Goethe and Schiller. There was great interest in "dime novels" of the day, but "reading novels was only permitted in the afternoon," as it was considered "lazy" to be caught spending more than a small portion of the day reading fiction. Although Natchez was a small town, throughout the postwar period traveling theatrical troupes or musicians would present plays and concerts at Institute Hall (a part of the Natchez Institute complex, which housed the public school for white children), including *The Count of Monte Cristo* and *H.M.S. Pinafore*, and this activity was a favorite among children of the merchant class. These children also wore nice clothing and the newest fashions, either purchased locally or in New Orleans or even Cincinnati, with many articles hand-tailored by a local seamstress, dressmaker, or female family members. In the Lowenburg household the "sewing women came by the week and the women in the household helped. . . . It was quite indecent not to have a half dozen of each garment in reserve for everyone."[27]

Most of all, Natchez merchant families placed a high premium on education for their children. Many went to local private schools or tutors, boarding schools in larger cities, and on occasion even to Europe. There were several small private parochial schools run by the Episcopal, Presbyterian, and Catholic churches, as well as the Jewish temple. There were also small nonaffiliated privately owned schools run by the sisters of Confederate general William T. Martin and Professor A. D. Campbell. The Lowenburg children attended a private school with those of the Geisenbergers and Carpenters, while Ann E. Abbott's children went to school at the Presbyterian Church and those of the Perraults to the Catholic cathedral. In the early 1880s Julius Weis was advised by his doctors to take a couple of years off from the stresses of his cotton factorage firm in New Orleans, and, as a German expatriate, he decided to take the "cure" in Europe. As a consequence, he took his children and those of the Lowenburgs along and placed them in European boarding schools while there. Thus Sim Lowenburg attended two years of boarding school in Switzerland, while his sister Clara attended a women's school in Frankfurt, Germany, where they learned French, German, as well as the classics; while in Europe Clara was also able to buy the "latest fashions" in Paris. About the same time, the Lowenburgs sent their other daughter, Sallie, to a private boarding school in Cincinnati, while Nathaniel Leslie Carpenter was sent to a private school in Jackson, Mississippi. The mercantile emphasis on the importance of education continued into college, as N. Leslie Carpenter attended Vanderbilt University, Phillip Beekman completed his education at Bellevue Medical College in New York City, and Sim Lowenburg studied engineering at the University of Cincinnati before taking over I. Lowenburg & Co. when his father died. Access to higher education produced several doctors and lawyers among Natchez merchant sons, but, as in Lowenburg's case, regardless of their education, many mercantile sons followed their fathers' footsteps into trade. The Carpenters, Beekmans, Perraults, Abbotts, Friedlers, and Jacobses all had such sons.[28]

Many Natchez merchant families were well traveled and worldly and often spent summers in Northern resorts and occasionally Europe. It had long been a tradition among the planter class and Natchez residents of means to flee the oppressive heat and humidity of the Mississippi summers, and this tradition continued among the postwar merchant class, whose business was slowest at that time of year, affording the best opportunity for travel. The German Jewish immigrants had strong ties to their homeland, and as early as the summer of 1871 Isaac Lowenburg took his family to visit Germany—only to experience difficulty getting home because the Franco-Prussian War had begun while they were there—while Vidalia merchant Isaac Friedler took his wedding trip to Germany in 1874. In the Carpenter family, "For many years it was the custom of Mr. Carpenter to make extended summer tours, always returning in the fall with a well stored memory of information that his observant mind had gathered in Europe or the remote parts of this continent." The wealthy New Orleans commission merchant Julius Weis spent many summers in Europe during the 1870s and 1880s, and by the 1890s had taken to staying at a summerhouse in Manchester-by-the-Sea, north of Boston. Members of the Jacobs family would go to St. Louis to stay with friends, while Sim and Clara Lowenburg often stayed summers with their respective families at Elkhorn Lake in Wisconsin. Ailing merchants and their families would also travel to stateside health resorts or European spas to take the "cure" in times of illness. In the months before Isaac Lowenburg died in 1888, "so that he could seek a renewal of health. . . . he went to a number of the healing resorts in the country, but could only obtain temporary relief." Shortly before his death the following year, Simon Jacobs "took a trip to Europe hoping to be benefited, and indeed he was, but a short time since he was attacked by another relentless foe . . . [and] quietly passed away."[29]

One historian of the Southern antebellum merchant class has noted, "The family was the center of southern merchant culture. The ties between husband and wife, parent and child, brother and sister provided the ultimate foundation for merchant values . . . [and] families incorporated varying degrees of affection, materialism, paternalism, and racism, but the peculiar blend of those qualities within the merchant family made it unique." In a real sense, the same sort of social construct dominated merchant life in postwar Natchez as well. The immediate and extended family was the bedrock of mercantile life, providing support, belonging, and a deep sense of purpose that drove these trade families in their social and business endeavors. The merchant family was not only the source of business partners, clerks, and potential marriages or a means of consolidating and perpetuating wealth. Through its lifestyle it inculcated bourgeois values. The family was the prime beneficiary of the often difficult demands of business life, and the reward for involvement in a stressful and consuming profession was the material comforts and advantages that merchants relentlessly pursued. Natchez merchant families were distinct in that they were not quite urban but certainly not "country," at once closely tied to the land and the city in equal parts, and they enjoyed advantages and comforts well beyond what might be expected for an emerging small-town middle class. And the strength of their strong-rooted family lives or "strong ties" provided both a solid base and a ready conduit into the larger affairs of the community and what social and economic power it held, enabling merchants to reinvent both themselves and their environs in the process.[30]

❖ ❖ ❖

> Natchez has now a population of 11,000 inhabitants; they are intelligent, energetic, industrious and liberal. . . . It is not to be marveled at that the busy hum of industry is heard on every side . . . shown in the various manufacturing enterprises—having in our midst two

extensive cotton factories, who ship the result of their looms, not only to New York, San Francisco, but also to foreign countries. We have also two cotton seed oil mills, a batting mill, ice factory, saw mills; one of the largest cotton compresses . . . and today Natchez has become a well recognized cotton market. We also have a freight elevator, street railway . . . [and] trade and commerce . . . extends for hundreds of miles up and down the Mississippi River, Tensas and Quachita Rivers, bring us much trade every year. The Natchez & Jackson, Mississippi Valley, Red River & Texas Railroads add much to our commerce. Gentlemen, we do not fear for the future.[31]

Merchant Isaac Lowenburg's final speech as the mayor of Natchez, on December 30, 1886, is a striking example of rising New South "boosterism," a driving Gilded Age desire among the "New Men" of the South to cast off the "curse of slavery" and remake the South in a Northern image by furthering manufacturing, commerce, technological development, and social improvement. Embracing a growing movement of leading Southern proponents of change like Atlanta newspaperman Henry Grady, by the early 1880s Natchez civic and commercial leaders were constantly at work seeking ways to improve local economic conditions and living standards in a push to build Natchez into a more modern little city. At the forefront of this local movement was the Natchez merchant class, which increasingly emulated and resembled the rising Southern business culture in the South's premier cities like Atlanta. This phenomenon was described by one Southern newspaperman as "a new race of rich people [who] have been gradually springing up among us, who owe their wealth to successful trade and especially manufactures. . . . [They] are taking the leading place not only in our political and financial affairs, but are pressing to the front for social recognition." While Natchez never came close to attaining the level of size, wealth, or sophistication of first-tier Southern cities, the Natchez elite followed much of the same social and economic trajectory as the leaders of those cities to achieve their status and goals. Indeed, Natchez merchants built and consolidated their economic and social power-base through a host of means—religious organizations, civic and charitable groups, and business associations. They used their increasing economic means, and the social status provided by these organizations, to enter and dominate local politics; used their influence to push for civic and technological improvements; and parlayed their business alliances into new local corporate entities representative of the modernized business practices sweeping the nation. These developments also brought the merchant class into league with other powerful local social and economic elements, especially local banking, legal, and business professionals and, increasingly, the planter class. If the family and business firm provided a strong base for Natchez mercantile endeavor and lifestyle, it was the weaker social ties formed of friends, organizations, and institutions that helped merchants ascend to a higher level of power, influence, and economic clout.[32]

✳ ✳ ✳

Reputation was a key element for a successful business or civic leader, and membership in a religious organization was one venue for establishing one's reputation and demonstrating civic involvement and leadership. Religion had always been a major social institution in the South. In postwar Natchez, the churches and Jewish temple provided key social contacts and support, and were particularly important among the large immigrant merchant communities. The Catholic Church and the Jewish temple also had affiliated social organizations or "lodges" that provided key venues to participate in religious and community affairs, do charitable work, and foster friendships and business associations that played into the larger Natchez social community and solidified social and business standing. St. Mary's Cathedral was an important social nexus for several groups—particularly the Irish and Italian merchant communities but also the professional and planter classes—and membership in the church provided a crucial opportunity to "meet and greet" on a weekly basis, as well as cement one's position among peers and gain respectability and social visibility. Also, the various religious communities supported each other's religious institutions with contributions, sponsorships, and attendance at each other's events, building bonds and goodwill among the different groups and their businessmen.[33]

The membership rolls of St. Mary's included leading Irish merchantmen George T. Payne, John O'Brien, James Carradine, Lawrence Marron, and Patrick Burns, as well as top Italian traders John Botto, John Grillo, and Joseph Reale, and the entire French Perrault family. Newspaper owner James W. Lambert, City Clerk Joseph Arrighi, City Treasurer Fred Maher, and several important planter families, including the Kennedys, Fowlers, and Alexanders, also attended regularly. The church offered the opportunity for leading members of these groups to work together on a host of functions, including fund-raising for building upkeep, relief of poverty, and particularly the operation of the St. Mary's and D'Evereux Hall Orphanages, important Natchez charitable institutions. This cross-association between mercantile, business, and planter factions aided in familiarity and mutual trust and provided social opportunities, not just among the men but also among women who were deeply involved in fund-raising. The church was closely associated with four separate social and charitable clubs—the Knights of Columbus, the St. Joseph's Total Abstinence Society, the Italian Benevolent Association, and the Hibernian Benevolent Association—all of which met monthly at the cathedral. The Hibernians were the leading Irish social club in Natchez—and a bastion of social capital in the Irish merchant community—and their officers received this letter of thanks from the Catholic Church for their charitable work in 1880:[34]

Natchez, Miss., Feb. 21st, 1880

Messrs. Lawrence Marron, Geo. T. Payne, Peter Walsh and Patrick Burns, Committee of the Hibernian Society of Natchez:

Gentlemen—With very warm thanks I acknowledge the receipt from you of six hundred and twenty-six dollars, twenty-five cents, ($626.25), Collected in Natchez, Vidalia and the vicinity for the relief of the sufferers in Ireland. I am glad to inform you that I had previously received $156 by the collection made in the Cathedral Jan. 18th; $35.35 from the entertainment given by ex-pupils of the Cathedral school Feb. 9th; $54.50 collected by some charitable ladies, and $64.65 through the church box and from various individuals—making a total of $936.65.[35]

In much the same way, the Temple B'Nai Israel served as a major focal point for the Jewish mercantile community. These merchants enhanced their local influence by drawing upon their own cultural ties within the larger Natchez community, ties that not only enriched them socially but also advanced them economically. Aaron Beekman, Isaac Lowenburg, Simon Jacobs, and Henry Frank all served as congregation president, while every Jewish merchant in this study or their sons served on the temple's board of trustees, presiding over large sums of money and dictating how that money was spent. One had to petition and be voted on to become a member, and, as in other religious congregations, an internal hierarchy was established by the paying of "pew assessments," which separated members by economic importance and dictated seating rights at religious services. Consequently, the socially prominent or highly successful businessmen usually paid the most and sat up front. One pew assessment from the mid-1870s lists Beekman, Frank, and Lowenburg as the largest contributors at $250, $255, and $260, respectively, per year—a significant cost for that measure of social prominence. As officers and trustees, these men handled considerable sums of temple funds for the building of the first temple and securing the Jewish cemetery. The men also determined which charities received money and support, which interestingly including the Poor Children's Christmas Tree Fund started by Catholic newspaperman James W. Lambert, a good example of mutual support among different religious communities. Assuming leadership in the temple provided social prominence and helped cement one's position within the larger Natchez community, and local businessmen undoubtedly understood the considerable economic clout wielded by temple members as a highly cohesive mercantile force.[36]

Perhaps the most important social and economic power base within the Jewish community was Ezra Lodge #134, Independent Order of B'Nai Brith (I.O.B.B.). Membership lists for the lodge contain just about every prominent Natchez Jewish merchant of the era, and there is strong evidence that Jewish powerbrokers used this forum to advance their business interests. One striking feature of this organization is that the lodge loaned money to prominent members out of "excess" lodge funds when they needed it. At one meeting in July 1878, for example, the lodge loaned merchants Isaac Lowenburg and Henry Frank $250 each at 10 percent interest with a "thirty day call." Board members would vote on this or hold a raffle to the highest bidder—often the same individuals who were recipients of these loans—but even loans among themselves required paying the going interest rate, often 8 to 10 percent. Many Jewish merchants received these loans at one time or another during the period 1873 to 1910; Wolfe Geisenberger and Lowenburg twice received funds. In every case the funds went to an influential member of the Jewish merchant community, perhaps for land purchases. Other networking advantages arose through membership in the lodge as well. The organization also represented the local Jewish businessmen on a national level through annual meetings held in Cincinnati. It is probable that a great many issues concerning the local Jewish business community were decided among these leaders at the lodge meetings, and membership also served as a "coming of age" rite of passage for mercantile sons joining the business community. By the 1890s the lodge included the sons of every Jewish merchant family in this study, solidifying business ties among families and serving as an extension of the social and economic relationships formed by extensive intermarriage between prominent families. Sons and daughters of prominent families married into other influential families, power and wealth accumulated, and before long the sons turned up at the lodge meetings with their power-broker fathers, continuing the tradition as soon as they finished school and joined the business community.[37]

The same sort of networking opportunities occurred in other religious communities as well. At Trinity Episcopal Church, the Carpenter family was deeply involved with a host of local business and planter class leaders, while much the same happened at First Presbyterian, where the Abbotts and Flemings attended. But there were also many other local fraternal and social organizations, not tied to religion, that brought the members of the different mercantile, business, and planter communities together in new social configurations that fed the local business scene. By the late 1870s Natchez had several Masonic chapters that met monthly at the expansive brick Masonic Hall on Main Street, and their membership brought together a disparate collection of local leaders. In 1877 the officers of Natchez Royal Arch Chapter No. 1, for example, included merchants Cassius L. Tillman of I. Lowenburg & Co. and John A. Dicks of Carpenter, Dicks & Co.; banker George W. Koontz of Britton & Koontz Bank; lumber supplier R. F. Learned of Learned Sawmill Co.; insurance broker E. George De Lap of P. A. Barker & Co.; and leading planter E. J. Van Court. There were also two lodges of the Independent Order of Odd Fellows, and Wildey Encampment No. 1 included members from the Irish, Italian, and Jewish merchant communities, with L. M. Patterson, Antonio Druetta, and Aaron Beekman as officers. In a striking example of increasing socialization between planter and merchant classes, in 1900 the sons of the Beekman, Friedler, Lowenburg, and Jacobs mercantile families joined with other local business leaders—particularly younger members of leading planter families such as the Ogdens, Shields, and Stantons—to incorporate "Natchez Lodge No. 553 of the Benevolent Order of Elks . . . created for social, fraternal, benevolent, and charitable purposes." Around the same time, many of the same individuals incorporated the downtown Prentiss Club and Standard Club, major venues for the new Natchez elite to talk business and socialize, extending their influence and solidifying their importance in the Natchez business community and social circles.[38]

❉ ❉ ❉

Of the numerous social groups in Natchez at the time, perhaps the most honored was the Adams Light Infantry, an organization comprised of local Civil War veterans who had served in various Confederate units during the war. Service in the Confederacy represented the pinnacle of postwar Natchez honor, esteem, and respect, and the rolls were filled with leaders of the merchant, business, and planter classes. Members included merchants Joseph N. Carpenter, William Abbott, S. D. Stockman, and the Perrault brothers, among a host of others—notably the much-honored Judge William T. Martin, the highest-ranking officer from Natchez in the Confederate army. One interesting facet of this society included the appointment of "honorary members" who were important friends and associates of, but not actually members of, the Adams Light Infantry or who were not even Confederate veterans. The list of honorary members who never served in the Confederacy included much of the crème de la crème of Natchez business and society: bankers Audley C. Britton and George W. Koontz, wealthy planters James Surget and Stephen Duncan Jr., Northern newcomer and newspaper editor Thomas Grafton, and merchants George T. Payne, Andrew Fleming, and former Union army lieutenant Henry M. Gastrell. Like Gastrell, Isaac Lowenburg and Henry Frank were honorary members who came to Natchez with the occupying Union forces. Apparently this ironic change of allegiance did not bother the local elites and ardent Southerners in this organization, and this is good indication that these two important businessmen were found acceptable and considered equals by their important local peers, money and influence speaking louder than former loyalties.[39]

If social organizations and networks brought like-minded merchants and businessmen together and smoothed the way for their cooperation, the social capital engendered came to fruition in the explosion of new business associations and incorporated commercial concerns that defined the era and brought technological improvements and modernity to Natchez by the turn of the century. The Natchez Board of Trade was formed in the early 1870s to provide a business forum for local mercantile firms, and its membership was comprised of "All the principle merchants of Natchez." A more social venue, the first with a business focus, was the Natchez Club, formed in 1883 for the purpose of furthering local business concerns. The club's membership consisted of about "seventy-five citizens from the leading representatives of its various trades and professions." The club offered an "agreeable relaxation from the cares and toils of business, by providing to its members . . . an extensive collection of daily, weekly and monthly publications, from the leading [business] journals of this country and England."[40] Three years later, in 1886, many of the same local businessmen formed the most important local business association of the era, and soon the local newspaper issued its own broadside aimed at New South "Boosterism" and trumpeted that

> our businessmen, realizing the benefits to be derived from cooperative organization, secured a charter from the State of Mississippi and established "The Natchez Cotton and Merchants Exchange." . . . Their headquarters are fitted up in . . . the heart of the city, and there they receive daily reports of he world, which are posted on the board for the edification of the members. Their organization and the building of our large cotton compresses last year brought a flood of cotton buyers, who competed successfully with New Orleans, and induced an increase in cotton receipts of over 20,000 bales. . . . [It] is one of the solidest organizations in the city.[41]

Established by leading merchants, including Joseph N. Carpenter, Simon Mayer, Theodore Wensel, George T. Payne, Henry Frank, and Isaac Lowenburg, in league with local bankers and planters, the Natchez Cotton and Merchants Exchange developed as the premier "booster" of Natchez mercantile and cotton trade well into the twentieth century, and a prime supporter of new manufacturing concerns: the Rosalie Cotton Mills and the Natchez Cotton Mills.[42]

Local merchants, planters, and bankers had begun to gather together to forward the idea of creating a local cotton mill in the early 1870s. It was not until April 1877 that a host of local leaders—including banker A. C. Britton; merchants Joseph N. Carpenter, John C. Schwartz, and John A. Dicks; and planters James Surget, A. D. Rawlings, and Wilmer

Shields—joined their capital and incorporated the Natchez Cotton Mills to process locally produced cotton into a finished product for trade and export. This first large-scale manufacturing endeavor in Natchez was initially capitalized at $70,000 through shares issued in $5,000 increments. It soon consumed an entire city block. By the early 1880s it was joined by another mill, the Rosalie Cotton Mills. Observer Mark Twain noted that "I was not expecting to live to see Natchez and these other river towns become manufacturing strongholds and railway centers," but that is exactly how he described Natchez in *Life on the Mississippi* in 1882:[43]

> The Rosalie Yarn Mill, of Natchez, had the capacity of 6,000 spindles and 160 Looms, and employs 100 hands. The Natchez Cotton Mills Company began operations four years ago in a two-story building of 50 x 190 feet, with 4,000 spindles and 128 looms; capital $105,000, all subscribed in the town. Two years later, the same stockholders increased their capital to $225,000; added a third story to the mill, increased its length to 317 feet; added machinery to increase the capacity to 10,300 spindles and 304 looms. The company now employ[s] 250 operatives, many of whom are citizens of Natchez. "The mill works 5,000 bales of cotton annually and manufactures the best quality of brown shirtings and sheetings and drills, turning out 5,000,000 yards of these goods per year." A close corporation—stock held at $5,000 per share, but none in the market.[44]

The *Natchez Democrat* boasted in 1887 that, between the two mills, about 7,000 bales of local cotton were consumed in the above-named products as well as "blue cloth and a variety of other grades of goods," while providing $7,000 in wages for the hundreds of mill workers every month—a huge boost to the local economy. The cotton mills also served as a vanguard of a host of new local business endeavors that the merchant class was deeply involved in bringing to fruition. The Carpenter family partnered with John A. Dicks as Carpenter, Dicks & Co. to open the Lee Oil Works about the same year the mills opened, and by the late 1880s these investors were also instrumental in the formation of the Adams Manufacturing Co., which included "Two large Cotton seed mils, employing about seventy-five men each . . .[and] a Batting Mill where lint from the cotton seed is manufactured into neat rolls of cotton batting which are shipped north. . . . The works of these two institutions occupy nearly two blocks, and are a portion of the greatest industrial enterprise ever started in the south." Local merchants were also part of the construction of the Natchez Compress Co., which in 1887 brought "15,000 bales of cotton to this market more than usual." A host of other local business institutions sprang up as diverse as "two mineral water bottling establishments with a capacity each of 180 dozen bottles," and "three manufacturing confectioners, two of whom make 1,200 pounds of candy per day," and even "a beer bottling institution of large capacity." The list goes on: during the explosion of business endeavors in the last quarter of the nineteenth century, local merchants and businessmen presided over the incorporation of a plethora of businesses for the purpose of packet shipping, warehousing, banking, investment, insurance, canning, land development, and oil and lumber production, among others.[45]

❀ ❀ ❀

During the 1880s and 1890s the merchants and businessmen who formed the vanguard of the local commercial boom also participated in and pushed for elements of technological modernization sweeping the nation at that time. The merchants and their business associates were instrumental in constructing or were some of the first local customers of new Gilded Age technological improvements like telephone service (1881), manufactured ice (1882), municipal railways (1887), municipal water and sewer service (1889), electricity (1889), and finally indoor plumbing (1891). The Carpenter family once again led the way by combining with other businessmen to incorporate the Natchez Ice Co. in 1882 to mechanically produce thirty tons of ice daily. They achieved another first in 1890 by combining with bankers A. C. Britton and G. W. Koontz, planter Steven Duncan Jr., and fellow merchants John A. Dicks and S. E. Rumble to open the Hotel Natchez—the first building in town to feature indoor plumbing, hot and cold running water, and electric lights and elevators. About the same time, Sim Lowenburg installed indoor plumbing and electricity in his new house in Clifton Heights, one of the first private residences in Natchez to enjoy these modern conveniences. Merchants put electric lights and telephones into their stores, enabling them to monitor their far-flung interests in other counties and parishes on a daily basis by telephone. Contracts, documents, and other correspondence from Aaron Beekman & Son Co. begin to appear in typewritten form in the early 1890s, followed soon by I. Lowenburg & Co. Paradoxically, merchants were among the first to use new typewriters in official records at a time when others carried on using handwritten forms for another ten years, yet, as demonstrated earlier, merchants still kept their books in the time-honored handwritten business ledgers. Ledgers aside, local merchants were also among the first Natchez citizens to purchase automobiles: in the summer of 1901 Sim Lowenburg bought a "Pope Toledo," and James Fleming purchased a "White Steamer" soon after. Clearly, as a class the merchants proved ready and eager to employ new technologies, and they appeared to thrive with the new improvements.[46]

Perhaps the most salient form of the drive toward modernization was railroad construction. All Natchez merchants and businessmen stood to benefit from improved rail connections for a town that still relied upon the Mississippi River for the lion's share of its commerce. Local business leaders began pushing for a rail connection soon after the war ended. By 1900 they had been directly involved in at least six major railroad construction schemes, including four that were backed by local capital and incorporated in either Natchez or Vidalia. A clique of local mercantile, planter, and business "boosters" drove most local railroad efforts. Merchants Henry Frank, Isaac Lowenburg, Henry Gastrell, Samuel Block, and Isaac Friedler; bankers A. C. Britton and G. W. Koontz; planter James Surget; lumberman R. F. Learned; and judges-lawyers Thomas Reber, William T. Martin, and Hiram Steele were the leaders. These boosters were never far from any local railroad building effort, and several lent their prestige to these projects or pushed for public funding through bond issues. Although occasionally they were able to profit directly from their involvement, the push for railroads was not just about losses and gains. It also represented a significant local attempt to form modern business structures that employed hierarchal management over distances and provided key links to the interior that aided commerce, and began to eclipse river traffic as the key method of freight and passenger transportation.[47]

Chartered in 1870, the first successful local railroad effort—the Natchez, Jackson, & Columbus Railroad Co., or "Little J"—had by 1882 connected Natchez with Jackson and with much of the nation via the railway links there, changing life in Natchez forever. Headed by former Confederate general and judge William T. Martin, the railroad employed a hierarchal management team that included a board of directors, composed of major shareholders, and a salaried superintendent who directed employees, including engineers and agents as well as mechanics and roadmen who maintained the equipment, railroad depots, sidings, platforms, and fueling and watering stations. This "smooth-running narrow gauge railroad" maintained a regular schedule with a train leaving daily at 11:00 a.m. and arriving in Jackson five hours later. From there, connections to New Orleans, Vicksburg, Cincinnati, and other destinations could be had and enabled formerly unheard-of travel times. The railroad's securities were backed by public funds in the form of bonds issued by the city of Natchez ($200,000) and Jackson-area Hinds County ($146,000), held through a New York City securities firm and made negotiable through the local Britton & Koontz Bank. The railroad's opening also coincided with Natchez Cotton Mills coming on line. In this way, the Natchez business community developed, with allies, a local system of vertical integration that tied local agriculture, industry, commerce, and transportation together. To work in conjunction with the new Little J facilities, judge Thomas Reber worked with several merchants to install two municipal railroad projects to service the Rosalie Mills–Mississippi River landing area with a funicular incline freight-loading apparatus and a connecting local street railway system for the city.[48]

This project inspired a spate of other railroad schemes and ventures. About the same time that the Little J was getting off the ground, Natchez hardware merchant Henry H. Gastrell, Vidalia plantation supplier Samuel Block, and judge Thomas Reber used their own funds to form the Vidalia & Western Railroad Co. The first rail line in Concordia Parish that laid track connecting interior cotton plantations to Vidalia, it was a boon for Vidalia merchants like Block and Isaac Friedler. In 1881 the railroad boosters bought out the Vidalia & Western in the first real attempt to connect as far west as Texas, when they incorporated the Natchez, Red River, & Texas Railroad Co. This was followed by a host of local railroad incorporations: the New Orleans, Natchez, & Fort Scott Railroad Co. in 1886, which the city of Natchez backed with another $250,000 bond issue to connect with rail lines in Arkansas, and the Mississippi Valley Railroad Co., which filed incorporation paperwork in 1895 to consolidate the several existing local railway projects. As late as 1904 a second generation of Natchez boosters incorporated the Natchez & Gulf Railroad Co. to connect with the coastal city of Gulfport, Mississippi. Boosters not only aided their businesses but also profited directly. While secretary of the Natchez, Red River, & Texas in 1881, merchant Isaac Lowenburg received $17,520 in company stock in return for his role in securing a right-of-way through Concordia Parish, when he bought over 6,000 acres of unimproved land for $277 at a tax sale and then sold the railroad over 3,000 acres in consideration for the stock. Lowenburg was secretary on the board of the railroad company when he completed the transaction, using inside information gained as an officer of the company to profit on land speculation. In addition to the money Lowenburg made on the right-of-way and stock transaction, he also collected an annual salary for the secretary post, perhaps as much as $2,000 per annum. The railroad incorporation papers indicate that all the board officers collected a salary and that the president of the company, Hiram R. Steele, made $3,500 a year. Lowenburg also used his position as secretary on the board of the Little J in 1877 to secure and build his own whistle-stop town in Jefferson County—Lowenburg Station.[49]

✤ ✤ ✤

Finally, the merchant community was deeply involved in local politics. While this was another venue that brought the various local factions together—particularly the mercantile-business and planter classes—politics also occasionally brought competing groups into conflict as well. During Reconstruction, local politics on both sides of the river were dominated by the Republican Party and in fact included large numbers of freed black politicians. With the end of Union occupation, however, the Democratic Party would soon dominate under an increasingly racist program. After Redemption, there were very few Republican or "carpetbagger" politicians among the Natchez business class, and in fact subscription to the "lost cause" was almost a prerequisite for local success. There were at least four political organizations in which members of leading merchant families and their close associates held political office: the police jury in Concordia Parish, the board of alderman for the city of Vidalia, the Adams County Board of Supervisors, the board of alderman for the city of Natchez, and the Natchez office of mayor.[50]

In Concordia Parish, for example, Isaac Friedler served as a member of the Vidalia Board of Aldermen during the 1880s and later as president of the parish police jury during the 1890s. His store also frequently sold dry goods, supplies, and merchandise to the city and the parish, a perk of close ties to local government. Plantation supply merchant Isadore Lemle served during the 1870s and 1880s as the official recorder for the

Concordia clerk's office, recording all chattel mortgages, trust deeds, and land deeds in the parish. Every contract carried out in the parish crossed his desk, even those of his clients or business competitors—providing a significant source of inside information of local business. Railroad boosters Thomas Reber and Hiram Steele were Concordia Parish circuit court judge and district attorney, respectively. Steele was required to sign off on the legality of the incorporation papers of the Natchez, Red River, & Texas Railroad Co.—the same paperwork that made him president of that firm. This was so even though in the rural Concordia Parish, the planter class dominated politics, and in the city of Vidalia, four of the mayors elected between 1880 and 1908 were sons of large antebellum planters. Political players often posted surety bond for other local political candidates within their business or social circles. A case in point was Isaac Friedler. He posted a $1,000 surety bond for fellow merchant and parish recorder Isadore Lemle in 1877, and another $1,000 bond for Lemle's boss, E. W. Wall, as parish clerk, and this habit continued with a $1,000 surety bond he posted for planter's son C. C. Campbell in 1896 as court clerk for the Eighth Judicial District. His association with Vidalia politics ended shortly thereafter, and he moved across the river to Natchez, where he built a house in Clifton Heights, the new enclave for prominent merchants and businessmen.[51]

The merchant class was very active in politics on the Mississippi side of the river as well. As in the antebellum period, Natchez city politics were a merchant-class stronghold. But merchants' influence remained weak on the county board of supervisors—long dominated by planters living in their agricultural countryside districts. When merchants had increased interest by virtue of their growing plantation holdings and beholden cropper constituencies, this began to change. In 1870, for example, all five seats were held by agricultural or planter families. But after 1875 the merchant class generally controlled the First District, which included the city of Natchez. Two long-running presidents of the board, Henry C. Pollock (1876–1884) and James S. Fleming (1896–1907), were merchants. By 1896, moreover, three out of five supervisors had mercantile backgrounds, and the county board would remain split thereafter. The county supervisors were very important to merchants, businessmen, and plantation owners alike, because they set the valuations of all property in the county and therefore determined property taxes, a significant burden to both large landowners and owners of highly valued commercial property. Also, both the city and the county taxed all the inventory and facilities contained within a store or business. Consequently, every August a parade of both planters and merchants appeared before the board to plead for reductions, with mixed success. Just about every merchant or planter family was either a happy recipient or victim of reassessment at one time or another. In August 1886, for example, the board gave I. Lowenburg & Co. a reduction in assessed store inventory from $20,000 to $18,000, but then turned around and raised the assessed value on Mayor Lowenburg's house on Commerce Street from $4,000 to $4,500. Local merchants sold a large amount of goods to the county, particularly for facilities or road construction and upkeep, and on several occasions ran the county "poor farm" for profit. They also held salaried county offices on occasion: I. Lowenburg & Co. partner Cassius L. Tillman served as county sheriff and then treasurer in the 1880s and 1890s, while merchant Charles H. Perrault served as county sheriff from 1904 to 1908.[52]

But Natchez is where members of the merchant class really left their political mark. Natchez was divided into four wards that elected two aldermen each, and throughout the period local businessmen dominated these offices. In fact, members of almost every mercantile family included in this study were elected to serve on the Natchez Board of Alderman or in the mayor's office, and in some cases more than one member of a business firm or mercantile family served over time, often holding the same seat. For example, merchant Isaac Lowenburg served as an alderman from the Third Ward from 1873 to 1878, and then his business partner Cassius L. Tillman held the same seat from 1880 to 1881, followed by Lowenburg's son Simon, who served in the same ward during 1897–1898. In another case, cousins Aaron F. Jacobs and Albert C. Jacobs, co-owners of A. F. Jacobs & Bros. (cotton merchants) and Adolf Jacobs & Son Banking Co., respectively, served as aldermen from the Second and Third Wards at the same time in 1906 and 1907. Prominent merchants George T. Payne, Ben C. Geisenberger, William Abbott, Armand Perrault, Joseph Reale, Joseph O'Brien, and S. E. Rumble, among others, served at least one term as aldermen; feisty Irishman George T. Payne served three terms in the Second Ward. While all the political leaders mentioned were elected as Democrats, occasionally these aldermen elections could have a political component that pitted one cultural merchant group against another. Besides the "native" Mississippi faction, which was the strongest local group politically, the constituents of the immigrant Irish, Jewish, and Italian communities vied to get members of their groups elected and achieved notable success. They placed at least two Italian, six Irish, and thirteen Jewish tradesmen in the aldermen's office over a thirty-year period. Also, in another indication of the increasing incorporation of the planter class into the town's business and political ranks, planters' sons lawyer Wilmer H. Shields and bookkeeper D. S. Bisland served as aldermen from the Third Ward from 1906 to 1908.[53]

But if the aldermen's offices were important, the Natchez mayor's office was the premier local political prize, offering significant prestige and influence to those who held the position. Largely middle-class merchants had occupied the mayor's office in the years before the war, and during Reconstruction Robert H. Wood became Natchez's first African American mayor in 1871. Following Redemption, however, the local merchant class again began to dominate the office, and in the greatest political achievement of the period for the Jewish merchant community, Isaac Lowenburg defeated incumbent Henry C. Griffin in the 1882 mayoral race to become the city's first Jewish and immigrant mayor. Lowenburg ran as a proponent of civic improvements, promising the construction of a new Natchez hospital and installation of electric power and the municipal gasworks. Natchez enjoyed a significant period of prosperity and growth while he was in office. In his first month as mayor, Lowenburg went to New York to lobby the president of the New Orleans & Northwestern Railroad Co. to divert its line through Natchez. Out of this junket grew a railroad plan that would interconnect four separate railroads in the Natchez-Vidalia area, making Natchez a strategic crossroads city and connecting it with the Northeast and Far West. Lowenburg supported a commitment by the Natchez municipality to issue $320,000 in municipal bonds to finance the connection of the New Orleans & Northwestern with the New Orleans, Natchez, & Fort Scott rail line in Vidalia, with ferry service across the Mississippi to complete the connection in Natchez with the existing Natchez, Red River, & Texas railroad and the Natchez, Jackson, & Columbus Railroad on the Mississippi side. New facilities would be built in Natchez and Vidalia, and these rail lines would be connected to the local track system of the new Natchez Municipal Railway Co. Lowenburg easily won a second mayoral term in the 1884 and served until 1886, when ill health forced him to retire from politics. He was replaced by the local wholesale grocer William H. Mallery, followed in 1888 by former Natchez clerk and merchant William G. Benbrook, who served as mayor for almost a quarter-century. All of these mercantile administrations demonstrated a liberal-minded concern for the improvement of Natchez, presided over key technological and civic improvements, and brought the area into the modern era.[54]

❧ ❧ ❧

Perhaps the leading booster of the emerging, altered, and improved way of doing things in the postwar South, Atlanta newspaperman Henry Grady proclaimed in 1886 that "there is a New South, not through protest against the old, but because of new conditions, new adjustments and, if you please, new ideas and aspirations." Grady could not have been more right about the outlook and desires of the Natchez postwar merchant class, if the reality of their new world was somewhat less than the grand New South pronouncements. The merchant-businessmen of Gilded Age Natchez were transitional figures, in some respects steeped in the older ways of merchant capitalism, yet constantly forced, or indeed motivated, to change and update their practices to keep in step with the new. They embraced the unrestrained new local marketplace with a vengeance, and it was responsible for their success, yet that same marketplace was still intimately tied to elements of the old, as King Cotton still dominated the Natchez economy. They almost uniformly honored the "lost cause" in their social circles and politics, all the while maintaining a distinct Natchez version of Old South grandeur with their stately homes, black servants, and uncommon privileges. Yet, as Harold Woodman has noted, "Although there was no industrial revolution in the South, there were significant changes in agriculture and trade, changes which supported a new class in the postwar south . . . [and] members of this new class were urban oriented even when they were urban dwellers." Indeed, Natchez merchants were often well-off, worldly, urban oriented, and exposed to and indoctrinated in the latest advances, styles, and education. At the same time, however, they were still essentially small-town or semirural entrepreneurs. Natchez traders differed considerably from the "New Men" of the South who inhabited the larger booming cities of Atlanta or Louisville. They still maintained direct, local, hands-on ties to cotton agriculture as plantation owners, after all, and dealt with other agricultural owners and the workers themselves. Yet they nevertheless embraced new forms of business endeavor and organization wholeheartedly, immersed themselves in modern social configurations and networks that mimicked those of contemporary big city businessmen of the era, and lost no time in seeking available improvements in business, transportation, organization, and technology. Thanks to their efforts, the world they inhabited in 1900 was far different from the one from which they emerged in 1865, even if in other ways it was still quite similar.[55]

CHAPTER 6

A Dangerous Business

IN THE SPRING OF 1876 HENRY M. GASTRELL SEEMINGLY HAD IT all. Since bursting onto the Natchez mercantile scene as a fresh twenty-two-year-old trader in October 1865 with the advertisement, "New Store. H. M. Gastrell & Co., *Dealers in all kinds of* Hardware and Cutlery, Stoves, Tin Ware, Lamps, Lanterns, and Plantation Implements," the lively Englishman from Bristol had built a bustling concern, which by the mid-1870s was equal to any in the district. Arguably the youngest upper-tier merchant in Natchez, Gastrell had come as a former Union officer with few or no local ties, yet proved he had what it took to build a thriving business where a host of other newcomers failed. He weathered the severe economic downturn following the panic of 1873 in fine form and in fact built a small fortune specializing in farm tools and equipment, billing himself as the "HEADQUARTERS FOR AGRICULTURAL IMPLEMENTS. . . . H. M. GASTRELL OFFERS SPECIAL INDUCEMENTS IN SCRAPERS, DOUBLE SHOVEL PLOWS, [and] JUMPER PLOWS." It was a good business that probably generated more hard-currency cash flow than other local lines more dependent on offering petty credit through the crop lien system, although he almost certainly had a significant amount of collectable credit extended himself. He lived in the beautiful home Twin Oaks on a fine section of Homochitto Street, backed by a wife from his hometown, surrounded by children and two black live-in servants. He even had his nephew helping him run his thriving business. As if this were not enough, he also owned a large interest in a river steamboat named after his wife, the *Lucy E. Gastrell*, a controlling share in a small, local, narrow-gauge rail line, two farms, and 15,000 acres of agricultural land: truly he was a self-made man of the new age. But as it often happens with men who clawed their way upward from nothing, he was full of hubris, and the local R. G. Dun credit agent noted his braggadocio skeptically: "[Gastrell] States that he has clear [assets of] $231,000," an improbably large sum, indicative of his larger dreams. Gastrell certainly had plenty, but he had come too far, too fast, and his little empire was highly leveraged and largely built on credit and would soon come crashing down around him.[1]

Speculation. It was at once the panacea and nemesis of countless nineteenth-century business climbers, and, in Gastrell's case, railroad speculation—a gamble that a large investment in a small Concordia Parish railroad would monopolize all the localized cotton and mercantile shipping trade and act in tandem with his related land and boat ventures—brought on a descending spiral of debt that would relegate him to business oblivion and, soon enough, kill him outright. By taking credit offered to his business in the form of merchandise, Gastrell had taken his profits and invested them in his railroad, and for a time paid his creditors without any problem. But as land acquisition, construction, and equipment purchase costs mounted without sufficient return, Gastrell found himself without further cash reserves and had to dig deeper into his available credit, mortgaging his store stock and borrowing from important friends around town, securing the debts with his numerous properties, thereby creating an unsustainable debt load. Word began to circulate around Natchez in the spring of 1878 that Gastrell "Has got in trouble over heavy investment in his baby and own 'Vidalia & Western R.R.,'" and sure enough, and even though his word was still good, Gastrell was in too deep and falling perilously behind in his obligations.[2] By the spring of 1879 he was on the brink, and the local R. G. Dun agent noted that Gastrell "Has written to his largest creditors asking for an extension of time offering 25% cash balance in 4 + 6 months with int. secured by mort. paper. He claims that he owes $14,180.23. . . . We learn that he stands well here and is regarded 'as an active energetic pushing man, parties do not hesitate to accept his proposition.'"[3] Perhaps, but his standing was fading fast in a business where reputation was everything, and only a few short months later, in November 1879, the same R. G. Dun agent portrayed him in a far less savory light, indicative of just how fast a merchant's name and fortunes could fall: "He is regarded honest but too ambitious to do large irons in the fire. . . . He is also stubborn + gets angry when forced to pay. . . . He is looked upon as a dangerous man to do bus. with + long or large credit is not recommended."[4]

Gastrell's freefall had thus commenced as debt-collection suits filed at the Adams County courthouse mounted and the first of wave of judgments and their ramifications began to appear. The following February the word about Natchez held that "the sheriff yesterday levied on 'HMG' who is unable to pay 4 NY or more + took into possession part of his stk (store stock) + has it advertised for sale." That spring, in a testament to Gastrell's tenacity, he desperately clung to his business as its constituent parts were unceremoniously disassembled. But on the particularly frightful day of April 10, 1880, in Natchez Eleventh District Circuit Court, Gastrell was laid bare with no less than ten separate defaults in debt suit judgments totaling $5,930.24 plus court costs and accruing 6 percent interest forthwith, to such diverse creditors as "Alfred Field & Co. . . . N.Y., N.Y.," "A. Bradley & Co. . . . Pittsburgh, Penn.," and "E. P. T. Hobcraft Co. . . . Alton, Ind." The stunned and prostrate Gastrell did not even attend or send his attorney to the day's proceedings, during which four more debt suits totaling an additional $2,139.75 plus costs and interest were set over to a later date, only to be lost the following month. In fact, during the period 1880–1884 an untold number of debt suits cycled through circuit court against Gastrell, who fought several of the multiple proceedings with the help of Natchez attorney Frank J. Winchester, but to little avail. Gastrell began selling his assets to satisfy the judgments, and on April 3, 1881, signed over his "baby," the Vidalia & Western Railroad Co., for $50,000 in $2,500 cash and the remainder in deferred payments dependent on the success of the railroad's imminent bond issue. It is unclear how much Gastrell actually collected from the sale, as the purchaser, the Natchez, Red River & Texas Railroad Co., experienced a host of its own financial difficulties and later was sold at a loss at least twice. But the infusion was apparently enough to save Gastrell's hardware firm, although it now existed as a shell of its former self. Gastrell limped along in business, but gone were the cocksure attitude, the splashy newspaper ads, the expansive plantation lands, the steamboat *Lucy E. Gastrell*; Gastrell died a broken man a few years later of "congestion of the brain" at a mere forty-five-years old, and his widowed wife was left to her own devices. The last anyone ever heard of H. M. Gastrell & Co. could have well served as both his and many a postwar merchantman's epitaph:[5]

Closing Out Sale!
GASTRELL STOCK AT 211 MAIN ST.,
will be closed out regardless of cost at auction,
sales daily from 11 a.m. to 2 p.m.
A good chance to get bargains.
MRS. H. M. GASTRELL[6]

The history of business in Natchez was both festooned with remarkable success stories and littered with grinding failures. The last half of the nineteenth century was certainly no different. In fact, it was an especially explosive business environment. The fickle cotton market was challenge enough, but modernization offered additional challenges as new venues for investment and speculation could yield great returns or turn bad at a moment's notice, in the wake of an economic downturn or after any number of unforeseen circumstances. And bad things could happen with alarming alacrity in a more modern and less isolated marketplace. King Cotton had never been a forgiving master, but the nature of the constrained postwar labor market, depressed cotton prices, changing international cotton markets, emergent cotton futures trading, debilitating reliance upon outside credit, and enduring dearth of significant local capital all combined to ensure a volatile business environment. Merchants in particular felt this pressure, not only as the leading providers of petty agricultural and consumer credit but also as the prime keepers and perpetuators of an unequal and pernicious system of liens and credit that poisoned the future growth of Natchez. And mercantile trade had by its very nature always been a risky endeavor. While one keen nineteenth-century observer exaggerated when writing that among merchants, "a very large majority, even ninety-seven in a hundred, are sure to fail," probably at least half of all postwar Natchez merchants succumbed between 1865 and 1910. Financial panic, speculation, merchant competition, as well as crop failure, low cotton prices, the inability to collect debts, bad personal habits or health, and poor business practices or reputation all took their toll.[7]

The trader's ability to garner credit from business-hungry merchandise wholesalers and manufactures was remarkably easy. On the other hand, often the credit costs were high, and the lien credit system was fraught with peril, as "the furnishing merchant carried on his business in the context of a dependant south . . . a very risky business." After all, he relied on a single crop and dealt "with a farmer who could give virtually no security for his loans except the forthcoming crop." This perilous condition made the merchant a bad credit risk as well, and he was "virtually forced to exploit the tenant if he [were] himself to survive." And Natchez merchants found that selling the merchandise was easy compared to collecting the money and paying their own debts, and only the prudent or lucky maintained sufficient capital to weather a bad crop year, financial panic, or failed investment. Even in the best of times the system was still predicated upon layers upon layers of credit. When Gastrell gambled on his railroad, he was compounding risk by making himself dependent on long-term shipping proceeds generated by planters and croppers who made a risky gambit every time they planted a crop of cotton, often only one bad crop away from financial oblivion themselves. It was a dangerous business. With upward of 75 percent of all mercantile business in the district being conducted on credit, the postwar Natchez traders were often prisoners and victims to the same pernicious system of debt they themselves perpetuated.[8]

If the postwar merchant was limited, and made to accept high risk, as a result of the lack of Southern capital and the layers of debt created by the crop lien system, he also was beset by a host of other problems, both those that resulted from the system as well as exterior forces beyond local control. The yearly paying and collection of debts precipitated an endless round of lawsuits comprised of seizures of land, chattels, and cotton; storage of seized items; and sheriff's sales, none of which remedies was guaranteed to collect the amounts owed and often cost more than what was recovered. Merchants were intimately acquainted with the sheriffs in every locality of the district, constantly forced to push magistrates for land and chattels seizures for court judgments or failed contracts. Even if they did make recoveries, they then had to store everything from plows to herds of cattle until they could be sold, a huge logistical nightmare that carried no certainty of sufficient resale prices for used and damaged items or underfed and sick livestock. Because of this, merchants often spent freely to provide surety bonds for their local sheriffs to curry favor and support, and in a few cases ran for sheriff themselves. Much the same held true with local lawyers, as merchants were by far their best customers and spent large sums for legal fees yearly, on top of countless filing, collection, court, advertising, and transportation fees. There was no guarantee of winning lawsuits either, as merchants often lost substantial amounts in legal disputes, particularly with suppliers and planters. If a merchant, like Gastrell, got behind in his own supplier debt, he was soon beset with creditors clamoring for payment, and debt resolutions through judicial judgment or "assignments"—where a merchant would sign over his goods and assets to a trustee to liquidate and pay his creditors—occurred with startling frequency and reduced many a Natchez trader. One bad crop year could decimate a merchant's income, and naturally, creditors wanted to be paid regardless. These credit and debt dilemmas existed in what was already a very competitive marketplace, where a valued customer could be enticed away by a competitor at any time, putting constant pressure upon the merchants to match or beat prevailing local prices, bad year or not. And regardless of a merchant's financial condition, the heavy local inventory, property, and levee taxes bore down and were collected every year, on top of business licensing fees.[9]

The risks facing the merchant were not just in business either. The Natchez District had never been an exceptionally safe or healthy environment, with near yearly visitations from malaria and other subtropical maladies, especially yellow fever, which took countless lives and often completely shut down all local business by quarantine during the peak of cotton season in the late summer or fall. Low-lying cotton fields and the town of Vidalia were regularly inundated with flooding by springtime swells of the Mississippi River, destroying businesses, homes, and crops alike, while the area was also prone to severe rains or droughts, a major source of crop failure and business downturn. If flooding did not destroy a crop, insects could, and infestations of armyworms and cotton worms attacked crops regularly until the appearance of the cotton boll weevil in 1907 shattered the local economy. The wooden structures of the district were at constant peril from fire in an age of kerosene lamps, coal heating, and, later, natural gas appliances, destroying houses and storefronts with alarming regularity. In a social sense, the crop lien system created significant backlash in the form of Populism, and several attempts to remove the merchants from the supply equation were made by local planters and farmers, who formed mercantile cooperatives. Class divisions were on the rise as well, as wage-earning workers who lived in ramshackle tenements and worked at the cotton mills or other manufacturing concerns conducted strikes on several occasions, while the uncertain cotton markets repeatedly put the mills out of business, and speculative local railroads often failed. Local racism also grew steadily worse: by 1901 African Americans had practically disappeared from local political office and voter rolls, and rising violence by "White Caps" south of Natchez threatened both black croppers and their Jewish merchant-landlords. The eventual effects of rising Jim Crow, in combination with cotton boll weevil devastation, created an exodus of farmers and, in turn, merchants, severely reducing the local economy. In addition, the national economy suffered at least three devastating downturns between 1865 and 1914, including an enduring "long-wave" depression from the mid-1870s until the late 1890s, restricting currency and credit in a dependent region and destroying businesses in its wake. Perhaps worst of all, a combination of new foreign competition, overproduction, high tariffs, and rising speculation through new venues of cotton futures trading drove cotton prices steadily downward after 1870. Except for brief respites, prices resided under $.10 a pound by the 1890s, making cotton unprofitable and beginning the exodus of the farmers and the attendant merchant class in the opening wave of the Great Migration.[10]

Finally, there were the merchant families themselves, at once bastions of support but also frequently serious detriments to continued business success. In many ways, merchant families were victims of their own success, as affluent sons and daughters of first-generation postwar merchants were schooled in or traveled to other regions, and simply wanted little part of the small-town life that their fathers had built. Gentrification took its toll, as merchants' sons took positions in other major cities to further their own careers, leaving behind their family businesses to wither in the twentieth century—particularly after the boll weevil devastated local commerce. The intertwined and carefully built family ties and fortunes suffered as people began to leave in search of a better life in larger cities with more opportunities and conveniences. Even if a mercantile family with means remained in Natchez, the passing of the original patriarch could create a nasty succession fight among siblings and heirs, rending families and destroying continuity and support networks. Too, tragedy struck with frequency in the form of disease, infant mortality, and sheer exhaustion from overwork. In fact, the tensions created by conducting business in the uncertain boom-and-bust economy often pushed merchants and their families to the precipice. A spate of suicides occurred in Natchez, starting in the 1890s, and continued throughout the cotton boll weevil onslaught. At least two major actors in this study and several mercantile family members died, while others exhibited "lunacy" and were committed. Meanwhile, in the midst of the boll weevil devastation and cotton production decline, a major Natchez bank failed with several merchants in key positions, ruining countless deposit holders, sending community leaders to jail, and creating a huge rift between mercantile families and groups, in the process destroying perhaps the most storied mercantile firm of the postbellum period. Thus a host of forces, both internal and external, were converging to corrode the position and profitability of the Natchez merchant class, and by the second decade of the twentieth century Natchez merchants were in serious decline, signaling the beginning of the end of postwar Natchez mercantile supremacy.[11]

※ ※ ※

The best investment which any man can make, and the first which he should make, is to purchase his own liabilities. In a word the very best use of money is paying one's debts. If outstanding obligations have still a time to run, to pay them off with whatever interest is due upon them at the time. . . . Many a shrewd businessman practice this, and secure double good, the improvement of their credit, and the actual reaping of profit. . . . If everybody, rich and poor, followed this safe course, the "fluctuations of trade" would be diminished to a wonderful degree.[12]

There is a good chance that John Fleming and Hiram Baldwin read the above advice in their local newspaper just at a time when they wished they had followed its precepts more than anything. Perhaps no postwar mercantile firm had been better positioned to succeed than Fleming & Baldwin, yet like H. M. Gastrell, they, too, fell prey to fiscal overextension as a result of speculation—excessive investment in cotton planting. By 1871 their plantation supply house was probably the largest in the region, and they commanded ownership or leases on at least eight plantations, with thousands of acres of cotton under cultivation by croppers drawing their supplies from the firm. But in the speculative postwar rush for quick cotton profits, they had thrown caution aside and bet heavily on planting, far too heavily. And what was worse is that they knew better, having been in business since the 1840s and having seen countless men fail in the cotton business. They had survived the war intact, and had always been viewed as "safe" and "prudent" "men of integrity [and] of superb business capacity and deserve[d] success." But the prospect of quick riches does strange things to people. Even after taking huge losses in the shattering crop failures of 1866 and 1867, they still pumped further capital into land and planting, with as much as $300,000 invested and a perilous level of debt pending to Natchez's Britton & Koontz Bank, cotton factors S. B. Newman & Co., and New York financier David Withers. As 1872 commenced, in a last-ditch attempt to extricate themselves, they mortgaged their mansions Dunleith, the Towers, and 125 mules to refinance a defaulting $41,000 note at 10 percent interest to Britton & Koontz, as well as another 120 mules and "wagons, implements, [and] gear" to David Withers for two notes of $12,500 and $25,000 at 8 percent interest, in addition to selling several tracts of land. Most of this debt was due by that fall, and they bet everything on the hopes of a windfall crop year to pay their debts, which also included mounting wholesaler bills. But cotton proceeds in 1872 did not come close to covering the expected payments, and as 1873 began they were going down fast. S. B. Newman & Co. now owned a lien on every bit of cotton they produced. The inevitable lawsuits began in circuit court. The firm's plight was compounded by the emerging financial panic that year, making creditors doubly anxious to collect. Hiram Baldwin died broke that summer of "congestive fever" (likely yellow fever), and by November the R. G. Dun agent unceremoniously noted that Natchez's number one firm was now "dissolved.... 'B's' estate is insolvent, [and] 'F's' is insolvent also." Fleming might have wished he had died, too, as the process of liquidating his assets would continue for years, while he apparently eked out a living as a small grocer. Decades later the *Natchez Democrat* noted of Fleming that "as a member of the firm of Fleming & Baldwin he aided in building up one of the largest commercial houses that ever operated in Natchez, but the magnificent business his wonderful energy had established was swept away in one of the financial crises that came a few years after the war, and all he had was lost."[13] The *Democrat* was being overly kind; speculation killed Fleming & Baldwin.

The spectacular failures of H. M. Gastrell and Fleming & Baldwin—as large as any during the postwar era—were indicative of the perils of overextension and speculation, but a host of lesser Natchez mercantile firms failed in less exciting but equally compelling ways. Almost always tied to mercantile debt owed and customer debt never collected, a merchant's resolution to his creditors usually ended in a circuit court judgment, a "deed of assignment," or a "chattel conveyance." The Bankruptcy Act of 1867 allowed for formal bankruptcy proceedings on the federal level, but apparently few Natchez cases made their way to New Orleans federal court because of the costs, time, and distance involved. The act was repealed in 1878, leaving local lawsuits, assignments, and conveyances as the preeminent local debt resolution vehicles into the twentieth century—if collection could not be had through a trustee on an existing deed of trust. Debt collection lawsuits were often brought forth for large sums by outside creditors (out-of-state wholesalers, manufacturers, and cotton factors) through local attorneys, although this could very well occur with local creditors, too, if the amounts owed were large or the animosity was high. Usually the local attorneys would file suit and petition for a "writ of attachment," freezing assets and forcing the defendant to put up a surety bond to ensure the debtor's appearance in court, frequently backed by another merchant associate. In H. M. Gastrell's case, for example, many of the plaintiffs were out-of-state creditors represented in common by the local law firm Carson, Shields, & Carson, and for whatever reason Gastrell did not fight many of the initial suits, in which he sacrificed bond and was levied with quick judgments in absentia that went straight to sheriff Robert H. Wood for asset seizure and sale. Other times this process could drag on for years: Gastrell was still in court four years later, fighting other suits, bleeding both the plaintiffs and himself of legal fees, apparently buying time to stash a few assets in his wife's name and raise more money. Much the same occurred in John Fleming's case. He still had assets for sale by a trustee nearly a decade after going broke. But a judgment was often no great benefit to creditors, who usually accepted cents on the dollar from ruined merchantmen, who had little, while creditors paid substantial legal bills just to get that much.[14]

By far the simplest and most common scenario involved a deed of assignment or a chattel conveyance, an informal agreement where a merchant who had reached the end of credit with his suppliers was forced to sign over his remaining stock and store assets to a trustee (usually another prominent merchant) to liquidate and satisfy creditors—of which two-thirds had to agree to the proceeding. A large amount of local mercantile credit and goods was actually supplied by large local wholesalers, who acted as middlemen for out-of-state suppliers, particularly in the case of smaller, second-tier local merchants. In one interesting example of a simple chattel conveyance to satisfy both local and out-of-state supply debt, Irish merchant Thomas Hart was indebted to local suppliers Rumble & Wensel, Henry Frank Co., and I. Lowenburg Co. in the amount of $3,500, with a secondary interest held by New Orleans cotton factor Richard Flower & Co.[15] Hart signed over

> all the stock of goods, wares, and merchandize consisting of dry goods, groceries, clothes, tobacco, cigars, notions, and general merchandize . . . and also all the book accounts, rights, credits, cotton, chattel mortgages, notes &c, to us due and to become due; and also the following livestock and chattels, to wit: (including over 25 mules, cattle, and oxen). . . . Subject, however, as to cotton, chattel mortgages, and livestock to an indebtedness due by us to the firm of Richard Flower & Co. of New Orleans, Louisiana, for the satisfaction of which indebtedness I pledged the same.[16]

It is unclear what amounts were owed individually to I. Lowenburg & Co., Rumble & Wensel, Henry Frank Co., and Richard Flower & Co., but this resolution brings up a valuable point: in a settlement on the local level conducted by local creditors, the local creditors often received the lion's share of the settlement, as the primary collectors and liquidators of the debt, and then subordinated a negotiated settlement of any further proceeds to the outsider at a reduced settlement amount. Another factor in Thomas Hart's failure was that he apparently was not well respected in the business community, because the R. G. Dun agent had noted that "he keeps a mulatto girl for a mistress, I am always afraid of men who lead such a life . . . the inevitable tendency to debase + degrade + destroy all pride of char[acter]. He is intemperate, of doubtful honor + not altogether reliable." Poor reputation and character was a businessman's scourge, yet Hart's problems with drinking and women was apparently a fairly common theme of failure among many of his contemporaries, including M. L. Cary, who also had problems with drink and women, as the Dun agent sniffed he was "Drunk all the time, no cap[ability] or cr[edit]. . . . Quit business, left, played out, woman at the bottom."[17]

Just as common as a chattel conveyance, a deed of assignment ended many a Natchez merchantman's career. The primary difference lay in the appointment of a trustee to liquidate store assets to pay creditors, who were often classified in "classes," which determined the hierarchy of who was to be paid first. Samuel Block, for example, was a prominent member of the German Jewish community; had been a large plantation supply merchant in Concordia Parish since 1867, with hundreds of accounts; and had owned and leased several plantations for years, but lost heavily as a part owner in H. M. Gastrell's Vidalia & Western Railroad Co. when it failed in 1881. By 1885 he was deeply in debt to factor V. & A. Meyer Co. of New Orleans, and soon was selling off plantation assets to pay creditors.[18] Apparently, he closed his store in Vidalia and tried for a new start, reopening in Natchez, but to no avail, as he was soon beset by creditors in that city who forced him to accept the following deed of assignment to trustee Aaron Beekman Jr. in 1890:

> Samuel Block of the City of Natchez doing business in the said city at No. 522 Franklin Street . . . [whereas] by reason of misfortunes in business, and the inability to collect debts and outstanding accounts is insolvent, financially embarrassed, and unable to pay his debts at maturity in full; and is desirous of providing for their payment and assigning his property for that purpose as hereinafter stipulated. . . . Doth grant, bargain, sell, convey, assign, transfer, and set over . . . all and singular his estate, goods, chattels, effects, credits, classes in action, notes, book accounts and property both real and personal of every name and kind belonging to said business and in the store.[19]

For a merchant to have his store and stock handed over to a fellow merchant, particularly a rival from the same tight-knit Jewish religious and business community, was likely the epitome of degradation and humiliation, and in Block's case his creditors may have wanted him humbled. Assignment deeds usually did not carry such strong wording as "insolvent" and "embarrassed," but in this case he was defaulting to powerful members of his synagogue and Ezra Lodge #134, including "Simon Ullman . . . note dated Dec. 20th, 1886 at the rate of eight per cent per annum from date for . . . $585.20," and "Julius W. Roos, Chairman of the Endowment Fund of the I.O.O.B., two notes due Jan'y 1–4, 1891 . . . one bearing interest at the rate of (9) nine per cent per annum . . . [and] one bearing interest at the rate if eight (8) per cent per annum, both dated 1st day of Jan'y 1890 for $500.00." This episode may have been personal in the Jewish community, because these two debts were listed as "Class No. One" debts to be paid first, ahead of $7,000 owed to Britton & Koontz Bank, which was listed as a "Class No. Two" creditor, to be paid second, even though the bank was owed many times as much. During the following year leading

Jewish businessmen Henry Frank and the Scharff brothers sued Block and received judgments in circuit court for thousands more. Block was ruined, but he remained in town until at least 1910 as a "planter" on leased lands. However, he had clearly lost his standing and reputation in his own community. It was a business death to default to creditors, but it was also a social and personal death to default to local friends, family, and associates.[20]

If avoiding supply debt and financial ruin was a difficult mercantile task, collecting on one's outstanding accounts could be even worse. Attempts to collect on chattel mortgage or deed of trust debt precipitated a constant round of legal filings, seizures, and sheriff's sales—all time-consuming and expensive proceedings from which often only the attorneys profited. Merchants generally would try to collect small amounts generated by chattel mortgage debt through rolling over debt from year to year or would try to reach a resolution through negotiation. This process occurred without fail year after year, usually in the months of October through December, when the year's supply bill was due and the cotton crop was in, the best time of year to catch the debtor with a little money in his pocket or cotton to seize. Depending on the merchant, even fairly small amounts could generate legal activity against croppers who had little or nothing to begin with. For example, between January 1878 and January 1881 the litigious Isaac Friedler filed at least twelve collection lawsuits for overdue annual supply bills against croppers on at least six different plantations in Concordia Parish. The total sought was $2,444.88, or an average of $203.74 per suit. All were backed by crop liens on cotton, and in a testament to the inferior legal position of the croppers, and perhaps the abilities of his lawyers, Mayo & Boatner, Friedler won each case plus court costs and 8 percent interest until paid, although whether he ever collected on all these judgments is unknown. At least three must have paid or negotiated arrangements, however, because Charles Washington on Carter's Lake ($124.78 plus costs), and Wilson Johnson and Jake Davis on Minorca ($240 and $397.45 plus costs, respectively) recorded further supply accounts with Friedler over many years.[21]

Other times the croppers might have cotton or chattels that could be seized under the conditions of the lien, and the merchant would then be forced to file for a "replevin writ"—essentially an order for the local sheriff to seize property that was signed away as a condition of a chattel mortgage and therefore was already considered rightful property of the merchant. This was to force those with delinquent accounts to pay their outstanding supply bill or rent. Armed with a replevin writ the sheriff would travel out to the plantation and seize the items in question, usually taking possession for transport back to Natchez. In November 1876, for example, Wolfe Geisenberger's attorney, Frederick Parsons, appeared before Natchez Justice Court and was given a replevin writ for "10 bales cotton" owed by croppers Abe Perry, Frank Johnson, Tom Brown, and Isaac Payne, who were working as a squad on Mandamus plantation in Adams County. To resolve an overdue supply bill as well as unpaid rent in cotton, sheriff Robert H. Wood rode out to the plantation the same day the writ was issued, and the croppers agreed to an immediate settlement in cotton. This gave Geisenberger the ten bales as payment, but left him to pay for the filing fee, attorney's cost, and the sheriff's mileage and transportation of the cotton, which should have been delivered to him without the additional expense to begin with. Livestock such as mules, cattle, and oxen traded hands in the same manner with yearly regularity. In just one example, I. Lowenburg & Co. seized two mules from Joseph Murdock on Waveland in 1895 for overdue supply bills of $446.98 and 223.45 plus 8 percent interest and costs. Two mules were certainly not worth the amount and the time and trouble the company invested in this seizure almost thirty miles from Natchez, but the firm later recouped a small additional amount when awarded title to Murdock's land. Cattle seized was of often dubious value, because, while mules in good condition (which they frequently were not) could be rented or resold for around $100, cattle required pasturage or stock pens and had to be fed and were not worth anything close to a mule—more trouble than they were worth. The chattels seized for debt could also include farm implements, and there was no guarantees the merchant would keep what was taken: in 1903 A. F. Jacobs & Bros. seized some cattle and a wagon and buggy from cropper William Alexander for unpaid supply debt on Hunters Hall, and the judge allowed Jacobs to keep the cattle but made him return the wagon and buggy.[22]

The same collection sequence could occur with a planter as well. In January 1874 top Natchez attorney and judge William T. Martin filed suit and received a replevin writ for I. Lowenburg & Co. against old-line planter Daniel S. Farrar, who owed over $1,000 on a supply bill from 1872 and 1873. Sheriff William McCary then traveled out and seized eighteen bales of cotton from Farrar on his Allendale plantation. This was to ensure that Farrar would appear in a forthcoming lawsuit in the April term of circuit court. Just to get the cotton (to be stored until a possible judgment),

Lowenburg spent $3.55 on the clerk's fee, $7.55 on the sheriff's fee, plus travel costs of eighteen miles at $1.80 a mile, not to mention whatever Martin charged as his legal fee, which probably ran well over $100. Lowenburg apparently received a judgment that April, but the collection of the debt dragged on until July 1874, when Farrar finally deeded over the title to Allendale (393 acres) for a forgiveness of $1,690.43 in supply debt. This means that I. Lowenburg & Co. had to pay all the associated costs and its own supply debts in advance, only to receive the land but no cash in return, requiring substantial capital to float the entire cost and giving no guarantees that the land would generate income immediately. Thus even the collection of a debt was fraught with risk and required substantial capital to stay in business waiting for resolution. And there was no guarantee the merchant would win a debt suit at all. Sim Lowenburg, of I. Lowenburg & Co., lost a debt dispute with his former agent and overseer Mike Phelen in the Eighth Judicial Court in Concordia Parish in 1896, and the court ordered Lowenburg's Fletcher plantation seized and sold, with the proceeds partitioned to pay Phelen. Lowenburg apparently refused to give up a plantation that had been in his family for two decades, so at a sheriff's sale he bought his own plantation back for $3,000, made a $1,433.74 payment to Phelen and also absorbed $132.50 in court costs and $150 in attorney's fees only to give up on Fletcher and sell it later. Merchant lawsuit losses were common: N. L. Carpenter & Son lost a cotton gin to a replevin writ by planter Anna E. Smith on one occasion and lost substantial lease proceeds in cotton to planter Wilmer H. Shields on another. Isaac Friedler paid $4,104.53 in one dispute with suppliers Fuzz & Backer, and in another lost a $4,465.50 judgment versus the police jury in Concordia Parish over the payment of old Reconstruction-era municipal bonds. As with cropper debt, even if the merchant won his suit, payment might come at cents on the dollar or in the form of hard-to-sell livestock or used farm implements that required storage. Isaac Friedler received farming equipment in a $563.15 judgment versus planter A. M. Swayze, while I. Lowenburg & Co. and Henry Frank Co. took well over 100 head of livestock and assorted equipment in the default of merchant-planter I. S. Simon.[23]

While supply debt and the resulting collection efforts and legal trouble were a vexing and financially draining part of every crop year and ruined many Natchez merchants, myriad local taxes and business licensing requirements were also a constant source of trouble. In Mississippi and Louisiana, state, county, and city taxes, when applicable, were levied on personal and real property, in addition to assessments for levee construction and upkeep, or for repayment of municipal railroad or infrastructure improvement bonds, which, when combined, added up to a substantial expense. In addition, in Mississippi an "inventory tax" was levied on the merchandise contained in a merchant's store. This was assessed by the county tax assessor and subject to review by the equalization board, comprised of community leaders working for the county supervisors. It was collected by the county tax collector (the sheriff) and divided with the city, depending upon the merchandise's assessment as "capital employed in merchandise," essentially placing city merchants in the unenviable position of being taxed twice for the same merchandise. There was a constant battle by merchants to get their inventory assessments lowered by both the Natchez Board of Aldermen and the Adams County supervisors. In a sample of city assessments, in 1882–1883 I. Lowenburg & Co. was assessed for $15,000 in merchandise; Aaron Beekman & Son, $6,000; Marx Lemle Co., $7,000; and Henry Frank Co. an expansive $35,000. Once the goods were given a value, a complex formula was applied, where the assessed value would be multiplied by 15 percent and then multiplied by a "millage" rate (1/10 of one cent per mill)—17.7 mills in Adams County in 1874. The millage on $10,000 in goods would generate a tax bill of $262.50. In addition to mercantile taxes, add on taxes on personal property, real estate, and municipal bond indebtedness, as well as the poor tax, school tax, and state taxes, and a Natchez merchant's tax bill could easily approach $1,000 a year. And it could be a lot more than that if the merchant owned significant plantation lands that were also taxed. The high postwar property taxes that stressed the planter class and caused a spate of land tax sales hit the new merchant-planters hard as well. While difficult to gather entire totals, with less than $10,000 employed in merchandise, for example, Aaron Beekman paid $631 for his inventory tax, personal property tax, and poll tax in Adams County alone in 1886–1887, and almost certainly paid many hundreds of dollars more for his property taxes on several city properties and plantation lands in three counties. In low-lying Concordia Parish, merchants, who suffered high state and parish taxes, also had to pay steep levee taxes, also calculated in mills and raised frequently, particularly after devastating flooding in the 1880s.[24]

Cities in addition required some form of license or tax as a requirement to run or conduct a business. The city of Natchez, for example, required a "privilege tax" to operate a business in the city limits, as well as another for the right to sell alcoholic beverages—a key and highly profitable item in many a store. In the 1880s the privilege tax ran $150 a year, and failure to pay brought a prompt grand jury indictment: the mercurial Irishman George T. Payne apparently hated to pay his and was indicted twice by a grand jury, forced to relinquish the $150, and assessed a steep fine and court costs on both occasions. A liquor license was an additional $100 and had to be renewed yearly. It also required a petition signed by residents of the ward in question to be submitted to the board of alderman for approval. Perfectly in character, on one occasion Payne was also charged with illegally selling less than one gallon of "spirituous liquor" (one pint of whisky), and had the same scenario play out before the grand jury, ruining his chances of getting a liquor license for several years. To make matters worse, in 1901 the state of Mississippi moved to collect back taxes on interest income or "solvent credits" generated by trust deeds, mortgages, and other loans dating back to the 1880s. In an effort that shattered merchants, planters, and bankers alike—anyone who loaned money or goods at interest—the state sent a special revenue agent to Natchez who methodically went through all deed, mortgage, and conveyance records and compiled strikingly accurate lists of special assessments on a host of local businessmen. Probably over 100 new assessments were issued and applied on top of existing taxes to be paid by December 15 of that year. In a few examples, A. F. Jacobs & Bros. was assessed an additional $12,245; Adolf Jacobs Co., $13,141; Ann E. Abbott (Abbott Groceries Co.), $14,948; and Britton & Koontz Bank a staggering $175,253. In a sign that planter and businessman were now practically one and the same, sharing the same financial troubles, leading planter James Surget was levied an enormous $84,174 dating back to 1888 on chattel mortgages and trust deeds issued by him on his many plantations. The heavy assessments came at a time when cotton prices were low, local cotton production was stressed, and mercantile profits were shrinking. This assessment was another sign of an impending mercantile crisis due to a host of external factors that had been building for decades, and the appearance of one particularly unwelcome new resident, the cotton boll weevil:[25]

> There is no doubt but that we will suffer from the ravages of the pest until we can adapt ourselves to the new conditions, but in less than three years, business will adjust itself. . . . There is no method of killing the weevil in the field. We can only hope to lessen its damage

by adopting the "cultural methods." . . . If you attempt to plant your present acreage and use present methods . . . the result will be your ruin.[26]

When the weevil invaded the Natchez District sometime in 1907, some results were immediately felt; others played out over years. The weevil meant a quantum shift in the social and economic nature of the region and heralded the local end of King Cotton. As the primary keepers of the local postwar system of debt, tenancy, and cotton marketing, the Natchez merchant class was among the first to feel the sting, and within a few short years the ranks of Natchez merchants would be greatly reduced. Many of the factors that fed the decline of the local traders had actually been building for years, and the boll weevil merely provided the impetus to topple the rotting edifice of an unstable and pernicious system, built upon the backs of the unfortunate and predicated upon an unsustainable, dangerous business. In an immediate sense, crop yields began to fall appreciably after 1907, reducing the profits from the production and handling of cotton, creating a commensurate contraction in the plantation supply business and the local economy in general. There was also the specter of *fear*, the anxiety that cotton would never again reach levels of previous profitability. This caused farmers to plant less acreage and tighten their expenditures, which in turn forced merchants to assume austerity and retrench in their efforts. The primary advice rendered by the agricultural experts at the time was diversification and self-sufficiency in food, to "plant about one-third as much cotton as formerly, and the remaining two-thirds is to be put in corn and forage crops." Grow food. Be self-sufficient. Reduce your dependency upon credit. If only someone had followed that advice thirty years earlier, there might not have been such a merchant class or system of debt. Of course, a handful of local Grangers and Populists had expounded as much for years, but the simple fact was that the search for immediate profits by farmers, as well as the security demanded by the merchants as the cost of their credit in the absence of local capital, perpetuated the local mono-agriculture that ruined land, ruined farmers, and soon ruined merchants. King Cotton had consumed all in its path, and now it was going to consume the king's attendants.[27]

In many ways, it was a wonder that Natchez and its merchant class prospered to any degree at all after the war, a testament to the energy of its citizens in an area beset on all sides by perils largely beyond their control.

The state of the national economy had subjected the district to boom-and-bust cycles driven by currency expansion and constriction, while at least three periods of financial panic and a long-lasting economic downturn, which endured from the 1870s through the 1890s, plagued Natchez. Northerners and locals alike largely built the initial postwar recovery in the district on speculation in cotton, and while the initial burst of vitality helped solidify the new merchant class, the shattering crop failures of 1867 and 1868 reduced many of the first wave of entrepreneurs. And with the almost complete absence of local capital, the lien system quickly became entrenched and threatened both the merchant and the cropper and planter alike. There was probably no viable alternative, but the systematic reliance upon "flawed institutions" of credit offering would guarantee eventual trouble and failure. No sooner had the district got back on its feet after the initial speculation-driven debacle when the panic and currency constriction, driven by a rising dollar of the 1870s, created a second wave of business failures because of a lack of local capital and tightening credit. These factors contributed to the failure of firms like Fleming & Baldwin and H. M. Gastrell Co., who exercised gross fiscal overextension in a tightening credit environment and were victims of their own excess and speculation. In the 1880s the district once again recovered and, indeed, boomed, engendering a local explosion of investment in railroads, cotton mills, and other New South manufacturing and financial businesses, only to fall prey to plummeting cotton prices and a new round of panic and constriction in the 1890s:[28]

> By the year 1893 the time had come: credit was used up, prosperity was at an end. . . . Prices struck new low levels . . . and cotton at less than five cents a pound, debts merely compounded . . . in ever dearer dollars. Small businessmen who depended upon the farmers' trade suffered almost as acutely as the farmers themselves. Even the country merchants of the South, who protected themselves by high credit prices to the last possible limit, failed by the hundreds.[29]

That round of financial troubles—in combination with generational change and fresh ideas about modern business practices, new products, and new types of businesses—fed an increasing willingness to abandon strictly cotton-related mercantile pursuits or, at least, supplement them with more diversified business interests. In fact, local merchantmen may have had intimations of the imminent downfall of their cotton-related businesses as early as the 1880s. Certainly they did by the 1890s, when they began actively seeking new businesses and diversification. This was a decade or two before the severe reduction of the local cotton business. But the prevailing excitement and expansive attitudes engendered by the new century and an emerging and powerful modern America seem to have still provided sufficient hope for the future to keep plenty of firms in the old plantation supply regime, only to be shattered again by both financial panic and the appearance of the boll weevil in 1907. Natchez had always had a boom-and-bust economy and was never a very safe place to do business, and the nature of the local and national economy from the end of the Civil War until 1914 made doing business there particularly risky.[30]

If the general economy was uncertain, the cotton business and marketplace were exponentially so and changing fast, and the two were intimately intertwined in Natchez. Several factors drove the volatility of cotton prices, and in many ways the situation was getting worse. First was the emergence of cotton futures trading, which had been in existence in a rudimentary form of "forward contracts"—where a speculator buys a position on future crop delivery at a certain price—on the New York and Liverpool cotton exchanges since the 1850s. But by the 1880s formal rules and clearing houses had been established, and active trading in a modern form occurred at cotton or commodities exchanges in New York, Chicago, and New Orleans, which became a key trading venue for Natchez cotton. Morton Rothstein has noted, "Many contemporary (nineteenth century) critics were suspicious of a form of business in which one man sold what he did not own to another who did not want it." This view is based on sound reason, because increasingly cotton prices were driven and manipulated by speculators with no interest in the actual crop, and prices no longer reflected actual supply and demand. While this factor would lead one to suspect that speculation would drive prices higher, market manipulators could profit by depressing prices and "hedging," or betting on lower prices. This brought the other two reasons into play: increasing global cotton production in tandem with extreme overproduction in the United States. Partly as a result of the Union embargo of the South during the Civil War, textile producers in England had found and developed new sources of production in India, Egypt, and Brazil. After an initial spike in demand following the war, the world market was increasingly glutted with a surplus of cotton, reducing the Deep South market share at a time when vast cotton lands in Texas, Arkansas, and California added to already excessive Southern production. Yet Southern croppers and planters continued to put more acreage into mono-crop cotton production, making the surplus of cotton on the market worse, while becoming ever more dependent in the process, because they put less into food and other crops. Of course, Southern merchants deserve a healthy measure of blame due to their demands for cotton production to back their risks in the crop lien credit system.[31]

Even the grand ventures to build local manufacturing and other infrastructure at least partly failed to bolster the local economy, even when they did not turn out to be ill-advised speculations. As we have seen, railroad investment was risky at best, and many local merchants and businessmen lost money through local or even national railroad schemes. The same company that bought out H. M. Gastrell's failing little railroad in 1881, the Natchez, Red River & Texas Railroad Co., was backed with $10,000 investments (100 shares each) by a host of leading merchants, including Henry Frank, S. E. Rumble, Samuel Block, Isaac Friedler, and Julius Weis, among others. All of these investors apparently lost their money when the railroad was sold for taxes in April 1885 to a New Orleans investor, who failed later as well. Even the successful Little J railroad, connecting Natchez to Jackson, defaulted on its 3.5 percent interest payments to the city of Natchez for $225,000 in municipal bonds in 1885, and was bailed out by a group of local leaders working behind closed doors with Mayor Isaac Lowenburg. On another occasion, in 1892, when Natchez was obligated with $320,000 in bonds to build the New Orleans & Northwestern Railroad (successor to another failed city-backed venture, the New Orleans, Natchez & Fort Scott Railroad), the *Natchez Democrat* sarcastically commented, "The people of this community have been very patient with the road under its promises and hopes which must eventually be fulfilled, but patience grows weary in the failure of fruition." That road was actually finished, but not before it bled all parties involved dry, only to be put into receivership in 1902. In another example of planters becoming businessmen, perhaps the largest and most successful remnants of the old planter class—brother and sister team James Surget and Kate Minor—found serious railroad troubles themselves in 1877, as the R. G. Dun agent noted: "[Surget] took his sister Mrs. K. S. Minor in [and] has lost heavily by investing in RR stock &c." The local cotton mills faced their share of troubles as well. After a rapid and profitable start in the 1880s, the

Natchez Cotton Mills experienced a disastrous boiler explosion in 1887, killing three, spawning a host of lawsuits, and greatly reducing its value. Due to stiff competition, plummeting textile prices, and vanishing credit, during the 1890s both the Natchez Cotton Mills and Rosalie Cotton Mills experienced severe financial troubles and were closed briefly. Britton & Koontz Bank was given a bill of sale on the Rosalie Cotton Mills in 1896 for a defaulted $20,000 debt, and a year later the estate of Mrs. Armand Perrault declared, "The stock held by the said estate in the Rosalie Cotton Mills Co. of Natchez, was absolutely worthless." Meanwhile, the Natchez Cotton Mills was reopened in 1902, but only after an infusion of $350,000 in new capital.[32]

In addition to the economic troubles, everyday life in the Cotton Kingdom was a fairly uncertain proposition. A plethora of local environmental and physical hazards bore down on Natchez at different times. While local boosters touted Natchez's "beautiful location, its delightful climate, [and] its phenomenal healthfulness," the simple fact was the district had never been especially healthful. The area's subtropical climate brought almost yearly visitations from malaria and yellow fever in the late summer or early fall. Greatly feared, yellow fever reached epidemic proportions many times during the nineteenth century, producing "death, confusion, and despair, paralyzing commercial, political, and church activities and bringing the life of the community to a standstill for weeks." The local elite had always spent summers away if possible, but with crops being harvested September through November, the end of the crop season was a crucial time for local merchants to be attending business at their stores and plantations, even though it was at the height of yellow fever danger. During one particularly virulent episode in 1871, for example, 1,200 cases in Natchez alone produced at least ninety-nine deaths, and many more in swampy flatlands across the river in Vidalia and Concordia Parish. Many people fled town for the countryside or beyond, and by September local business came to a standstill. Isaac Lowenburg saved his family by moving them to a rented farmhouse north of town, but his partner, John Hill, "was taken sick at his and papa's grocery store. . . . When the doctor declared it yellow fever . . . there were no nurses to be had even for pay . . . to take care of him until he died a few days later." Just about every mercantile family in this study lost at least one member to yellow fever between 1865 and 1905, and the 1871 epidemic took merchants Hiram Baldwin and brothers Jacob and Abram Lorie. It also nearly killed Lowenburg's brother, Samuel, who never fully recovered. Natchez became virtually abandoned, as a strict quarantine was enforced and the epidemic dragged on into late October, ruining business and prompting the *Democrat* to note: "Natchez now presents the unusual spectacle of stores unusually well stocked with goods of all kinds, and nobody to buy them. The face of a country customer is rarely seen, and even our own city people with rare exceptions, keep close to home. The streets look deserted." Actually, deserted streets were not so unusual, because almost yearly the city and county governments hired able-bodied men to enforce a quarantine on the county roads, boat landings, and train entry points, at gunpoint if necessary, following the first sign of trouble. They restricted the afflicted to the "pest house," and burned their bedding, clothing, and other household and personal items. Regardless of the danger, local merchants hated quarantine almost as much as yellow fever itself, as the following petition signed by every merchant in town and presented to the Natchez aldermen during the outbreak of the 1899 fever season indicates: "The undersigned merchants and taxpayers of the city of Natchez respectfully protest the rigid quarantine system or regulations now in force . . . especially the placing of guards upon the public roads of this county."[33] The last serious outbreak occurred in 1905, by which time the mosquito had been identified as the culprit and authorities had developed countermeasures. But yellow fever, in combination with malaria, diphtheria, smallpox, and other outbreaks, taxed the local populace regularly and hurt business on practically a yearly basis. People grew tired of the incessant subtropical maladies, quarantines, and difficult summers—one reason that many moved on when the cotton business began to falter.[34]

There were other substantial local perils to life and business as well. Natchez lay in an area renowned for its weather extremes, including tornados. The second most deadly tornado in American history destroyed a good portion of the town and the river landing in 1840, killing over 300 people. Another tornado destroyed several buildings in the Pine Ridge area north of Natchez in 1908, including the Pine Ridge Presbyterian Church and plantation home Mount Repose. And while no other major cyclone smashed the Natchez area during the postwar period, immoderate rains or droughts were a constant bane to local cotton and damaged or ruined crops with alarming frequency, in turn distressing local business and merchants.[35] On one occasion in July 1887 the *Democrat* noted:

We interviewed several of our country planters who came in yesterday and all agree that we are having entirely too much rain. The present rains have been very general, extending all over the country, and . . . their continuance is becoming a detriment to both cotton and corn. In the cleanest fields before the rains began the weeds and grass are growing rank, and unless there is an early dry spell they will greatly retard the growth of the cotton.[36]

While planters, croppers, and merchants alike cast anxious eyes toward the sky yearly, they also had to look to the river. Natchez, on the bluff, did not flood, but expansive plantation lands north and south of town, and especially the excellent flatland across the river in Concordia Parish, were usually flooded at least two or three times in a decade, the result of large springtime overflows of the Mississippi River. On the Mississippi side, although some local efforts had been made at levee construction, many rural areas had little or no protection, and a late flood could set back planting by a month or more, practically ensuring a small or stunted crop. On one occasion in 1906, severe flooding on forty-two unprotected plantations and farms in Adams County resulted in a change in their assessed value from $233,800 to $153,850. This was due to the damage to the lands from "unusual and unprecedented overflow in each case." Across the river in Concordia and Tensas Parishes, flooding made the vast alluvial plains, full of sediments, so rich to begin with, but floods were a serious problem, completely inundating the town of Vidalia on several occasions. The local police jury responded with a massive levee-building project in the 1880s, but that was also a bane of sorts, because of the cost, as levee tax assessments skyrocketed. And regardless of rain or flood, insect damage was a constant peril long before the boll weevil appeared. A combination of armyworms and flooding had decimated crops in 1867–1868, but their cousins cotton worms and cutworms also made a regular appearance, prompting one local to note in 1882:[37] "The crop prospects in Concordia parish are not the most favorable desired this year. The cut worms are eating both cotton and corn in some localities. . . . Many places the ravages of the worms have been sufficient to necessitate a replanting of the cotton crop."[38]

If rain troubles, flooding, and insects were not enough, crop yields throughout the district had been falling for years because of "tired lands." The fields were depleted of nutrients by mono-crop planting with little or no crop rotation, increasingly requiring guano and chemical fertilizer to get much yield. Decades of planting also had caused serious soil erosion problems, particularly in the rolling hills of Adams County. Large "gashes" appeared in and between cultivated fields as drainage patterns were changed by clearing forests without proper accounting for run-off. The cumulative effect of these mounting troubles was making cotton less and less profitable, slowly eroding the will and vigor of both producer and merchant alike.[39]

Even if a good crop could escape myriad troubles and make it to the merchant's warehouse in town for processing, sale, and shipment, it could still fall victim to perhaps the most persistent peril in the district: fire. In the wooden frame and brick buildings on district plantations and city streets alike, countless conflagrations burned cotton gins, cotton warehouses, mercantile firms, cotton and lumber mills, and private residences with startling regularity. Aaron Beekman had his store building burned to the ground on two separate occasions, while S. & A. Jacobs, A. F. Jacobs & Bros., Henry Frank Co., and Samuel Lowenburg lost their buildings and stock on at least one occasion. R. G. Dun reports for the period are replete with comments like "Lately burned out" or "Burn't out . . . lost ½ his stock . . . rapidly becoming insolvent." In fact, James Carradine & Co. was worth around $100,000, and Carradine was considered "one of our best citizens" until "losing his residence + contents by fire uninsured," starting a downward spiral that shocked even the Dun agent: "I can hardly conceive that he wd [would] be in so much debt. He got behind 2 yrs. ago, when he lost his dwlg [dwelling] by fire." It was a testament to the importance of purchasing fire insurance, which was not cheap, because Carradine & Co. collapsed a year later. Even with insurance, it might take a lawsuit to get the insurance company to pay, and while the city maintained several volunteer fire companies, their steam-driven water pumpers were woefully inadequate—one major reason for a local push to build a municipal water system with hydrants. But fires continued throughout the period, and some were spectacular. One huge blaze at Cotton Square in 1891 consumed cotton and merchandise worth many tens of thousands of dollars and burned or damaged no less than five mercantile establishments, the Natchez Cotton and Merchants Exchange, and the Britton & Koontz Bank. In 1887 boiler explosions blew apart both the Natchez Cotton Mills and Chamberlain's Sawmill, killing four people. Within a two-week period in the spring of 1908, a huge fire burned ten houses and knocked out electric power and telephone service to the city for days, followed by a shattering gas explosion that leveled the new Natchez Drug Co. building, killing ten people.[40]

Significant local social and economic resistance had existed against merchants for some time, while racism was getting steadily worse, with particularly ominous ramifications for the merchantmen. Often acting in league with the beleaguered planter class, particularly as the new century got closer, local merchants had also been the focal point of considerable ire among planters and farmers because of their credit-debt practices. In the early 1870s the *Natchez Almanac* complained on the planters' behalf:

> Pshaw! Planters have no friends while they have cotton. If their staple gets just as low as it can get, the merchants, through their brokers, will kindly take it as a settlement for advances, and get their profit in a rise.... We are not blaming the cotton merchant. We are only showing the pitiful case of the man who deals with him.[41]

The explosion of rural discontent that pushed the "Greenbackers," Grange, and Populists onto the national stage after the "Crime of 1873" existed in the Natchez District as well, although never to the same extent as in some other Southern agricultural states such as Texas or Georgia. Nonetheless, several old-line planter families, including the Bayards, Stowers, Dardens, and Farrars, banded together with others to form Grange ("Patrons of Husbandry") chapters in Pine Ridge, north of town, and in Kingston, to the south. Local Grange leaders George W. Bayard and Orange S. Miles— Miles had been in serious supply debt to I. Lowenburg & Co. and Meyer, Weis, & Deutsch during the 1870s and almost lost his land—formed the Natchez Co-Operative Ass'n Grange Store in 1877 to remove the merchants and their high credit rates from the plantation supply equation. The R. G. Dun agent noted in 1879 that Orange S. Miles was the manager of a "corporation composed of planters," with a worth of $10,000. He also made clear that "their prospects of success will depend almost entirely on grange patronage." The Grange store lasted only a few years in the face of withering local mercantile competition, and ironically, Orange Miles's wife, Eliza, lost their entire estate, after he died in 1885, to Perrault & Co. at a debt sale. But by their existence, the Grange and its local store make it clear that significant resistance to merchant practices existed among local planters and farmers.[42]

But if there was passive resistance to the merchants through the Grange, a new force was emerging south of town, in Amite County. It threatened the Jewish merchant class and black croppers alike with racial violence. In 1892, as a part of rising local racism, "an organization known as White Caps was begun for the purpose of controlling Negro labor of the county and to break up the apparent combine between Jewish merchants and Negro labor." Supposedly formed of the "best citizens" of Amite County (twenty-five miles southeast of Natchez), the White Caps were upset that, by offering excessive inducements, the Jewish merchants had lured most of the counties' African American workforce to work on farms owned by Jews, and under "such circumstances the Negroes were not willing to work for white farmers." The White Caps ordered all blacks to leave these farms no later than January 1, 1893, and advised the Jewish merchants to "stop buying land and mules for the Negroes, and not to furnish them except through the (white) farmers." While the end result is not entirely known, apparently one black cropper was murdered, several others were "whipped" by bands of White Caps to drive them off lands that Jews owned, and a few merchants were ruined and forced out of business. Not wanting to lose their workforce, White Cap leaders tried to assure the African Americans that the violence was directed at Jews and not at the black tenants per se. Only those who had business with Jews faced trouble, but the local African Americans banded together to demand that the violence stop, or they would leave the state. Natchez Jews were aware of the troubles, and Jewish firms Aaron Beekman & Son, I. Lowenburg & Co., and Wolfe Geisenberger & Son all owned or supplied plantations in nearby Wilkinson County; by the turn of the century all three had sold their assets or quit business in the area, another sign of an impending Jewish mercantile diaspora from the district.[43]

If local Jews were starting to feel uncomfortable, local African Americans felt much worse as racism was building throughout the district. Soon it would reach a point of no return, eventually feeding an outward migration of the black croppers who provided the backbone of local agriculture. Blacks had made significant inroads in the Natchez District during Reconstruction and for a time thereafter, producing a host of local, state, and federal politicians; gaining ownership of many local plantations; and participating in railroad and other business endeavors with their white counterparts. But by the late 1880s most African American politicians had vanished with the post-Redemption decimation of the Republican Party and the rise of the Democrats, and the tenor of local white racial views was changing in an ominous fashion, as the *Democrat* commented:[44]

> When the Government of the United States emancipated the Negro, it did but a simple act of justice . . . but when the government clothed him with the elective franchise it made a mistake. He should not have been granted this greatest of rights until he was able to decipher the names on the tickets. . . . The negro in politics has thus far been a failure.[45]

In 1890 the state of Mississippi approved a new constitution that included a poll tax, a literacy test, and an understanding clause, effectively disenfranchising thousands of poor black, and white, voters in the Natchez District. Many beseeched the Natchez aldermen and Adams County supervisors for an "abatement" of their poll taxes, to little avail: in the Natchez aldermen's elections, the number of eligible voters in the heavily black Third Ward fell from ninety-three in 1899 to just nine in 1901. Local African Americans were losing their rights on a daily basis. Washington Ives was lynched in Adams County in 1888 for a suspected attempted rape (possibly of a white woman), while the Ku Klux Klan was known to operate in the rural areas north of Natchez near Washington, and south of town in Kingston. Meanwhile, White Caps were terrorizing blacks and Jews alike in Amite County.[46] The situation was rapidly deteriorating for African Americans, as Jim Crow took hold of the Natchez environs, and the racist rhetoric in the newspaper increased greatly as well with columns that shouted: "The black is incapable of receiving and using more than rudiments of education . . . [and] the present generation is retrograding to the status of the savage and might be ruled by force. This is shown by the constant disregard of the laws, repeated resistance of arrest and shooting down of white men who attempt to control them."[47]

Meanwhile, the continued debt-credit system perpetuated by the merchant class left the vast majority of local black landowners and croppers facing increasingly fraught conditions, as the local cotton business deteriorated. What had begun as a trickle of out-migration of African Americans in the 1890s gathered impetus in the first decade of the new century. It became a strong flow after the boll weevil arrived, and turned into a torrent when World War I–related Northern manufacturing jobs beckoned after 1914. The family of cropper Nathan Wright, father of the noted black author Richard Wright and longtime supply customers and debtors to Natchez merchants George T. Payne and Adolf Jacobs on Rucker plantation, finally gave up on Natchez, cotton, and debt and moved to Memphis in 1912. The same year, perhaps the most powerful African American politician in Mississippi, plantation owner John R. Lynch, also a customer and debtor of Adolf Jacobs, gave up his cotton interests and moved to Chicago. Some of the best merchant customers were leaving the district, and so were many merchants themselves.[48]

The social and economic conditions in the district had been less than ideal for some time, and developments after the turn of the century accelerated this trend. Yet despite myriad troubles facing the Natchez merchant class from exterior and systemic forces, some of the greatest threats to their continued success came from within. The families and strong merchant groups had been the bedrock of postwar merchant success, but gentrification, succession issues, and the natural process of death and generational change that induced migration were reducing the ranks of the merchant elite. The sons of the first-generation postwar merchants left the trade for other professions, or new opportunities in cities with better physical, social, and economic climates. Joseph N. Carpenter's son Nathaniel Leslie, the potential inheritor of the largest and wealthiest local mercantile-manufacturing complex, left his family's many successful businesses and storied past behind to seek his own fortune. He worked first as a banker in Bessemer, Alabama, and then as a cotton broker in Liverpool and, later, New York City, becoming partners in perhaps the largest cotton brokerage in the world, Carpenter, Baggott & Co. The Carpenter family's many local businesses largely ceased to exist after Joseph N. Carpenter died in 1925, and his son never returned to live in Natchez, although he did leave a huge philanthropic legacy to the city with his substantial fortune.[49]

The two sons of Aaron Beekman also left to attend medical school in New York and New Orleans, before practicing medicine in Memphis and, later, Natchez, where Drs. Phillip and Marcus Beekman became much-respected local figures in the medical, not the mercantile, realm. Their other brother, Samuel, remained in the plantation supply business for a time after Aaron Beekman died in 1901, but was out of business by 1912—the first time since the 1840s that a Beekman was not in the wholesale grocery and plantation supply business in Natchez, and the end of a local trade dynasty. Also not in the business for the first time since the 1840s was the Perrault family, as the two remaining Perrault brothers, Frank and Thomas, were local electrical contractors by 1912. And the Flemings were also out of the business, as James S. Fleming had made a large investment in pecan farming. William Abbott Jr. continued his family's wholesale grocery into the second decade of the twentieth century but was selling real estate by 1920. Adolf and Albert Jacobs gave up their plantation supply business in 1907 to open a small bank, while cousins Aaron and Hymen Jacobs gave up on their A. F. Jacobs & Bros. about the same time. In fact, with the general deterioration of the cotton business, countless merchant and planter sons sought new careers in law, medicine, engineering, insurance, banking, and real estate—even selling automobiles. By 1912 only two credit-offering wholesale grocer–cotton merchant–plantation supply firms remained in their original postwar forms: I. Lowenburg & Co. and Rumble & Wensel, although Geisenberger & Friedler Co. remained in that business as a combination of those two families. Perhaps the best barometer of the mercantile decline in Natchez was the exodus of the Jewish merchant community. In control of as many as a third of all local firms in 1900, after reaching a peak in 1905 the Jewish community began a steep decline, following the introduction of the boll weevil. As many as 300 Jews had fled Natchez by the 1920s, dropping their numbers by two-thirds and removing a host of firms from the marketplace.[50]

Other factors existed as well. While death is a natural part of life, it had been particularly unkind to several of the merchant families. The substantial business and planting interests held by Marx Lemle were sold to support his wife and daughter, and the business ended there, because he had no male heir. Much the same happened when the never-married George T. Payne died intestate in 1891, leaving his two sisters to petition in probate court to gain control of his large estate, which they sold off piecemeal for years in order to survive. And even when there was a will and interested, viable heirs, there was no guarantee that things would go smoothly. When Isaac Lowenburg died, his business partner, Cassius L. Tillman, remained with the firm, but apparently the Lowenburg heirs were not altogether happy with his presence.[51] Lowenburg's daughter Clara complained: "The business [I. Lowenburg & Co.] had gone down a great deal during papa's long illness, and which he had had to leave management of his partner, Cassius Tillman. Papa loved and trusted him, but Cassius was more interested in politics and speculating in cotton at that time than he was in the business. . . . He was drinking a lot too, with his political friends."[52]

Sim Lowenburg was later able to buy Tillman out and install his good friend and brother-in-law, Emanuel Samuels, as his partner in I. Lowenburg & Co., but only after considerable wrangling and expense. In fact, probate court could spell serious trouble for a mercantile family, and probably the most spectacular family meltdown and succession fight occurred among the many Perraults between 1897 and 1904. Armand Perrault had died in 1885 and left everything to his wife, Elizabeth, who ran the family businesses and plantations with the help of her four sons. But when she died in 1897, she had stipulated that the many cotton plantations and two stores be divided among no less than thirty-two living heirs, setting off a cascade of lawsuits in at least three counties. After intense legal fighting that pitted brothers against brothers against wives and grandchildren and saw one brother die in the process, a judge in 1904 decreed that the proceeds of the estate be divided and distributed to the thirty-two separate heirs in percentages ranging from "5936/20480" for a major heir (a Perrault son), to the fraction "171/20480" for some grandchildren, effectively diluting the economic power of the residual estate and forever rending the large family. Several small mercantile fortunes were dissipated in such a fashion, breaking the strong family ties that had cemented the merchant communities together.[53]

And it was not just that merchants or their family members died, in many cases it was how they died. Life was still precarious in the last half of the nineteenth century, and a person could go at a moment's notice or could suffer a gruesome malady for months before passing away. Isaac Lowenburg, for example, was bedridden for several months with liver and heart disease and suffered from "terrible paroxysms of asthma and suffocation [that] came on every night," necessitating "giving him morphine [injections] and increasing the doses so much that toward the end, no amount seemed to quiet the terrible paroxysms of pain." Life was short and often full of heartbreak. Lowenburg had lost his first wife at only twenty-six years old, remarried, but promptly lost two children from that marriage to various health problems, while his two surviving children in turn both lost infant children as well. Every merchant family in this study suffered at least one similar tragedy and often several. Especially after the boll weevil appeared, the building stress of the marketplace and demands of business gave rise to another form of malady: mental illness and suicide. John C. Schwartz, the wealthiest and most successful hardware purveyor in town, who had survived the crucible of war and every business trial that followed intact and indeed prospering, hanged himself in 1890. The Perrault brothers committed their youngest brother, James, shortly thereafter to an asylum in New Orleans for being "an insane." Clara Lowenburg's husband and prominent Natchez merchant-banker Abraham Moses was so distraught by the pressures of business and the death of their child that he suffered a complete mental breakdown and had to be committed in Cincinnati, where he committed suicide in 1899. Joseph N. Carpenter's twenty-four-year-old niece, Julia, had apparently been suffering from "melancholia" and shot herself in the head in 1901, and her planter father, Allen Delos, followed suit a few months later in 1902. After the boll weevil arrived, a spate of suicides plagued both planters and businessmen alike: merchant Charles Patterson committed suicide, and planter-businessman John C. Jenkins died of a self-inflicted gunshot in 1908; leading Natchez land developer, entrepreneur, businessman, and judge Thomas Reber shot himself in the head in 1912; and in 1914 planter William Wood, merchant-planter George Zurhellen, and banker George W. Koontz all ended their lives with gunshots to the head. It was a dangerous business in a dangerous place in an uncertain world, and King Cotton's attendants were going the way of the king himself.[54]

※ ※ ※

The town of Natchez had been buzzing with word of the failure of the First Natchez Bank since the fall, but on April 4, 1914, it was official, as the headlines in the *Democrat* screamed, "Forty-Five Charges Against The First Natchez Bank Officials." The bank's officers, businessman and president Andrew Campbell, senior vice president and merchant Sim Lowenburg, junior vice president and planter Robert Lee Wood, and cashier and planter H. B. Gaither all received at least ten charges before the circuit court grand jury, ranging from "receiving deposits in an insolvent bank" to "conspiracy to commit fraud" and "perjury," all stemming from the bank's sudden closing the previous October 29. The bank was now in receivership. It seems that the officers allowed the bank to lend very heavily to local planters and planting companies for the crop year 1913, but it started raining in late July and never stopped, completely ruining the local cotton crop by September. First Natchez was the city's largest bank, and court-appointed auditors stated that "the assets of First Natchez Bank must shrink by almost $275,000 before any loss falls on the depositors."

But the complete failure of the year's cotton crop meant countless planters could not repay their agricultural loans, coming due in September and October, by which time A. G. Campbell and Sim Lowenburg were frantically seeking an extension on the bank's credit from their creditors. But the condition of the year's crop was well known, and no other institution was willing to extend First Natchez any further credit, so the bank finally toppled with outstanding balances far exceeding cash on hand by almost $1 million—ruining hundreds of depositors in the process. At the trial that spring, all four defendants were jailed briefly before gaining a delay until the fall term and had to post large bail. Meanwhile, many citizens of Natchez, especially the ruined depositors, were in an uproar and wanted the blood of the defendants for what they viewed as a case of complete mismanagement and fraud, while the families and supporters of the defendants were vocal about their innocence, splitting the town into bitter factions. This was especially the case among the Jewish community, where on one side the prominent merchant Sim Lowenburg and his supporters proclaimed his innocence, while equally prominent Dr. Phillip Beekman, one of the largest depositors to lose money in the bank failure, led the other faction; never before had the local Jewish community been so divided.[55]

That fall of 1914, with Europe now locked in a mortal struggle that would soon have sweeping ramifications in the far-off Natchez District, it was clear that the position of the defendants was untenable. Investigators had determined that "the bookkeeping employed by the bank was wholly inadequate for the preservation of important records," while new allegations had surfaced. After the bank failed, the charge was that it had paid $5,284.78 to Tensas River Planting Co., in which Lowenburg had an interest and his partner at I. Lowenburg & Co., Emanuel Samuels, held the presidency. Apparently, the bank had paid out funds after closing to protect Lowenburg's and Samuels's planting business interests. Despite the best legal representation available, Lowenburg, Gaither, and Wood all pleaded nolo contendre to multiple charges, receiving hefty fines but escaping jail time. President A. G. Campbell faced the most serious charges and pleaded not guilty, and he went on to a jury trial. He was convicted on all counts and sentenced to three years in the Mississippi State Penitentiary, where he died later of gangrene. Sim Lowenburg was levied with a $30,000 fine plus all court costs on top of his attorney's fees, a huge sum, and was forced to sell many of his assets to make the payment, while he and his partner were now both outcasts in the eyes of the community.

Seeing no future in Natchez, Lowenburg and Samuels soon elected to distance themselves from I. Lowenburg & Co.—in business since 1863 and one of the last great wholesale grocers and cotton merchant firms still in existence—and move to New Orleans, never to return. In an improbable story of success and failure, over the course of fifty years the Lowenburgs had risen from nothing to the pinnacle of success in Natchez, only to have their fortunes upended and their good name disgraced. Thus began the end of the storied firm I. Lowenburg & Co., the oldest and most iconic of the postwar Natchez plantation supply firms. Its passing would mark the demise of a proud but troubled past consumed by an uncertain new age.[56]

Summary and Conclusion

THE TRAJECTORY OF THE BUSINESS CAREERS AND SOCIAL INTERactions of these ten mercantile families reveals much about the social and economic conditions that existed in the postwar Natchez District of Mississippi and Louisiana, and the changing economic demographics of the New South. The emergence of the postbellum merchant class as the new socioeconomic elite of the Natchez District was a complex process over time that actually had its roots in the antebellum period. The postwar explosion of mercantile influence was predicated on a host of factors converging at just the right time, in the right way, to elevate a formerly second-tier social and economic group to first-citizen status. The new merchant elite was comprised of a diverse combination of initially dissimilar social and economic communities, which, as the postwar period progressed, became more alike, increasingly intermarried, and formed new social, political, and business configurations that crossed former social and ethnic lines and were indicative of larger socioeconomic changes sweeping the nation. The emerging merchant elite made much of their advance at the expense of the formerly dominant planter class, but never completely replaced the local gentry. Instead, in a twist of irony, the sons of the planter and the merchant alike were becoming more similar. "Planter" and "merchant" increasingly became "businessman" of the New South. Both classes found their social and economic fate intimately intertwined and firmly tied to the unequal system of labor and credit that was built on the backs of freed blacks.

From the very beginning the planters and the merchants were never that far separated in social or economic terms. The Natchez District was first settled and built as a colonial trading center dominated by merchants, not planters, long before cotton agriculture made its appearance in the district. Even as slaves were introduced to the area and first indigo and then cotton agriculture became the primary and most successful economic endeavor in the region, several initial planter fortunes and family dynasties were built largely by mercantile pursuits, not planting wealth. Many leading early planters entered into the mercantile arena just to supply their own needs on the American frontier. After Mississippi achieved statehood and the antebellum period was in full swing, the importance of the merchant class remained, if somewhat overshadowed by the blinding success of planters and the accumulating fortunes found locally. The explosion of the Mississippi River trade, by flatboat and then steam packet, made Natchez perhaps the most important regional center in the Old Southwest, ensuring the continued importance of the local mercantile trade. As the antebellum period progressed, several large mercantile houses and cotton-factoring firms developed locally and rivaled those of New Orleans. In contrast, a growing cadre of middle-class and bourgeoisie traders began to develop and increasingly influence local city politics, social circles, and urban economic life. The influx of immigrants during the 1840s and 1850s greatly added to this growing class of indigenous middling traders with eager and shrewd German Jewish, Irish, Italian, and other foreign-born merchantmen who learned their mercantile trade in the European tradition. These elements of the growing bourgeoisie were not on the same level as the vaunted planters on the eve of the Civil War, but many had substantial worth, property, and numbers of slaves. This middle-class element would, in combination with energetic newcomers, build the new merchant elite of the postwar era.

The coming of the Civil War forever changed the social and economic composition of the district and created the conditions that provided postwar mercantile success. The war and ensuing blockade quickly destroyed the supply chains and credit sources emanating from New Orleans and elsewhere, and early Union success on the Gulf Coast ensured that both planters and merchants alike were stressed to their limits as early as 1862. While a handful of local merchants eked out a living as smugglers or purveyors of scarce goods at a premium, the first two years of war largely destroyed the large local cotton commission houses and plantation supply firms, particularly those with strong planter-class ties and large amounts of capital tied up in land and slaves. The Union occupation of the Natchez District in mid-1863 marks the pivotal point of change: once local slaves were freed, the character of the marketplace was irrevocably changed in the merchants' favor. Blacks had always been the key to labor—and in turn agricultural success—in the Cotton Kingdom and would continue to be so in the postbellum scene, but now the added element of the emerging African American market for goods and credit caused the marketplace to explode. As Northern and immigrant opportunists flooded the district in search of quick fortunes in renewed cotton production at high wartime prices, equal numbers of shrewd merchantmen from both the North and the South quickly realized there was a huge opportunity in servicing the African American market. This is the true nexus of postwar mercantile success: the emergence of a huge new market providing goods and credit to freed blacks.

Newcomers and local traders alike found the new marketplace a chaotic milieu of both burgeoning opportunity and stinging competition. A great many did not survive the first years of Reconstruction. At that juncture the importance of familial, religious, ethnic, and social networks became crucial as a support mechanism for traders in the bustling but perilous new market. For those who banded together, intermarried, pooled their resources, and formed strong mercantile communities, the new agricultural lien laws in 1867 gave them a near stranglehold on the local plantation supply and cotton-handling business—not a territorial monopoly gained by location, as some historians have posited, but a legal monopoly, derived by law. The superior liens merchants could levy on the cotton crops of their debtor customers, both struggling planter and small cropper alike, is the second most important tier of postwar mercantile success. Cotton factors in New Orleans and elsewhere still existed and conducted a significant trade, mainly with the shrinking remnants of the proud planter class. But the use of the local crop as security made local "hands-on" monitoring of crops and careful metering of credit a necessity to negate the risks of a highly speculative business that could fail on a yearly basis from any of a host of maladies that assaulted the cotton crops.

By the mid-1870s the crop lien system was firmly entrenched, and the merchant class was clearly in the ascendancy, often at the expense of the planter class. Failed crops, new and increased taxes, lack of capital, and shrinking land values reduced the planters, and increasingly merchant-planters took their place as the new landed class of the Natchez District. But merchants were driven by a different set of goals in their planting activities. Their plantation-furnishing businesses came first and usually were what initially made them wealthy, not cotton planting. In fact, their venture into agriculture was more driven by their ability to profit off a near-captive market of supply accounts that resided on their plantations. In addition, their growing control of the cotton itself and its processing, shipping, and selling augmented their profits. Many of the lands garnered by the merchant class were acquired by resolution of debt with struggling small or middle-tier planters who did not have the capital to conduct planting without merchant credits. In addition, freed blacks had a well-known aversion to dealing their former masters, if possible. This led them to favor doing business with the new merchant class, even if they did not receive better terms financially or in living standards. Ironically, the very nature of the new credit and lien system of labor also united planter and merchant in a strange partnership of sorts. They both needed to control African American labor to continue in business, and the share-tenancy system helped provide just that by "keeping the blacks down" not only in social and racial terms, but beholden in economic terms as well, locked into a cycle of debt that perpetuated their interest-bearing mercantile accounts year after year while keeping them firmly mired on the plantation.

During the next two decades the merchant class became near-masters of the Natchez District. Armed with growing fortunes gathered by their plantation supply, ownership, and cotton-handling activities, they changed the face of the district—particularly the developing urban landscape. They used their position in the cash-credit nexus and their growing control of local political and civic organizations to foster countless changes and improvements in the region: building and developing railroads, infrastructure, cotton mills and manufactors, and commercial and residential buildings, all the while becoming leading proponents of Gilded Age business, organizational, and technological innovations. For the first time local incorporated businesses brought the leaders of the emerging business class of the New South together in combinations, where Confederate war hero sat next to Yankee carpetbagger in the boardrooms of local business combinations, breaking down cultural and social divisions in a new world dominated by the almighty dollar and its commensurate profits. This development also enveloped the planter class, as the antebellum planter's son now attended university and became a member of the professional or business classes alongside the son of an immigrant trader who made good in the business of dealing with African Americans. This is the third component of postbellum mercantile success: the ability to change with a rapidly emerging modern world, and to use institutional advantages to penetrate and eventually dominate all local social, political, and business configurations. Some of the family names and financial fortunes made during this peak of mercantile influence would endure for decades. A few endure to this day.

But the same unequal system of credit and debt backed by racial control that made the merchant class would eventually reduce its members in a painful decline. Many merchants seemed to recognize as early as the 1880s that the cotton business was headed for a serious decline, and as a result several attempted to diversify their business concerns to escape from their reliance on King Cotton. In a great irony, many former merchantmen became bankers. This new, favored business form largely usurped their core business of petty agricultural lending by the early 1900s, thus having a hand in the destruction of their own class. But the simple fact was that the very core of their business and legal advantages—be it mercantile plantation supply, petty lending, or larger banking—still depended on a fickle cotton business that had never been stable since its inception a century earlier. In fact, all that there was in Natchez still depended on cotton. But new forms of marketing and speculation in the cotton business, in combination with rising competition from a host of sources and declining productivity of tired local lands, sent local cotton profitability and productivity into a sharp downward spiral, starting at some point in the 1890s, never to fully recover. Working in tandem with this development was the rising tide of Southern racism; the Natchez District had its fair share of racial hatred and while not an epicenter of Ku Klux Klan activity and lynching, by 1900 local African Americans had lost most if not all the rights they had enjoyed in Reconstruction. Once again, African Americans, their labor, and their marketplace were key. Once local African American croppers tired of years of debt, falling cotton prices, and virulent racism, they began to leave the district in search of new opportunities—largely sealing the fate of the merchant class. The appearance of the boll weevil in 1907 and its near destruction of local cotton production proved to be the tipping point, although the problems of the cotton economy had been building for half a century. By 1914, when war jobs began drawing local croppers away en masse, the Natchez mercantile scene was already reduced by a third and sinking fast. Perhaps as many as half of this story's ten featured merchant families left Natchez for good by the mid-twentieth century, including the Beekmans, Jacobses, and

Lowenburgs, while descendants of the Abbotts, Carpenters, and Geisenbergers still reside in Natchez today.

In retrospect, perhaps the most fitting epitaph of these Natchez merchants is that they were very good businessmen. They emerged in a time of chaos and social change, endowed with a keen eye for whatever opportunities came their way in Natchez, which were considerable. They left few stones of profit unturned and deftly used all the assets at their disposal to prosper and become some of the largest landowners in the region. The merchant trade was difficult and risky, even with the prevailing mercantile advantages after the war, and many other merchants failed to prosper. But these families made money from just about every segment of the agrarian economy open to them. Clearly, they did this because of their sound business sense, their practical assessment of the economic area in which they operated, and their willingness to diversify their operations to every possible arena of business—always with a sharp eye for the bottom line in their ledger books. There can be little doubt that these merchants played a vital part in the survival and development of the Natchez District's postwar economy. They provided a timely infusion of Northern credit and goods when it was needed most. There were Northern goods on the shelves of I. Lowenburg & Co. and Aaron Beekman & Co. in 1863, when the traditional supply system was still largely disrupted or destroyed. Area merchants were able to translate Northern credit on goods into local credit that benefited the planters and the emerging freedmen sharecroppers at a time when few local planters, or even the federal government, were able to undertake such enterprise. Without adequate supplies of goods and credit, it is likely that many of the formerly enslaved people of the district would have suffered even more than they did in the transition from slavery to a paid labor force. At the time, the merchants provided a valuable service in a world torn apart by war and the destruction of its social order. These merchants also reinvested their profits in the local economy, and their enterprise accounted for much of the economic activity that went on in the area over the next two generations. Indeed, their enterprise underwrote much of the economic recovery experienced by Natchez in the postwar years. No other group was as responsible for the economic health of the town and its hinterland as were the merchants, who invested in land, railroads, cotton mills, and numerous civic undertakings over the years. Even today, the community's historical memory credits these men with having saved Natchez from economic collapse and ruin in the aftermath of the war. Their houses and store buildings are pointed to with pride by present-day Natchezians, who note the degree to which these postbellum traders were accepted and valued as the saviors of Natchez.

There is, of course, another side to this story. In the antebellum period, several merchant families were active participants in, and supporters of, slavery. Whether they accepted all the racial aspects of slavery or simply took advantage of slavery as part of the given social milieu is unknown. But in the postwar era, there can be little question that the merchants profited from the plight of the area's debtors, both black and white. Nor did they ever do much to alleviate the situation by using their resources to assist in the creation of a system of tenancy leading to farm ownership or self-sufficiency. Such issues were never part of their agenda as entrepreneurs or as community leaders. In fact, there is little in what these merchants accomplished that indicates a great deal of social concern, particularly toward African Americans, other than politically motivated and self-serving civic projects that promoted business and benefited white Natchez and their own associates. These merchants were all about business, and they manipulated and exploited the people and resources available to them to an amazing degree. They used their positions to prey upon the less advantaged while they accommodated those in stronger positions. Perhaps there was nothing that could be done given the sorry state of the economy, perpetually declining cotton prices, a labor force just out of slavery, and no social safety nets available once Reconstruction ended. It is fair to say, moreover, that had these merchants not provided the services they did, someone else would have stepped in. In the end, this is the perplexing dichotomy of a class that at once used every unequal advantage to climb to the social and economic pinnacle of the Natchez District, giving and taking in large measure, clearly tarnished but undoubtedly the true builders of a New South.

1) The Franklin Street "Cotton Square" during the busy harvest season. Aaron Beekman & Co., in the center, was located directly across the street from I. Lowenburg & Co. to the left (ca. 1880s). (Courtesy Mississippi Department of Archives and History)

2) Shopkeepers and passersby before the storefronts of A. Beekman and V. Druetta companies on Franklin Street in 1880. (Courtesy of Special Collections, LSU Libraries, Louisiana State University)

3) J. C. Schwartz Co., perhaps the oldest and most successful Natchez hardware firm, was located on 91 Main Street (1890). (Courtesy of Special Collections, LSU Libraries, Louisiana State University)

4) I. Lowenburg & Co., located on 92 Franklin Street, sold a wide range of goods, including plantation supplies, groceries, and liquor—often on credit (ca. 1880s). (Courtesy of Special Collections, LSU Libraries, Louisiana State University)

5) A woman laden with scissors, hammers, and other goods models the products available at Schwartz & Stewart Hardware Co. at the 1891 "Businessmen's Jubilee." (Courtesy of Special Collections, LSU Libraries, Louisiana State University)

6) Former slave and plantation owner Alex Mazique. The Mazique family prospered in the postwar period and owned China Grove and Oakland plantations in Adams County. (Courtesy of Special Collections, LSU Libraries, Louisiana State University)

7) A well-equipped Natchez barbershop in 1900 with electric light fixtures, fans, and hot and cold running water. The cabinet in the background likely held the individualized shaving mugs of regular customers. (Courtesy of Special Collections, LSU Libraries, Louisiana State University)

8) An incline railcar brings cotton bales from the Natchez bluff top down to the under-the-hill Mississippi River steamship landing. Built in the 1880s, the system greatly aided transport of goods to and from river packets to the town above. (Courtesy of Special Collections, LSU Libraries, Louisiana State University)

9) Three generations of the very successful Carpenter family on the steps of their mansion, Dunleith. J. N. Carpenter (front with mustache) could make cotton prices rise and fall "with a couple of words." (Courtesy of the Historic Natchez Foundation)

10) Former slave and U.S. congressman John R. Lynch was one of the most important local African American politicians and a plantation owner. (Courtesy of Special Collections, LSU Libraries, Louisiana State University)

11) A large cotton field attended by workers with mules, plow, wagon, and buggy ca. 1900. (Courtesy of Special Collections, LSU Libraries, Louisiana State University)

12) Men, women, and children picking cotton at harvest time. Often, two or more cropper families pooled their labor and worked as "squads" to farm and bring in their crops. (Courtesy of the Historic Natchez Foundation)

13) D. Moses Cheap Cash Store and other firms on Silver Street under-the-hill ca. 1880. Out of frame to the left is the river landing, and the street rises up to Natchez proper in the background. (Courtesy of Special Collections, LSU Libraries, Louisiana State University)

14) The Carpenter family lived in Dunleith from the 1870s until the mid-twentieth century, when this image was taken. (Courtesy of the Historic Natchez Foundation)

15) A steamship ferry off-loading a train engine and cars under-the-hill sometime after 1910. The Natchez and Louisiana Transfer Co. began similar service across the Mississippi River from Vidalia, Louisiana, to Natchez in 1900. (Courtesy of Special Collections, LSU Libraries, Louisiana State University)

16) Fire was a constant danger in the age of kerosene and early gas appliances. Firemen and the pumper *Walter McBee* put out the ruined A. & M. Moses and S. & A. Jacobs stores, ca. 1890s. (Courtesy of Special Collections, LSU Libraries, Louisiana State University)

17) A mule team pulls a wagon loaded with cotton bales and workers. Cotton bales averaged 450 pounds, and mule-drawn wagons moved most cotton to local gins and markets well into the 1900s. (Courtesy of the Historic Natchez Foundation)

18) R. F. Learned's sawmill on the Mississippi River under-the-hill, ca. 1880s. The lumber business made Learned one of the wealthiest Natchez businessmen, and he also served as the president of the Natchez Cotton Mills. (Courtesy of the Historic Natchez Foundation)

19) The Lowenburg children in 1885. Partially educated in Europe, the affluent Lowenburgs were very influential in the Natchez social, business, and commercial community. (Courtesy of Special Collections, LSU Libraries, Louisiana State University)

20) A firemen's parade passes the *Natchez Democrat* newspaper building on the corner of Main and Pearl Streets, ca. 1890s. Note the telephone and power lines overhead, and the trolley tracks on the roadway. (Courtesy Mississippi Department of Archives and History)

21) Looms and machinery inside the Natchez Cotton Mills. In 1882 Mark Twain noted its "10,300 spindles and 304 looms" consumed "5,000 bales of cotton annually and manufactures the best quality of brown shirtings and sheetings." (Courtesy of Special Collections, LSU Libraries, Louisiana State University)

22) The Natchez Cotton Mills on Canal Street began operation in 1878. The three-story, 317-foot-long mill covered an entire city block, employed 250 workers, and produced five million yards of textiles per year. (Courtesy of Special Collections, LSU Libraries, Louisiana State University)

23) Part of the building boom of the 1880s and 1890s, the Natchez Savings Bank was also one of many new banks opened during the period. Note the telephone lines and finished sidewalks, ca. 1890. (Courtesy of Special Collections, LSU Libraries, Louisiana State University)

24) Aerial panorama of Natchez facing northwest, ca. 1880s. Note the cotton mills, buildings under construction, and Mississippi River with Concordia Parish, Louisiana, in the background. (Courtesy of Special Collections, LSU Libraries, Louisiana State University)

25) The Natchez under-the-hill riverboat landing filled with steamships assembled to honor a visit from President Taft in 1908. (Courtesy of Special Collections, LSU Libraries, Louisiana State University)

26) The steamship *John A. Scudder* fully loaded with cotton bales moored at the riverboat landing, ca. 1890. Steamships could carry up to 5,000 bales of cotton, and remained important passenger and freight carriers until the 1900s. (Courtesy of Special Collections, LSU Libraries, Louisiana State University)

27) The residence of successful hardware merchant W. P. Stewart, ca. 1890s. Local businessmen constructed many beautiful homes in the downtown area during this period. (Courtesy Mississippi Department of Archives and History)

28) The interior of an unknown local mercantile firm, possibly a grocery, liquor, confectioners, or cigar store. Note the full-length display cases and high wall shelving loaded with goods. (Courtesy of Special Collections, LSU Libraries, Louisiana State University)

29) The Natchez Temple B'Nai Israel Synagogue in 1880. Built in 1872, the temple was the oldest and largest in Mississippi, and served a vibrant Jewish community that counted the proprietors of one-third of local mercantile firms as members. (Courtesy of Special Collections, LSU Libraries, Louisiana State University)

30) A large crowd gathered at the Natchez train station, ca. 1890s. First built in the 1870s, by the 1880s Natchez railways offered connections nationwide and carried increasing volumes of freight and passenger traffic. (Courtesy Mississippi Department of Archives and History)

Notes

Introduction

1. *Natchez Daily Democrat*, January 11, 1898, 6.

2. Harrison Ross to Wolf Geisenberger, Chattel Mortgages, February 27, 1895, January 27, 1896, February 8, 1897, January 11, 1898; Anderson and Mary Ross to Wolf Geisenberger, Chattel Mortgage, February 22, 1882; Lawrence Woods et al. to Wolf Geisenberger, Chattel Mortgage, January 11, 1894, Office of Records, Adams County, Natchez, Mississippi; Ronald L. F. Davis, *The Black Experience in Natchez: 1720–1880* (Denver: U.S. Department of the Interior, National Park Service, 1994), 162–170; 1886 Natchez City Census, Natchez Collection, California State University, Northridge; U.S. Census (1880, 1900) Population Schedules, Adams County, Mississippi.

3. Harrison Ross to Wolf Geisenberger, Chattel Mortgages, May 6, 1880, February 27, 1895, January 27, 1896, February 8, 1897, January 11, 1898, Office of Records, Adams County, Natchez, Mississippi; Ronald L. F. Davis, *Good and Faithful Labor* (Westport, Conn.: Greenwood Press, 1982), 1–9, 58–59, 169–184; Davis, *Black Experience*, 158–170; U.S. Census (1880, 1900) Population Schedules, Adams County, Mississippi.

4. Some historians have contended that the system of tenant farming was not all that new and in fact was a continuation of prevalent practices in upcountry cotton-producing areas with few slave owners. However, the Natchez District was an epicenter of large plantations run with slave labor. See Frederick A. Bode and Donald E. Ginter, *Farm Tenancy and the Census in Antebellum Georgia* (Athens: University of Georgia Press, 1988), 1–20.

5. Don H. Doyle, *New Men, New Cities, New South: Atlanta, Nashville, Charleston, Mobile, 1860–1910* (Chapel Hill: University of North Carolina Press, 1990), xi–xvi; C. Vann Woodward, *Origins of the New South, 1877–1913* (Baton Rouge: Louisiana State University Press, 1951), 291–349.

6. The ten merchant families chosen for this research were the combined Abbotts/Flemings, Beekmans, Carpenters, Friedlers, Geisenbergers, Jacobses, Lemles, Lowenburgs, Paynes, and Perraults. Their individual histories, members, and attributes will be covered completely in chapter 2.

7. Harold D. Woodman, *King Cotton and His Retainers: Financing and Marketing the Cotton Crops of the South, 1800–1925* (Lexington: University of Kentucky Press, 1968), 199–345; Davis, *Good and Faithful Labor*, 1–9, 58–59, 169–184; Michael Wayne, *The Reshaping of*

Plantation Society: The Natchez District, 1860–1880 (Baton Rouge: Louisiana State University Press, 1983), 31–52; Roger L. Ransom and Richard Sutch, *One Kind of Freedom: The Economic Consequences of Emancipation* (1977, repr., New York: Cambridge University Press, 2001), 126–148, 171–199; Woodward, *Origins of the New South*, 291–349; Doyle, *New Men, New Cities, New South*, xi–xvi; David Carlton, *Mill and Town in South Carolina, 1880–1920* (Baton Rouge: Louisiana State University Press, 1982), 58–63; Louis Kyriakoudes, "Lower-Order Urbanization and Territorial Monopoly in the Southern Furnishing Trade: Alabama, 1871–1890," *Social Science History* 26 (Spring 2002): 179–198.

Chapter 1. Old Ways and New Realities

1. Natchez had informally been surrendered by Mayor John Hunter to Commander James S. Palmer of the USS *Iroquois* on May 13, 1862. But in the intervening months, with almost all able-bodied men now in uniform on Confederate battlefronts, no one was left to defend Natchez save for an underage-overage militia. Natchez citizens grew increasingly edgy as Union gunboats passed frequently, Confederate guerrillas raided cotton plantations in the surrounding countryside, and the very large local slave population grew restive with the anticipation of their liberation with occupation—spawning fears of slave uprisings. See the *Natchez Weekly Courier*, May 14, 1862, 1; Davis, *Black Experience in Natchez*, 126–127; Edith Wyatt Moore, *Natchez Under-the-Hill* (Natchez, Miss.: Southern Historical Publications, 1958), 98–99; Charles L. Dufor, "The Conquest of the Mississippi," in *The Guns of '62*, Vol. 2 of *The Image of War, 1861–65*, ed. William C. Davis (Garden City, N.J.: Doubleday, 1982), 255–322.

2. See Commodore W. D. Porter's report quoted in Thomas Reber, *Proud Old Natchez* (Natchez, Miss.: self-published, 1909), 39; see also Moore, *Natchez*, 99.

3. Moore, *Natchez*, 99; Robert Gordon Pishel, *Natchez: The Museum City of the Old South* (Tulsa, Okla.: Magnolia Publishing, 1959), 84, 103.

4. By one Southern account a small detachment of the local militia "Silver Grays" was led that day by a seriously wounded Major Douglas Walworth, home from the front recovering, and it was he who gave the order to fire on a larger force of "fifteen or twenty bluejackets" coming ashore—much to his later regret. See Moore, *Natchez*, 99; *Natchez Weekly Courier*, September 3, 1862, 1.

5. In addition to Rosalie Beekman, Natchez mayor Henry Hunter may have died of a heart attack during the excitement of the shelling or its immediate aftermath. See Moore, *Natchez*, 100; Reber, *Proud Old Natchez*, 41–41; Leo E. Turitz and Evelyn Turitz, *Jews in Early Mississippi* (Jackson: University Press of Mississippi, 1983), 12; Natchez Jewish History, Research File, Historic Natchez Foundation; David G. Sansing et al., *Natchez: An Illustrated History* (Natchez, Miss.: Plantation Publishing, 1992), 119; Natchez City Cemetery, Jewish Burial Grounds, Tombstone of Rosalie Beekman; Aaron Beekman, Last Will and Testament and Estate File, June 12, 1901, Cause No. 1703, File Box No. 237, Office of Records, Adams County, Natchez, Mississippi.

6. Moore, *Natchez*, 102; Davis, *Black Experience*, 126–128; Sansing et al., *Natchez Illustrated*, 110; *Natchez, Mississippi On Top, Not "Under the Hill"* (Natchez, Miss.: Daily Democrat Steam Press, 1888), 10.

7. Moore, *Natchez*, 102.

8. Thomas D. Clark, *Pills, Petticoats, and Plows* (Indianapolis, Ind.: Bobbs-Merrill, 1944), 22; Woodman, *King Cotton*, 299; Davis, *Good and Faithful Labor*, 121–122.

9. The term "nabob" emerged sometime during the early nineteenth century to denote a "man of great wealth," and, while not always necessarily meant to be flattering in nature, has over time come to epitomize the aristocratic class of antebellum Natchez grandees like no other. See D. Clayton James, *Antebellum Natchez* (Baton Rouge: Louisiana State University Press, 1968), 136–139; Wayne, *Reshaping of Plantation Society*, 5–28; William K. Scarborough, *Masters of the Big House: Elite Slaveholders of the Mid-Nineteenth-Century South* (Baton Rouge: Louisiana State University Press, 2003), 128–129, 409–410.

10. Dunbar Rowland, ed., *History of Mississippi* (Jackson, Miss.: S. J. Clarke, 1925), 1:125–130, 193–199.

11. Daniel H. Usner, *Indians, Settlers, and Slaves in a Frontier Exchange Economy* (Chapel Hill: University of North Carolina Press, 1992), 24–25; *Goodspeed's Biographical and Historical Memoirs of Mississippi* (Chicago: Goodspeed Publishing, 1891), 2:159; Rowland, *History of Mississippi*, 1:199–203; Davis, *Black Experience*, 1–4; Moore, *Natchez*, 11; James, *Antebellum Natchez*, 8; Morton Rothstein, "The Remotest Corner: Natchez on the American Frontier," in *Natchez before 1830*, ed. Noel Polk (Jackson: University Press of Mississippi, 1989), 94.

12. Rowland, *History of Mississippi*, 1:225–236; *Goodspeed's Biographical and Historical Memoirs*, 2:159; Davis, *Black Experience*, 6; Federal Writers Project of the Works Progress Administration, *Mississippi: A Guide to the Magnolia State* (New York: Hastings House, 1938), 238.

13. Rowland, *History of Mississippi*, 1:253–254, 264–269; *Goodspeed's Biographical and Historical Memoirs*, 2:159; Moore, *Natchez*, 15–16; James, *Antebellum Natchez*, 17.

14. Davis, *Black Experience*, 7; James, *Antebellum Natchez*, 19–20; *Goodspeed's Biographical and Historical Memoirs*, 2:159–160.

15. There is some strong evidence that Oliver Pollock was also a relative to the wealthy antebellum and postbellum Natchez merchant Thomas C. Pollock, who served as a popular president of the Adams County Board of Supervisors from 1876 to 1884. See Moore, *Natchez*, 16; Robert V. Haynes, *The Natchez District and the American Revolution* (Jackson: University Press of Mississippi, 1976), 19–23, 34–35, 56–73; James, *Antebellum Natchez*, 21–23;

16. Rowland, *History of Mississippi*, 1:273–294; James, *Antebellum Natchez*, 31–52.

17. Gayoso socialized with the planter and mercantile elite at his mansion home Concord, which was one of the first Natchez mansions constructed and was later the family home of the powerful Minor family—which Stephen Minor received directly from Gayoso as acting Spanish governor when the American takeover was imminent. Gayoso and the wealthy elites felt an "aristocratic" kinship of sorts, and, in fact, he married not only one daughter of planter Stephen Watts but, after her death, a second. See Rowland, *History of Mississippi*, 1:273–294; James, *Antebellum Natchez*, 31–52; Sansing et al., *Natchez Illustrated*, 40; Davis, *Black Experience*, 10.

18. Rothstein, "Remotest Corner," 94–95; James, *Antebellum Natchez*, 48–49; Moore, *Natchez*, 24. The italics are included in the original text of James's *Natchez*.

19. Theodora Britton Marshall, *They Found It in Natchez* (New Orleans: Pelican Publishing, 1939), 45.

20. Rothstein, "Remotest Corner," 95; James, *Antebellum Natchez*, 20, 37–38, 48–49.

21. Rowland, *History of Mississippi*, 1:312–319; James, *Antebellum Natchez*, 40–52, n70; Federal Writers Project, *Mississippi*, 239; Arthur H. DeRosier Jr., *William Dunbar: Scientific*

Pioneer of the Old Southwest (Lexington: University Press of Kentucky, 2007), 53–60, 87; Rothstein, "Remotest Corner," 98; Davis, *Black Experience*, 16.

22. DeRosier, *William Dunbar*, 100–104; James, *Antebellum Natchez*, 52; John Hebron Moore, *The Emergence of the Cotton Kingdom in the Old Southwest* (Baton Rouge: Louisiana State University Press, 1988), 1–19.

23. The slave population of the district was climbing precipitously and reached 2,110 by 1798, 40 percent of the total population, while prices rose commensurately and ranged from around $500 to over $1,000 for a prime field hand—cheap by later standards but still a considerable sum for the time, indicative of the income level cotton production was generating. See James, *Antebellum Natchez*, 45–52; Davis, *Black Experience*, 16; Rothstein, "Remotest Corner," 98; Federal Writers Project, *Mississippi*, 239; Moore, *Emergence of the Cotton Kingdom*, 1–19; DeRosier, *William Dunbar*, 108.

24. In this and in several following newspaper advertisements, small changes in word spellings were made by the author to account for nineteenth-century typesetting and spelling practices to make the advertisements clearly readable and understandable. For example, the letter "f" was often substituted for the letter "s," wherein the original spelling of "instant" or "Rose" appeared "inftant" and "Rofe." However, typographical errors such as the repeated use of the word "in" remain. See the early Natchez newspaper the *Intelligencer*, October 13, 1801, 3.

25. Advertisements, Job Routh, Stephen Douglas, and John Lynd, *Intelligencer*, October 6, 1801, 2, October 13, 1801, 2, December 8, 1801, 2; *Mississippi Herald and Natchez City Gazette*, May 28, 1804, March 25, 1806, November 27, 1807; Woodman, *King Cotton*, 5–14; James, *Antebellum Natchez*, 148.

26. James, *Antebellum Natchez*, 183; Woodman, *King Cotton*, 11.

27. Advertisements, John Callender & Co., M. Snyder, and Claiborne and Wooldridge, *Mississippi Herald and Natchez City Gazette*, May 28, 1804, June 29, 1804, October 5, 1804.

28. Rothstein, "Remotest Corner," 98–101; Advertisement, Samuel Postlethwaite & Co., *Intelligencer*, October 13, 1801, 2.

29. Martha Jane Brazy, *An American Planter: Stephen Duncan of Antebellum Natchez and New York* (Baton Rouge: Louisiana State University Press, 2006), 10–11: Rothstein, "Remotest Corner," 98–101.

30. James, *Antebellum Natchez*, 150.

31. Marshall, *Found It in Natchez*, 73.

32. Rothstein, "Remotest Corner," 101; James, *Antebellum Natchez*, 112, 269; Sansing et al., *Natchez Illustrated*, 49–64; Rowland, *History of Mississippi*, 1:419–425; Advertisement, Ferguson & Woolley Co., *Intelligencer*, December 8, 1801, 2.

33. Future president Abraham Lincoln was a frontier merchant in Illinois and apparently made the flatboat trip to Natchez and New Orleans himself with a cargo of produce in 1828. See *Natchez Democrat*, August 19, 2008, A8; Charles S. Sydnor, *A Gentleman of the Old Natchez District: Benjamin L. C. Wailes* (Westport, Conn.: Greenwood Press, 1970), 22–23; James, *Antebellum Natchez*, 77, 162; Federal Writers Project, *Mississippi*, 239–240; Marshall, *They Found It in Natchez*, 98–105; Robert H. Gudmestad, *A Troublesome Commerce: The Transformation of the Interstate Slave Trade* (Baton Rouge: Louisiana State University Press, 2003), 24–27; Davis, *Black Experience*, 17; Advertisement, M. Robitaille, *Natchez Gazette*, May 18, 1825, 4.

34. Davis, *Black Experience*, 17; Federal Writers Project, *Mississippi*, 239–240; Marshall, *They Found It in Natchez*, 118–119; James, *Antebellum Natchez*, 192–198; Brazy, *American Planter*, 15.

35. Woodman, *King Cotton*, 4–83; Louis E. Atherton, *The Southern Country Store, 1800–1860* (Baton Rouge: Louisiana State University Press, 1949), 19–86; Moore, *Emergence of the Cotton Kingdom*, 232–240.

36. Ibid.

37. Wayne, *Reshaping of Plantation Society*, 13–14; James, *Antebellum Natchez*, 164–165.

38. Ibid. The complexities of the district's planter class always had defied any clear-cut absolutes concerning intermarriage and gentry membership. Another young Pennsylvania doctor, John Carmichael Jenkins, married the granddaughter of William Dunbar in 1839, while former store clerk and merchant Samuel H. Lambdin wed a member of the wealthy Bisland family in 1842, both during the financial upheaval following the panic of 1837. See Scarborough, *Masters of the Big House*, 128–129; William Ransom Hogan and Edwin Adams Davis, eds., *William Johnson's Natchez: The Ante-bellum Diary of a Free Negro* (Baton Rouge: Louisiana State University Press, 1993), 3–4; Herbert Weaver, "Foreigners in Ante-bellum Mississippi," *Journal of Mississippi History* 16 (Spring 1954): 151–156.

39. Scarborough, *Masters of the Big House*, 138–142; James, *Antebellum Natchez*, 164–65; Frank J. Byrne, *Becoming Bourgeois: Merchant Culture in the South, 1820–1865* (Lexington: University Press of Kentucky, 2006), 1–120; Charles Sellers, *The Market Revolution: Jacksonian America, 1815–1846* (New York: Oxford University Press, 1991), 279–281; Natchez Jewish History, Research File, Historic Natchez Foundation; Turitz and Turitz, *Jews in Early Mississippi*, xvii, 11–28.

40. Scarborough, *Masters of the Big House*, 131–132; Moore, *Emergence of the Cotton Kingdom*, 239–240; James, *Antebellum Natchez*, 158–159, 220; Hogan and Davis, *William Johnson's Natchez*, 302n.

41. Morton Rothstein, "The Antebellum South as a Dual Economy: A Tentative Hypothesis," *Agricultural History* 41 (October 1967): 373–382; Moore, *Emergence of the Cotton Kingdom*, 193–196; James, *Antebellum Natchez*, 190–191, 203–210.

42. Moore, *Emergence of the Cotton Kingdom*, 190–191; Davis, *Black Experience*, 17; James, *Antebellum Natchez*, 159–160, 183–184; U.S. Census (1860), MS Population and Slave Schedules, Adams County, Mississippi; 1858 Natchez City Business Directory, Historic Natchez Foundation.

43. Davis, *Good and Faithful Labor*, 59; Rebecca M. Dresser, "The Minor Family of Natchez: A Case of Southern Unionism" (M.A. thesis, California State University, Northridge, 2000), 1–25.

44. Davis, *Labor*, 59–61; Wayne, *Reshaping of Plantation Society*, 31–52; Federal Writers Project, *Mississippi*, 240; Woodman, *King Cotton*, 205–215; Benjamin Wailes quoted in James, *Antebellum Natchez*, 293.

45. Turitz and Turitz, *Jews in Early Mississippi*, xvii, 15–16; Davis, *Labor*, 1–9; Permits to Purchase Cotton Ledger, Natchez District, March 1864, 22–25; Permits to Ship Goods, June 13, 1864, Natchez District, Natchez Collection, California State University, Northridge; Natchez Board of Alderman's Meeting Minute Books, 1882–1886, City Hall, Natchez, Mississippi.

46. Advertisements, John Mayer & Son and Fleming & Baldwin Co., *Natchez Daily Courier*, June 26 and July 8, 1863; Advertisements, F. H. Clark & Co., Hoppe, Wolff & Co., and E. G. Tuttle & Co., *Natchez Courier*, September 18 and 22, 1863; Advertisements, D. B. Smith and C. W. Ford, *Natchez Courier*, November 10 and December 11, 1863; various advertisements, *Natchez Courier*, July 12, 1864.

47. The Jackson area was very close to Union lines in Vicksburg and would soon fall as part of that campaign. Also, the purchase of hardware stock with $5,000 of inflated Confederate currency was worth far less in the coming U.S. currency after July 1863—considerably less than half. See John C. Schwartz "Daybook, 1859–1865," J:23, Vol. 2A:204–210, John C. Schwartz Papers, Louisiana and Lower Mississippi Valley Collections, Louisiana State University Library, Baton Rouge (hereafter cited as John C. Schwartz Papers, LSU).

48. Ibid.

49. John C. Schwartz "Cashbook, 1863–1881," J:23, Vol. 1A:3, John C. Schwartz Papers, LSU.

50. John C. Schwartz "Cashbook, 1864–1875," J:23, Vol. 1B:5–16, John C. Schwartz Papers, LSU.

51. John C. Schwartz "Cashbook, 1863–1881," J:23, Vol. 1A:3–4; John C. Schwartz "Daybook, 1859–1865," J:23, Vol. 2A:215–220, John C. Schwartz Papers, LSU; Advertisements, Meyer, Deutsch, & Co., Fleming & Baldwin, Pollock & Mason, and Rickey, Shelton & Co., *Natchez Courier*, July 12, 1864, May 11 and June 22, 1865; Advertisements, Rumble & Wensel, Henry Frank, and H. M. Gastrell & Co., *Natchez Democrat*, June 22 and October 2, 1865; Rickey, Shelton & Co., Mississippi, Vol. 2, p. 104, R. G. Dun & Co. Ledgers, Harvard Business School, Baker Library Historical Collections, Cambridge, Massachusetts.

52. Scarborough, *Masters of the Big House*, 348, 368–369; Henry C. Minor to Katharine Minor, December 12, 1863, and Henry C. Minor to William J. Minor, March 23, 1864, Box 2, Folder 18, William J. Minor and Family Papers, Louisiana and Lower Mississippi Valley Collections, Louisiana State University Library, Baton Rouge.

53. Advertisements, A. B. Holmes and "A,B,C," *Natchez Courier*, May 11, 1865, 2.

Chapter 2. Merchant Communities

1. An underage Carpenter was purportedly so determined to join the Confederate ranks—and had been so vocal about it—that he was jailed by Union authorities after the occupation of Natchez in July 1863, and his father had to post a gold bond to have him released; whereupon he ran away anyway to join the Confederate army in Tennessee. See Dunbar Rowland, ed., *Mississippi: Comprising Sketches of Counties, Towns, Events, Institutions, and Persons* (Atlanta: Southern Historical Publishing Association, 1907), 3:178–180; Obituary of Joseph N. Carpenter, *Natchez Democrat*, March 4, 1925, 1, 8; Multiple credit ledger entries, N. L. Carpenter & Son, J. N. Carpenter & Co., and Carpenter, Dicks & Co., Mississippi, Vol. 2, pp. 111, 113, and 178, R. G. Dun & Co. Ledgers, Harvard Business School.

2. Multiple entries contained within the complete lists of Natchez Confederate units and war veterans. See Land Conveyance Ledger Book 4I, pp. 269–294, Office of Records, Adams County, Natchez, Mississippi; U.S. Census (1860–1870), MS Population Schedules, Adams County, Mississippi; 1858 Natchez City Business Directory, Historic Natchez Foundation.

3. Obituary of N. L Carpenter, *Natchez Democrat*, December 24, 1892, 2; Rowland, *Mississippi*, 3:178–180; Wayne, *Reshaping of Plantation Society*, 167; *Sheppard's Mississippi State Gazetteer and Shippers Guide for 1866–67* (Cincinnati: J. S. Sheppard, 1866), 131–135; U.S. Census (1870), MS Population Schedules, Adams County, Mississippi; Record of Naturalizations, 1854–1904, Circuit Court of Adams County, Office of Records, Adams County, Natchez, Mississippi, 1–193; Pamela Walker Laird, *Pull: Networking and Success since Benjamin Franklin* (Cambridge, Mass.: Harvard University Press, 2006), 1–10.

4. U.S. Census (1860), MS Population Schedules, Adams County, Mississippi; 1858 Natchez City Business Directory, Historic Natchez Foundation. The figures and percentages are presented for comparison purposes to demonstrate the changing nature of the Natchez marketplace. In the postbellum period, few merchants would be inclined to list themselves as planters or "farmers" first and foremost, even though as the period progressed many owned lands in cotton production. Postwar merchants are more defined by their mercantile and entrepreneurial pursuits within the marketplace, and these activities were usually the basis of their wealth, at least initially. When running their own cotton plantations, they are more clearly characterized as "landlord-merchants" renting to croppers in the new tenant-farming and sharecropping regime. This emerging labor system, and the merchant's role in it, will be fully explored in the next chapter.

5. U.S. Census (1860), MS Population Schedules, Adams County, Mississippi; 1858 Natchez City Business Directory, Historic Natchez Foundation; Record of Naturalizations 1854–1904, pp. 1–193, Circuit Court of Adams County, Office of Records, Natchez, Mississippi; Turitz and Turitz, *Jews in Early Mississippi*, xii–xiii.

6. U.S. Census (1860), MS Population Schedules, Adams County, Mississippi; 1858 Natchez City Business Directory, Historic Natchez Foundation; Record of Naturalizations 1854–1904, pp. 1–193, Circuit Court of Adams County, Office of Records, Natchez, Mississippi; Turitz and Turitz, *Jews in Early Mississippi*, xii–xiii.

7. U.S. Census (1860–1870), MS Population Schedules, Adams County, Mississippi; Turitz and Turitz, *Jews in Early Mississippi*, xii–xiii, 11–28; 1858 Natchez City Business Directory, 258–269, Historic Natchez Foundation; *Sheppard's Mississippi State Gazetteer*, 131–135; N. L. Carpenter, *Natchez Democrat*, December 24, 1892, 2.

8. U.S. Census (1860–1870), MS Population Schedules, Adams County, Mississippi; Multiple credit ledger entries, Henry Frank Co. and Abbott, Henderson & Stone Co., Mississippi, Vol. 2, pp. 100, 104, R. G. Dun & Co. Ledgers, Harvard Business School.

9. Advertisement, S. D. Stockman & Co., *Natchez Weekly Democrat*, October 14, 1867, 2.

10. U.S. Census (1840–1870), MS Population Schedules, Adams County, Mississippi; Natchez Confederate Veterans, Land Conveyance Ledger Book 4I, pp. 269–294, Office of Records, Adams County, Natchez, Mississippi; James, *Antebellum Natchez*, 95, 156–157, 212; Wayne, *Reshaping of Plantation Society*, 152.

11. Advertisement, S. B. Newman and S. D. Stockman & Co., *Natchez Weekly Democrat*, October 14, 1867, 2.

12. Credit ledger entries, Buckner & Newman Co., Mississippi, Vol. 2, p. 7, R. G. Dun & Co. Ledgers, Harvard Business School; Wayne, *Reshaping of Plantation Society*, 152.

13. The original notations that were included in the R. G. Dun and Co. credit ledger entries are used in this and later direct quotations to portray the unique nature of these fascinating references. However, in each case, a "key" will be included in the notes for any new abbreviations used: "amt." (amount), "+" (and), "N.O." (New Orleans), "cr." (credit), "bus." (business), "pers" (personally), "reliab" (reliable), "250 NY" ($250,000), "thr" (their), "capl" (capital). See the credit ledger entry, S. D. Stockman & Co., Mississippi, Vol. 2, p. 7, R. G. Dun & Co. Ledgers, Harvard Business School.

14. Advertisement, Aetna Insurance Co., S. D. Stockman Agent, *Natchez Weekly Democrat*, November 16, 1865, 2. Portions of this advertisement were omitted due to its length.

15. U.S. Census (1840–1870), MS Population Schedules, Adams County, Mississippi; Davis, *Good and Faithful Labor*, 135–136; John G. and Jeanette Fleming to James N. Stockman (Trustee for Fleming & Baldwin Co.), Trust Deed, March 25, 1856; James T. Roach to James

N. Stockman (Trustee for Fleming & Baldwin Co.), Trust Deed, December 20, 1858, Land Conveyance Ledger Books, Office of Records, Adams County, Natchez, Mississippi. The "John G. Fleming" listed in the first trust deed is part of another branch of Flemings that had been planters in the district since at least 1804, and his sons, Holliday and Benton, were significant planters in the postwar era. There is some evidence that this branch of Flemings also emerged from Virginia and that they were related to the mercantile Flemings.

16. Credit ledger entry, Fleming & Baldwin Co., Mississippi, Vol. 2, p. 6, R. G. Dun & Co. Ledgers, Harvard Business School. New abbreviations key: "yr" (year), "Per" (personal), "prop" (property), "abt" (about), "$5m." ($5,000), "RE" (real estate), "char" (character), "habts" (habits), "cap" (capacity), "Cap" (capital), "prob" (probably), "@" (and, or).

17. John and Mary Fleming to S. Dryden Stockman, Deed, April 1, 1861; James Metcalfe et. ux to John Fleming (Trustee of Buckner & Newman and S. D. Stockman), Trust Deed, April 4, 1866, Land Conveyance Ledger Books, Office of Records, Adams County, Natchez, Mississippi; U.S. Census (1870–1880), MS and LA Population Schedules, Adams County, Mississippi, and Orleans Parish, Louisiana.

18. Rowland, *Mississippi*, 3:177–180; U.S. Census (1840–1850), MS Population Schedules, Adams County, Mississippi; L. A. Basaucon to N. L. Carpenter, Agreement, June 24, 1837; N. L. Carpenter and Wife to Stephen Duncan, Mortgage, August 7, 1844; N. L. Carpenter to Thomas Leathers, Agreement, February 27, 1854; N. L. Carpenter to Hannah H. and Lineas W. Risley, Apprentice Agreement, November 13, 1854, Land Conveyance Ledger Books, Office of Records, Adams County, Natchez, Mississippi.

19. Advertisement, N. L. Carpenter, *Natchez Courier*, October 5, 1865, 2; Rowland, *Mississippi*, 3:177–180.

20. Advertisement, N. L. Carpenter & Sons Co., *Natchez Weekly Democrat*, October 14, 1867. Allen D. Carpenter, N. L. Carpenter's other son and J. N. Carpenter's older brother, was technically part of "N. L. Carpenter & Sons" for a couple of years, but by 1868 the firm's name had been changed to N. L. Carpenter & Son, and A. D. Carpenter became a full-time cotton planter on Point Place, which he operated until the early twentieth century.

21. Rowland, *Mississippi*, 3:177–180; U.S. Census (1870–1880), MS Population Schedules, Adams County, Mississippi; William S. Cannon to N. L. Carpenter and J. N. Carpenter, Mortgage, March 21, 1868; Edward Dixon and Wife to Sarah E. Carpenter, Mortgage, March 12, 1868; J. N. Carpenter to Britton & Koontz, Trust Deed, November 23, 1870; J. N. Carpenter and Wife to J. R. Stockman (Trustee for Britton & Koontz), Trust Deeds, July 19, 1873, and February 13, 1874, Land Conveyance Ledger Books, Office of Records, Adams County, Natchez, Mississippi. N. L. Carpenter may also have had brothers or cousins named Ira and Samuel in Natchez and received some capital from them. Ira Carpenter was listed as a "late merchant" in the 1850 census, and after he died sometime after 1860, his widow, Sarah, often furnished capital for various endeavors related to N. L. Carpenter & Son.

22. The number preceding the credit ratings denotes the local agent's identification number in the R. G. Dun ranks. It is included when appropriate because often a firm's credit rating could literally change overnight if a new agent appeared—which also raises the question of whether some sort of favors or payment influenced credit ratings. Also, the type of business is not always included in the agent's ratings, but when it was it will be included. See credit ledger entries, N. L. Carpenter & Son, Vol. 2, p. 111, R. G. Dun & Co. Ledgers, Harvard Business School. New abbreviations Key: "oof" (zero, nothing), "gd." (good), "wor." (worth).

23. Obituaries of William Abbott and Ann E. Abbott, *Natchez Democrat*, December 27, 1884, 2, and June 9, 1903, 5; Advertisement, Henderson & Peale Co., *Natchez Weekly*

Democrat, October 14, 1867, 2; U.S. Census (1860–1880), MS Population and Slave Schedules, Adams County, Mississippi; Natchez Confederate Veterans, Land Conveyance Ledger Book 4I, pp. 269–294, Office of Records, Adams County, Natchez, Mississippi.

24. Multiple credit ledger entries, Henderson & Peale Co., Abbott, Henderson, & Stone, Abbott & Henderson Co., William Abbott & Co., Vol. 2, p. 104, R. G. Dun & Co. Ledgers, Harvard Business School. New abbreviations key: "Liabs" (liabilities), "sm" (small), "chars" (characters), "H+A" (Henderson and Abbott).

25. H. G. Newcomb and Wife to William Abbott (Trustee for Robert E. McClure), Trust Deed, April 17, 1877; Alfred Blanton et al. to William Abbott (Trustee for Thomas L. Mellon), Trust Deed, March 3, 1880; Alex Mazycque to James S. Fleming (Trustee for William Abbott), Trust Deed, May 5, 1884, Chattel Mortgage Ledger Books, 1884–1903, Office of Records, Adams County, Natchez, Mississippi; Notice of Power-of-Attorney and Management, Ann E. Abbott of William Abbott & Co. to James S. Fleming, *Natchez Democrat*, December 27, 1884, 2.

26. Advertisements, Rumble & Wensel Co., Pollock & Mason, and E. B. Baker & Sons, *Natchez Weekly Democrat*, October 5 and 12, 1865; U.S. Census (1860–1870), MS Population Schedules, Adams County, Mississippi; *Sheppard's Mississippi State Gazetteer*, 131–135. George G. Klapp was a carpetbagger planter who appeared soon after the war and operated several rented plantations in Concordia Parish across the river from Natchez. In the early 1870s he teamed up with J. N. Carpenter in the formation of J. N. Carpenter & Co. and became intimately involved in the many entrepreneurial activities of the Carpenter family for over two decades. See Lawrence N. Powell, *New Masters: Northern Planters during the Civil War and Reconstruction* (New Haven, Conn.: Yale University Press, 1980), 136–139; Wayne, *Reshaping of Plantation Society*, 167.

27. Multiple Notices of Attachment, *Babcock & Co. et al. v. Rickey, Shelton & Co.*, and *Charles Dedreck & Co. et al. v. Murphy & Gairnes*, *Natchez Weekly Democrat*, March 11, 1867, 2; Credit ledger entries, Ricky Shelton & Co., Vol. 2, p. 104, R. G. Dun & Co. Ledgers, Harvard Business School. New abbreviations key: "consid'd" (considered), "embarr'd" (embarrassed), "estab'd" (established).

28. Advertisement and Cotton Statement, S. D. Stockman & Co., *Natchez Weekly Democrat*, July 5, 1869, 3.

29. One of the Yankee sutlers was John Hill, a German immigrant who was not Jewish but Catholic. He was a close friend of Lowenburg and his family, and would be Lowenburg's partner until he died in 1871. But Hill was never part of the Jewish religious community and did not marry a Jew, and as such, is not mentioned here where Jewish familial interconnections are discussed. See Turitz and Turitz, *Mississippi Jews*, xii–xxii, 11–32; Wendy Machlovitz, *Clara Lowenburg Moses: Memoir of a Southern Jewish Woman* (Jackson, Miss.: Museum of the Southern Jewish Experience, 2000), 3–9, 41–48; U.S. Census (1840–1860), MS Population and Slave Schedules, Adams County, Mississippi; Natchez Confederate Veterans, Land Conveyance Ledger Book 4I, pp. 269–294, Office of Records, Adams County, Natchez, Mississippi.

30. Ibid.; 1858, 1871, 1877, 1892 Natchez City Business Directories, Historic Natchez Foundation; *Sheppard's Mississippi State Gazetteer*, 131–135; Joan Gandy, "Jewish History," Research File, Historic Natchez Foundation.

31. Stephen J. Whitfield, "Commercial Passions: The Southern Jew as Businessman," *American Jewish History* 71 (March 1982): 342–357; Turitz and Turitz, *Mississippi Jews*, xii–xiii, 11.

32. Gandy, "Jewish History"; Turitz and Turitz, *Mississippi Jews*, xii–xxii, 11–32.

33. Julius Weis quoted in Turitz and Turitz, *Mississippi Jews*, xvii.

34. Weis apparently was in a dry goods partnership with Meyer Eiseman in Fayette, Jefferson County, before he removed to Natchez and in fact may have been in Natchez making supply contacts. See Turitz and Turitz, *Mississippi Jews*, 31–32; Credit ledger entry, Julius Weis, Vol. 2, p. 76, R. G. Dun & Co. Ledgers, Harvard Business School; U.S. Census (1860–1880), MS and LA Population Schedules, Adams County, Mississippi, and Orleans Parish, Louisiana; Wayne, *Reshaping of Plantation Society*, 171. Meyer, Deutsch & Weis partner Joseph Deutsch relocated to New York City after the war and opened a branch of their business there, providing access to New York capital markets. Many major cotton merchants mentioned in this study—Buckner & Newman, Fleming & Baldwin, S. D. Stockman, and Meyer, Deutsch & Weis—all had access to New York financing, and by proxy that financing trickled down to those they financed themselves. New abbreviations key: "pedler" (peddler), "ppy" (property).

35. The Goldring/Woldenburg Institute of Southern Jewish Life, "Digital Archive: Natchez," http://; Turitz and Turitz, *Mississippi Jews*, xii–xxii, 11–32; Machlovitz, *Clara Lowenburg Moses*, 3–9, 41–48; U.S. Census (1840–1860), MS Population and Slave Schedules, Adams County, Mississippi; 1852 Natchez City Tax Assessment Rolls, Natchez Collection, California State University, Northridge.

36. Beekman may have been partnered or associated with David Moses's Cheap Cash Store while in business under-the-hill in the early 1850s because his early R. G. Dun ratings are listed under Beekman & Moses, but photographs of his store in the Cotton Square after his move uptown in 1858 clearly show the name A. Beekman. See credit ledger entry, Beekman & Moses, Vol. 2, p. 58, R. G. Dun & Co. Ledgers, Harvard Business School. New abbreviations key: "bot" (bought), "wh" (which), "w" (with), "sm" (small).

37. Credit ledger entry, Aaron Beekman, Vol. 2, p. 29, R. G. Dun & Co. Ledgers, Harvard Business School; Turitz and Turitz, *Mississippi Jews*, 11–27; Machlovitz, *Clara Lowenburg Moses*, 3–9, 41–48; Aaron Beekman, Last Will and Testament (Estate File), June 12, 1901, Cause No. 1703, File Box No. 237, Office of Records, Adams County, Natchez, Mississippi. New abbreviations key: "mak'g (making), "c" (etc.).

38. Credit ledger entry, Marx Lemle, Vol. 2, p. 28, R. G. Dun & Co. Ledgers, Harvard Business School; Peter Grant and Wife to Marks Lemle, Deed, February 3, 1858; Office of Records, Adams County, Natchez, Mississippi; Land Conveyance Ledger Books, 1860–1900, General Mortgage Ledger Books, 1866–1900, Office of Records, Concordia Parish, Vidalia, Louisiana; U.S. Census (1850–1860), Population Schedules, Adams County, Mississippi; Marx Lemle, Last Will and Testament (Estate File), March 10, 1883, Cause No. 789, File Box No. 204, Office of Records, Adams County, Natchez, Mississippi; *William Gay v. Marx Lemle*, Circuit Court, April Term 1855, Drawer 366, Box 9–71, Historic Natchez Foundation; Adams Light Infantry Roster, Temple B'Nai Israel, Natchez, Mississippi. New abbreviations key: "stk" (stock).

39. Turitz and Turitz, *Mississippi Jews*, 14–16; Machlovitz, *Clara Lowenburg Moses*, 3–9, 41–48; Credit ledger entries, I. Lowenburg & Co. and Henry Frank Fancy Store, Vol. 2, pp. 120, 135, R. G. Dun & Co. Ledgers, Harvard Business School; Land Conveyance Ledger Books, 1860–1900, Office of Records, Adams County, Natchez, Mississippi; *Natchez, Mississippi On Top, Not "Under the Hill,"* 1–28. New abbreviations key: "dg" (doing).

40. Advertisement, I. Lowenburg & Co., *Natchez Weekly Courier*, February 12, 1870, 2.

41. The Geisenbergers were related to or intermarried with the Mayers, Weises, Beekmans, Lowenburgs, Franks, Ullmans, Benjamins, Laubs, and Friedlers. Jewish intermarriage and business partnerships get complicated—but are of great importance to these families. In just one brief example, Geisenberger's son Sam married Isaac Friedler's daughter Julia, and his daughter married Aaron Beekman's son Abe, and his son Sam also went into the dry goods business with Friedler's son Joseph. See Turitz and Turitz, *Mississippi Jews*, 17–20; Credit ledger entries, Geisenberger & Benjamin, Vol. 2, p. 125, R. G. Dun & Co. Ledgers, Harvard Business School. New abbreviations key: "marr'd" (married), "hab" (habits).

42. Obituary of Isaac Friedler, *Natchez Democrat*, July 12, 1911, 7; Entry for Ignatz Friedler, December 14, 1854, New York Passenger Lists, 1820–1957, National Archive microfilm roll M237-148, list 1647, http://www.Ancestry.com/search/rectype/default; U.S. Census (1860) Population Schedules, Ashtabula County, Ohio; U.S. Census (1870–1880) Population Schedules, Concordia Parish, Louisiana; Concordia Parish Tax Assessment Rolls, 1867, Natchez Collection, California State University, Northridge; Turitz and Turitz, *Mississippi Jews*, 17; Rosa Friedler, Estate File, March 21, 1927, Cause No. 5193, File Box No. 305, Office of Records, Adams County, Natchez, Mississippi. New abbreviations key: "fr" (frisk), "est" (estimated).

43. U.S. Census (1860) Population Schedules, St. Louis County, Missouri; U.S. Census (1870–1880) Population Schedules, Adams County, Mississippi; Obituary of Simon Jacobs, *Natchez Democrat*, February 7, 1889, 2; Credit ledger entries, Simon Jacobs and S. & A. Jacobs, Vol. 2, pp. 125, 154, R. G. Dun & Co. Ledgers, Harvard Business School; Machlovitz, *Clara Lowenburg Moses*, 11–12; Gandy, "Jewish History"; State of Mississippi to Adolf Jacobs & Son Banking Co., Corporate Charter, November 12, 1906, Office of Records, Adams County, Natchez, Mississippi. New abbreviations key: "marr'd" (married), "hab" (habits).

44. Robert Somers quoted in Woodman, *King Cotton*, 304; Sansing, et al., *Natchez*, 140.

45. David Rattray quoted in Turitz and Turitz, *Mississippi Jews*, xviii.

46. Entry for A. Perrault, May 7, 1835, New Orleans Passenger Lists, 1820–1945, National Archive microfilm roll M259-12, http://www.Ancestry.com/search/rectype/default; U.S. Census (1830–1850) Population Schedules, Orleans Parish, Louisiana; U.S. Census (1840) Population Schedules, Jefferson County, Kentucky; U.S. Census (1850–1880) Population Schedules, Adams County, Mississippi; Credit ledger entries, A. Perrault Co., G. T. Payne, T. E. Perrault, and McPherson & Perrault, Vol. 2, pp. 9, 73, 93, 123, 184, R. G. Dun & Co. Ledgers, Harvard Business School; John C. Schwartz "Daybook, 1859–1865," J:23, Vol. 2A, pp. 204–210, John C. Schwartz Papers, LSU; Natchez Confederate Veterans, Land Conveyance Ledger Book 4I, pp. 269–294, Chattel Mortgage Ledger Books, 1875–1903, Land Conveyance Ledger Books, 1850–1910, Office of Records, Adams County, Natchez, Mississippi.

47. Religion was often a binding factor in marriage or formation of mercantile associations, in many cases overriding national origin or ethnic loyalties. See the U.S. Census (1830–1910) Population Schedules, Adams County, Mississippi; *Natchez, Mississippi On Top, Not "Under the Hill*," 1–28; "Abstracts from St. Mary's Cathedral Church Announcements in Church Books," http://www. natchezbelle.org/adams-ind/church/htm.

48. U.S. Census (1850–1880) Population Schedules, Adams County, Mississippi; Record of Naturalization, 1854–1904, p. 46, Circuit Court of Adams County, Office of Records, Adams County, Natchez, Mississippi.

49. Credit ledger entries, G. T. Payne, Vol. 2, pp. 9, 73, R. G. Dun & Co. Ledgers, Harvard Business School. New abbreviations key: "variet" (variety), "form'ly" (formerly).

50. U.S. Census (1860) Population Schedules, Adams County, Mississippi; Jacob B. Davis and Wife to George T. Payne, Deed, July 26, 1862; Pascal J. Penn to George T. Payne, Deed,

March 26, 1863; Ambrose J. Foster to George T. Payne, Deed, April 13, 1863; Natchez Confederate Veterans, Land Conveyance Ledger Book 4I, pp. 269–294; Natchez City Alderman's Meeting Minutes, 1879–1882; Adams County Supervisor's Meeting Minutes 1875–1891, Office of Records, Adams County, Natchez, Mississippi; Credit ledger entries, G. T. Payne, Vol. 2, pp. 73, 108, R. G. Dun & Co. Ledgers, Harvard Business School; *State of Mississippi v. George T. Payne and Dan Cryder* (Marx Lemle Complainant), April 28, 1868, Box 14, File 1, Circuit Court Cases 1860–1880 Ledger, Historic Natchez Foundation; Wayne, *Reshaping of Plantation Society*, 181; *Natchez, Mississippi On Top, Not "Under the Hill,"* 1–28.

51. 1877 Natchez City Business Directory, 43, Historic Natchez Foundation.

52. Natchez Confederate Veterans, Land Conveyance Ledger Book 4I, pp. 269–294, Office of Records, Adams County, Natchez, Mississippi; Credit ledger entry, T. E. Perrault Clothing, Vol. 2, p. 123, R. G. Dun & Co. Ledgers, Harvard Business School.

53. 1877 Natchez City Business Directory, 43, Historic Natchez Foundation; Credit ledger entry, J. C. Schwartz Hardware, Vol. 2, p. 103, R. G. Dun & Co. Ledgers, Harvard Business School; Eustis Surget to Christina Schwartz, Isaac Lowenburg, and John Hill, Lease of "Morville," January 5, 1871, Office of Records, Concordia Parish, Louisiana. New abbreviations key: "excell't" (excellent).

54. 1877 Natchez City Business Directory, 43, Historic Natchez Foundation.

55. Frank O'Brien and Samuel J. Perrault to Hugh McGinty, Deed, March 4, 1883; Frank O'Brien and Samuel J. Perrault to Frank J. Arrighi, Trust Deed, June 4, 1883; Charles H. Perrault to Frank J. Arrighi, Trust Deed, May 2, 1887, Natchez Confederate Veterans, Land Conveyance Ledger Book 4I, pp. 269–294, Elizabeth M. Perrault, Estate File, April 13, 1897, Cause No. 1444, File Box No. 230, Office of Records, Adams County, Natchez, Mississippi; U.S. Census (1850–1900) Population Schedules, Adams County, Mississippi; Elizabeth M. Perrault, Estate File, April 13, 1897, Cause No. 1444, File Box No. 230, Office of Records, Adams County, Natchez, Mississippi; Credit ledger entry, E. J. Perrault Confectioner, Vol. 2, p. 166, R. G. Dun & Co. Ledgers, Harvard Business School; 1877 Natchez City Business Directory, Historic Natchez Foundation; Rowland, *Mississippi*, 3:489. New abbreviations key: "bot" (bought), "M+C" (Carrie).

56. Entry for Mary Maher, February 15, 1860, New Orleans Passenger Lists, 1820–1945, National Archive microfilm roll M259–48, http://www.Ancestry.com/search/rectype/default; U.S. Census (1860–1900) Population Schedules, Adams County, Mississippi, and Orleans Parish, Louisiana; Ann E. Miles to Fred Maher (Trustee for Perrault & Co.), Trust Deed, July 6, 1885; Fred Maher (Trustee) to the Perrault Co., Trustees Deeds, February 2, 7, and 23, 1887, Office of Records, Jefferson County, Fayette, Mississippi; Armand L. Perrault, Estate File, April 28, 1885, Cause No. 869, File Box No. 204; Chattel Mortgage Ledger Books, 1890–1903; Natchez City Alderman's Meeting Minutes, 1889–1910, Office of Records, Adams County, Natchez, Mississippi; 1892 Natchez City Business Directory, Historic Natchez Foundation.

57. Obituary of Henry M. Gastrell, *Natchez Daily Democrat*, April 18, 1889, 2; U.S. Census (1870–1880) Population Schedules, Adams County, Mississippi.

58. Advertisement, "H. M. Gastrell & Co.," *Natchez Weekly Democrat*, October 2, 1865, 3.

59. "Railroad Committee," *Natchez Weekly Democrat*, July 12, 1869, 1; Credit ledger entry, H. M. Gastrell Hardware & Stoves, Vol. 2, pp. 179, 186, R. G. Dun & Co. Ledgers, Harvard Business School; 1877 Natchez City Business Directory, Historic Natchez Foundation.

60. *Natchez, Mississippi On Top, Not "Under the Hill,"* preface.

Chapter 3. Crop Liens, Freedmen, and Planters

1. Davis, *Black Experience in Natchez*, 129–149; U.S. Census MS Population and Slave Schedules (1850, 1860), MS Population Schedules (1870, 1880, 1900), Adams County, Mississippi; Entries for James and Nathan Wright, Washington County, Adams County, Mississippi, 1890 Veterans Schedules, National Archive microfilm series M123, http://www.search.ancestry.com/cgi-bin/sse.dll?rank=1&gsfn=nathan&glsn=wright&=&_82004024_gpid=27&_82004043=adam.

2. U.S. Census (1870) MS Population Schedules, Adams County, Mississippi; Nathan Wright to George T. Payne, Chattel Mortgages, April 11, 1873, May 24, 1874, June 1, 1875; George Wright to George T. Payne, Chattel Mortgages, March 28, 1873, March 27, 1874, March 9, 1875, March 8, 1876, February 5, 1877, May 24, 1878; Peter C. Rucker to J. W. Roos, Deed, October 20, 1887; Nathan Wright to Adolf Jacobs & Son, Chattel Mortgage, March 8, 1902, Office of Records, Adams County, Natchez, Mississippi; Richard Wright, *Black Boy (American Hunger): A Record of Childhood and Youth* (New York: HarperCollins, 1998), xiii–xvi, 3–77; Hazel Rowley, *Richard Wright: The Life and Times* (New York: Henry Holt, 2001), 1–27.

3. Davis, *Good and Faithful Labor*, 1–9, 58–59; Clark, *Pills, Petticoats and Plows*, 313–336; Atherton, *Southern Country Store*, 19–86; Woodman, *King Cotton*, 241–247; Wayne, *Reshaping of Plantation Society*, 31–52; Allison Davis, Burleigh B. Gardner, and Mary Gardner, *Deep South: A Social Anthropological Study of Caste and Class* (Chicago: University of Chicago Press, 1941), 264

4. Davis, *Good and Faithful Labor*, 1–9, 59–88; Woodman, *King Cotton*, 204–16; Davis, *Black Experience*, 158–170; Harold D. Woodman, *New South—New Law* (Baton Rouge: Louisiana State University Press, 1995), 1–27.

5. Davis, *Black Experience*, 158–176; Davis, *Good and Faithful Labor*, 169–184, 193–196; Eric Foner, *Reconstruction: America's Unfinished Revolution, 1863–1877* (New York: Harper and Row, 1988), 564–601.

6. Wayne, *Reshaping of Plantation Society*, 75–109; 150–196; Davis, *Good and Faithful Labor*, 121–145; Land Conveyance Ledger Books, 1860–1910, Record of Leases 1875–1890, Office of Records, Adams County, Natchez, Mississippi; Land Conveyance Ledger Books, 1860–1910, General Mortgage Ledger Books, 1866–1910, Office of Records, Concordia Parish, Vidalia, Louisiana; Land Deed Ledgers, 1860–1900, Office of Records, Tensas Parish, St. Joseph, Louisiana; Land Deed Ledgers, 1871–1910, Office of Records, Jefferson County, Fayette, Mississippi; Land Deed Ledgers, 1874–1910, Office of Records, Franklin County, Meadville, Mississippi; Land Deed Ledgers, 1871–1910, Office of Records, Wilkinson County, Woodville, Mississippi.

7. Wayne, *Reshaping of Plantation Society*, 75–109, 150–196; Davis, *Good and Faithful Labor*, 121–145, 158–176; Natchez Jewish History, Research File, Historic Natchez Foundation; Turitz and Turitz, *Jews in Early Mississippi*, 11–28; *Natchez, Mississippi On Top, Not "Under the Hill,"* 10–14; Nathan Wright to George T. Payne, Chattel Mortgage, April 11, 1873; Nathan Wright to Adolf Jacobs & Son, Chattel Mortgage, March 8, 1902, Office of Records, Adams County, Natchez, Mississippi.

8. Henry and Lucinda Lincoln to I. Lowenburg & Co., Chattel Mortgage, March 26, 1869, Office of Records, Adams County, Natchez, Mississippi.

9. Ibid.; U.S. Census (1870–1880) MS Population Schedules, Adams County, Mississippi.

10. Davis, *Good and Faithful Labor*, 1–9, 59–73; Wayne, *Reshaping of Plantation Society*, 31–52.

11. Davis, *Good and Faithful Labor*, 4, 73–82, 172–173; Davis, *Black Experience*, 129–149; Wayne, *Reshaping of Plantation Society*, 31–52; Foner, *Reconstruction*, 185–227.

12. One major difference between sharecropping and tenant farming is in the extent of supervision over the farmers and the amount of the crop divided between workers, suppliers, and landowners. Share-tenants paid a set share of the crop, or a set rent in cotton, to the landlord, whereas sharecroppers received a share of the crop for their labor as wages, and these "shares" of cotton could range from one-third to two-thirds of the total cotton crop produced by the cropper. See Davis, *Good and Faithful Labor*, 73–82.

13. Ibid., 60, 73–82; Woodman, *King Cotton*, 295–318; Woodman, *New South—New Law*, 1–27.

14. Davis, *Good and Faithful Labor*, 60, 73–82, 121–151; Woodman, *King Cotton*, 295–318; Woodman, *New South—New Law*, 1–27; Wayne, *Reshaping of Plantation Society*, 150–196; Clark, *Pills, Petticoats and Plows*, 313–336.

15. *Sheppard's Mississippi State Gazetteer and Shippers Guide*, 131–135; 1871, 1877, and 1892 Natchez Business Directories; Natchez Jewish History, Research File, Historic Natchez Foundation.

16. Credit ledger entries, G. T. Payne, Mississippi, Vol. 2, p. 73, R. G. Dun & Co. Ledgers, Harvard Business School; Clark, *Pills, Petticoats, and Plows*, 313–336; Davis, *Good and Faithful Labor*, 121–151; Woodman, *King Cotton*, 295–318; Wayne, *Reshaping of Plantation Society*, 150–196; Permits to Purchase Cotton Ledger, Natchez District, March 22–25, 1864; Permits to Ship Goods, June 13, 1864, Natchez District, Natchez Collection, California State University, Northridge; Charles P. Roland, *The American Iliad: The Story of the Civil War* (New York: McGraw-Hill, 1991), 194–195.

17. Adams Light Infantry Membership Roster, Temple B'Nai Israel, Natchez, Mississippi; Permits to Purchase Cotton Ledger, Natchez District, March 22–25, 1864, July 6, 1864, October 12, 1864, June 21, 1865, July 28, 1865; Permits to Ship Goods, June 13, 1864, August 1–30, 1864, May 16–18, 1865, Natchez District, Natchez Collection, California State University, Northridge; Wayne, *Reshaping of Plantation Society*, 180–181.

18. Clark, *Pills, Petticoats and Plows*, 313–336; Davis, *Good and Faithful Labor*, 121–151; Wayne, *Reshaping of Plantation Society*, 150–196; Woodman, *King Cotton*, 295–318. See Chattel Mortgage Ledger Books, 1875–1903, Land Conveyance Ledger Books, 1865–1910, Record of Leases 1875–1890, Office of Records, Adams County, Natchez, Mississippi; Land Conveyance Ledger Books, 1865–1910, General Mortgage Ledger Books, 1866–1900, Office of Records, Concordia Parish, Vidalia, Louisiana; Land Deed Ledgers, 1865–1910, Office of Records, Tensas Parish, St. Joseph, Louisiana; Land Deed Ledgers, 1871–1910, Chattel Mortgage Lender Books, 1875–1910, Office of Records, Jefferson County, Fayette, Mississippi; Land Deed Ledgers, 1874–1910, Chattel Mortgage Ledgers, 1871–1903, Office of Records, Franklin County, Meadville, Mississippi; Land Deed Ledgers, 1871–1910, Office of Records, Wilkinson County, Woodville, Mississippi.

19. Davis, *Good and Faithful Labor*, 121–151; Wayne, *Reshaping of Plantation Society*, 150–196; Woodman, *King Cotton*, 295–318; Charlotte Surget to Isaac Lowenburg, Sale and Mortgage, August 21, 1867, Office of Records, Concordia Parish, Vidalia, Louisiana; Patrick Harris to Miller & Marsh, Agreement, February 23, 1867; William Hall to Fleming & Baldwin, Agreement, December 19, 1867; P. E. Jones to George T. Payne, Agreement, April 28, 1868; Thomas R. Shields and the Freedmen and Freedwomen of Hermitage Plantation,

Agreement, July 16, 1868, Henry and Lucinda Lincoln to I. Lowenburg & Co., Chattel Mortgage, March 26, 1869; Charles Woods et al. to Mark Lemle, Contract, April 4, 1870, Office of Records, Adams County, Natchez, Mississippi.

20. Chattel Mortgage Ledger Books, 1875–1903, Land Conveyance Ledger Books, 1865–1910, Record of Leases 1875–1890, Office of Records, Adams County, Natchez, Mississippi; Land Conveyance Ledger Books, 1865–1910, General Mortgage Ledger Books, 1866–1900, Office of Records, Concordia Parish, Vidalia, Louisiana; Land Deed Ledgers, 1865–1910, Office of Records, Tensas Parish, St. Joseph, Louisiana; Land Deed Ledgers, 1871–1910, Chattel Mortgage Lender Books, 1875–1910, Office of Records, Jefferson County, Fayette, Mississippi; Land Deed Ledgers, 1874–1910, Chattel Mortgage Ledgers, 1871–1903, Office of Records, Franklin County, Meadville, Mississippi; Land Deed Ledgers, 1871–1910, Office of Records, Wilkinson County, Woodville, Mississippi.

21. Ibid.
22. Ibid.
23. Ibid.
24. Ibid.
25. Ibid.
26. Ibid. Friedler had a store and riverboat landing in St. Joseph, Louisiana, in Tensas Parish across the river from Port Gibson, Mississippi, but local records contain land deeds only, with no chattel mortgage contracts for Friedler. We know this because Friedler recorded a five-year lease on L'Argent and Pocahontas plantations on the Mississippi River in December 1887. This lease details some of his plans to open a store there and a new riverboat landing on the Mississippi to service the town of St. Joseph and the surrounding area, conveniently located across the river from bustling Port Gibson, and only a short distance downriver from Vicksburg, a fairly large city. Also, he received this lease from a prominent local Jewish merchant in St. Joseph, Simon Marx, and the contract specifies that Marx cannot open or operate a store in St. Joseph for the term of the lease. See Simon Marx to Isaac Friedler, Lease, December 5, 1887, Office of Records, Tensas Parish, St. Joseph, Louisiana.

27. See Chattel Mortgage Ledger Books, 1875–1903, Land Conveyance Ledger Books, 1865–1910, Record of Leases 1875–1890, Office of Records, Adams County, Natchez, Mississippi; Land Conveyance Ledger Books, 1865–1910, General Mortgage Ledger Books, 1866–1900, Office of Records, Concordia Parish, Vidalia, Louisiana; Land Deed Ledgers, 1865–1910, Office of Records, Tensas Parish, St. Joseph, Louisiana; Land Deed Ledgers, 1871–1910, Chattel Mortgage Lender Books, 1875–1910, Office of Records, Jefferson County, Fayette, Mississippi; Land Deed Ledgers, 1874–1910, Chattel Mortgage Ledgers, 1871–1903, Office of Records, Franklin County, Meadville, Mississippi; Land Deed Ledgers, 1871–1910, Office of Records, Wilkinson County, Woodville, Mississippi.

28. Ibid. These distances involved are significant, particularly to interior areas where riverboat service was unavailable and a trip by wagon could take a day or two or more, depending on the weather. Railroads mitigated this aspect later in the period by connecting these areas to the Mississippi River and Natchez proper, and several of the merchants featured in this work were closely involved in these railroad-building efforts, which is understandable since they had much to gain by improved transportation. See Permits to Purchase Cotton Ledger, Natchez District, March 1864, 22–25; Permits to Ship Goods, June 13, 1864, Natchez District, Natchez Collection, California State University, Northridge.

29. H. B. and Oraline White to Aaron Beekman, Chattel Mortgage, February 1, 1893; H. B. and Oraline White to Aaron Beekman, Judgment, March 4, 1896, Office of Records,

Concordia Parish, Vidalia, Louisiana. Rufus and Emma Ford to Aaron Beekman, Deed, October 16, 1882, Office of Records, Franklin County, Meadville, Mississippi; W. K. Penny to Aaron Beekman and Son, Deed, March 13, 1885, Office of Records, Jefferson County, Fayette, Mississippi; Sina Hastings to Aaron Beekman, Conveyance, November 7, 1882, Office of Records, Wilkinson County, Woodville, Mississippi. See Chattel Mortgage Ledger Books, 1875–1903, Land Conveyance Ledger Books, 1865–1910, Record of Leases 1875–1890, Office of Records, Adams County, Natchez, Mississippi; Land Conveyance Ledger Books, 1865–1910, General Mortgage Ledger Books, 1866–1900, Office of Records, Concordia Parish, Vidalia, Louisiana; Land Deed Ledgers, 1865–1910, Office of Records, Tensas Parish, St. Joseph, Louisiana; Land Deed Ledgers, 1871–1910, Chattel Mortgage Lender Books, 1875–1910, Office of Records, Jefferson County, Fayette, Mississippi; Land Deed Ledgers, 1874–1910, Chattel Mortgage Ledgers, 1871–1903, Office of Records, Franklin County, Meadville, Mississippi; Land Deed Ledgers, 1871–1910, Office of Records, Wilkinson County, Woodville, Mississippi.

30. Ibid.; Ransom and Sutch, *One Kind of Freedom*, 126–148; Kyriakoudes, "Lower-Order Urbanization," 179–198.

31. In 1877 Friedler recorded at least thirteen liens on Lowenburg's, totaling $1,395.53 in supply accounts for that year. See Charlotte B. Surget to Isaac Lowenburg, Lease, November 21, 1870; Sundry Persons to Isaac Lowenburg, Affidavit for Supplies Furnished (Merchant Lien), March 6 and July 7, 1876; Sundry Persons to Isaac Friedler, Affidavit for Supplies Furnished (Merchant Lien), November 28, 1876; Sundry Persons to Isaac Friedler, Affidavit (Merchant Lien), July 17, 1877, Office of Records, Concordia Parish, Vidalia, Louisiana.

32. Clarence Wade to Marx Lemle, Trust Deeds, March 18, 1875, June 6, 1875; Charles Sanders et al. to Marx Lemle (twelve contracts), Chattel Mortgages, March 31, 1876–February 28, 1883; George Hardiman to George T. Payne, Chattel Mortgage, May 25, 1878; James Ross to George T. Payne, Chattel Mortgage, July 5, 1882; James Anderson et al. to Wolfe Geisenberger (six contracts), Chattel Mortgages, March 15, 1879–April 10, 1880; Henry Richardson to Armand Perrault, Chattel Mortgage, March 6, 1877; Thirty-seven Chattel Mortgages from assorted croppers to Marx Lemle & Co., S. & A. Jacobs, Adolf Jacobs & Co., A. F. Jacobs & Bros., I. Lowenburg & Co., Wolfe Geisenberger & Co., George Payne & Co., and the William Abbott Co. (with James S. Fleming) on A. D. Carpenter's Point Place, May 15, 1877–March 4, 1902, Chattel Mortgage Ledgers, Office of Records, Adams County, Natchez, Mississippi.

33. Davis, *Good and Faithful Labor*, 99-106; Wayne, *Reshaping of Plantation Society*, 188–190; Delinquent Tax List, 1873, 1–48, Ledger R, General Mortgages; Barnell Bailey to Isaac Friedler, Merchant Lien, March 4, 1874; William Williams to Isaac Friedler, Merchant Lien, March 14, 1874; Isaac Friedler to Sundry Persons, Affidavit (Merchant Lien), August 12, 1874; John Harris to Isaac Friedler, Lease, November 3, 1874, Office of Records, Concordia Parish, Vidalia, Louisiana; Caroline Bowman et al. to Aaron Beekman (twenty-nine contracts), Chattel Mortgages, May 19, 1883–April 22, 1897; Oliver Anderson to Wolfe Geisenberger, Chattel Mortgage, February 22, 1886, Chattel Mortgage Ledgers, Office of Records, Adams County, Natchez, Mississippi.

34. Friedler started listing rent amounts in cotton in some contracts in the mid-1870s for "fixed rent tenants," and over the next few years the amounts on Waverly varied from two to seven bales per contract, depending on how many tenants were part of that contract, and also how much land they had to farm, which averaged around twenty acres per family or a small squad. For tenants who were sharecroppers in the sense of being more like wage hands than renters, the amount left to Friedler might have been as much as two-thirds of their

crop, generating even more cotton for Friedler. I use this figure of three bales as an "average" for this plantation for the purposes of re-creating how this arrangement might work, and do not mean to say that this number is the exact amount of cotton collected. This instance was chosen because there was a manageable and clearly defined number of contracts issued for that plantation in that year. For examples of cotton rent amounts on Waverly, see Steven Mackie to Isaac Friedler, Merchants Lien and Rent Agreement, December 29, 1874; Cornelius Johnson to Isaac Friedler, Merchants Lien and Rent Agreement, December 29, 1874; Jordan Cartwright to Isaac Friedler, Merchants Lien and Rent Agreement, December 29, 1874; Barnell Bailey to Isaac Friedler, Merchants Lien and Rent Agreement, December 28, 1874; John Harris to Isaac Friedler, Lease, November 3, 1874, Office of Records, Concordia Parish, Vidalia, Louisiana. For a reasonable explanation of this complex system, see Davis, *Good and Faithful Labor*, 89-145; Davis, *Black Experience in Natchez*, 162–170; Wayne, *Reshaping of Plantation Society*, 150–196.

35. Wayne, *Reshaping of Plantation Society*, 181–182; B. B. Parham to Carpenter, Dicks & Co., Contract and Lien, March 1, 1887, Office of Records, Concordia Parish, Vidalia, Louisiana. See Chattel Mortgage Ledger Books, 1875–1903, Land Conveyance Ledger Books, 1865–1910, Record of Leases 1875–1890, Office of Records, Adams County, Natchez, Mississippi; Land Conveyance Ledger Books, 1865–1910, General Mortgage Ledger Books, 1866–1900, Office of Records, Concordia Parish, Vidalia, Louisiana; Land Deed Ledgers, 1865–1910, Office of Records, Tensas Parish, St. Joseph, Louisiana; Land Deed Ledgers, 1871–1910, Chattel Mortgage Lender Books, 1875–1910, Office of Records, Jefferson County, Fayette, Mississippi; Land Deed Ledgers, 1874–1910, Chattel Mortgage Ledgers, 1871–1903, Office of Records, Franklin County, Meadville, Mississippi; Land Deed Ledgers, 1871–1910, Office of Records, Wilkinson County, Woodville, Mississippi.

36. Wayne, *Reshaping of Plantation Society*, 171, 180–181.

37. Livestock could be a good moneymaker for the sharecropper, in theory, because of the natural increase of the animals. Mules did not reproduce, of course, nor did draft animals that were worked to the point of exhaustion. See Chattel Mortgage Ledger Books, 1875–1900; Aaron Beekman to A. Eltringham and Company, Lease, November 1, 1883, Office of Records, Adams County, Natchez, Mississippi; General Mortgage Ledger Books, 1866–1900; Isaac Friedler to Sundry Persons, Affidavit (Merchants Lien), July 27, 1876; Edward Wilkinson to Isaac Lowenburg, Chattel Mortgage, February 11, 1880; Calliss Reed to Marx Lemle, Merchants Lien, May 8, 1879; Hunter Jenkins to Marx Lemle, Merchants Lien, December 30, 1879; Thomas N. Coleman to Isaac Friedler, Deed, July 14, 1881; Julius Weis to Ignatz Friedler, Deed, January 9, 1884, Office of Records, Concordia Parish, Vidalia, Louisiana.

38. *Isaac Friedler v. Jake Davis*, Judgment, January 1, 1878; *Isaac Friedler v. Monday Williams*, Judgment, January 15, 1878; *Isaac Friedler v. William Ridgely*, Judgment, June 16, 1878; *Isaac Friedler v. Charles Washington*, Judgment, November 23, 1878; *Isaac Friedler v. Mark Littleton*, Judgment, December 13, 1878; *Isaac Friedler v. Wilson Johnson*, Judgment, December 13, 1878, Record of Judgments and Pleadings, 1878–1882, Office of Records, Concordia Parish, Vidalia, Louisiana.

39. Ibid.; *Isaac Friedler v. John Hart*, Pleading, May 31, 1886, Record of Judgments and Pleadings, Office of Records, Concordia Parish, Vidalia, Louisiana.

40. Daniel Jackson to George T. Payne (six contracts), Chattel Mortgages, February 24, 1877–January 24, 1883; Daniel Jackson to Wolfe Geisenberger (six contracts), Chattel Mortgages, February 24, 1886–May 8, 1897, Office of Records, Adams County, Natchez, Mississippi; U.S. Census (1870–1910), MS Population Schedules, Adams County, Mississippi. There

is good evidence that Jackson had another son, Daniel Jr., who may have worked for many years with his father on Brandon Hall before moving to Locust Grove plantation in the same neighborhood and cropping there until 1908, while Murphy and Daniel Sr. both vanish from the records after 1900.

41. Aaron and Elizabeth B. Stanton to Aaron Beekman, N. L. Carpenter & Son, J. N. Carpenter & Co., and I. Lowenburg & Co. (thirty-five contracts), Chattel Mortgages and Trust Deeds, January 1, 1874–November 3, 1898, Office of Records, Adams County, Natchez, Mississippi; U.S. Census (1850–1930) MS Population Schedules, Adams County, Mississippi.

42. Gavin Wright, *The Political Economy of the Cotton South: Households, Markets, and Wealth in the Nineteenth Century* (New York: W. W. Norton, 1978), 158–184; Davis, *Good and Faithful Labor*, 1–9, 143–145; Woodman, *King Cotton*, 295–315; Wayne, *Reshaping of Plantation Society*, 163–183; Atherton, *Southern Country Store*, 39–62; Clark, *Pills, Petticoats, and Plows*, 271–291.

43. Ibid.; Davis, *Black Experience*, 158–171.

44. Ibid.

45. Whitfield, "Commercial Passions," 352–353.

46. Ibid.; Davis, *Black Experience*, 158–171; Ronald L. F. Davis, interview with author, November 2, 2004, California State University, Northridge.

47. Davis, *Good and Faithful Labor*, 1–19, 89-111; Davis, *Black Experience*, 158–171; Wayne, *Reshaping of Plantation Society*, 110-114, 150–151; Woodman, *King Cotton*, 295–315; Clark, *Pills, Petticoats, and Plows*, 271–291.

48. Davis, *Black Experience*, 171–175; Aaron Stanton to Isaac Lowenburg, Trust Deed, January 1, 1874; Mary Phipps to Isaac Lowenburg, Quitclaim Deed, December 23, 1874; John Henderson and Wife to Isaac Lowenburg, Deed of Trust, April 13, 1875; Maria Bowie to Isaac Lowenburg, Chattel Mortgage, March 29, 1876; Jack and Caroline Allen to Beekman & Meyer, Chattel Mortgage, March 9, 1875; Carroll Dancy to Isaac Lowenburg, Chattel Mortgage, March 31, 1877; John Travers et al. to Aaron Beekman, Chattel Mortgage, March 10, 1879; Quilly and Kesiah Dorsey to Wolfe Geisenberger, March 15, 1879; Charles and Patricia Woods to Marx Lemle, March 18, 1879; Major Clarke to Marx Lemle, Chattel Mortgage, March 28, 1879; Louis and Eliza Hall to Isaac Lowenburg, Chattel Mortgage, February 13, 1880; Randolph Mazique et al. to Wolfe Geisenberger, Chattel Mortgage, February 27, 1883; Louis J. Winston to A. H. Geisenberger (Trustee), Deed of Trust, August 4, 1890; Adams Building and Loan Association to A. H. Geisenberger (Trustee), Deed of Trust, October 13, 1890, Office of Records, Adams County, Natchez, Mississippi.

49. See Chattel Mortgage Ledger Books, 1875–1903, Land Conveyance Ledger Books, 1865–1910, Record of Leases 1875–1890, Office of Records, Adams County, Natchez, Mississippi; Land Conveyance Ledger Books, 1865–1910, General Mortgage Ledger Books, 1866–1900, Office of Records, Concordia Parish, Vidalia, Louisiana; Land Deed Ledgers, 1865–1910, Office of Records, Tensas Parish, St. Joseph, Louisiana; Land Deed Ledgers, 1871–1910, Chattel Mortgage Lender Books, 1875–1910, Office of Records, Jefferson County, Fayette, Mississippi; Land Deed Ledgers, 1874–1910, Chattel Mortgage Ledgers, 1871–1903, Office of Records, Franklin County, Meadville, Mississippi; Land Deed Ledgers, 1871–1910, Office of Records, Wilkinson County, Woodville, Mississippi.

50. Nelson and Cressy Page to Aaron Beekman, Chattel Mortgages, March 2, 1875, March 3, 1876, and February 5, 1877, Office of Records, Adams County, Natchez, Mississippi; U.S. Census (1870, 1880, 1900, 1910), MS Population Schedules, Adams County, Mississippi.

51. U.S. Census (1870, 1880, 1900, 1910), MS Population Schedules, Adams County, Mississippi; Henry Rice last appeared in the U.S. Census in the 1880 accounting as a sixty-nine-year-old widower, and it is possible he died after his contract with Beekman & Son in 1888, or perhaps moved from the district; he likely had a son, Daniel, living in Hinds County. See Henry Rice to Aaron Beekman, Chattel Mortgages, March 18, 1876, February 7, 1877, March 2, 1878, January 24, 1879, February 11, 1880, February 21, 1881, February 2, 1882, February 20, 1883, January 29, 1884, February 19, 1885, January 22, 1886, March 9, 1887, February 2, 1888, Office of Records, Adams County, Natchez, Mississippi; U.S. Census (1870, 1880, 1900), MS Population Schedules, Adams County, Mississippi.

52. U.S. Census (1870, 1880, 1900, 1910), MS Population Schedules, Adams County, Mississippi; Davis, Gardner, and Gardner, *Deep South*, 208–251; Davis, *Black Experience*, 160–84; Davis, *Good and Faithful Labor*, 121–145.

53. Grafton was still in the McGrew family in 1910, but apparently changed hands thereafter. See Fleming & Baldwin to Simon McGrew, Lease, January 12, 1872; Fleming & Baldwin to Simon McGrew, Deed, January 1, 1873; Simon McGrew and Simon McGrew Jr. to George T. Payne (eighteen contracts), Chattel Mortgages and Trust Deeds, March 7, 1873–January 22, 1891; Simon McGrew and Simon McGrew Jr. to A. F. Jacobs & Bros. and Adolf Jacobs Co. (five contracts), Chattel Mortgages, January 3, 1890–February 2, 1893, Office of Records, Adams County, Natchez, Mississippi; U.S. Census (1870–1910), MS Population Schedules, Adams County, Mississippi.

54. Quoted in Clark, *Pills, Petticoats, and Plows*, 271.

Chapter 4. A New Kind of Planter

1. At least forty miles from Natchez, this Jefferson County plantation supply account and land transaction is a good example of these merchants' geographic reach. There were five members of the McCoy family who inherited Galilee from James McCoy Sr., but James Jr. and Richard clearly operated the plantation for the several members of this large planter family. See James H. McCoy et al. to Isaac Lowenburg, Chattel Mortgage, March 19, 1874; R. A. McCoy to Isaac Lowenburg, Chattel Mortgage, March 20, 1874; James H. McCoy et al. to John R. Bledsoe (Trustee for I. Lowenburg & Co.), Trust Deed, August 4, 1876; John R. Bledsoe (Trustee), Sheriff's Deed, Office of Records, Jefferson County, Fayette, Mississippi.

2. Lowenburg was very active in this area of Jefferson County and gained many plantations in a like fashion. He received title on the adjacent Allendale a year earlier from old-line planter Daniel S. Farrar, who had also fallen in debt over a supply bill backed by a mortgage in 1873, and had deeded over Allendale for debt forgiveness and a cash payment a year later. See Daniel S. Farrar and Wife to Isaac Lowenburg, Mortgage, April 4, 1873; Daniel S. Farrar and Wife to Isaac Lowenburg, Deed, July 17, 1874; Tax Collector to Isaac Lowenburg, Tax Deed, March 3, 1873; James H. McCoy to Isaac Lowenburg, Quitclaim Deed, August 3, 1874; James H. McCoy et al. to Isaac Lowenburg, Chattel Mortgage, March 19, 1874; R. A. McCoy to Isaac Lowenburg, Chattel Mortgage, March 20, 1874; James H. McCoy et al. to John R. Bledsoe (Trustee for I. Lowenburg & Co.), Trust Deed, August 4, 1874; John R. Bledsoe (Trustee) to Isaac Lowenburg, Sheriff's Deed, April 17, 1876; James McCoy to Aaron Beekman & Son, Mortgage, April 3, 1896, Office of Records, Jefferson County, Fayette, Mississippi; Richard McCoy to John R. Bledsoe (Trustee for I. Lowenburg & Co.), Trust Deed, August 4, 1874;

James H. McCoy to Isaac Lowenburg, Deed, August 4, 1874; Land Sale Record for Delinquent Taxes 1872–1873, p. 4, Office of Records, Adams County, Natchez, Mississippi.

3. Lowenburg almost certainly knew about the proposed route of the Natchez, Jackson, & Columbus Railroad when he became involved with the McCoys and their lands, as he is listed on the right-of-way deed as "Secretary of the Board of Directors for the Natchez, Jackson, & Columbus Railroad Company." Also, Lowenburg was exercising his ability to branch out into new areas of business and compete for the cotton and supply trade in Jefferson County, a considerable distance from his Natchez base, which the new railroad made possible. The advent of interior rail lines came to define the means of interior cotton shipping in the 1880s as river traffic began to lose its hold, and I. Lowenburg & Co. made strategic inroads at the beginning of this trend with the company's geographic reach. Lowenburg's store was on a 151-acre parcel he received from Thomas Buie at a sheriff's sale in July 1877, which was part of the original Galilee plantation and sold by the McCoys in 1874 to help pay their debt with I. Lowenburg and Co. See Isaac Lowenburg to the Natchez, Jackson, & Columbus Railroad Co., Deed, February 6, 1877, Office of Records, Adams County, Natchez, Mississippi; James McCoy et al. and Isaac Lowenburg to Thomas Bowie, Deed, July 16, 1874; John R. Bledsoe (Trustee) to Isaac Lowenburg, Sheriff's Deed, July 21, 1877, Office of Records, Jefferson County, Fayette, Mississippi.

4. Joseph H. Ingraham quoted in James, *Antebellum Natchez*, 144; Land Conveyance Ledger Books, 1860–1910, Record of Leases, 1875–1898, Office of Records, Adams County, Natchez, Mississippi; Land Conveyance Ledger Books, 1860–1910, General Mortgage Ledger Books, 1866–1900, Office of Records, Concordia Parish, Vidalia, Louisiana; Land Deed Ledgers, 1860–1910, Office of Records, Tensas Parish, St. Joseph, Louisiana; Land Deed Ledgers, 1860–1910, Office of Records, Jefferson County, Fayette, Mississippi; Land Deed Ledgers, 1865–1910, Office of Records, Franklin County, Meadville, Mississippi; Land Deed Ledgers, 1865–1910, Office of Records, Wilkinson County, Woodville, Mississippi.

5. Davis, *Good and Faithful Labor*, 121-45; Wayne, *Reshaping of Plantation Society*, 31-52; Woodman, *King Cotton*, 204-216, 241–247.

6. 1858, 1871, 1877 Natchez City Business Directories, Historic Natchez Foundation; *Sheppard's Mississippi State Gazetteer*, 131–135; 1892 Natchez City Directory, Historic Natchez Foundation; Gandy, "Jewish History"; Ezra Lodge #134 I.O.O.B. Meeting Minute Book, 1878–1909, Temple B'Nai Israel, Natchez, Mississippi; Trinity Episcopal Meeting Minutes, 1822–1890, Trinity Episcopal Church, Natchez, Mississippi; Natchez City Alderman's Meeting Minutes, 1879–1910; Adams County Land Rolls, 1875, 1883, 1887; Natchez City Land Rolls, 1887, Office of Records, Adams County, Natchez, Mississippi.

7. Thomas D. Giles and Wife to N. L. Carpenter & Son, Deed, November 11, 1876; Multiple Land Deeds, Land Conveyance Ledger Books, 1860–1910, Record of Leases 1875–1898, Office of Records, Adams County, Natchez, Mississippi; Land Conveyance Ledger Books, 1860–1910, General Mortgage Ledger Books, 1866–1900, Office of Records, Concordia Parish, Vidalia, Louisiana; Land Deed Ledgers, 1860–1910, Office of Records, Tensas Parish, St. Joseph, Louisiana; Land Deed Ledgers, 1860–1910, Office of Records, Jefferson County, Fayette, Mississippi; Land Deed Ledgers, 1865–1910, Office of Records, Franklin County, Meadville, Mississippi; Land Deed Ledgers, 1865–1910, Office of Records, Wilkinson County, Woodville, Mississippi.

8. Isaac Lowenburg and Thomas Reber to the Lowenburg-Reber Addition, Plat Map (Woodlawn Subdivision), June 28, 1882; Isaac Lowenburg to the Clifton Addition, Plat Map, May 18, 1888; Multiple Land Deeds, Land Conveyance Ledger Books, 1860–1910, Record of

Leases 1875–1898, Office of Records, Adams County, Natchez, Mississippi; Land Conveyance Ledger Books, 1860–1910, General Mortgage Ledger Books, 1866–1900, Office of Records, Concordia Parish, Vidalia, Louisiana; Land Deed Ledgers, 1860–1910, Office of Records, Tensas Parish, St. Joseph, Louisiana; Land Deed Ledgers, 1860–1910, Office of Records, Jefferson County, Fayette, Mississippi; Land Deed Ledgers, 1865–1910, Office of Records, Franklin County, Meadville, Mississippi; Land Deed Ledgers, 1865–1910, Office of Records, Wilkinson County, Woodville, Mississippi.

9. Advertisement, William Dix & Co., *Natchez Courier*, June 22, 1865, 2.

10. Stephen Duncan Jr. quoted in Powell, *New Masters*, 47–48, 137–138; Davis, *Good and Faithful Labor*, 90–99; Wayne, *Reshaping of Plantation Society*, 59; C. D. Carter et al. to J. N. Carpenter et al. (J. N. Carpenter & Co.), Lease, December 19, 1885, Office of Records, Concordia Parish, Vidalia, Louisiana.

11. J. W. Labouisse quoted in Wayne, *Reshaping of Plantation Society*, 160, also cited on 68, 159–161; Davis, *Good and Faithful Labor*, 121–145; Legal Notice, Adams County Sheriff, *Natchez Democrat*, March 11, 1867, 2.

12. Advertisement, Fleming & Baldwin Co., *Natchez Courier*, June 22, 1867, 2.

13. Wayne, *Reshaping of Plantation Society*, 68; Credit ledger entry, Fleming & Baldwin Co., Mississippi, Vol. 2, p. 73, R. G. Dun & Co. Ledgers, Harvard Business School; John Fleming and Hiram Baldwin to Audley Britton and George Koontz, Mortgage and Deed, January 2, 1872; John Fleming and Hiram Baldwin to David D. Withers, Mortgage and Deed, March 28, 1872, Office of Records, Wilkinson County, Woodville, Mississippi; John N. Routh to Fleming & Baldwin, Deed, November 1, 1869; Charles Howard to Fleming & Baldwin, Contract and Lien, April 10, 1871; Fleming & Baldwin to S. B. Newman & Co., Act of Sale, January 15, 1873, Office of Records, Tensas Parish, St. Joseph, Louisiana; Fleming & Baldwin to Hiram Revels, Deed, April 24, 1871; Fleming & Baldwin to Simon McGrew, Lease, January 12, 1872, Office of Records, Adams County, Natchez, Mississippi.

14. Davis, *Good and Faithful Labor*, 121–151; Wayne, *Reshaping of Plantation Society*, 31–71, 150–196.

15. This is closely related to trust deeds in that both featured property seized for debt and put in the "trust" of a third party or trustee to see that the debt was paid. Chattel Mortgage Ledger Books, 1875–1903, Office of Records, Adams County, Natchez, Mississippi; General Mortgage Ledger Books, 1866–1910, Office of Records, Concordia Parish, Vidalia, Louisiana; Land Deed Ledgers, 1860–1910, Office of Records, Tensas Parish, St. Joseph, Louisiana; Land Deed Ledgers, 1871–1910, Office of Records, Jefferson County, Fayette, Mississippi; Land Deed Ledgers, 1874–1910, Office of Records, Franklin County, Meadville, Mississippi; Land Deed Ledgers, 1871–1910, Office of Records, Wilkinson County, Woodville, Mississippi.

16. Ibid. A quitclaim deed is a legal instrument used to release one person's right, title, or interest to another without providing a guarantee or warrantee on the title. See Woodman, *King Cotton*, 311–313; Wayne, *Reshaping of Plantation Society*, 191–195.

17. Land Conveyance Ledger Books, 1860–1910, Record of Leases 1875–1890, Chattel Mortgage Ledger Books, 1875–1903, Office of Records, Adams County, Natchez, Mississippi; Land Conveyance Ledger Books, 1860–1910, General Mortgage Ledger Books, 1860–1900, Office of Records, Concordia Parish, Vidalia, Louisiana; Land Deed Ledgers, 1860–1900, Office of Records, Tensas Parish, St. Joseph, Louisiana; Land Deed Ledgers, 1860–1910, Office of Records, Jefferson County, Fayette, Mississippi; Land Deed Ledgers, 1874–1900, Chattel Mortgage Ledger Books, 1871–1900, Office of Records, Franklin County, Meadville, Mississippi; Land Deed Ledgers, 1860–1910, Office of Records, Wilkinson County, Woodville, Mississippi.

18. Ibid.

19. Permits to Purchase Cotton Ledger, Natchez District, March 1864, 22–25; Permits to Ship Goods Ledger, June 13, 1864, Natchez District, Natchez Collection, California State University, Northridge; Credit ledger entry, I. Lowenburg & Co., Mississippi, Vol. 2, p. 148, R. G. Dun & Co. Ledgers, Harvard Business School; Charlotte B. Surget to Lowenburg and Hill, Lease, November 21, 1870; Eustis Surget to Christian Schwartz, Isaac Lowenburg, and John Hill, Lease, January 5, 1871; Isaac Lowenburg and George W. Jones to Willis Cook et al., Contract, March 6, 1876; Eliza Brady to Isaac Lowenburg, Deed, December 24,1885, Office of Records, Concordia Parish, Vidalia, Louisiana.

20. Samuel L. Winston to Marx Lemle, Chattel Mortgage, April 30, 1875, Record of Leases 1875–1877, Historic Natchez Foundation; Richard Lewis to Wolf Geisenberger, Chattel Mortgage, March 3, 1879, Office of Records, Adams County, Natchez, Mississippi; J. S. Harris to Isaac Friedler, Lease, November 3, 1874, September 25, 1876; Isaac Friedler to Sundry Persons, Affidavit for Supplies Furnished, July 27, 1876; LeGrand Page to Isaac Friedler, Lease, January 4, 1886; Dunbar Marshall to Carpenter & Dicks, Lease, December 1, 1884; C. D. Carter et al. to J. N. Carpenter et al. (J. N. Carpenter & Co.), Lease, December 19, 1885; Isaac Lowenburg to M. Phelen (Agent), Lease, September 8, 1883, Office of Records, Concordia Parish, Vidalia, Louisiana; Simon Marx to Isaac Friedler, Lease, December 5, 1887, Office of Records, Tensas Parish, St. Joseph, Louisiana; Wayne, *Reshaping of Plantation Society*, 150–196; Woodman, *King Cotton*, 310-311.

21. Credit ledger entry, Aaron Beekman, Vol. 2, p. 29, R. G. Dun & Co. Ledgers, Harvard Business School; Thomas Kenny and Wife to Armand Perrault, Deed, November 14, 1862; Armand Perrault to Charles N. Rowley and Wife, Deed and Mortgage, January 20, 1863; Alfred Swayze and Wife to Armand Perrault, Deed, January 29, 1863; Armand Perrault to Steven Guice, Deed, November 20, 1865; Charles N. Rowley and Wife to Armand Perrault, Deed, December 2, 1866; Armand Perrault to Susan R. Guice, Deed and Lien, November, 20, 1875, Office of Records, Adams County, Natchez, Mississippi.

22. Lowenburg & Hill to Ann Eliza Miles, Deed, March 4, 1871; Ann Eliza Miles to Lowenburg & Hill, March 4, 1871; Ann Eliza Miles to Isaac Lowenburg (Trustee for Meyer Weis & Co.), Trust Deed, February 27, 1872; Gustavus Calhoun to J. N. Carpenter, Deed, May 4, 1870; Rufus and Emma Ford to Aaron Beekman, Deed, October 10, 1882, Office of Records, Franklin County, Meadville, Mississippi.

23. Julius Weis to Ignatz Friedler, Deed, January 9, 1884; LeGrand Page with Julius Friedler, Articles of Co-Partnership, June 25, 1886; Isaac Friedler and LeGrand Page to Julius Weis and Company, Pledge, July 31, 1886; Isaac Friedler (By Sheriff) to Julius Weis, Tax Deed, January 3, 1886; Ignatz Friedler (By Sheriff) to Isaac Friedler, Sheriff's Deed, March 7, 1887, Office of Records, Concordia Parish, Vidalia, Louisiana.

24. Julius Weis to Isaac Friedler, Power of Attorney, October 17, 1882; Le Grand Page with Julius Friedler, Articles of Co-Partnership, June 25, 1886; Isaac Friedler and LeGrand Page to Julius Weis and Company, Pledge, July 31, 1886, Office of Records, Concordia Parish, Vidalia, Louisiana.

25. Wayne, *Reshaping of Plantation Society*, 84; Land Conveyance Ledger Books, 1860–1900, Office of Records, Adams County, Natchez, Mississippi; Land Conveyance Ledger Books, 1860–1900, Office of Records, Concordia Parish, Vidalia, Louisiana; Land Deed Ledgers, 1860–1900, Office of Records, Tensas Parish, St. Joseph, Louisiana; Land Deed Ledgers, 1871–1900, Office of Records, Jefferson County, Fayette, Mississippi; Land Deed Ledgers,

1874–1900, Office of Records, Franklin County, Meadville, Mississippi; Land Deed Ledgers, 1871–1900, Office of Records, Wilkinson County, Woodville, Mississippi.

26. Probate and succession often generated tax sales because the heirs or estate itself often was unable to pay sizable tax bills on big plantations. See S. D. Marshall (By Sheriff) to Isaac Lowenburg, Tax Deed, November 23, 1872; Estate of L. R. Marshall (By Sheriff) to Isaac Lowenburg, Tax Deed, June 6, 1873; Smith and Dunning (By Sheriff) to Isaac Lowenburg, Tax Deed, December 8, 1875; Isaac Lowenburg to Julius Weis, Deed, March 24, 1880; Joseph Auseline (By Sheriff) to Isaac Lowenburg, Tax Deed, May 9, 1882; Amended Charter of the Natchez, Red River & Texas Railroad, October 4, 1881, Office of Records, Concordia Parish, Vidalia, Louisiana.

27. Tax Collector to Isaac Lowenburg, Tax Deed, March 3, 1873; State of Mississippi to Isaac Lowenburg, State Tax Deed, April 14, 1877, Office of Records, Jefferson County, Fayette, Mississippi; State of Mississippi to S. & A. Jacobs, State Tax Deed, November 1, 1888; James H. Rowan et al. to William C. Martin (Trustee for S. & A. Jacobs), Trust Deed, January 7, 1889, Office of Records, Adams County, Natchez, Mississippi.

28. Much like the case of the McCoy plantation and Lowenburg in Jefferson County, Beekman and Lowenburg demonstrated an amazing ability to penetrate other Natchez District markets, even when a large distance was involved. Woodville is thirty-five miles from Natchez and Fayette forty miles, a difficult distance before the railroads linked these areas. Also, we do not know the exact amount of the initial trust deeds because the ledger that contained the contracts was destroyed by flood in the 1880s—but we do know that the contracts existed because the index for these ledgers still survives and lists the trust deed. See Chattel Deed Book, Index 4, 433; Deed Book, 5, 87; William Hastings to Aaron Beekman, Trust Deed, March 24, 1877; William Hastings to Aaron Beekman, Trust Deed, February 16, 1878; Sina Hastings to Aaron Beekman, Conveyance, November 7, 1882, Office of Records, Wilkinson County, Woodville, Mississippi.

29. Lowenburg & Hill to Ann Eliza Miles, Deed, March 4, 1871; Ann Eliza Miles to Lowenburg & Hill, March 4, 1871; Ann Eliza Miles to Isaac Lowenburg (Trustee for Meyer Weis & Co.), Trust Deed, February 27, 1872; Ann E. Miles to the Perrault & Co., Trust Deed, July 6, 1885; Fred Maher (Trustee for the Perrault & Co.), Trustees Deed, February 21, 1887; Perrault & Co. to A. J. Shelvy, Lease, March 2, 1887; Vincent Perrault to H. Marshall Gaither (Trustee First Natchez Bank), Trust Deed, December 31, 1903; Vincent Perrault to Etta Clure, Deed, April 19, 1907, Office of Records, Jefferson County, Fayette, Mississippi; Clara Lowenburg Moses, "My Memories," 82–84, Collection No. 702, Clara Lowenburg Moses Papers, American Southern Jewish Experience and Jewish Studies Collection, Tulane University Library, New Orleans.

30. L. H. D'Armond to Isaac Friedler, Deed, April 9, 1877; William Majors, Lease, November 6, 1877, Office of Records, Concordia Parish, Vidalia, Louisiana; Clarence J. Wade to Marx Lemle, Trust Deed and Deed, March 18, 1875, June 6, 1875; Lucy P. Barnett et al. to Marx Lemle, Deed, December 13, 1875; John R. Lynch to Henry R. Griffin (Trustee for Adolf Jacobs & Son), Trust Deeds, January 18 and 31, 1886; John R. Lynch to A. C. Jacobs, Conversion Deed, December 22, 1904; John W. Lambert (Sheriff) to Ann E. Abbott, Sheriff's Deed, May 11, 1891; Calvin S. Bennett to Ann E. Abbott, Trust Deed, June 12, 1888; Calvin S. Bennett to Ann E. Abbott, Deed, February 11, 1892, Office of Records, Adams County, Natchez, Mississippi; Office of Records, Tensas Parish, St. Joseph, Louisiana.

31. Charter of Incorporation of the Safe Deposit & Trust Co. of Natchez, August 17, 1889; Charter of Incorporation of the First Natchez Bank, March 12, 1895; Charter of Incorporation

of People's Savings Bank, June 30, 1902, Office of Records, Adams County, Natchez, Mississippi; Charter of Incorporation of The Bank of Visalia, March 13, 1903; Daniel A. Britton to W. M. Gordon (Agent for the American Mortgage Bank of Scotland), Mortgage Deed, March 3, 1902, Office of Records, Concordia Parish, Vidalia, Louisiana; J. W. Martin to Albert Calowell (Agent for De Nederlandsche Amerikaanishe Land Maatschappy), Mortgage Deed, February 19, 1887, Office of Records, Tensas Parish, St. Joseph, Louisiana.

32. Wecama Planting Co. (By W. A. S. Wheeler, President) to I. Lowenburg & Co., Mortgage, March 3, 1899; Charter of Incorporation of Concordia Planting Co., January 16, 1903; Charter of Incorporation of Dunbarton Planting Co., December 7, 1906, Office of Records, Concordia Parish, Vidalia, Louisiana; Charter of Incorporation of the Natchez Investment & Insurance Agency, September 7, 1907, Office of Records, Adams County, Natchez, Mississippi.

33. Charter of Incorporation of I. Lowenburg & Co., September 10, 1913, Office of Records, Adams County, Natchez, Mississippi.

34. Advertisement, Aaron Beekman, *Natchez Daily Democrat*, June 30, 1882, 2.

35. Elam Bowman and Wife to Aaron Beekman, Deed, March 1, 1862; Adams County Land Rolls, 1875, 1883, 1887, Office of Records, Adams County, Natchez, Mississippi.

36. This type of activity transpired primarily in Natchez and Vidalia. See Land Conveyance Ledger Books, 1860–1910, Office of Records, Adams County, Natchez, Mississippi; Land Conveyance Ledger Books, 1860–1910, Office of Records, Concordia Parish, Vidalia, Louisiana.

37. Credit ledger entries, Fleming & Baldwin, A. Perrault, and G. T. Payne, Mississippi, Vol. 2, pp. 6, 9, 73, R. G. Dun & Co. Ledgers, Harvard Business School; N. L. Carpenter to Steven Duncan, Mortgage, August 7, 1844; Martha Gibbs to Armand Perrault, Deed, April 7, 1856; Peter Grant and Wife to Marks Lemle, Deed, February 3, 1858; Administrators of Peter Little to Aaron Beekman, February 16, 1858; Elam Bowman and Wife to Aaron Beekman, Deed, March 1, 1862; Douglas L. Rivers and Wife to Marx Lemle, Deed, August 13, 1862; Ambrose J. Foster and Wife to George T. Payne, Deed, March 26, 1863, Office of Records, Adams County, Natchez Mississippi; Advertisement, N. L. Carpenter & Sons Co., *Natchez Weekly Democrat*, October 14, 1867.

38. Jacob Lorie was the brother of prominent Vidalia Jewish merchant Nathan Lorie, whom Isaac Friedler partnered with during this early period, and they received merchandise from Aaron Beekman's Natchez store. See Robert Carter to Aaron Beekman and David Moses, Deeds, October 15 and 19, 1866; Aaron Beekman and David Moses to Jacob Lorie, Lease, April 25, 1870, Office of Records, Concordia Parish, Vidalia, Louisiana; Lyman D. Aldrich to Marx Lemle, Deed, February 24, 1866; John Mayer and Wife to Isaac Lowenburg, Deed and Mortgage, January 5, 1866; George T. Payne to Letitia Payne, Deed, January 4, 1873; Molcie Lowenburg to Phelina J. Pendleton, Mortgage, July, 10, 1873, Office of Records, Adams County, Natchez, Mississippi.

39. James W. Coleman to I. Lowenburg & Co., Mortgage, September 24, 1869; Michael Mack to I. Lowenburg & Co., Mortgage, September 24, 1869; James W. Coleman to Isaac Friedler, January 18, 1871, Office of Records, Concordia Parish, Vidalia, Louisiana; Mary A. Bondurant to Julia Jacobs, Deed, July 1, 1874; M. Frank to Wolf Geisenberger, Sale Agreement, August 28, 1876, Office of Records, Adams County, Natchez, Mississippi.

40. Davis, *Good and Faithful Labor*, 121–151; Wayne, *Reshaping of Plantation Society*, 31–71, 150–196; Credit ledger entries, I. Lowenburg & Co. and Philip Wexler Dry Goods, Mississippi, Vol. 2, pp. 102, 148, 153, R. G. Dun & Co. Ledgers, Harvard Business School.

41. Peter Grant and Wife to Marks Lemle, Deed, February 3, 1858; Isaac Jones and Wife to Marx Lemle, Deed, February 11, 1859; Marx Lemle et al. to Ellen Cochran, Deed, March 14, 1870; Marx Lemle to Matilda Frank, Deed, April 2, 1875; James Frank and Wife to Wolf Geisenberger (Trustee), Deed of Trust, December 1, 1875; M. Frank to Wolf Geisenberger et al., Agreement, December 29, 1876; Wolf Geisenberger to Walter McCrea, Deed of Trust, April 15, 1884, Office of Records, Adams County, Natchez, Mississippi; Thomas Brady to Isaac Friedler, Deed, January 9, 1872; Alexander Eltringham to Isaac Friedler, Deed, April 14, 1873; C. W. Scott to Isaac Lowenburg (By Sheriff), Sheriff's Deed, June 13, 1874; Anna E. Winston to Isaac Lowenburg, Deed, November 23, 1874; Isaac Lowenburg to William B. Spencer, Deed, October 2, 1876; Samuel Lowenburg to Isaac Lowenburg, Deed, July 24, 1877; Isaac Lowenburg to Morris Wexler, Deed, January 7, 1878; Pauline Carter to Isaac Friedler, Deed, January 28, 1882; Isaac Friedler to Louis F. Broussard, Deed, December 8, 1891; Isaac Friedler to Charlotte Simmons, Deed, January 30, 1897, Office of Records, Concordia Parish, Vidalia, Louisiana; Credit ledger entries, Isaac Friedler, Louisiana Vol. 4, p. 229, R. G. Dun & Co. Ledgers, Harvard Business School.

42. Carpenter, Dicks & Co. to Frank Arrighi (Trustee Paul A. Botto and James W. Lambert), Trust Deed, January 3, 1877; Adolf Kastor to Aaron Beekman, Deed, September 10, 1879; J. N. Carpenter et al. to Adams Manufacturing Co., Deed, July 27, 1882; Aaron Beekman to A. Eltringham & Co., Lease, November 1, 1883; J. N. Carpenter and John A. Dicks to Carpenter, Dicks & Co., Deed, July 31, 1886; George F. Warner and Wife to Joseph N. Carpenter, Deed, October 27, 1886, Office of Records, Adams County, Natchez, Mississippi; Margaret Baylan (By Commissioner) to Isaac Lowenburg, Deed, September 27, 1881, Office of Records, Concordia Parish, Vidalia, Louisiana.

43. "Local News," *Natchez Daily Democrat*, June 7, 1882, 2.

44. Advertisement, Lowenburg & Reber, *Natchez Daily Democrat*, July 4, 1882, 4. Portions of this advertisement have been omitted due to its length.

45. Citizens Bank of Louisiana to Isaac Lowenburg et al., Deed and Plat Map, June 2, 1882; Isaac Lowenburg et al. to Annie V. Reber, Deed, February 1, 1883; Isaac Lowenburg et al. to Narcissa Phipps, Deed, January 12, 1883; Isaac Lowenburg et al. to Olivia P. Harvey, Deed, February 1, 1883; Isaac Lowenburg et al. to William R. Parker, Deed, February 7, 1883; Isaac Lowenburg et al. to Mary W. Bauer, Deed, February 9, 1883; Isaac Lowenburg et al. to Lewis Wells, Deed, February 9,1883; Isaac Lowenburg et al. to Blanche Myers, Deed, February 9, 1883, Office of Records, Adams County, Natchez, Mississippi.

46. "Local News," *Natchez Daily Democrat*, September 5, 1882, 2; Ullman and Laub to Isaac Lowenburg, Deed, December 22, 1883; Isaac Lowenburg et al. to Clifton Addition, Plat Map, May 3, 1888; Osborne K. Field to N. L. Carpenter, Deed, February 3, 1890; Joseph N. Carpenter to the Mallery Grocery Store, Deed, January 19, 1893; Joseph N. Carpenter to the Mallery Grocery Store, Deed, May 1, 1893; Plan of the Arlington Addition, October 14, 1897; Joseph N. Carpenter to the Carpenter Addition, Plat Map, April 30, 1902; Isaac D. Scharff to the Maple Terrace Addition, Plat Map, November 16, 1907, Office of Records, Adams County, Natchez, Mississippi; Advertisement, Natchez Hotel Co., *Natchez Daily Democrat*, July 25, 1890, 3; Sansing et al., *Natchez*, 138–152.

47. *Natchez, Mississippi On Top, Not "Under the Hill,"* 5–26; Carol Dubie et al., "Inventory and Evaluation of Historic Natchez Bluffs Area, Mississippi," National Historic Register of Historic Places, National Park Service, Washington, D.C., January 1, 1985, 3–5; Machlovitz, *Clara Lowenburg Moses*, 6–7; Isaac Lowenburg to the Trustees of Windy Hill Church, Deed, February 24, 1882; Samuel J. and Vincent L. Perrault to the Devereux Orphanage Asylum,

Deed, January 5, 1888; Nathaniel Leslie Carpenter to the City of Natchez, Deed of Gift, September 10, 1909, Office of Records, Adams County, Natchez, Mississippi.

48. Sansing et al., *Natchez*, 149; Gavin Wright, *Old South, New South: Revolutions in the Southern Economy since the Civil War* (New York: Basic Books, 1986), 84–85.

49. Doyle, *New Men, New Cities, New South*, xiii; *Natchez, Mississippi On Top, Not "Under the Hill,"* 15.

Chapter 5. Merchant Life and Social Capital

1. Charter of Natchez, Red River & Texas Railroad Co., January 20, 1881; H. M. Gastrell to Hiram R. Steele (President of the Natchez, Red River & Texas Railroad Co.), Act of Sale, April 23, 1881; Amended Charter of Natchez, Red River & Texas Railroad Co., September 30, 1881; Multiple Land Conveyances, Samuel Block and Isaac Lowenburg to Natchez, Red River & Texas Railroad Co., Deeds, 1881; Multiple Right-of-Way Conveyances, Isaac Lowenburg et al. to Natchez, Red River & Texas Railroad Co., Right-of-Way, 1881, Office of Records, Concordia Parish, Vidalia, Louisiana.

2. "Railroad Committee," *Natchez Weekly Democrat*, July 12, 1869, 12; *Natchez, Mississippi On Top, Not "Under the Hill,"* 5–6; Isaac Lowenburg to the Natchez, Jackson, & Columbus Railroad Co., Deed, February 6, 1877, Office of Records, Adams County, Natchez, Mississippi; Alfred D. Chandler, *The Visible Hand: The Managerial Revolution in American Business* (Cambridge, Mass.: Belknap Press of Harvard University Press, 1977), 1–12, 81.

3. Rothstein, "Antebellum South as a Dual Economy," 373–382; Davis, *Good and Faithful Labor*, 30–43; Moore, *Emergence of the Cotton Kingdom*, 193–196; James, *Antebellum Natchez*, 190–191, 203–210; Scott Marler, "Merchants and the Political Economy of Nineteenth-Century Louisiana: New Orleans and Its Hinterlands" (Ph.D. diss., Rice University, 2007), 407–412; Chandler, *Visible Hand*, 15; *Natchez, Mississippi On Top, Not "Under the Hill,"* 5–28; Woodward, *Origins of the New South*, 140–141; Doyle, *New Men, New Cities, New South*, xi–xvi; Carlton, *Mill and Town in South Carolina*, 58–63.

4. James S. Coleman, "Social Capital in the Creation of Human Capital," *American Journal of Sociology* 94 (Spring 1988): S96; Laird, *Pull*, 11–50; Wayne, *Reshaping of Plantation Society*, 101–103, 106–109, 194–195; Doyle, *New Men, New Cities, New South*, 87–96; Rowland, *Mississippi*, 3:156–157, 267–268; Walter Nesbit Taylor and George H. Etheridge, eds., *Mississippi: A History* (Jackson, Miss.: Historical Record Association, n.d.), 4:1698–1701.

5. Moses, "My Memories," 1–178; John C. Schwartz "Daybook, 1864–1875," J:23, Vol. 2A, p. 210, John C. Schwartz Papers, LSU; Schwartz & Stewart "Price List Ledger" Z/1273.001, Box 12, p. 1; "Account Ledger, 1878–1882," Box 13, pp. 1–25, in Z/1273.001, Schwartz and Stewart Co. Records, Accretion, Mississippi Department of Archives, Jackson; Mark Wahlgren Summers, *The Gilded Age, or The Hazard of New Functions* (Upper Saddle River, N.J.: Prentice-Hall, 1997), 43–48, 80–81; Doyle, *New Men, New Cities, New South*, xi–xvi; Wayne, *Reshaping of Plantation Society*, 194–195; Davis, *Good and Faithful Labor*, 121–145.

6. "Local News," *Natchez Daily Democrat*, December 17, 1879, 2, December 30, 1900, 2; U.S. Census (1900) Population Schedules, Adams County, Mississippi; 1892 Natchez City Business Directory, 26, 33, Historic Natchez Foundation; Gandy, "Jewish History"; *Natchez, Mississippi On Top, Not "Under the Hill,"* 5–28.

7. Harriet Ligon to A. H. Geisenberger (Trustee for Adolf Jacobs & Son), Trust Deed, January 1, 1901; Robert Lee and Isaiah Ligon to A. H. Geisenberger (Trustee for A. F. Jacobs

& Bros.), Trust Deed, January 1, 1901; Scott Washington to A. H. Geisenberger (Trustee for Adolf Jacobs & Son), Trust Deed, January 1, 1901; Joseph Hargrave to A. H. Geisenberger (Trustee for Adolf Jacobs & Son), Trust Deed, January 1, 1901; George Walker and Wife to A. H. Geisenberger (Trustee for Adolf Jacobs & Son), Trust Deed, January 1, 1901; Multiple Chattel Mortgage Contracts, 1874–1903, Office of Records, Adams County, Natchez, Mississippi; Multiple Chattel Mortgage Contracts, General Mortgage Ledger Books, 1870–1910, Office of Records, Concordia Parish, Vidalia, Louisiana; Multiple Chattel Mortgage Contracts Land Deed Ledgers, 1870–1910, Office of Records, Tensas Parish, St. Joseph, Louisiana; Multiple Chattel Mortgage Contracts, Chattel Mortgage Ledger Books, 1874–1910, Office of Records, Jefferson County, Fayette, Mississippi; Office of Records, Franklin County, Meadville, Mississippi; Office of Records, Wilkinson County, Woodville, Mississippi.

8. Mark Twain, *Life on the Mississippi* (1883; repr., Pleasantville, N.Y.: Reader's Digest Association, 1987), 241; Doyle, *New Men, New Cities, New South*, xi–xvi; Andrew White Sr. to Adolf Jacobs, Chattel Mortgage, January 8, 1894; Alf Burke to Adolf Jacobs, Chattel Mortgage, January 8, 1894; State of Mississippi to Adolf Jacobs & Son Banking Co., Corporate Charter, November 12, 1906; Multiple Chattel Mortgages and Land Conveyances, 1874–1910, Office of Records, Adams County, Natchez, Mississippi; Multiple Chattel Mortgages and Land Conveyances, 1874–1910, Office of Records, Jefferson County, Fayette, Mississippi; Office of Records, Franklin County, Meadville, Mississippi; Office of Records, Wilkinson County, Woodville, Mississippi.

9. Clark, *Pills, Petticoats, and Plows*, 313–336; Byrne, *Becoming Bourgeois*, 31–44; Atherton, *Southern County Store*, 66–67, 157–163; Mark S. Granovetter, "The Strength of Weak Ties," *American Journal of Sociology* 78 (May 1973): 1360–1380.

10. Turitz and Turitz, *Jews in Early Mississippi*, xii–xiii, 11–28; Moses, "My Memories," 1-130; Obituary of Mary Fleming, *Natchez Weekly Democrat*, February 7, 1900, 2; Credit ledger entries, A. Perrault Co., G. T. Payne, T. E. Perrault, and McPherson & Perrault, Mississippi, Vol. 2, pp. 9, 73, 93, 123, 184, R. G. Dun & Co. Ledgers, Harvard Business School; George T. Payne, Estate File, June 20, 1891, Cause No. 1140, File Box No. 230, Office of Records, Adams County, Natchez, Mississippi; U.S. Census (1840–1880), MS and LA Population Schedules, Adams County, Mississippi, and Orleans Parish, Louisiana.

11. Moses, "My Memories," 15, 27, 35; Machlovitz, *Clara Lowenburg Moses*, 19–20, 43–44; James, *Antebellum Natchez*, 82;

12. Clark, *Pills, Petticoats, and Plows*, 55–56; Byrne, *Becoming Bourgeois*, 39.

13. Byrne, *Becoming Bourgeois*, 39.

14. Advertisement, I. Lowenburg & Co., *Natchez Daily Democrat*, June 27, 1882, 2; "Local News," *Natchez Daily Democrat*, July 29, 1882, 2, September 30, 1882, 2.

15. Loose-leaf correspondence and invoices, Mss. 385, 4732, Series IX, Box 1, Folders 1, 6, and 14, John C. Schwartz Papers, LSU; Schwartz & Stewart "Invoice Book, 1875–1880," Z/1273.001, Box 9, entries June 3 and 9, 1876, Schwartz & Stewart Co. Records Accretion, Mississippi Department of Archives and History, Jackson.

16. Clark, *Pills, Petticoats, and Plows*, 314-315; Schwartz and Stewart, "Daily Journal, September 27, 1877–May 1, 1878," Z/1273.001, Box 8, entries for September 28, 1877, Schwartz & Stewart Co. Records Accretion, Mississippi Department of Archives and History.

17. John C. Schwartz "Daybook, 1864–1875," J:23, Vol. 2A, p. 210, and "Cashbook, 1864–1875," J: 23, Vol. 1B, Cover Page, John C. Schwartz Papers, LSU.

18. Moses, "My Memories," 34–35; Obituaries, Nathaniel L. and Joseph N. Carpenter, *Natchez Daily Democrat*, December 24, 1892, 2; March 4, 1925, 1, 8; Isaac Lowenburg,

Natchez Weekly Democrat, September 12, 1888, 2; William Abbott, *Natchez Daily Democrat*, December 27, 1884, 2; Ann Abbott, *Natchez Daily Democrat*, June 10, 1903, 5.

19. Byrne, *Becoming Bourgeois*, 33–36; Moses, "My Memories," 2, 43; "Local News," *Natchez Daily Democrat*, May 3, 1882, 2, July 13, 1882, 2, September 6, 1882, 2.

20. Moses, "My Memories," 29–31.

21. 1892 Natchez City Business Directory, Historic Natchez Foundation; U.S. Census (1880, 1900) Population Schedules, Adams County, Mississippi; *Natchez, Mississippi On Top, Not "Under the Hill,"* appendix.

22. Moses, "My Memories," 13, 29–30.

23. U.S. Census (1880, 1900, 1910, 1920) Population Schedules, Adams County, Mississippi, and Orleans Parish, Louisiana.

24. Jane Turner Censer quoted in Byrne, *Becoming Bourgeois*, 78, 80–92.

25. Moses, "My Memories," 31.

26. Since 1837, Mississippi was one of the few states in the nation to have a married women's property law that allowed married women to own property in their own names, which could not be touched by the creditors of their husbands. Moses, "My Memories," 4, 14, 19, 38, 70; Anne Firor Scott, *The Southern Lady: From Pedestal to Politics, 1830–1930* (Charlottesville: University Press of Virginia, 1970), 23–44, 106–163; Byrne, *Becoming Bourgeois*, 78–92.

27. Moses, "My Memories," 20, 47, 49, 70–72, 90–91; Byrne, *Becoming Bourgeois*, 78–92.

28. *Natchez, Mississippi On Top, Not "Under the Hill,"* 7-14; Moses, "My Memories," 22–23, 44–45, 49–51, 56–66; Rowland, *Mississippi*, 3:464; Taylor and Etheridge, *Mississippi*, 649, 800–801, 1698-1701; 1892 and 1912 Natchez City Business Directories, Historic Natchez Foundation; U.S. Census (1880, 1900, 1910) Population Schedules, Adams County, Mississippi, and Concordia Parish, Louisiana.

29. Obituaries, Isaac Lowenburg, Simon Jacobs, and Nathaniel L. Carpenter, *Natchez Daily Democrat*, September 12, 1888, 2, February 6, 1889, 2, December 24, 1892, 2; Moses, "My Memories," 3-121.

30. Byrne, *Becoming Bourgeois*, 77.

31. Farewell Speech of Mayor Isaac Lowenburg, Natchez Board of Aldermen Minutes, December 30, 1886, Office of Records, Natchez Mississippi

32. Doyle, *New Men, New Cities, New South*, xi–xvi, 1, 18–19, 87–96; *Natchez, Mississippi On Top, Not "Under the Hill,"* 1–28.

33. Laird, *Pull*, 49–50, 69–70, 86; 1877 Natchez City Business Directory, Historic Natchez Foundation.

34. "Announcements in Church" 1863–1895, Natchez St. Mary's Cathedral, http://www.Natchezbelle.org/adams-ind/church.htm.

35. Open Letter to the Hibernian Association, February 21, 1880, "Announcements in Church" 1863–1879, Natchez St. Mary's Cathedral, http://www.Natchezbelle.org/adams-ind/church.htm.

36. Hevra Kadusha Society Minutes and Temple B'Nai Israel Meeting Minutes, October 9, 1864, August 21, 1870, July 2, 1871, November 26, 1871, March 14, 1872, July 7, 1872, February 10, 1873, June 4, 1873, Temple B'Nai Israel, Natchez, Mississippi; Gandy, "Jewish History"; Elaine Lehman, interview with author, February 25, 2004.

37. Ezra Lodge #134 I.O.O.B. Meeting Minute Book, May 26, 1878, July 14 and 17, 1878, April 13, 1879, July 13, 1884, August 14, 1887, February 22, 1891, December 27, 1891, April 2,

1905; Ezra Lodge #134 Endowment Record Book, April 10 and 13, 1873, August 10, 1879, September 1, 1887, May 13, 1888, June 24, 1888, Temple B'Nai Israel, Natchez, Mississippi.

38. Trinity Episcopal Church Meeting Minutes Book, March 9, 1822–November 3, 1890, Trinity Episcopal Church, Natchez, Mississippi; 1877 and 1892 Natchez City Business Directories, Historic Natchez Foundation; *Natchez Daily Democrat*, July 12, 1911, 7; Machlovitz, *Clara Lowenburg Moses*, 7; State of Mississippi to Natchez Lodge No. 553 of the Benevolent Order of the Elks, Charter, October 3, 1900; State of Mississippi to Prentiss Club, Charter, July 3, 1903, Office of Records, Adams County, Natchez, Mississippi.

39. Adams Light Infantry Honorary Member Roster, Temple B'Nai Israel, Natchez, Mississippi; Natchez Confederate Veterans, Land Conveyance Ledger Book 4I, pp. 269–294, Office of Records, Adams County, Natchez, Mississippi.

40. 1877 Natchez City Business Directory, Historic Natchez Foundation; *Natchez, Mississippi On Top, Not "Under the Hill,"* 14-15.

41. *Natchez, Mississippi On Top, Not "Under the Hill,"* 14-15.

42. Ibid.

43. Wayne, *Reshaping of Plantation Society*, 106–107; John Botto to Rufus F. Learned et al. in trust for Rosalie Yarn Mills, Deed, January 20, 1880, Office of Records, Adams County, Natchez, Mississippi; Twain, *Life on the Mississippi*, 241.

44. Twain, *Life on the Mississippi*, 241. Twain was astounded with the changes he witnessed in Natchez from the antebellum town he knew from decades earlier, and his figures were derived from an article appearing in the *New Orleans Times-Democrat*, August 26, 1882.

45. *Natchez, Mississippi On Top, Not "Under the Hill,"* 8-11; Multiple Charters and Business Incorporations, 1877–1910, Land Deed Ledgers, Office of Records, Adams County, Natchez, Mississippi.

46. Moses, "My Memories," 149–150; Reber, *Proud Old Natchez*, 61–62; Sansing et al., *Natchez*, 142–143; Summers, *Gilded Age*, 1–9; Federal Writers Project, *Mississippi*, 237–239; Isaac Lowenburg Last Will and Testament (Estate File), September 10, 1888, Cause No. 995, File Box No. 222; Natchez Electric Light, Heat, & Power Co. to Walter McCrea (Trustee for Van Deporle Electric Manufacturing Co.), Deed of Trust, March 20, 1889; D. F. Alexander to Aaron Beekman, Chattel Mortgage, February 15, 1894, Office of Records, Adams County, Natchez, Mississippi.

47. "Railroad Committee," *Natchez Weekly Democrat*, July 12, 1869, 12; Charter of Natchez, Red River & Texas Railroad Co., January 20, 1881; H. M. Gastrell to Hiram R. Steele (President of the Natchez, Red River & Texas Railroad Co.), Act of Sale, April 23, 1881; Amended Charter of Natchez, Red River & Texas Railroad Co., September 30, 1881; Multiple Land Conveyances, Samuel Block and Isaac Lowenburg to Natchez, Red River & Texas Railroad Co., Deeds, 1881; Multiple Right-of-Way Conveyances, Isaac Lowenburg et al. to Natchez, Red River & Texas Railroad Co., Right-of-Way, 1881; Charter of the New Orleans, Natchez, & Fort Scott Railroad Co., August 10, 1886; Mississippi Valley Railroad Co. to Hiram R. Steele, Resolution of the Board of Directors, November 13, 1895, Office of Records, Concordia Parish, Vidalia, Louisiana; Charter of the Natchez & Gulf Railroad Co., November 29, 1904, Office of Records, Adams County, Natchez, Mississippi; *Natchez, Mississippi On Top, Not "Under the Hill,"* 5–6; Chandler, *Visible Hand*, 1-12.

48. Natchez, Jackson, & Columbus Railroad Co., Report of the President and Directors, December 31, 1881, pp. 1–3, Call Number 385 N19, Archival Reading Room, Mississippi Department of Archives and History; *Natchez Daily Democrat*, June 6, 1882, 2, July 6, 1882, 1,

July 13, 1882, 2, July 27, 1882, 4, September 6, 1882, 2; Isaac Lowenburg to Annie V. Reber, Deed, February 1, 1883; Isaac Lowenburg to Natchez Street Railway Co., Right-of-Way, May 19, 1888, Office of Records, Adams County, Natchez, Mississippi; *Natchez, Mississippi On Top, Not "Under the Hill,"* 5–6.

49. In the space of a decade merchant Isaac Lowenburg served as secretary of the board of trustees of three separate railroad companies—the Natchez, Jackson, & Columbus Railroad Co.; the Natchez, Red River, & Texas R.R. Co.; and the New Orleans, Natchez, & Fort Scott Railroad Co.—and as such was probably the greatest railroad booster of any local business leader. See Isaac Lowenburg to the Natchez, Jackson, & Columbus Railroad Co., Deeds, February 6, 1877, and May 5, 1877; Isaac Lowenburg to Natchez Street Railway Co., Right-of-Way, May 19, 1888; Charter of the Natchez & Gulf Railroad Co., November 29, 1904, Office of Records, Adams County, Natchez, Mississippi; Charter of Natchez, Red River & Texas Railroad Co., January 20, 1881; H. M. Gastrell to Hiram R. Steele (President of the Natchez, Red River & Texas Railroad Co.), Act of Sale, April 23, 1881; Isaac Lowenburg to the Natchez, Red River, & Texas Railroad Co., Deed, July 10, 1881; Amended Charter of Natchez, Red River & Texas Railroad Co., September 30, 1881; Charter of the New Orleans, Natchez, & Fort Scott Railroad Co., August 10, 1886; Mississippi Valley Railroad Co. to Hiram R. Steele, Resolution of the Board of Directors, November 13, 1895, Office of Records, Concordia Parish, Vidalia, Louisiana.

50. Davis, *Black Experience in Natchez*, 158–184.

51. The police jury in Concordia Parish would be similar to modern county board of supervisors, and the board of aldermen is the same as a city council. See Natchez Jewish History, Research File, Historic Natchez Foundation; Rosa L. Friedler to Natchez Building and Loan Association, Trust Deed, June 25, 1894; Adams County Board of Supervisor's Minutes, 1870–1910; Natchez Board of Alderman's Meeting Minute Books, 1879–1910, City Hall and Office of Records, Natchez, Mississippi; Isadore Lemle to the Governor of Louisiana, Recorder's Bond, May 12, 1877; E. W. Wall to the Governor of Louisiana, Clerk's Bond, May 12, 1877; C. C. Campbell to Governor of Louisiana, Court Clerk Bond, June 17, 1896; Isaac L. Friedler to J. L. Rountree, Deed and Mortgage, January 11, 1897, General Mortgage Ledgers, 1880–1910; Vidalia Board of Alderman's Meeting Minute Books, 1903–1910, City Hall and Office of Records, Concordia Parish, Vidalia, Louisiana.

52. Adams County Board of Supervisor's Minutes, 1870–1910; specific entries July 30, 1870, July 9, 1874, January 4, 1876, June 30, 1884, August 7, 1886, April 2, 1888, January 6, 1896, January 4, 1904, January 8, 1908, Office of Records, Natchez, Mississippi.

53. Natchez Jewish History, Research File, Historic Natchez Foundation; 1877 and 1892 Natchez Business Directories; U.S. Census (1880, 1900, 1910) Population Schedules, Adams County, Mississippi; Natchez Aldermen's Minutes, 1879–1910, City Hall, Natchez, Mississippi.

54. The city of Natchez had previously issued $225,000 in municipal bonds at 3.5 percent interest annually to finance the Natchez, Jackson, & Columbus Railroad Co. See the Natchez Aldermen's Minutes, December 15, 1882, January 18, 1883, March 18, 1883, December 20, 1883, July 7, 1884, December 12, 1884, July 5 and 16, 1885, August 6, 1885, July 1, 1886, October 7, 1886, December 30, 1886, January 12, 1888, January 10, 1910, City Hall, Natchez, Mississippi; Isaac Lowenburg to Natchez, Jackson, & Columbus Railroad Co., Deed, February 6, 1877, Office of Records, Adams County, Natchez, Mississippi.

55. Henry Grady quoted in Woodman, *King Cotton*, 322–33; Summers, *Gilded Age*, 43–48, 80–81; Doyle, *New Men, New Cities, New South*, xi–xvi; Wayne, *Reshaping of Plantation Society*, 194–195; Davis, *Good and Faithful Labor*, 121–145.

Chapter 6. A Dangerous Business

1. Advertisement, H. M. Gastrell & Co., *Natchez Weekly Democrat*, October 21, 1865; Advertisement, H. M. Gastrell & Co., 1877 Natchez City Business Directory, 221, Historic Natchez Foundation; U.S. Census (1870, 1880), MS Population Schedules, Adams County, Mississippi; Credit ledger entry, "H. M. Gastrell Hardware & Stoves," Mississippi, Vol. 2, p. 179, R. G. Dun & Co. Ledgers, Harvard Business School.

2. Summers, *Gilded Age*, 84–89; Scott A. Sandage, *Born Losers: A History of Failure in America* (Cambridge, Mass.: Harvard University Press, 2005), 90–92; Robert Dabney Calhoun, "The History of Concordia Parish: 1768–1930," *Louisiana Historical Quarterly* (January 1932): 168–169; Credit ledger entry, "H. M. Gastrell Hardware & Stoves," Mississippi, Vol. 2, p. 179, R. G. Dun & Co. Ledgers, Harvard Business School.

3. Credit ledger entry, "H. M. Gastrell Hardware & Stoves," Mississippi, Vol. 2, p. 186, R. G. Dun & Co. Ledgers, Harvard Business School.

4. Ibid.

5. Ibid.; Record of Judgments, 1880–1885, 1–5, 67–68; Record of Judgments, 1878–1885, 397–409, Office of Records, Adams County, Natchez, Mississippi; H. M. Gastrell to Hiram R. Steele (President of the Natchez, Red River & Texas Railroad Co.), Act of Sale, April 3, 1881, Office of Records, Concordia Parish, Vidalia, Louisiana; Dunbar Rowland, ed., *Mississippi: Comprising Sketches of Counties, Towns, Events, Institutions, and Persons* (Atlanta: Southern Historical Publishing Association, 1907), 2:502-515; Entry, "Henry M. Gastrell, April 17, 1889," Natchez Sexton Records, October 4, 1825–September 30, 1908, http://www.Natchezbelle.org/adams-ind/sexton.htm; Obituary of Henry M. Gastrell, *Natchez Daily Democrat*, April 18, 1889, 2.

6. Notice, "Mrs. H. M. Gastrell," *Natchez Daily Democrat*, July 3, 1890, 3.

7. Henry David Thoreau quoted in Sandage, *Born Losers*, 7.

8. Woodman, *King Cotton*, 318–333, 356–357; Ransom and Sutch, *One Kind of Freedom*, 120–125, 142–144, 186–188: Wayne, *Reshaping of Plantation Society*, 172–173; Davis, *Good and Faithful Labor*, 136–138; Clark, *Pills, Petticoats, and Plows*, 271–282.

9. Assorted Court Cases, Filings, Judgments, and Tax Assessments, Record of Judgments, 1880–1885; Record of Judgments, 1878–1885; Land Deed Records, 1865–1910; Record of Leases 1875–1877, 1877–1890; Natchez City and Adams County Land Rolls, 1875–1900; Inventories and Appraisements, 1866–1898, Office of Records, Adams County, Natchez, Mississippi; Assorted Court Cases, Filings, and Judgments, Record of Judgments &c., 1878–1882; General Mortgages and Land Deed Records, 1865–1910, Office of Records, Concordia Parish, Vidalia, Louisiana.

10. James, *Antebellum Natchez*, 267–269; Reber, *Proud Old Natchez*, 44–45, 61–63; *Natchez, Mississippi On Top, Not "Under the Hill,"* 5–6, 23, 28; Jeremy Atack and Peter Passell, *A New Economic View of American History* (New York: W. W. Norton, 1994), 402–426; Davis, *Black Experience in Natchez*, 186–191; Woodman, *King Cotton*, 319–359; Adams County Board of Supervisor's Minutes, 1870–1910; Natchez Board of Alderman's Meeting Minute Books, 1879–1910, City Hall and Office of Records, Natchez, Mississippi; Multiple articles, *Natchez Daily Democrat* and *Natchez Weekly Democrat*, 1865–1914.

11. Multiple Probate Files, Office of Records, Natchez, Mississippi; Natchez Sexton Records, October 4, 1825–September 30, 1908, http://www.Natchezbelle.org/adams-ind/sexton.htm; Natchez City Death Records, Compilation, 1800–1921; Gandy, "Jewish History"; Ezra Lodge #134 I.O.O.B. Meeting Minute Book, 1878–1909, Temple B'Nai Israel, Natchez, Mississippi.

12. "Financial Advice," *Natchez Tri-Weekly Democrat*, November 11, 1871, 2.

13. Credit ledger entries, Fleming & Baldwin Co., Mississippi, Vol. 2, pp. 6, 165, R. G. Dun & Co. Ledgers, Harvard Business School; John Fleming and Hiram Baldwin to Audley Britton and George Koontz, Mortgage and Deed, January 2, 1872; John Fleming and Hiram Baldwin to David D. Withers, Mortgage and Deed, March 28, 1872, Office of Records, Wilkinson County, Woodville, Mississippi; John N. Routh to Fleming & Baldwin, Deed, November 1, 1869; Charles Howard to Fleming & Baldwin, Contract and Lien, April 10, 1871; Fleming & Baldwin to S. B. Newman & Co., Act of Sale, January 15, 1873, Office of Records, Tensas Parish, St. Joseph, Louisiana; Fleming & Baldwin to Hiram Revels, Deed, April 24, 1871; Fleming & Baldwin to Simon McGrew, Lease, January 12, 1872, Office of Records, Adams County, Natchez, Mississippi; Trustees Sale Announcement, *Natchez Weekly Democrat*, December 17, 1879, 4; Obituary of John Fleming, *Natchez Daily Democrat*, June 4, 1895, 2.

14. Most Natchez lawsuit cases from 1801 to 1870 have been cataloged and processed, and are available at the Historic Natchez Foundation; however, cases from 1870 to 1910 remain unprocessed and unavailable at present. See *Numerous Creditors v. Henry M. Gastrell*, Default Judgments, April and May Term, 1880; *J. C. Hayner & Co. v. Henry M. Gastrell*, Judicial Judgment, May 12, 1884, Record of Judgments, 1880–1885, 1–5, 67–68; Record of Judgments, 1878–1885, 397–409, Historic Natchez Foundation; *Notice for Trustee's Sale v. John Fleming*, *Natchez Daily Democrat*, December 17, 1879, 4.

15. A chattel conveyance simply transfers all rights in and possession of "chattels," which usually included goods, wares, furnishings, livestock, and any other sundry items that the mercantile firm had in the course of conducting business. See Thomas M. Hart to Henry Frank and Others, Chattel Conveyance, March 31, 1881, Record of Leases, 1877–1890, Historic Natchez Foundation.

16. Ibid.

17. Credit ledger entries, Thomas M. Hart Groceries and M. L. Cary Saddlery, Mississippi, Vol. 2, pp. 123, 144, R. G. Dun & Co. Ledgers, Harvard Business School.

18. Block had been partnered with Marx Lemle's brother Isadore, and they had a thriving business with supply accounts on tens of plantations, but they seem to have parted ways sometime in 1886, and Block's fortunes seemingly deteriorated from there. See Samuel Block to A. Beekman Jr., Assignment, December 26, 1890, Record of Leases, 1877–1890, Historic Natchez Foundation; Samuel Block to V. & A. Meyer Co., Mortgage, March 9, 1885; Samuel Block to A. R. Montgomery, Deed, February 13, 1886, Office of Records, Concordia Parish, Vidalia, Louisiana.

19. Samuel Block to A. Beekman Jr., Assignment, December 26, 1890, Record of Leases, 1877–1890, Historic Natchez Foundation.

20. "Captain" Sam Block was a cousin of Isaac Lowenburg and emigrated with him from Germany in 1858. This gave Block a powerful ally in the Jewish community, and Block seems to have enjoyed a measure of business respect for years, but after financial reverses in the 1880s and Lowenburg's death in 1888, he may have lost considerable support. Block was also distantly related by marriage to Henry Frank and Simon Ullman, who sued him during his downfall. See Samuel Block to Henry Frank, Scharff Bros., and Others (five cases total), Judicial Mortgages and Default Attachments, March 14, 1891; Samuel Block to A. Alder & Co., Judgment, May 22, 1891; Samuel Block to Schwartz & Stewart, Judgment, October 12, 1891, Office of Records, Concordia Parish, Vidalia, Louisiana.

21. *Isaac Friedler v. Charles Washington*, Judgment, November 23, 1878; *Isaac Friedler v. Wilson Johnson*, Judgment, December 13, 1878; *Isaac Friedler v. Jake Davis*, Judgment,

January 2, 1878; Monday Williams and Others (nine suits total), Judgments, January 15, 1878–January 26, 1881, Record of Judgments &C., 1878–1882; Charles Washington to Isaac Friedler, Chattel Mortgage, July 21, 1881; Wilson Johnson to Isaac Friedler, Chattel Mortgage, August 18, 1885; Jake Davis to Isaac Friedler, Chattel Mortgage, August 18, 1886, 4, Office of Records, Concordia Parish, Vidalia, Louisiana.

22. Sheriff Wood was black, an indicator that many blacks held office in Adams County at the end of Reconstruction in 1876. Sheriff William McCary, mentioned in the following paragraph, was also black. See *Wolfe Geisenberger v. Abe Perry et al.*, Affidavit and Replevin Writ, November 22, 1876, Box 12, File 58, Group 1870; *A. F. Jacobs & Bros. v. William Alexander*, Replevin Writ, May 19, 1903, Circuit Court Minutes, 1898–1903, Historic Natchez Foundation; Frank Johnson to Wolfe Geisenberger, Chattel Mortgage, February 27, 1877; William Alexander to A. F. Jacobs & Bros., Chattel Mortgage, March 4, 1902, Office of Records, Adams County, Natchez, Mississippi; Joseph Murdock to Sim Lowenburg, Attachment and Default, July 19, 1895; Joseph Murdock to Sim Lowenburg, Tax Deed, September 11, 1895, Office of Records, Tensas Parish, St. Joseph, Louisiana.

23. *Isaac Lowenburg v. Daniel S. Farrar*, Affidavit and Replevin Writ, January 8, 1874, Box 7, File 59, Group 1870; *Anna E. Smith v. N. L. Carpenter & Son*, Replevin Writ, October 6, 1866, Box 6, File 58, Group 1860, Historic Natchez Foundation; *Isaac Friedler v. Police Jury of Concordia Parish*, Judgment, October 4, 1879, Record of Judgments &C., 1878–1882; Isaac Lowenburg to M. Phelen, Agent, Lease, November 8, 1883; Isaac Friedler to Fuzz & Backer, Judicial Mortgage, April 4, 1886; A. M. Swayze to Isaac Friedler, Attachment, April 2, 1896; J. H. Lambdin to Sim H. Lowenburg, Sheriff's Deed, February 8, 1896, Office of Records, Concordia Parish, Vidalia, Louisiana; W. R. Easterling (Substitute Trustee) to I. Lowenburg & Co., Trustee's Deed, April 3, 1905, Office of Records, Jefferson County, Fayette, Mississippi; Announcement, *W. H. Shields v. Carpenter & Dicks*, *Natchez Daily Democrat*, April 29, 1885, 2.

24. Adams County Board of Supervisor's Minutes, 1870–1910; Natchez Board of Alderman's Meeting Minutes, 1879–1910, City Hall and Office of Records, Natchez, Mississippi; Police Jury of Concordia Parish Meeting Minutes, 1878–1886, Office of Records, Concordia Parish, Vidalia, Louisiana; Natchez City and Adams County Land Rolls, 1873, 1875, 1883, 1887; Land Sale Record for Delinquent Taxes, 1872–1873; Adams County Tax Collections, October 1886–November 1887, Historic Natchez Foundation; Wayne, *Reshaping of Plantation Society*, 78–81.

25. Ibid.; *State of Mississippi v. George T. Payne*, Multiple Indictments and Judgments, January 18–20, 1868, Box 20, File 19, Group 1860; Record of Judgments, 1880–1885, 46, 84, 130, Historic Natchez Foundation; Adams County Board of Supervisor's Minutes, July 1–3, 1901, August 5, 1901, Office of Records, Natchez, Mississippi.

26. "Be Self-Sustaining: The Boll Weevil Is an Old Chestnut," *Natchez Daily Democrat*, November 8, 1908, 5.

27. Ibid.; Wright, *Political Economy of the South*, 158–184; Woodman, *King Cotton*, 345–359; John D. Hicks, *The Populist Revolt: A History of the Farmers Alliance and the Peoples Party* (1931; repr., Omaha: University of Nebraska Press, 1961), 55–95; Ransom and Sutch, *One Kind of Freedom*, 160–163, 172–176; Clark, *Pills, Petticoats, and Plows*, 286–291.

28. Woodman, *King Cotton*, 345–359; Clark, *Pills, Petticoats, and Plows*, 286–291; Atack and Passell, *New Economic View of American History*, 376–400, 516–517; Summers, *Gilded Age*, 33, 45, 116, 139, 235–236, 285; Ransom and Sutch, *One Kind of Freedom*, 165–168.

29. Hicks, *Populist Revolt*, 309.

30. Woodward, *Origins of the New South*, 264–275; Woodman, *King Cotton*, ix–xxiv, 345–359; Clark, *Pills, Petticoats, and Plows*, 286–291; Atack and Passell, *New Economic View of American History*, 376–400, 516-517; Summers, *Gilded Age*, 33, 45, 116, 139, 235–236, 285; Ransom and Sutch, *One Kind of Freedom*, 165–168.

31. Morton Rothstein quoted in Joseph Santos, "A History of Futures Trading in the United States," EH.Net Encyclopedia, http://www.eh.net/encyclopedia/article/Santos.futures; Summers, *Gilded Age*, 44–45; Wright, *Political Economy of the South*, 158–159; Woodman, *King Cotton*, 288–294, 338–341.

32. Assessments Announcement, *Natchez Daily Democrat*, July 2, 1887, 2; Railroad Editorial, Natchez *Daily Democrat*, December 24, 1892, 2; Charter of Natchez, Red River & Texas Railroad Co., January 20, 1881; H. M. Gastrell to Hiram R. Steele (President of the Natchez, Red River & Texas Railroad Co.), Act of Sale, April 23, 1881; Amended Charter of Natchez, Red River & Texas Railroad Co., September 30, 1881; State Tax Collector (Natchez, Red River & Texas R.R. Co.) to L. A. Hale et al., Tax Deed, April 20, 1885; Charter of the New Orleans, Natchez, & Fort Scott Railroad Co., August 10, 1886; *Central Trust Company of New York v. New Orleans & Northwestern Railroad Co.*, Master's Deed, November 15, 1902, Office of Records, Concordia Parish, Vidalia, Louisiana; Natchez Board of Alderman's Meeting Minutes, August 6, 1885; Rosalie Cotton Mills (W. A. S. Wheeler President) to Britton & Koontz, Bill of Sale, September 16, 1896; E. M. Perrault, Estate File, April 13, 1897, Cause No. 1444, File Box No. 230, City Hall and Office of Records, Natchez, Mississippi; Credit ledger entries, James Surget and Kate Minor, Mississippi, Vol. 2, pp. 40, 161, R. G. Dun & Co. Ledgers, Harvard Business School; Calhoun, "History of Concordia Parish," 168–169; Narvell Strickland, "A History of Mississippi Cotton Mills and Cotton Villages," http://www.narvellstrickland1.tripod.com/cottonmillhistory2/index 1.html.

33. Natchez Board of Alderman's Meeting Minutes, September 29, 1899, City Hall, Natchez, Mississippi.

34. James, *Antebellum Natchez*, 266–270; Reber, *Proud Old Natchez*, 44–45; *Natchez, Mississippi On Top, Not "Under the Hill,"* 6, 23–24; Moses, "My Memories," 19–22, 40–41; *Natchez Tri-Weekly Democrat*, October 7, 1871, 1–2, October 19, 1871, 1–2; Adams County Board of Supervisor's Minutes, 1870–1910; Natchez Board of Alderman's Meeting Minutes, 1879–1910, City Hall and Office of Records, Natchez, Mississippi; Police Jury of Concordia Parish Meeting Minutes, 1878–1886, Office of Records, Concordia Parish, Vidalia, Louisiana; LAGenWeb, "1871 Yellow Fever Epidemic," http: www.rootsweb.ancestry.com/~laconcor/yellow.htm.

35. James, *Antebellum Natchez*, 272.

36. *Natchez Daily Democrat*, July 4, 1887, 2.

37. Davis, *Good and Faithful Labor*, 100-101, 124–125, 162–163; James, *Antebellum Natchez*, 271; Adams County Board of Supervisor's Minutes, 1870–1910; Assessment Reductions, August 12, 1908, Office of Records, Natchez, Mississippi; Police Jury of Concordia Parish Meeting Minutes, 1878–1886; Flooding and Levee Assessments, July 3, 1882, October 7, 1884, October 5, 1885, Office of Records, Concordia Parish, Vidalia, Louisiana; *Natchez Daily Democrat*, June 3, 1882, 2, September 6, 1882, 2.

38. *Natchez Daily Democrat*, June 3, 1882, 2.

39. Many Natchez District lands were considered "tired" even before the Civil War, and the availability of guano and ammonia-phosphate exploded after the war in recognition of the land condition. See Advertisement, Fleming & Baldwin, *Natchez Weekly Courier*, February 11, 1870, 3; James, *Antebellum Natchez*, 216.

40. Credit ledger entries, Aaron Beekman & Co., James Carradine Co., Henry Frank Co., and Sim Lowenburg, Mississippi, Vol. 2, pp. 29, 58, 98, 100, R. G. Dun & Co. Ledgers, Harvard Business School; Simon Jacobs, Estate File, October 19, 1891, Cause No. 1161, File Box No. 223, Office of Records, Natchez, Mississippi; *Seligman Schatz v. the Hartford Insurance Co.* (For the use of Aaron Beekman), Judgment, September 28, 1868, Box 22, File 28, Group 1860, Historic Natchez Foundation; *Natchez Daily Democrat*, July 22, 1887, 2, October 6, 1891, 2, December 7, 1907, 3; March 2, 1908, 1, March 19, 1908, 1, 5, 6, 8; James, *Antebellum Natchez*, 270–271.

41. "Prospectus of the Natchez Business Directory & Almanac For 1871," 20, 30, Historic Natchez Foundation.

42. Credit ledger entry, Natchez Co-Operative Ass'n Grange Store, Mississippi, Vol. 2, p. 90, R. G. Dun & Co. Ledgers, Harvard Business School; Lowenburg & Hill to Ann Eliza Miles, Deed, March 4, 1871; Ann Eliza Miles to Lowenburg & Hill, March 4, 1871; Ann Eliza Miles to Isaac Lowenburg (Trustee for Meyer Weis & Co.), Trust Deed, February 27, 1872; Ann E. Miles to Perrault & Co., Trust Deed, July 6, 1885; Fred Maher (Trustee for the Perrault & Co.), Trustees Deed, February 21, 1887, Office of Records, Jefferson County, Fayette, Mississippi; Wayne, *Reshaping of Plantation Society*, 100–101.

43. "Source Material for Mississippi History: Amite County Volume III, Part I," Compiled by the WPA State-Wide Historical Project, 1936–1939 (Liberty, Miss.: Amite County Historical and Genealogical Society, 2006), 219–227. The year of last contracts recorded in the area for the three Jewish merchants mentioned are: Beekman, 1900; Geisenberger, 1899; Lowenburg, 1899. See Frank Anderson to L. Goldsmith (Trustee for Sam Beekman), Trust Deed, January 19, 1900; Thomas J. Schropshire and Wife to A. H. Geisenberger (Trustee for Wolfe Geisenberger & Son), Trust Deed, January 27, 1899; Henry Frank et al. (Sim Lowenburg and others) to Wyatt Barnes, Deed, December 6, 1899, Office of Records, Wilkinson County, Woodville, Mississippi.

44. Davis, *Black Experience in Natchez*, 158–190.

45. *Natchez Daily Democrat*, July 8, 1887, 2.

46. Jerrold M. Packer, *American Nightmare: The History of Jim Crow* (New York: St. Martins Griffin, 2002), 66–69; Joel Williamson, *A Rage for Order: Black and White Relations in the American South since Emancipation* (New York: Oxford University Press, 1986), 117-151; Adams County Board of Supervisor's Minutes, 1890–1910; Natchez Board of Alderman's Meeting Minutes, 1890–1910; January 13, 1899, December 10, 1901, City Hall and Office of Records, Natchez, Mississippi; WPA, "Source Material for Mississippi History: Amite County," 219–227; Davis, *Black Experience*, 180–181; "Mississippi Lynchings, 1882–1930," http://users.bestweb.net/~rg/lynchings/Mississippi%20Lynchings.htm.

47. *Natchez Daily Democrat*, January 1, 1908, 1.

48. Davis, Gardener, and Gardener, *Deep South*, 255–257; Williamson, *Rage for Order*, 205; Multiple Chattel Mortgage Contracts, Nathan Wright to George T. Payne and Adolf Jacobs, 1873–1902; John R. Lynch to Henry R. Griffin (Trustee for Adolf Jacobs Co.), Trust Deeds, January 18 and 31, 1896, Office of Records, Natchez, Mississippi; Jay Mechling, "The Failure of Folklore in Richard Wright's *Black Boy*," *Journal of American Folklore* 104 (Summer 1991): 275–294; Davis, *Black Experience*, 186–187.

49. Taylor and Etheridge, *Mississippi*, 4:800–802, 1698-1702; 1892 and 1912 Natchez City Business Directories, Historic Natchez Foundation; Gandy, "Jewish History"; U.S. Census (1880, 1900, 1910, 1920, 1930) Population Schedules, Adams County, Mississippi; James S. Fleming, Estate File, February 18, 1933, Cause No. 321, File Box No. 6177, Office of Records,

Natchez, Mississippi; The Goldring/Woldenburg Institute of Southern Jewish Life, "Digital Archive: Natchez," http://www.isjl.org/history/archive/ms/natchez.htm.

50. Ibid.

51. Marx Lemle, Last Will and Testament (Estate File), March 10, 1883, Cause No. 789, File Box No. 204; George T. Payne, Estate File, June 20, 1891, Cause No. 1140, File Box No. 230; Isaac Lowenburg, September 10, 1888, Estate File, Cause No. 995, File Box No. 222, Office of Records, Adams County, Natchez, Mississippi.

52. Moses, "My Memories," 92

53. Ibid., 92, 181–182; Isaac Lowenburg, September 10, 1888, Estate File, Cause No. 995, File Box No. 222; Elizabeth M. Perrault, Last Will and Testament (Estate File), April 13, 1897, Cause No. 1444, File Box No. 230; *Vincent L. Perrault to Charles H. Perrault et al. v. James O. Perrault by T. K. Winchester*, Special Commissioner, Commissioners Deed, December 31, 1903, Office of Records, Adams County, Natchez, Mississippi; *Charles H. Perrault et al. v. James O. Perrault*, Distribution Order (By Court), March 1, 1904, Office of Records, Jefferson County, Fayette, Mississippi.

54. Moses, "My Memories," 5–6, 80, 90–91, 112-138; Entries, John C. Schwartz, February 1, 1890; Julia Francis Carpenter, September 22, 1901; A. D. Carpenter, January 17, 1902; John C. Jenkins, February 1, 1902, Natchez Sexton Records, October 4, 1825–September 30, 1908, http://www.Natchezbelle.org/adams-ind/sexton.htm; Entries, George W. Koontz, Thomas Reber, William Wood Jr., George N. Zurhellen, and Charles Patterson, pp. 48, 68, 95, 132, 134, Natchez City Death Records, Compilation, 1800–1921, Historic Natchez Foundation; Elizabeth M. Perrault, Last Will and Testament (Estate File), April 13, 1897, Cause No. 1444, File Box No. 230, Office of Records, Adams County, Natchez, Mississippi.

55. *Natchez Daily Democrat*, March 24, 1914, 1, 4, April 2, 1914, 1, April 7, 1914, 1, April 8, 1914, 1, 2, April 10, 1914, 1; *State of Mississippi v. Andrew G. Campbell, Sim H. Lowenburg, Robert Lee Wood, and H. M. Gaither*, Docket Nos. 3300–3325, March and November Terms 1914, 181–183, State Court Docket Ledger, November 1896–November 1926, Historic Natchez Foundation; Moses, "My Memories," 179–182.

56. Both Lowenburg and Samuels retained ownership of I. Lowenburg & Co. and held positions as corporate officers into the 1920s, but relinquished control of day-to-day operations with their move to New Orleans. In her account, Lowenburg's sister Clara writes that the First Natchez Bank trouble was disheartening enough that Samuels and his family moved soon after the trial, and the Lowenburgs followed within a year. Mortgage records indicate that Lowenburg sold the family home fully furnished in 1919, yet Clara wrote "they walked out with their clothes only" several years earlier. Regardless, the Lowenburgs lived on tony St. Charles Avenue in New Orleans by 1920 and clearly still had significant means, while a much-reduced I. Lowenburg & Co. continued in business in Natchez until around the time Sim Lowenburg died in 1928. See I. Lowenburg & Co. to I. Lowenburg & Co., Deed of Conveyance, November 29, 1913; Media E. and S. H. Lowenburg to Jeanna Smith, Deed of Conveyance, April 29, 1919; I. Lowenburg & Co. to V. B. Wheeler, Deed, June 6, 1927, Office of Records, Natchez, Mississippi; Moses, "My Memories," 179–192; U.S. Census (1920, 1930) Population Schedules, Orleans Parish, Louisiana.

Selected Bibliography

Primary Sources

Manuscripts

Austin, Texas. University of Texas Center for American History, Natchez Trace Collection.
  Pamphlet and Serials Collection.
  Winchester Family Papers.

Baton Rouge, Louisiana. Louisiana State University Hill Memorial Library, Louisiana and Lower Mississippi Valley Collections.
  Audley Clark Britton and Family Papers.
  Britton and Koontz Papers.
  Lemuel Parker Conner and Family Papers.
  Stephen Duncan and Stephen Duncan Jr. Papers.
  Henderson Family Papers.
  Katherine Surget Minor Letter.
  William J. Minor and Family Papers.
  John C. Schwartz Papers.
  Joseph D. Shields Papers.
  Shlenker-Hirsch-Moyse Papers.
  R. Viener and Co. Account Books.

Boston. Harvard University Baker Library Historical Collections.
  R. G. Dun and Co. Mercantile Agency Credit Ledgers.

Chapel Hill, North Carolina. Wilson Library, Southern Historical Collection.
  William Dunbar Account Book.
  Mary Susan Ker Papers.
  Minor Family Papers.

Fayette, Mississippi. Office of Records.
  Chattel Mortgage Ledgers for Jefferson County, 1873–1910.
  Land Deed Records for Jefferson County, 1865–1910.
  Liens and Mortgage Records for Jefferson County, 1865–1910.

Jackson, Mississippi. Mississippi Department of Archives and History, Natchez District Manuscript Collection.
    American Cotton Oil Co. Papers.
    Baker and Moss Co. Papers.
    T. Otis Baker Papers.
    Cohn Brothers Mercantile Records.
    First Natchez Bank Records.
    Charles P. Leverich Papers.
    Minor Family Papers.
    Salvo and Berndon Candy Co. Records.
    Schwartz & Stewart Co. Papers.
    Surget-McKittrick-MacNeil Family Papers.
    Trinity Episcopal Church Records, 1822–1890.
    Battaille Harrison Wade and Family Papers.

Meadville, Mississippi. Office of Records.
    Chattel Mortgage Ledgers for Franklin County, 1875–1903.
    Land Deed Records for Franklin County, 1865–1910.
    Liens and Mortgage Records for Franklin County, 1865–1910.

Natchez, Mississippi. City Hall.
    Minutes of the Mayor and Aldermen for the City of Natchez, 1878–1910.

Natchez, Mississippi. Historic Natchez Foundation.
    Circuit and Justice Court Cases for Adams County, 1865–1914.
    Circuit Court Minutes for Adams County, 1898–1914.
    Chattel Mortgage Ledgers for Adams County, 1875–1903.
    Land Sale Record for Delinquent Taxes for Adams County, 1872–1873.
    Natchez City Business Directories, 1858, 1867, 1871, 1877, 1892, 1912.
    Natchez City Death Records, 1800–1921.
    Natchez Jewish History, Research File.
    Record of Judgments for Adams County, 1878–1914.
    Record of Leases for Adams County, 1877–1899.
    Record of Naturalizations for Adams County, 1854–1904.
    Tax Collections for Adams County, 1886–1887.

Natchez, Mississippi. Office of Records.
    Adams County Land Rolls, 1873, 1875, 1883, and 1887.
    Chancery Records for Adams County, 1865–1910.
    Land Deed Records for Adams County, 1865–1910.
    Liens and Mortgage Records for Adams County, 1830–1910.
    Minutes of the Adams County Supervisors, 1878–1910.
    Natchez City Land Rolls, 1887.
    Natchez Sexton Records, 1825–1908.
    Probate Records for Adams County, 1865–1910.

Natchez, Mississippi. Temple B'Nai Israel.
   Ezra Lodge Endowment Record Book (1873–1890).
   Ezra Lodge #134 I.O.O.B. Lodge Meeting Minutes (1878–1905).
   Temple Meeting Minutes (1864–1875).

Natchez, Mississippi. Trinity Episcopal Church.
   Vestry Meeting Minutes Book, 1822–1890.

New Orleans. Tulane University Howard-Tilton Memorial Library, American Southern Jewish Experience and Jewish Studies Collection.
   Clara Lowenburg Moses Papers.

Northridge, California. California State University, Natchez Archive Collection.
   Manuscript Tax Rolls for Adams County, Mississippi, and Concordia Parish, Louisiana, 1866–1899.
   Natchez City Census, 1886.

St. Joseph, Louisiana. Office of Records.
   Land Deed Records for Tensas Parish, 1865–1910.
   Liens and Mortgage Records for Tensas Parish, 1865–1899.

Vidalia, Louisiana. Office of Records.
   Chancery Records for Concordia Parish, 1865–1899.
   Land Deed Records for Concordia Parish, 1865–1910.
   Liens and Mortgage Records for Concordia Parish, 1865–1899.
   Probate Records for Concordia Parish, 1899–1911.
   Record of Judgments and Pleadings for Concordia Parish, 1865–1899.

Washington, D.C. Department of Commerce, Bureau of the Census.
   U.S. Census (1850), Manuscript Agricultural, Population, and Slave Schedules for Adams, Franklin, Jefferson, and Wilkinson Counties, Mississippi, and Concordia and Tensas Parishes, Louisiana.
   U.S. Census (1860), Manuscript Agricultural, Population, and Slave Schedules for Adams, Franklin, Jefferson, and Wilkinson Counties, Mississippi, and Concordia and Tensas Parishes, Louisiana.
   U.S. Census (1870), Manuscript Agricultural and Population Schedules for Adams, Franklin, Jefferson, and Wilkinson Counties, Mississippi, and Concordia, Orleans, and Tensas Parishes, Louisiana.
   U.S. Census (1880), Manuscript Agricultural and Population Schedules for Adams, Franklin, Jefferson, and Wilkinson Counties, Mississippi, and Concordia, Orleans, and Tensas Parishes, Louisiana.
   U.S. Census (1900), Manuscript Agricultural and Population Schedules for Adams, Franklin, Jefferson, and Wilkinson Counties, Mississippi, and Concordia, Orleans, and Tensas Parishes, Louisiana.
   U.S. Census (1910), Manuscript Agricultural and Population Schedules for Adams, Franklin, Jefferson, and Wilkinson Counties, Mississippi, and Concordia, Orleans, and Tensas Parishes, Louisiana.

U.S. Census (1920), Manuscript Agricultural and Population Schedules for Adams, Franklin, Jefferson, and Wilkinson Counties, Mississippi, and Concordia, Orleans, and Tensas Parishes, Louisiana.

U.S. Census (1930), Manuscript Agricultural and Population Schedules for Adams, Franklin, Jefferson, and Wilkinson Counties, Mississippi, and Concordia, Orleans, and Tensas Parishes, Louisiana.

Woodville, Mississippi. Office of Records.
Chattel Mortgage Ledger Index for Wilkinson County, 1871–1885.
Land Deed Records for Wilkinson County, 1865–1910.
Liens and Mortgage Records for Wilkinson County, 1858–1899.

Newspapers

Intelligencer (Natchez), 1801–1802.
Mississippi Herald and Natchez City Gazette (Natchez), 1802–1807.
Natchez Daily Courier, 1820–1865.
Natchez Daily Democrat, 1860–1914.
Natchez Weekly Courier, 1820–1870.
Natchez Weekly Democrat, 1860–1890.
New Orleans Times-Democrat, 1881–1882.
Sentinel (Concordia), 1867–1869.

Books and Pamphlets

Goodspeed's Biographical and Historical Memoirs of Mississippi Vol. II. Chicago: Goodspeed Publishing, 1891.

Hogan, William Ransom, and Edwin Adams Davis, eds. *William Johnson's Natchez: The Ante-bellum Diary of a Free Negro*. Baton Rouge: Louisiana State University Press, 1993.

Linden, Glenn M. *Voices from the Reconstruction Years, 1865–1877*. Fort Worth, Tex.: Harcourt Brace College Publishers, 1999.

Machlovitz, Wendy. *Clara Lowenburg Moses: Memoir of a Southern Jewish Woman*. Jackson, Miss.: Museum of the Southern Jewish Experience, 2000.

Marshall, Theodora Britton. *They Found It in Natchez*. New Orleans: Pelican Publishing, 1939.

Natchez, Mississippi On Top, Not "Under the Hill." Natchez, Miss.: Daily Democrat Steam Press, 1888.

Olmstead, Frederick Law. *The Cotton Kingdom: A Traveler's Observations on Cotton and Slavery in the American Slave States*. 1861. Reprint, New York: Da Capo Press, 1996.

Reber, Thomas. *Proud Old Natchez*. Natchez, Miss.: self-published, 1909.

Reed, Richard F. *The Natchez Country from the Settlement By the French to the Admission of Mississippi as a State*. 1909? Reprint, Natchez, Miss.: News Publishing, 2002.

Reid, Whitelaw. *After the War: A Southern Tour, May 1, 1865 to May 1, 1866*. 1866. Reprint, New York: Harper Torchbooks, 1964.

Sheppard's Mississippi State Gazetteer and Shippers Guide for 1866–67. Cincinnati: J. S. Sheppard, 1866.

Somers, Robert. *The Southern States since the War, 1870–71*. 1871. Reprint, Tuscaloosa: University of Alabama Press, 2005.
"Source Material for Mississippi History: Amite County Volume III, Part I." Compiled by the WPA State-Wide Historical Project, 1936–1939. Liberty, Miss.: Amite County Historical and Genealogical Society, 2006.
Twain, Mark. "Concerning the Jews." 1898. Reprinted in *Collected Tales, Sketches, Speeches, and Essays, 1891–1910*. New York: Literary Classics, 1966.
———. *Life on the Mississippi*. 1883. Reprint, Pleasantville, N.Y.: Reader's Digest Association, 1987.
Wright, Richard. *Black Boy (American Hunger): A Record of Childhood and Youth*. 1945. Reprint, New York: HarperCollins Publishers, 1998.

Secondary Sources

Books

Aiken, Charles S. *The Cotton Plantation South since the Civil War*. Baltimore: Johns Hopkins University Press, 1998.
Alsburg, Henry G. ed. *The American Guide: The South and Southwest*. New York: Hastings House, 1949.
Armbrester, Margaret England. *Samuel Ullman and "Youth."* Tuscaloosa: University of Alabama Press, 1993.
Ash, Stephen V. *When the Yankees Came: Conflict and Chaos in the Occupied South, 1861–1865*. Chapel Hill: University of North Carolina Press, 1995.
Ashkenazi, Elliott. *The Business of Jews in Louisiana, 1840–1875*. Tuscaloosa: University of Alabama Press, 1988.
Atack, Jeremy, and Peter Passell. *A New Economic View of American History*. New York: W. W. Norton, 1994.
Atherton, Lewis E. *The Southern Country Store, 1800–1860*. Baton Rouge: Louisiana State University Press, 1949.
Ayers, Edward L. *Promise of the New South: Life After Reconstruction*. New York: Oxford University Press, 1992.
Bailey, Earl L. *A Look at Natchez: Its Economic Resources*. Natchez, Miss.: Natchez Association of Commerce, 1953.
Barth, Gunther. *City People: The Rise of Modern City Culture in Nineteenth-Century America*. New York: Oxford University Press, 1980.
Bauman, Mark K., ed. *Dixie Diaspora: An Anthology of Southern Jewish History*. Tuscaloosa: University of Alabama Press, 2006.
Beckert, Sven. *The Monied Metropolis: New York City and the Consolidation of the American Bourgeoisie, 1850–1896*. New York: Cambridge University Press, 2001.
Bentley, George R. *A History of the Freedmen's Bureau*. 1955. Reprint, New York: Octagon Books, 1970.
Blackford, Mansel G. *A History of Small Business in America*. 1992. Reprint, Chapel Hill: University of North Carolina Press, 2003.
Bode, Frederick A., and Donald E. Ginter. *Farm Tenancy and the Census in Antebellum Georgia*. Athens: University of Georgia Press, 1988.

Bodnar, John. *The Transplanted: A History of Immigrants in Urban America*. Bloomington: Indiana University Press, 1985.

Bolton, Charles C. *Poor Whites of the Antebellum South: Tenants and Laborers in Central North Carolina and Northeast Mississippi*. Durham, N.C.: Duke University Press, 1994.

Boorstin, Daniel J. *The Americans: The Democratic Experience*. New York: Random House, 1973.

Brazy, Martha Jane. *An American Planter: Steven Duncan of Antebellum Natchez and New York*. Baton Rouge: Louisiana State University Press, 2006.

Brundage, W. Fitzhugh. *The Southern Past: A Clash of Race and Memory*. Cambridge, Mass.: Belknap Press of Harvard University Press, 2005.

Byrne, Frank J. *Becoming Bourgeois: Merchant Culture in the South, 1820–1865*. Lexington: University Press of Kentucky, 2006.

Campbell, Gavin. *Archival Shadows of the Old Natchez District*. Chapel Hill: Center for the Study of the American South, 1996.

Carlton, David. *Mill and Town in South Carolina, 1880–1920*. Baton Rouge: Louisiana State University Press, 1982.

Cash, W. J. *Mind of the South*. 1941. Reprint, New York: Vintage Books, 1991.

Catton, Bruce, and James M. McPherson, eds. *The American Heritage New History of the Civil War*. New York: MetroBooks, 2001.

Chandler, Alfred D. *The Visible Hand: The Managerial Revolution in American Business*. Cambridge, Mass.: Belknap Press of Harvard University Press, 1977.

Clark, Thomas D. *Pills, Petticoats, and Plows*. Indianapolis, Ind: Bobbs-Merrill, 1944.

Coclanis, Peter A. *The Shadow of a Dream: Economic Life and Death in the South Carolina Low Country, 1670–1920*. New York: Oxford University Press, 1989.

Cohen, William. *At Freedom's Edge: Black Mobility and the Southern White Quest for Racial Control, 1861–1915*. Baton Rouge: Louisiana State University Press, 1991.

Cowley, Robert, ed. *With My Face to the Enemy: Perspectives on the Civil War*. New York: G. P. Putman's Sons, 2001.

Daniel, Pete. *Breaking the Land: The Transformation of Cotton, Tobacco, and Rice Cultures since 1880*. Chicago: University of Illinois Press, 1985.

Davis, Allison, Burlieigh B. Gardner, and Mary R. Gardner. *Deep South: A Social Anthropological Study of Caste and Class*. Chicago: University of Chicago Press, 1941.

Davis, Jack E. *Race Against Time: Culture and Separation in Natchez Since 1930*. Baton Rouge: Louisiana State University Press, 2001.

Davis, Ronald L. F. *Good and Faithful Labor: From Slavery to Sharecropping in the Natchez District, 1860–1890*. Westport, Conn.: Greenwood Press, 1982.

———. *The Black Experience in Natchez, 1720–1880*. Denver: U.S. Department of the Interior, National Park Service, 1994.

Davis, Ronald L. F., and Joyce L. Broussard, eds. *Natchez on the Mississippi: A Journey through Southern History, 1870–1920*. Northridge: School of Social and Behavioral Sciences, California State University, 1995.

Davis, William C. *The Lost Cause: Myths and Realities of the Confederacy*. Lawrence: University Press of Kansas, 1996.

———, ed. *The Guns of '62*. Vol. 2 of *The Image of War, 1861–65*. Garden City, N.J.: Doubleday, 1982.

Degler, Carl N. *Place Over Time: The Continuity of Southern Distinctiveness*. Baton Rouge: Louisiana State University Press, 1977.

DeRosier, Arthur H., Jr. *William Dunbar: Scientific Pioneer of the Old Southwest.* Lexington: University Press of Kentucky, 2007.
Dinnerstein, Leonard, and Mary Dale Palsson, eds. *Jews in the South.* Baton Rouge: Louisiana State University Press, 1973.
Doyle, Don H. *New Men, New Cities, New South: Atlanta, Nashville, Charleston, Mobile, 1860–1910.* Chapel Hill: University of North Carolina Press, 1990.
Dubie, Carol, Beth Savage, and Patrick Andrus. *Inventory and Evaluation of Historic Resources in the Natchez Bluffs Area, Mississippi.* Washington, D.C.: National Register of Historic Places, National Park Service, 1985.
Du Bois, W. E. B. *Black Reconstruction in America, 1860–1880.* 1935. Reprint, New York: Free Press, 1998.
Eaton, Clement. *The Growth of Southern Civilization, 1790–1860.* New York: Harper & Row, 1961.
Escott, Paul D., et al., eds. *Major Problems in the History of the American South.* Vol. 2. Boston: Houghton Mifflin, 1999.
Evans, Eli N. *The Lonely Days Were Sundays: Reflections of a Jewish Southerner.* Jackson: University Press of Mississippi, 1993.
Faulkner, William. *The Hamlet.* 1940. Reprint, New York: Vintage Books, 1991.
——. *The Unvanquished.* 1934. Reprint, New York: Random House, 1965.
Federal Writers Project of the Works Progress Administration. *Mississippi: A Guide to the Magnolia State.* New York: Hastings House, 1938.
Field, John. *Social Capital.* New York: Routledge, 2003.
Fogel, Robert William, and Stanley L. Engerman. *Time on the Cross: The Economics of American Negro Slavery.* Boston: Little, Brown, 1974.
Foner, Eric. *Politics and Ideology in the Age of the Civil War.* New York: Oxford University Press, 1980.
——. *Reconstruction: America's Unfinished Revolution, 1863–1877.* New York: Harper & Row, 1988.
Ford, Lacey K., Jr., ed. *Blackwell Companion to the Civil War and Reconstruction.* Boston: Blackwell Press, 2005.
Gandy, Joan W., and Thomas H. Gandy. *Natchez City Streets Revisited (Images of America: Mississippi).* Charleston, S.C.: Arcadia Publishing, 1999.
——. *Natchez Landmarks, Lifestyles, and Leisure (Images of America: Mississippi).* Charleston, S.C.: Arcadia Publishing, 1999.
Garner, James W. *Reconstruction in Mississippi.* 1901. Reprint, Baton Rouge: Louisiana State University Press, 1968.
Gaston, Paul M. *The New South Creed: A Study in Southern Mythmaking.* 1970. Reprint, Montgomery, Ala.: New South Books, 2002.
Genovese, Elizabeth Fox, and Eugene D. Genovese. *Fruits of Merchant Capital: Slavery and Bourgeois Property in the Rise and Expansion of Capitalism.* New York: Oxford University Press, 1983.
Genovese, Eugene D. *A Consuming Fire: The Fall of the Confederacy in the Mind of the White Christian South.* Athens: University of Georgia Press, 1998.
——. *Roll, Jordan, Roll: The World the Slaves Made.* New York: Pantheon Books, 1974.
——. *The World the Slaveholders Made.* New York: Vintage Books, 1971.
Goodwyn, Lawrence. *The Populist Moment: A Short History of Agrarian Revolt in America.* New York: Oxford University Press, 1978.

Gudmestad, Robert H. *A Troublesome Commerce: The Transformation of the Interstate Slave Trade.* Baton Rouge: Louisiana State University Press, 2003.

Gutman, Herbert G. *The Black Family in Slavery and Freedom, 1750–1925.* New York: Pantheon Books, 1976.

Hahn, Steven. *A Nation Under Our Feet: Black Political Struggles in the Rural South from Slavery to the Great Migration.* Cambridge, Mass.: Harvard University Press, 2003.

Halpern, David. *Social Capital.* Malden, Mass.: Polity Press, 2005.

Halttunen, Karen. *Confidence Men and Painted Women: A Study of Middle-Class Culture in America, 1830–1870.* New Haven, Conn.: Yale University Press, 1982.

Haynes, Robert V. *The Natchez District and the American Revolution.* Jackson: University Press of Mississippi, 1976.

Hicks, John D. *The Populist Revolt: A History of the Farmers Alliance and the Peoples Party.* 1931. Reprint, Omaha: University of Nebraska Press, 1961.

Higgs, Robert. *Blacks in the American Economy, 1865–1914.* New York: Cambridge University Press, 1977.

Holt, Michael F. *The Rise and Fall of the Whig Party: Jacksonian Politics and the Onset of the Civil War.* New York: Oxford University Press, 1999.

Horowitz, Daniel. *The Morality of Spending: Attitudes toward the Consumer Society in America, 1875–1940.* Baltimore: Johns Hopkins University Press, 1985.

James, D. Clayton. *Antebellum Natchez.* Baton Rouge: Louisiana State University Press, 1968.

Kane, Harnett. *Natchez on the Mississippi.* New York: William Morrow, 1947.

Kolchin, Peter. *American Slavery, 1619–1877.* New York: Hill and Wang, 1993.

Kyriakoudes, Louis M. *The Social Origins of the Urban South: Race, Gender, and Migration in Nashville and Middle Tennessee, 1890–1930.* Chapel Hill: University of North Carolina Press, 2003.

Laird, Pamela Walker. *Pull: Networking and Success since Benjamin Franklin.* Cambridge, Mass.: Harvard University Press, 2006.

Leach, William. *Land of Desire: Merchants, Power, and the Rise of a New American Culture.* New York: Vintage Books, 1993.

Linderman, Gerald F. *Embattled Courage: The Experience of Combat in the American Civil War.* New York: Free Press, 1987.

Litwack, Leon F. *Been in the Storm So Long: The Aftermath of Slavery.* New York: Vintage Books, 1980.

Mandle, Jay R. *Not Slave, Not Free: The African American Economic Experience since the Civil War.* Durham, N.C.: Duke University Press, 1992.

———. *The Roots of Black Poverty: The Southern Plantation Economy After the Civil War.* Durham, N.C.: Duke University Press, 1978.

McMillian, Neil R. *Dark Journey: Black Mississippians in the Age of Jim Crow.* Urbana: University of Illinois Press, 1990.

McPherson, James M. *Battle Cry of Freedom: The American Civil War Era.* 1989. Reprint, New York: Oxford University Press, 2003.

Mintz, Steven, and Susan Kellogg. *Domestic Revolutions: A Social History of American Family Life.* New York: Free Press, 1988.

Mokotoff, Gary. "Tracking Jewish-American Family History." In *The Source: A Guidebook to American Genealogy.* Salt Lake City, Utah: Ancestry, 1997.

Moore, Edith Wyatt. *Natchez Under-the-Hill.* Natchez, Miss.: Southern Historical Publications, 1958.

Moore, John Hebron. *Agriculture in Ante-Bellum Mississippi*. 1958. Reprint, New York: Octagon Books, 1971.
———. *The Emergence of the Cotton Kingdom in the Old Southwest, Mississippi, 1770–1860*. Baton Rouge: Louisiana State University Press, 1988.
Nash, Gerald D., ed. *Issues in American Economic History*. Lexington, Mass.: D. C. Heath, 1972.
Norris, James D. *R. G. Dun & Co., 1841–1900: The Development of Credit-Reporting in the Nineteenth Century*. Westport, Conn.: Greenwood Press, 1978.
Oakes, James. *The Ruling Race: A History of American Slaveholders*. New York: Vintage Books, 1982.
Olsen, Otto H., ed. *Reconstruction and Redemption in the South*. Baton Rouge: Louisiana State University Press, 1982.
Ownby, Ted. *American Dreams in Mississippi: Consumers, Poverty, and Culture, 1830–1998*. Chapel Hill: University of North Carolina Press, 1999.
Owsley, Frank L. *Plain Folk of the Old South*. 1949. Reprint, Baton Rouge: Louisiana State University Press, 1982.
Packer, Jerrold M. *American Nightmare: The History of Jim Crow*. New York: St. Martins Griffin, 2002.
Parker, William N., ed. *The Structure of the Cotton Economy of the Antebellum South*. Washington, D.C.: Agricultural History Society, 1970.
Percy, William Alexander. *Lanterns on the Levee*. New York: Alfred A. Knopf, 1941.
Pishel, Robert Gordon. *Natchez: The Museum City of the Old South*. Tulsa, Okla.: Magnolia Publishing, 1959.
Polk, Noel, ed. *Natchez before 1830*. Jackson: University Press of Mississippi, 1989.
Porter, Glenn. *The Rise of Big Business, 1860–1920*. Wheeling, Ill.: Harlan Davidson, 1973.
Porter, Glenn, and Harold C. Livesay. *Merchants and Manufacturers: Studies in the Changing Structure of Nineteenth-Century Marketing*. Baltimore: Johns Hopkins University Press, 1971.
Potter, David M., and Don E. Fehrenbacher, eds. *The Impending Crisis, 1848–1861*. New York: HarperPerennial, 1976.
Powell, Lawrence N. *New Masters: Northern Planters during the Civil War and Reconstruction*. New Haven, Conn.: Yale University Press, 1980.
Ransom, Roger L. *Conflict and Compromise: The Political Economy of Slavery, Emancipation, and the American Civil War*. New York: Cambridge University Press, 1989.
Ransom, Roger L., and Richard Sutch. *One Kind of Freedom: The Economic Consequences of Emancipation*. 1977. Reprint, New York: Cambridge University Press, 2001.
Rawski, Thomas G., ed. *Economics and the Historian*. Berkeley: University of California Press, 1996.
R. G. Dun. *The Mercantile Agency Reference Book, Louisiana*. Vol. 2. New York: R. G. Dun, 1917.
———. *The Mercantile Agency Reference Book, Mississippi*. Vol. 2. New York: R. G. Dun, 1917.
Roark, James L. *Masters without Slaves: Southern Planters in the Civil War and Reconstruction*. New York: W. W. Norton, 1977.
Rosengarten, Theodore. *All God's Dangers: The Life of Nate Shaw*. Chicago: University of Chicago Press, 1974.
Rothstein, Morton. *Resistance, Flight, and Adjustment: Natchez Elite Planters during and after the Civil War*. Davis: Agricultural History Center, University of California, 1985.

Rowland, Charles P. *The American Iliad: The Story of the Civil War*. New York: McGraw-Hill, 1991.
Rowland, Dunbar, ed. *History of Mississippi*. Vol. 1. Jackson, Miss.: S. J. Clarke, 1925.
———, ed. *Mississippi: Comprising Sketches of Counties, Towns, Events, Institutions, and Persons*. Vol. 2. Atlanta: Southern Historical Publishing Association, 1907.
———, ed. *Mississippi: Comprising Sketches of Counties, Towns, Events, Institutions, and Persons*. Vol. 3. Atlanta: Southern Historical Publishing Association, 1907.
Rowley, Hazel. *Richard Wright: The Life and Times*. New York: Henry Holt, 2001.
Royce, Edward. *The Origins of Southern Sharecropping*. Philadelphia: Temple University Press, 1993.
Sandage, Scott A. *Born Losers: A History of Failure in America*. Cambridge, Mass.: Harvard University Press, 2005.
Sansing, David G., et al. *Natchez: An Illustrated History*. Natchez, Miss.: Plantation Publishing, 1992.
Satcher, Buford. *Blacks in Mississippi Politics, 1865–1900*. Washington, D.C.: University Press of America, 1978.
Scarborough, William Kaufman. *Masters of the Big House: Elite Slaveholders of the Mid-Nineteenth-Century South*. Baton Rouge: Louisiana University Press, 2003.
———. *The Overseer: Plantation Management in the Old South*. 1966. Reprint, Athens: University of Georgia Press, 1984.
Schlereth, Thomas J. *Victoria America: Transformations in Everyday Life, 1976–1915*. New York: HarperCollins, 1991.
Schweikart, Larry. *Banking in the American South from the Age of Jackson to Reconstruction*. Baton Rouge: Louisiana University Press, 1987.
Schweninger, Loren. *Black Property Owners in the South, 1790–1915*. Urbana: University of Illinois Press, 1990.
Scott, Anne Firor. *The Southern Lady: From Pedestal to Politics, 1830–1930*. Charlottesville: University Press of Virginia, 1970.
Sellers, Charles. *The Market Revolution: Jacksonian America, 1815–1846*. New York: Oxford University Press, 1991.
Shore, Laurence. *Southern Capitalists: The Ideological Leadership of an Elite, 1832–1885*. Chapel Hill: University of North Carolina Press, 1986.
Smith, Mark M. *Mastered by the Clock: Time, Slavery, and Freedom in the American South*. Chapel Hill: University of North Carolina Press, 1997.
Stover, John F. *The Railroads of the South: A Study in Finance and Control*. Chapel Hill: University of North Carolina Press, 1955.
Summers, Mark Wahlgren. *The Gilded Age, or Hazard of New Functions*. Upper Saddle River, N.J.: Prentice-Hall, 1997.
———. *Railroads, Reconstruction, and the Gospel of Prosperity: Aid under the Radical Republicans, 1865–1877*. Princeton, N.J.: Princeton University Press, 1984.
Sydnor, Charles S. *A Gentleman of the Old Natchez District: Benjamin L. C. Wailes*. Westport, Conn.: Greenwood Press, 1970.
Taylor, Walter Nesbit, and George H. Etheridge, eds. *Mississippi: A History*. Vol. 4. Jackson, Miss.: Historical Record Association, n.d.
Turitz, Leo E., and Evelyn Turitz. *Jews in Early Mississippi*. Jackson: University Press of Mississippi, 1983.

Usner, Daniel H. *Indians, Settlers, and Slaves in a Frontier Exchange Economy.* Chapel Hill: University of North Carolina Press, 1992.
Wayne, Michael. *The Reshaping of Plantation Society: The Natchez District, 1860–1880.* Baton Rouge: Louisiana State University Press, 1983.
Weissbach, Lee S. *Jewish Life in Small Town America: A History.* New Haven, Conn.: Yale University Press, 2005.
Wells, Jonathan Daniel. *The Origins of the South Middle Class, 1800–1861.* Chapel Hill: University of North Carolina Press, 2004.
Wharton, Vernon Lane. *The Negro in Mississippi, 1865–1890.* 1947. Reprint, Greenwood Press, 1984.
Wiebe, Robert H. *A Search for Order, 1877–1920.* New York: Hill and Wang, 1967.
Wiener, Jonathan M. *Social Origins of the New South: Alabama, 1860–1885.* Baton Rouge: Louisiana State University Press, 1978.
Williamson, Joel. *A Rage for Order: Black and White Relations in the American South since Emancipation.* New York: Oxford University Press, 1986.
Willis, John C. *Forgotten Time: The Yazoo-Mississippi Delta after the Civil War.* Charlottesville: University of Virginia Press, 2000.
Woodman, Harold D. *King Cotton and His Retainers: Financing and Marketing the Cotton Crops of the South, 1800–1925.* Lexington: University of Kentucky Press, 1968.
———. *New South—New Law.* Baton Rouge: Louisiana State University Press, 1995.
Woodward, C. Vann. *Origins of the New South, 1877–1913.* Baton Rouge: Louisiana State University Press, 1951.
———. *Strange Career of Jim Crow.* New York: Oxford University Press, 1955.
Wright, Gavin. *Old South, New South: Revolutions in the Southern Economy since the Civil War.* New York: Basic Books, 1986.
———. *The Political Economy of the Cotton South: Households, Markets, and Wealth in the Nineteenth Century.* New York: W. W. Norton, 1978.
Wyatt-Brown, Bertram. *Southern Honor: Ethics and Behavior in the Old South.* New York: Oxford University Press, 1982.
———. *The Shaping of Southern Culture: Honor, Grace, and War, 1760–1880s.* Chapel Hill: University of North Carolina Press, 2001.

Articles and Essays

Anderson, George L. "The South and Problems of Post Civil War Finance." *Journal of Southern History* 9 (June 1943): 181–195.
Atherton, Lewis E. "The Problem of Credit Rating in the Ante-Bellum South." *Journal of Southern History* 12 (November 1946): 534–556.
Bigelow, Martha Mitchell. "Freedmen of the Mississippi Valley, 1862–1865." *Civil War History* 8 (March 1962): 38–47.
Bull, Jacqueline P. "The General Merchant in the Economic History of the New South." *Journal of Southern History* 18 (February 1952): 37–59.
Byrne, Frank J. "The Merchant in Antebellum Southern Literature and Society." *American Nineteenth Century History* 6 (March 2005): 33–55.
Cabaniss, Francis Allen, and James Allen. "Religion in Mississippi since 1860." *Journal of Mississippi History* 9 (January 1947): 207–216.

Calhoun, Robert Dabney. "A History of Concordia Parish, Louisiana, 1768–1931." *Louisiana Historical Quarterly* 15 (January 1932): 44–67; 15 (April 1932): 214–233; 15 (July 1932): 428–452; 15 (October 1932): 618–645: 16 (January 1933): 92-124.

Carlton, David L., and Peter A. Coclanis. "Capital Mobilization and Southern Industry, 1880–1905: The Case of the Carolina Piedmont." *Journal of Economic History* 49 (March 1989): 73–94.

Clark, Thomas D. "The Furnishing and Supply System in Southern Agriculture since 1865." *Journal of Southern History* 12 (February 1946): 24–44.

Coleman, James S. "Social Capital in the Creation of Human Capital." *American Journal of Sociology* 94 (Fall 1988): 95-120.

Cox, LaWanda. "The Promise Land for Freedmen." *Mississippi Valley Historical Review* 45 (December 1958): 413–440.

Daniel, Pete. "The Metamorphosis of Slavery, 1965–1900." *Journal of American History* 66 (June 1979): 88–99.

Davis, Ronald L. F. "The U.S. Army and the Origins of Sharecropping in the Natchez District- A Case Study." *Journal of Negro History* 62 (January 1977): 60–80.

Ellis, L. Tuffly. "The New Orleans Cotton Exchange: The Formative Years, 1871–1880." *Journal of Southern History* 39 (November 1973): 545–564.

Ferleger, Louis. "Sharecropping Contracts in the Late-Nineteenth-Century South." *Agricultural History* 67 (Summer 1993): 31–46.

Ford, Lacy K. "Rednecks and Merchants: Economic Development and Social Tensions in the South Carolina Upcountry, 1865–1900." *Journal of American History* 71 (September 1984): 294–318.

Granovetter, Mark S. "The Strength of Weak Ties." *American Journal of Sociology* 78 (May 1973): 1360-1380.

Greenberg, Kenneth S. "The Civil War and Redistribution of Land: Adams County, Mississippi, 1865–1870." *Agricultural History* 52 (April 1978): 292–307.

Higgs, Robert. "Race, Tenure, and Resource Allocation in Southern Agriculture, 1865–1910." *Journal of Economic History* 33 (March 1973): 149–169.

Huffman, Frank J., Jr. "Town and Country in the South, 1850–1880: A Comparison of Urban and Rural Social Structures." *South Atlantic Quarterly* 76 (Summer 1977): 366–381.

Jones, Lu Ann. "Gender, Race, and Itinerant Commerce in the Rural New South." *Journal of Southern History* 66 (May 2000): 297–320.

Kyriakoudes, Louis. "Lower-Order Urbanization and Territorial Monopoly in the Southern Furnishing Trade: Alabama, 1871–1890." *Social Science History* 26 (Spring 2002): 179–198.

Marler, Scott P. "'An Abiding Faith in Cotton': The Merchant Capitalist Community of New Orleans, 1860–1862." *Civil War History* 54 (Fall 2008): 247-276.

———. "Merchants in the Transition to a New South: Central Louisiana, 1840–1880." *Louisiana History* 42 (Spring 2001): 165–192.

Mechling, Jay. "The Failure of Folklore in Richard Wright's *Black Boy*." *Journal of American Folklore* 104 (Summer 1991): 275–294.

Neal, Ernest E., and Lewis W. Jones. "The Place of the Negro Farmer in the Changing Economy of the Cotton South, 1880–1950." *Rural Sociology* 15 (March 1950): 30–51.

Olegario, Rowena. "'That Mysterious People': Jewish Merchants, Transparency, and Community in Mid-Nineteenth-Century America." *Business History Review* 73 (Summer 1999): 161–189.

Reid, Joseph D. "Sharecropping as an Understandable Market Response: The Post-Bellum South." *Journal of Economic History* 33 (March 1973): 106–130.

Ross, Michael A. "Resisting the New South: Commercial Crisis and Decline in New Orleans, 1865–85." *American Nineteenth-Century History* 4 (Spring 2003): 59–76.

Rothstein, Morton. "The Antebellum South as a Dual Economy: A Tentative Hypothesis." *Agricultural History* 41 (October 1967): 373-382.

———. "The New South and the International Economy." *Agricultural History* 57 (Fall 1983): 385–402.

———. Review of *King Cotton and His Retainers: Financing and Marketing the Cotton Crop of the South*, by Harold D. Woodman. *Journal of Southern History* 34 (August 1968): 431–433.

Schlomowitz, Ralph. "The Origins of Southern Sharecropping." *Agricultural History* 53 (July 1979): 557–575.

Schweikart, Larry. "Secession and Southern Banks." *Civil War History* 31 (June 1985): 111–125.

Sitterson, J. Carlyle. "The Transition from Slave to Free Economy on the William J. Minor Plantations." *Agricultural History* 17 (October 1943): 216–224.

Somers, Dale A. "New Orleans at War: A Merchant's View." *Louisiana History* 14 (Winter 1973): 49–68.

Suarez, Raleigh A. "Bargains, Bills, and Bankruptcies: Business Activity in Rural Antebellum Louisiana." *Louisiana History* 7 (Summer 1966): 189–206.

Weaver, Herbert. "Foreigners in Ante-Bellum Mississippi." *Journal of Mississippi History* 16 (Spring 1954): 151–156.

Weiher, Kenneth. "The Cotton Industry and Southern Urbanization, 1880–1930." *Explorations in Economic History* 14 (1977): 120–140.

Wiener, Jonathan M. "Class Structure and Economic Development in the American South, 1865–1955." *American Historical Review* 84 (October 1979): 970–1006.

———. "Planter Merchant Conflict in Reconstruction Alabama." *Past and Present* 68 (August 1975): 73–94.

Whitfield, Stephen J. "Commercial Passions: The Southern Jew as Businessman." *American Jewish History* 71 (March 1982): 342-357.

Woodman, Harold D. "Class, Race, Politics and the Modernization of the Postbellum South." *Journal of Southern History* 63 (February 1997): 3–22.

———. "Class Structure and Economic Development in the American South, 1865–1955: Comments in AHR Forum." *American Historical Review* 84 (October 1979): 993-1001.

———. "The Decline of Cotton Factorage after the Civil War." *American Historical Review* 71 (July 1966): 1219–1236.

———. "Economic History and Economic Theory: The New Economic History in America." *Journal of Interdisciplinary History* 3 (Autumn 1972): 323–350.

———. "One Kind of Freedom After 20 Years: Comment." *Explorations in Economic History* 38 (November 2001): 48–57.

———. "Post–Civil War Southern Agricultural and the Land." *Agricultural History* 62 (January 1979): 319–337.

———. "The Political Economy of the New South: Retrospect's and Prospects." *Journal of Southern History* 67 (November 2001): 789–810.

———. "The Profitability of Slavery: A Historical Perennial." *Journal of Southern History* 29 (August 1963): 303–325.

———. "Sequel to Slavery: The New History Views the Postbellum South." *Journal of Southern History* 43 (November 1977): 523–554.

Wright, Gavin. "The Strange Career of the New Southern Economic History." *Reviews in American History* 67 (December 1982): 164–180.

Dissertations, Theses, and Unpublished Scholarship

Dresser, Rebecca M. "The Minor Family of Natchez: A Case of Southern Unionism." M.A. thesis, California State University, Northridge, 2000.

Marler, Scott P. "Merchants and the Political Economy of Nineteenth-Century Louisiana: New Orleans and Its Hinterlands." Ph.D. diss., Rice University, 2007.

The Natchez Jewish Experience. Produced and Directed by Edward Cohen. 18 min. Museum of the Southern Jewish Experience, 1994. Videocassette.

Vanderford, Chad V. "Peter Little: From Merchant to Planter." M.A. thesis, California State University, Northridge, 2000.

Index

A. F. Jacobs & Bros. Co., 95, 109, 147, 193, 196, 204, 209
Aaron Beekman & Co. (& Son), 82, 93, 96, 102, 112, 125, 172, 206, 219
Abbott, Ann (merchant), 52, 92, 130, 158–59, 196
Abbott, William (merchant), 41, 45, 51–52, 73, 81–82, 153, 168, 176
Abbott & Henderson Co., 51, 82
Abbott family (merchants), 8, 87, 221n6
Adams County, Miss.: board of supervisors of, 174, 195, 207, 223n15; building and loan association of, 128; census of, 43–44, 107; chattel contracts in, 84–85, 91–94, 107; courts in, 182, 188–93; flooding in, 203–4; government officials, 74, 106, 118, 138; plantations in, 3, 26, 31, 71, 95–96, 101, 113, 119, 129, 193; taxes in, 127, 195, 203–4, 207
Adams Manufacturing Co., 137, 170
Adolf Jacobs & Co. (& Son), 72, 76, 95, 109, 130, 147–48, 176, 196
Agriculture: financing of, 5, 50, 52, 89, 102–3, 148, 230n34; hazards to, 75, 80, 112, 118, 149, 184–88, 195–97, 201–5, 218, 254n39; mono-crop, 200, 203; self-sufficiency in, 108, 197, 220; technology and improvements of, 99, 144, 204
Allendale (plantation), 193–94, 239n2
Amite County, Miss., 206–7
Armand Perrault & Co., 34, 64, 66–68, 92, 95, 129, 134, 150, 205
Atlanta, Ga., 40–41, 144, 163, 178

Baker, E. B. (merchant), 52–53
Baldwin, Hiram H. (merchant), 119, 187–88, 201
Bank of Mississippi, 24
Basaucon, L. A. (newspaperman), 49
Bayridge (plantation), 127
Beekman, Aaron (merchant), 11, 29, 44, 57, 61, 83, 104, 123, 128, 132, 134, 136, 150, 153, 165, 191, 195, 204, 208, 243n28, 244n38
Beekman, Marcus (physician), 161
Beekman, Phillip (physician), 161, 212
Beekman, Rosalie, 12, 222n5
Beekman family, 7, 13, 54, 86–87, 92, 132, 161, 218, 221n6, 231n41
Bennett, Calvin S. (planter), 130
Bettman, Bloom & Co., 82
Bitterwood (plantation), 93, 128
Black Codes, 79, 105
Bledsoe, John R. (agent), 112–13
Block, Samuel (merchant), 58, 69, 142, 157, 172–73, 190–91, 200, 252n18
Blommart, John (merchant), 17–18
Blue Ridge (plantation), 68, 129
Boosterism (New South), 163, 169, 178, 250n49
Botto, Louis (merchant), 41, 68, 143, 164
Bourgeois (and middle class): antebellum role of, 143–44; lifestyle of, 149, 157, 159, 162; political influence of, 26, 177, 215; socio-economic status of, 30–31, 33, 39, 41–43, 45, 47–49, 52, 67, 73, 141, 157, 159, 215

Brandon, Gerard (governor), 102
Brandon, Samuel (planter), 77
Brandon Hall (plantation), 101–2, 237n40
Breckinridge, John C. (Confederate general), 40
Breckinridge Guards, 40, 51
Britton, Audley (banker), 168–69, 171–72
Britton and Koontz Bank, 50, 119, 153, 167, 173, 188, 191, 196, 201, 204
Buckner, Henry S. (cotton factor), 29, 46
Buckner and Newman Co., 43, 46–48, 81, 83, 119, 135, 230n34
Burns, Patrick (merchant), 65, 164
Burr, Aaron (vice-president), 25

Campbell family (planters and bankers), 160, 175, 211–12
Cannon, William S. (planter), 50, 85
Carlton, David, 10
Carpenter, Alan D. (planter), 49, 124, 150, 221, 228n20
Carpenter, Dicks & Co., 98, 136–37, 154, 167, 170
Carpenter, Joseph N. (merchant), 40, 44, 47–50, 73, 81, 116–18, 123–24, 136–37, 139, 150, 157–58, 168–69, 208, 211, 226n1
Carpenter, Nathaniel Leslie, I (merchant), 40, 44, 48–49, 150
Carpenter, Nathaniel Leslie, II (businessman), 161, 208
Carpenter family, 8, 41, 49, 50–51, 86–87, 92–94, 104, 124, 133, 137, 139, 155, 160–61, 167, 170–71, 219, 221n6
Carpetbaggers, 7, 37–38, 52, 174, 217, 229n26
Carradine, James (merchant), 45, 164, 204
Carter, Dr. Robert and Pauline (planters), 136
Carter's Lake (plantation), 192
Cedar Grove (plantation), 102
Chandler, Alfred, Jr., 143
Chattel mortgage. *See* Mortgages: chattel
Cheripa (plantation), 95, 122–23
Chicago, Ill., 199, 208
China Grove (plantation), 106
Churches-Synagogues. *See* Religion

Cincinnati, Ohio, 36, 52, 146, 160–61, 167, 173, 211
Civil War: battles of, 8, 11, 40–41, 54, 222n1, 222n3, 222n5; conditions during, 11–14, 31–38, 40, 53–54, 58–59, 65, 71, 78, 82–83, 199, 222n1, 222n3, 222n5, 226n1; eve of, 30, 42, 73, 215; mentioned, 4, 7, 9, 23, 26–27, 73, 126, 131; veterans of, 41, 52, 65, 81, 145, 168
Clermont (plantation), 116
Clifford (plantation), 130
Clifton (plantation), 124, 129
Clifton (villa and grounds), 37, 124, 129, 139
Clifton Heights. *See* Subdivisions
Commission merchants. *See* Merchants
Concordia Parish, La.: courts in, 100, 142, 192, 194–95; flooding in, 118, 149, 185, 195, 203; parish government of, 58, 174–75, 194, 203, 250n51; plantations in, 61, 67, 85, 93, 95–97, 99, 118, 122, 125–27, 195, 203, 229n26, 236n34; railroads in, 142, 172–74, 177, 181–82, 191
Concordia Planting Co., 131
Confederate States of America: army units of, 8, 40–42, 60, 66, 83, 168, 222n1, 226n1; currency of, 34, 58, 63–65, 123–24, 132–34, 226n47; government of, 34, 40, 222n1; guerillas of, 31, 78, 222n1; "lost cause" of, 13, 174, 178; veterans of, 7–8, 13, 40–41, 46, 52, 54, 60, 63, 65–68, 73, 81, 83, 142, 145, 160, 168, 172, 217, 226n1
Cotton: boll weevil, 88–89, 101, 185–86, 196–97, 199, 203, 207–11, 218; crops, 32, 72, 75–76, 80, 84, 99, 105, 110, 114, 118–19, 149, 152, 158, 185, 197, 200–203, 216, 221; futures trading of, 183, 186, 199; gins and ginning of, 40, 49–50, 117, 133, 153, 204; handling of, 21, 23, 27, 30, 40, 46, 48–49, 72, 75, 96–98, 100–101, 121, 126, 132, 135–36, 156, 197, 216–17; marketing of, 5, 10, 14, 27, 143, 197, 218; mills, 59, 65, 115, 136–37, 154, 163, 169–70, 173, 185, 195, 198, 200–201, 204, 217, 219, 249n44; prices of, 27, 29, 88, 90, 101, 108, 118–19, 183, 186, 196–99,

218, 220; shipping of, 23, 26, 30, 53, 65, 82–83, 94, 97–98, 110, 114, 119, 171, 181, 184, 217, 240n3
Credit. *See* Merchants
Crop Lien System, 74, 78, 80, 93, 101, 109, 115, 119, 180, 184–85, 216
Crop liens. *See* Mortgages
Crozet, Antoine (financier), 15
Culture: of business, 142–57, 163–64, 168–74; of education, 68, 160–61, 178, 207; household and domestic, 58, 64, 147, 158–60, 178, 180; of politics, 174–78; of travel, 146, 156–58, 160–62, 173

D'Armond (plantation), 129
Davis, Alfred V. (planter), 118
Davis, Ronald L. F., 9, 237n34
De Marco, Prospero (merchant), 68
Debt: foreclosure on, 9, 68, 75, 102, 112–14, 116, 120, 122, 135; mortgage, 6, 74–78, 84–89, 97, 107–9, 114–15, 120, 124–26, 128–30, 133–36, 148, 192, 196, 235n26, 239n1–2, 241n15; supply, 4, 72, 74–77, 93–94, 102, 112, 120, 122, 127–30, 189, 192–94, 205, 236n31; tax, 9, 75, 102, 112–14, 116, 118, 120, 125–28, 133, 142, 155, 174, 195–96, 203, 243n27
Deerpark (plantation), 122, 130, 148
Democratic Party, 174
Depressions, 30, 112, 186
Dicks, John A. (businessman), 47, 50, 117, 136–37, 139, 167, 169–71
Disasters: epidemic, 25, 122, 185, 188, 201–2; fire, 12, 47, 57, 185, 201, 204–5, 222; flooding, 3, 75, 85, 112, 118, 149, 185, 195, 203, 243n28; insects, 75, 185, 203; tornado, 202
Doyle, Don H., 10
Dunbar, William (planter), 18, 20–21, 24, 225n38
Dunbar (plantation), 107
Dunbarton Planting Co., 131
Duncan, Dr. Steven (planter), 24, 27–28, 49
Duncan, Steven, Jr. (planter), 118, 168, 171, 241n10
Dunleith (mansion), 137, 157, 188

E. B. Baker & Sons Co., 52–53
E. J. Perrault Co., 68
Education. *See* Culture
Egypt (plantation), 102
Ellicott, Andrew (U.S. commissioner), 20
Ellis Cliffs (plantation), 148
Ellis family (planters), 24
Emerald Mound (plantation), 68, 129
European: anti-Semitism, 54; colonial period, 15–21; goods, 15–23, 61; immigration, 6–7, 29, 41, 43–45, 55–56, 63–64, 104, 161, 215, 252n20; mercantile tradition, 29, 43; travel, 146, 158, 160–61

Factors. *See* Merchants
Farrar, Daniel S. (planter), 193–94, 239n2
Fayette, Miss., 112, 129, 230n34, 239n1–2, 240n3
First Natchez Bank, 129–30, 211, 243n31, 256n56
Fisk, Alvarez (merchant), 29
Flatboats, 20, 23
Fleming, James S. (merchant), 48, 52, 92, 159, 172, 175, 209
Fleming, John (merchant), 47–48, 52, 69, 150, 187
Fleming & Baldwin Co. 33, 37, 48, 51–52, 55, 73, 81, 83–84, 109, 118–19, 122, 133, 150, 187–88, 198, 230n34, 239n53
Fleming family (merchants), 8, 52, 221n6
Fletcher (plantation), 93, 95, 122–23, 131, 194
Ford, Emma and Rufus (planters), 124
Forest (plantation), 99, 125–26
Frank, Henry (merchant), 45, 54, 59, 61, 117, 127, 142, 156, 158, 165–66, 168–69, 172, 192, 200
Franklin County, Miss., 84, 91–93, 118, 124
Fraternal Organizations: Benevolent Order of Elks, 167–68; Ezra Lodge, 116, 166, 191; Hibernian Benevolent Association, 165; Italian Benevolent Association, 165; Knights of Columbus, 165; Odd Fellows, 167
Freedmen (African Americans): contraband camps and refugees, 13, 71–73, 78; as

farmers, 72, 74, 148, 186; as landowners and planters, 74, 106, 108–9, 121, 129–30, 207–8; marketplace of, 14, 32, 38, 55, 58, 71, 104–5, 140, 207–8, 215–16, 218; as politicians and officials, 74, 106, 129, 138, 174, 189, 193, 206–8, 253n22; racism against, 104–5, 158, 162, 185, 205–6, 218; as sharecroppers and tenants, 3–4, 72–78, 80–81, 101–4, 106–10, 192–93, 206–8; as Union soldiers, 32, 36, 71, 78

Freedmen's Bureau, 37, 73, 78–79, 105

Friedler, Isaac (merchant), 60–61, 73, 82, 87, 90–91, 95, 100, 123, 125–27, 129, 131, 135–36, 142, 147, 150, 153, 161, 172–75, 192, 194, 200, 235n26, 236n31, 236n34, 244n38

Friedler, Joseph (merchant), 61, 131, 150, 167, 209, 231n6

Friedler family, 7, 86–87, 93, 104, 161, 221n6, 231n6

Gaither, H. B. (banker), 211–12

Galilee (plantation), 112–13, 239n1, 240n3

Galvez, Bernardo de (Spanish governor), 18

Gastrell, Henry M. (merchant), 69, 82, 168, 172–73, 180–85, 187–89

Gayoso de Lemos, Manuel (Spanish governor), 18, 223n17

Geisenberger, Abraham H. (lawyer), 106, 147, 231n41

Geisenberger, Benjamin C., 60, 176

Geisenberger, Sam (merchant), 4, 61, 131, 231n41

Geisenberger, Wolfe (merchant), 4, 60–61, 73, 83, 90, 92, 106, 135–36, 147, 154, 158, 166, 193, 255n43

Geisenberger & Benjamin Co., 60

Geisenberger & Friedler Co., 61, 131, 147, 167, 209

Geisenberger family (merchants), 7, 60, 87, 90, 92, 104, 160, 219, 221n6, 231n40

George T. Payne & Co., 72, 87, 95–98

Gilded Age, 8, 39, 130, 140, 143, 150, 163, 171, 178, 217

Good Hope (plantation), 123

Grady, Henry (newspaperman), 163, 178

Grafton (plantation), 109, 119, 239n53

Grafton, Thomas (newspaperman), 168

Grange (and Populism), 185, 205–6

Grant, Ulysses S. (U.S. general), 11, 13, 32, 53, 59, 71, 83

Great Migration, 186

Griffin, Henry C. (mayor), 143, 177

Grove (plantation), 74, 102

H. M. Gastrell & Co., 37, 69, 82, 180–83, 198, 201

Harding, Lyman (lawyer), 25

Hart, John (merchant and planter), 65, 100

Hart, Thomas (merchant), 41, 65, 189–90, 252n15

Hastings, William and Sina (planters), 128, 243n28

Hedges (plantation), 74

Henderson, John (merchant), 20, 22

Henderson, John W. (merchant), 45, 51, 82

Henderson, Thomas (merchant), 12, 42, 45

Henderson & Co., 22–23

Henderson & Peale Co., 51

Henry Frank & Co., 37, 57–59, 61, 189–90, 194–95, 204, 252n15, 252n20

Hill, John Henry (merchant), 60, 82–83, 122–23, 229n29

Homestead (plantation), 119

Homochitto (plantation), 74, 148

Hunt, Abijah (merchant), 24–25

Hutchins, Anthony (planter), 17–18

Hutchins, John (planter), 19

Illnesses: diphtheria, 202; infant mortality, 186, 210; malaria, 186, 201–2; mental, 210–11; smallpox, 202; yellow fever, 25, 122, 185, 188, 201–2

Immigrants: English, 7, 28, 43–45, 61–64, 68; French, 7, 43, 62–64, 66, 164; German and German Jewish, 7, 12, 29, 32, 41–45, 54–55, 57–58, 61–63, 134, 150, 160–61, 190, 215, 229n29; Irish, 6–7, 17, 28–29, 41, 43–45, 62–68, 150, 164–65, 167, 176–77, 189, 215; Italian, 7, 41, 43–45, 63–64, 67–68, 150, 164–65, 167, 176–77, 215; Russian Jewish, 7, 43–45, 61–62

Ingleside (plantation), 74
Intelligencer, The, 21, 23, 224n24
Isaac Friedler & Co., 87, 90–91, 95–97, 99–100, 106, 123, 125–27
Isaac Lowenburg & Co., 57–60, 76–77, 80, 84–85, 87, 92–93, 95, 97, 99, 102, 106, 112–14, 121–24, 127, 130–31, 134–38, 143, 161, 167, 172, 176, 189–90, 193–95, 205–6, 209–10, 212–13, 219, 239n1–3, 243n28, 256n56

J. C. Schwartz Hardware Co., 33–37, 66–67, 154–55
J. N. Carpenter & Co., 102, 118, 123–24, 137, 226n1
Jackson, Daniel and Louisa (farmers), 101, 237–38n40
Jackson, Miss., 34, 143, 156, 161, 172–73, 200, 226n47
Jacobs, Aaron (merchant), 147, 176, 209
Jacobs, Adolf (merchant), 61, 135, 147–48, 208–9
Jacobs, Albert C. (merchant), 131, 147, 176, 208–9
Jacobs, Simon (merchant), 61–62, 135, 162, 165
Jacobs family (merchants), 7, 60, 62, 86–87, 90, 94, 140, 147–48, 150, 161, 167, 218, 221n6
Jefferson County, Miss., 56, 68, 84, 85–86, 92–94, 112, 114, 121, 124, 126, 129, 143, 174, 230n34, 239n1–3
John Mayer & Son Co., 33, 57
Jones, George W. (planter), 122, 127
Julius Weis & Co., 98

Kibbeville (plantation), 93, 124
Klapp, George G. (planter), 50, 52, 117–18, 137, 229
Kyriakoudes, Louis, 10, 94

La Salle, Robert Cavalier de (explorer), 15
Lambert, James (newspaperman), 143, 164, 166
L'Argent (plantation), 123, 235n26
Learned, Rufus F. (businessman), 167, 172

Leathers, Thomas P. (steamboat captain, *Natchez* vs. *Robert E. Lee*), 3, 49
Lehmann family (merchants), 55, 61
Lemle, Isadore (merchant), 174–75
Lemle, Marx (merchant), 54, 57–58, 83–84
Lemle family, 7, 54, 58, 86–87, 91, 104, 129, 134–36, 158, 209, 221n6
Lien laws. *See* Crop Lien System
Ligon, Harriet, and sons (planters), 148
Lincoln, Abraham (president), 77, 83, 224n33
Lincoln, Henry and Lucinda (farmers), 77
Lintot family (planters), 18, 20
Liverpool, England, 21, 27, 103, 199, 208
Livestock, 17, 72, 85, 89, 99, 113, 117, 125, 133, 157, 184, 190, 193–94, 237n37, 252n15
Loch Leven (plantation), 82–83, 119, 122
Loch Ness (plantation), 93
Lochdale (plantation), 119
Locust Hill (plantation), 119
Lone Pine (plantation), 93
Lorie family (merchants), 61, 82, 134, 201, 244n38
Louisiana: chattel mortgage system in, 78, 80, 84, 86, 91; freed slaves from, 78–80, 109; mentioned, 28, 31, 58, 137, 142; Natchez District of, 5, 16, 214; taxes in, 113, 126, 194
Louisville, Ky., 27, 36, 63, 146, 153, 156, 178
Lowenburg, Isaac (merchant), 7–8, 32, 54, 59, 62, 67, 73, 82–83, 112, 126–28, 134, 136–37, 139, 142, 153, 155–56, 161–62, 165–66, 168–69, 172–73, 176–77, 200–201, 209–10, 236n31, 239n1–2, 240n3
Lowenburg, Ophelia Mayer, 59, 159–60, 210
Lowenburg, Samuel (merchant), 59, 204
Lowenburg, Simon "Sim" (merchant), 130–31, 158, 161, 171–72, 194, 210–13, 256n56
Lowenburg family, 7, 92–93, 104, 116, 134, 139, 155–56, 158–61, 213, 219, 221n6, 231n41, 256n56
Lyman, Phineas and Thaddeus (soldier settlers), 17
Lynch, John R. (congressman and planter), 74, 106, 129, 208
Lynch, William (planter), 106

Maher, Fred (merchant), 68–69, 129, 164
Mallery, William H. (merchant), 139, 177
Manufacturing, 30, 50, 81, 117, 136–37, 143–44, 150, 162–63, 169–71, 185, 198, 200, 207–8
Manuscript census, 6, 31, 42–45, 49, 65, 72, 101, 107
Marron, John (merchant), 41, 65, 164–65
Marsh, Cyrus (merchant), 42, 83–84
Marshall, Levin R. (planter), 127, 273n26
Martin, William T. (Confederate general and lawyer), 13, 142, 160, 168, 172, 193–94
Marx Lemle & Co., 58, 91, 95, 97–99, 195
Mayer, John (merchant), 13, 33, 54, 57, 59, 134, 150, 158
Mayer, Simon (merchant), 41, 169
Mayer family (merchants), 54, 57, 59, 60, 69, 134, 150, 158, 160, 231n41
Mazique, August and Sarah (planters), 106
McCoy, James, Richard, and family (planters), 112–14, 121, 126, 239n1, 239n3
McCoy Place (plantation), 112–14, 127, 243n28
McGrew, Simon, and family (planters), 109, 239n53
McPherson, John (merchant), 66
McPherson & Perrault Co., 66
Mellon, William F., and family (lawyers and businessmen), 49, 150
Memphis, Tenn., 11, 27, 33, 72, 208
Merchants: antebellum role of, 14, 19–33, 42–43, 55–58, 63–65, 73, 104, 123, 133–34, 140; clerks of, 8, 29, 41, 44, 52, 145–46, 149, 151–52, 154–55, 162; competition of, 29, 68, 94–96, 104, 183, 205, 216; cultural communities of, 6–8, 10, 40–70, 104, 110, 115, 144–45, 150, 164–67, 176–77, 210, 214–16, 231n47; factors and coastal commission merchants, 5, 21, 27–32, 46, 57, 81, 92, 94, 98, 100, 103, 110, 124, 143, 188–89, 216; family life of, 149–52, 155–62; gentrification of, 186, 208–9; investments of, 115–17, 123–26, 130–31, 134–39, 143, 169–71, 173–74, 180–83, 187–88, 198–200, 209; as landlords, 8, 52, 55, 64, 81–82, 94–98, 115–17, 122–25, 129, 132–33, 155, 227n4; litigation of, 99–100, 182, 184, 188–94, 211–13; monopolies of, 10, 94, 216; plantation ownership of, 25, 52, 63–66, 68, 75, 92–96, 99, 109, 112–17, 119–32, 140–41, 155, 175, 178, 182, 188, 205, 216–17, 239n2; as providers of credit and supplies, 4–5, 8–10, 14, 19–23, 25–29, 31–32, 38, 50–52, 55, 62, 71–132, 140–41, 146–49, 153–55, 180, 183–85, 197–98, 200, 205–7, 209, 214–19; work routine of, 149–57
Metcalfe, James (planter), 48
Meyer, Weis, and Deutsch Co., 57, 59, 124
Miles, Orange and Ann (planters), 124, 128–29, 205
Minor, Henry C. (planter), 37
Minor, Katherine Surget (planter), 154, 200
Minor, Steven (planter), 221, 223n17
Minor family (planters), 18, 25, 37, 223n17
Minorca (plantation), 192
Mississippi: delta, 28, 30; river, 11, 15, 20–21, 59, 61, 63, 91, 139, 170, 172–73, 185, 205, 215, 235n26, 235n28; river steamships, 3, 26–27, 40, 49, 69, 117, 156, 180, 182; river valley, 78; state government, 26–27, 74, 80, 102, 127, 196, 207; state taxes, 194–96, 207
Mortgages: chattel, 6, 78, 84–89, 94, 103, 106–7, 120–21, 148, 175, 190, 192, 196, 235n26; crop liens, 4, 76–78, 80–92, 99, 101–2, 109–10, 115–16, 119–20, 180, 184–85, 192, 200, 216; general, 84–85; trust deeds, 85–93, 102, 106, 109, 112–15, 120–21, 124–30, 147, 175, 196, 227n15, 241n15, 243n28
Morville (plantation), 122
Moses, Clara Lowenburg, 155–61, 209–11, 256n56
Moses, David, and family (merchants), 54, 58, 150, 211, 230n36, 244n78
Mount Welcome (plantation), 74, 106, 119

N. L. Carpenter & Sons, 40, 49–50, 228n20
Nabobs. *See* Planters
Nalle & Cammack Co., 65, 98
Nashville, Tenn., 30, 40

Natchez: board of trade, 169; city government of, 8, 26, 46, 74, 106, 130, 143, 162–64, 166, 173–78, 194–96, 200, 202, 207, 250n54; city taxes, 195–96; cotton and merchants exchange, 59, 62, 65, 67, 167, 204; cotton mills, 59, 65, 136–37, 169–71, 173, 201; cotton square, 132; district, 4–10, 13–24, 27, 31, 38–39, 60, 73–80, 83–98, 101, 106–8, 110, 115–17, 133, 142, 178, 185, 197, 205–7, 212, 214–20, 243n28, 254n39; Fencibles, 41, 51; forks-in-the-road, 26; Indians, 16; justice court, 193–94, 252n14; Light Guards Infantry, 41, 66, 168; under-the-hill and river landing, 11–12, 15, 17, 19–20, 122

Natchez Democrat, 18, 137–38, 143, 170, 188, 200

Natchez Weekly Courier, 12

New Orleans, La., 3, 11, 16–19, 21–23, 27, 29–30, 35–37, 46, 48–51, 56–57, 61, 63, 65, 68, 81–83, 96–98, 100, 103, 119, 122, 124–26, 143–44, 146, 156–58, 160–61, 169, 173, 189–91, 199–200, 208, 211, 213, 215–16, 224n33, 256n56

New York, N.Y., 27, 29, 31, 48–49, 56–57, 60, 62, 103, 119, 156, 161, 163, 173, 177, 188, 199, 208, 230n34

Newman, Samuel B., and Samuel B., Jr. (cotton factors), 46, 48

Oakland (plantation), 106
Ober Atwater & Co., 83
O'Brien, Frank, and family (businessmen), 67, 150, 156
O'Brien & Co., 67
Ogden family (planters), 16, 167
Olmstead, Frederick Law, 104
Orphanages, 139, 165

Page, LeGrand (planter), 125
Page, Nelson and Cressey (farmers), 107–8
Palatine (Hill) (plantation), 84, 122
Panmure, Fort (Fort Rosalie), 15–16
Payne, George T. (merchant), 7, 63–66, 72, 76, 83–84, 98, 104, 109, 124, 150, 153, 157–58, 164–65, 168–69, 176, 193, 208–9

Payne family (merchants), 7, 150, 209, 221n6
Payne Place (plantation), 92
Pennsylvania, 24, 225n38
Perrault, Armand (merchant), 7, 59, 63–65, 104, 123–24, 133, 152, 176, 210
Perrault, Armand, Jr. (merchant), 68
Perrault, Charles (merchant and sheriff), 176
Perrault, Edward (merchant), 41, 68
Perrault, Elizabeth, 201, 210
Perrault, Frank (merchant), 209
Perrault, James (merchant), 216
Perrault, Thomas (merchant), 66–67, 209
Perrault, Vincent (merchant), 68, 129, 139
Perrault & Maher Co., 68, 129
Perrault family (merchants), 7, 63–64, 66–69, 87, 129, 150, 160–61, 164, 168, 210–11, 221n6
Phelen, Mike (agent), 123, 194
Philadelphia, Penn., 17, 19, 21, 24
Pipes, Louis (planter), 4
Pittsfield (plantation), 118, 123, 130
Planters: antebellum role of, 5, 10, 17–32, 80–81, 175, 214–15, 227n4, 227n16; intermarriage of, 24, 28, 30, 102; land grants of, 16–18; nabobs, 14, 16, 18, 21, 24, 26, 28–29, 37, 42, 45, 48, 50, 52, 70, 118–19, 223n9; postwar reduction of, 10, 32, 37–38, 71–81, 95, 110, 112–37, 140–41, 184, 200, 211, 212, 216–19; relationship with merchants, 19–24, 27–30, 32, 36–38, 46–48, 50–56, 57, 61, 73–76, 80–103, 109–15, 118–29, 135, 143–44, 147–48, 151, 184–85, 200, 205, 215–19; transition to businessmen, 142–45, 168–69, 172, 196, 200, 211; wealth of, 5, 21–22, 25–26, 28, 30–31, 45, 73, 168, 215
Point Place (plantation), 95, 124, 228n20
Politics, 26, 42, 59, 106, 146, 163, 174–75, 177–78, 206, 209, 215
Pollock, Henry C. (merchant), 175, 223n15
Pollock, Oliver (merchant), 17–18, 223n15
Pollock & Mason Co., 37, 52–53, 65
Porter, William "Dirty Bill" (U.S. naval officer), 11–12
Postlethwaite, Samuel, and family (merchants), 24–25, 27–28, 45
Providence (plantation), 74, 130

R. G. Dun & Co. (and agents), 29, 47–48, 51–53, 56–62, 64–69, 83, 119, 122–23, 136, 181, 188, 190, 200, 204–5, 222n13, 228n16, 228n22, 229n24, 229n27, 230n36–37, 230n39, 231n41, 231n43, 231n49
Railroads: Natchez, Jackson, & Columbus, 114, 142–43, 156, 172, 177, 240n3, 250n49, 250n54; Natchez, Red River & Texas, 127, 142, 173, 175, 177, 182, 200, 243n26, 250n49; New Orleans, Natchez, & Fort Scott, 173, 177, 250n49; Vidalia & Western, 173, 181–82, 191
Ransom, Roger, 10
Reale, Joseph (merchant), 68, 164, 176
Reber, Thomas (businessman and judge), 116, 137–38, 142, 154, 172–73, 175, 211
Redemption (southern political), 105, 174, 177, 206
Religion: Baptist (Windy Hill Baptist Church), 139; Catholic (St. Mary's Basilica), 64, 68, 160, 164–66, 229n29; Episcopal (Trinity Episcopal Church), 160, 167; Jewish (Temple B'Nai Israel), 160, 164–66; Presbyterian (First Presbyterian Church and Pine Ridge Church), 160, 167, 202
Revels, Hiram (senator), 74, 106
Rice, Henry (farmer), 107–8
Richard Flower & Co., 190
Rickey, Shelton & Co., 37, 53
Roos family (merchants), 62, 72, 150, 191
Rosalie, Fort, 15–16
Ross, Harrison (farmer), 3–4
Rothstein, Morton, 199, 254n31
Routh, Job, and family (merchants and planters), 22, 30, 119
Rowandale (plantation), 127
Rucker family (and plantation), 71–72, 78, 208
Rumble, S. E. (merchant), 127, 143, 171, 176, 200
Rumble & Wensel Co., 37, 52, 55, 189–90, 200, 209

S. & A. Jacobs Co., 61–62, 95, 98, 127, 153, 204
S. B. Newman & Co., 46, 188
S. D. Stockman & Co., 48, 53
Samuels, Emanuel (merchant), 130–31, 150, 210, 212–13, 256n56
Sandy Creek (plantation), 74, 102, 106
Saragossa (plantation), 74
Scharff family (merchants), 56, 62, 150, 192
Schwartz, Christian (planter), 67, 157
Schwartz, John C. (merchant), 33–36, 63, 66–67, 150, 152–55, 169, 210, 226n47
Schwartz & Stewart Co., 152–55
Scotland (plantation), 123
Seltzertown (plantation), 77, 108
Shamrock (plantation), 98
Sharecropping. *See* Tenancy
Shields, Gabriel B. (planter), 25, 37
Shields, Wilmer (planter), 106, 169, 177, 194
Shields family (planters), 142, 167, 189
Signaigo, A. J., and family (merchants), 67–68, 105
Slavery, 3–5, 9–10, 13, 38, 54, 73–74, 76–77, 101, 103–6, 109, 163, 219–20
Social Capital, 28, 42, 142–79
Social Clubs, 145, 165, 167–69
Sojourner family (planters), 4, 138
Somerset (plantation), 119
Spokane (plantation), 130
St. Catherine's Creek, 15–16, 123
St. Genevieve (plantation), 123
St. Joseph, La., 123, 235n26
Stampley Place (plantation), 127
Stanton, Frederick, and family (merchants and planters), 12, 29, 36, 42–44, 46, 101–2
Steele, Hiram (attorney and businessman), 142, 156, 172, 174–75
Stockman, Samuel Dryden, and family (merchants), 36, 41, 44–50, 53, 55, 57, 150, 168
Subdivisions: Arlington Addition, 139; Carpenter Addition, 139; Clifton Heights, 8, 61, 117, 139, 171, 175; Maple Terrace Addition, 139; Reed & Brandon Addition, 139; Woodlawn, 116, 137–39
Surget, Charlotte (planter), 85, 122, 236n31
Surget, James (planter), 142, 154, 168–69, 172, 196, 200

Surget family (planters), 18, 25, 37, 103, 122, 154, 200
Sutch, Richard, 10
Swayze family (planters), 16, 194

Tacony (plantation), 131
Tate (plantation), 124
Tekoa (plantation), 127
Tenancy (agricultural): on fixed rents, 79, 97, 236n34; on shares (sharecropping), 3–6, 9–10, 73–75, 78–79, 82, 95–96, 100–101, 104–5, 108–10, 217, 227n4, 234n12
Tensas Parish, La., 84, 86, 91, 93–94, 119, 123, 163, 203, 212, 235n26
Tillman, Cassius L. (merchant), 167, 176, 209–10
Thomas Henderson & Co., 42, 46, 48, 51
Towers, The (mansion), 157, 188
Treaties, 16, 18, 20
Twain, Mark, 148, 170, 249n44

Ullman, Samuel, and family (merchants), 60, 139, 150, 191, 252n20
United Sates of America (Union): army and occupation forces of, 6–8, 11, 13–14, 32–34, 37–38, 40, 53–54, 59, 69, 71, 73, 75, 78, 82–83, 88, 122, 134, 139, 151, 168, 174, 215, 226n1, 226n47; currency of, 32, 34–36, 123–24, 132–34; embargo of, 11, 31, 199, 215; federal authorities and courts of, 37, 73–75, 79, 103–5, 188–89, 206, 219; navy of (USS *Essex*), 11–12, 132, 222n1; soldiers of, 32, 36, 69, 71–73, 82, 110, 168, 180

Via Mede (plantation), 119
Vicksburg, Miss., 3, 11, 13, 30–31, 78, 173, 226n47, 235n26
Vidalia, La.: businesses in, 58–59, 61, 82, 91, 93, 95, 106, 130, 172, 191; courts in, 100, 102; flooding in, 185, 201, 203; land dealings in, 115–16, 127, 129, 134–36; mentioned, 161, 165; politics in, 174–75; railroads in, 142, 173, 177, 181–82, 191
Vousdan, William, and family (planters), 18, 21, 25

Wade, Battaille H. (planter), 53
Wade, Clarence J. (planter), 95, 129
Wade's Woodyard (plantation), 95, 129
Wage labor, 5, 73, 78–79, 82, 84, 137, 185, 236–37n34
Waveland (plantation), 193
Waverly (plantation), 96, 123, 236–37n34
Wayne, Michael, 9
Wecama Planting Co. (and plantation), 130
Weis, Julius (cotton factor), 54, 56, 59, 61, 124–25, 127–28, 143, 156–58, 160–61, 200
West Florida (Spanish and British), 16, 18
Western Company (Company of the Indies), 15
Whigs, 31
White Hall (plantation), 68, 129
Wilkins, James (merchant), 25
Wilkinson County, Miss., 83–86, 92–94, 119, 122, 128, 206, 243n28
William Abbott & Co., 51–52, 92, 95
Willing, James, and family (merchants), 17–18
Windy Hill (plantation), 102
Winston, Louis J. (lawyer and county clerk), 74, 106, 138
Wolfe Geisenberger & Son Co., 4, 60, 95–97, 101–2, 147, 206
Wood, Robert H. (mayor and sheriff), 177, 189, 193, 253n22
Wood, Robert Lee (businessman), 211–12
Woodland (plantation), 48, 148
Woodman, Harold, 9, 178
Woodville, Miss., 243n28
Woodward, C. Vann, 10, 144
World War I, 207, 212
Wright, Nathaniel, and family (farmers), 71–73, 76, 78, 207–8
Wright, Richard (author), 73, 208

www.ingramcontent.com/pod-product-compliance
Lightning Source LLC
Chambersburg PA
CBHW030335240426
43661CB00052B/1645